WILEY SERIES ON PERSONALITY PROCESSES

IRVING B. WEINER, *Editor*
Case Western Reserve University

INTERACTION IN FAMILIES
by Elliot G. Mishler and Nancy E. Waxler

SOCIAL STATUS AND PSYCHOLOGICAL DISORDER: A Causal Inquiry
by Bruce P. Dohrenwend and Barbara Dohrenwend

PSYCHOLOGICAL DISTURBANCE IN ADOLESCENCE
by Irving B. Weiner

ASSESSMENT OF BRAIN DAMAGE: A Neuropsychological Key Approach
by Elbert W. Russell, Charles Neuringer, and Gerald Goldstein

BLACK AND WHITE IDENTITY FORMATION
by Stuart Hauser

THE HUMANIZATION PROCESSES: A Social, Behavioral Analysis of Children's Problems
by Robert L. Hamblin, David Buckholdt, Daniel Ferritor, Martin Kozloff, and Lois Blackwell

ADOLESCENT SUICIDE
by Jerry Jacobs

TOWARD THE INTEGRATION OF PSYCHOTHERAPY
by John M. Reisman

MINIMAL BRAIN DYSFUNCTION IN CHILDREN
by Paul Wender

LSD: PERSONALITY AND EXPERIENCE
by Harriet Linton Barr, Robert J. Langs, Robert R. Holt, Leo Goldberger, and George S. Klein

TREATMENT OF THE BORDERLINE ADOLESCENT: A Developmental Approach
by James F. Masterson

PSYCHOPATHOLOGY: Contributions from the Biological, Behavioral, and Social Sciences
edited by Muriel Hammer, Kurt Salzinger, and Samuel Sutton

ABNORMAL CHILDREN AND YOUTH: Therapy and Research
by Anthony Davids

PSYCHOTHERAPY WITH CHILDREN
by John M. Reisman

AVERSIVE MATERNAL CONTROL: A Theory of Schizophrenic Development
by Alfred B. Heilbrun, Jr.

INDIVIDUAL DIFFERENCES IN CHILDREN
edited by Jack C. Westman

AVERSIVE MATERNAL CONTROL:

A Theory of Schizophrenic Development

ALFRED B. HEILBRUN, JR.

Professor of Psychology
Emory University

About the Author

ALFRED B. HEILBRUN, JR., is Professor of Psychology at Emory University, Atlanta. He was previously Assistant and then Associate Professor at the University of Iowa and Visiting Associate Professor at the University of California, Berkeley. Dr. Heilbrun received a Ph.D. degree in psychology at the University of Iowa. He is the author of 120 research or critical papers and contributed chapters.

A WILEY-INTERSCIENCE PUBLICATION

JOHN WILEY & SONS, New York • London • Sydney • Toronto

Library of Congress Cataloging in Publication Data:

Heilbrun, Alfred B. *1924-*
Aversive maternal control.

(Wiley series on personality processes)
"A Wiley-Interscience publication."
1. Schizophrenia. 2. Mother and child.
I. Title. [DNLM: 1. Maternal behavior. 2. Parent-child relations.
3. Schizophrenia, Childhood. WM 203 H466a 1972]

RC514.H43 618.9'28'982071 72-8882 ISBN 0-471-36895-4

Printed in the United States of America

10 9 8 7 6 5 4 3 2 1

To Marian and my children

Kirk, Lynn, Kim, Leigh, and Mark

SERIES PREFACE

This series of books is addressed to behavioral scientists interested in the nature of human personality. Its scope should prove pertinent to personality theorists and researchers as well as the clinicians concerned with applying an understanding of personality processes to the amelioration of emotional difficulties in living. To this end, the series provides a scholarly integration of theoretical formulations, empirical data, and practical recommendations.

Six major aspects of studying and learning about human personality can be designated: personality theory, personality structure and dynamics, personality development, personality assessment, personality change, and personality adjustment. In exploring these aspects of personality, the books in the series discuss a number of distinct but related subject areas: the nature and implications of various theories of personality; personality characteristics that account for consistencies and variations in human behavior; the emergence of personality processes in children and adolescents; the use of interviewing and testing procedures to evaluate individual differences in personality; efforts to modify personality styles through psychotherapy, counseling, behavior therapy, and other methods of influence; and patterns of abnormal personality functioning that impair individual competence.

Irving B. Weiner

Case Western Reserve University
Cleveland, Ohio

PREFACE

If these remarks had been recorded before this book was written, their character certainly would be more tentative than it is now. In the course of completing the manuscript, evidence from our research laboratory has continued to provide increasing confidence in the veridicality of our theoretical proposals. However, final verdicts on theory in the behavioral sciences have a way of suffering infinite postponement, so in the meantime each reader must serve as his own judge of the scientific assumptions and methodologies that went into our research and the theoretical alignment of the evidence that came out of it.

Where concepts included in the book were originated by others, credit has been given. In the main, the ideas which went into the research and came out of it are my own, a fact which up to this time has been a mixed blessing. I find at the point in the book where most writers offer their appreciation to colleagues or institutions for encouragement, collaborative effort, financial support, or helpful suggestions concerning the manuscript that no acknowledgment is specifically called for.

I would like to offer appreciation, however, to the graduate students who have chosen to work with me on programmatic research and to the many female graduate students who, for nine consecutive years, have worked as experimenters and somewhat underaged surrogate "mothers." Special gratitude is extended to Mrs. Jeanne Fletcher, my assistant, who has almost single-handedly absorbed the labor of manuscript preparation into an already taxing schedule.

Alfred B. Heilbrun, Jr.

Atlanta, Georgia
October 1972

CONTENTS

AVERSIVE MATERNAL CONTROL:
A THEORY OF SCHIZOPHRENIC DEVELOPMENT

CHAPTER 1

The Nature of Schizophrenia

The purpose of this book is to trace the development of a theory which explains how schizophrenia may be learned. Our investigation of the learning antecedents to schizophrenia has been based upon a larger body of systematically interlocking research studies than any previous effort to date, this book culminating some thirteen years of inquiry by me and my graduate student associates. While this program of research and the theory of schizophrenia which it generated will be our focus of interest in this book, proper exposition requires that we initially consider several basic issues. The first of these has to do with the nature of schizophrenia itself. What are the behaviors that require developmental explanation?

Extremely rich descriptions of schizophrenic symptomatology are available elsewhere (e.g., Weiner, 1966; 1970), and there is little to be gained from reviewing them here. Our concern will be with the major systems of behavior which tend to become pathologically involved in schizophrenia and serve as hallmarks of the disorder, since it is only with these general behavior systems that our theory of schizophrenic development can hope to contend at the present time. Meehl (1962) has suggested that the behavioral facts that lead to the diagnosis of schizophrenia may be usefully reduced to four categories. The first of these is thought disorder or, as he prefers, "cognitive slippage." Cognitive problems of schizophrenics range from the most basic loss in associative linkages and loss of language communication function to serious malfunctioning of perceptual screening in hallucinations and the faulty judgment that denies reality testing to the paranoid.

The second behavioral fact that serves to identify the schizophrenic is interpersonal aversiveness. A pervasive sense of fear, distrust, and unlovability and an expectation of rejection, all of which are highly resistant to corrective experience, overdetermine his superficial mode of relating socially or his more complete social withdrawal.

Anhedonia, the loss of pleasure capacity, and ambivalence round out the major identifying signs of schizophrenia in Meehl's list of four. Just as Meehl points out that additional schizophrenic signs may be subsumed under his four categories, it serves our purpose in attempting to explain schizophrenic development to reduce his four to the two major behavioral systems that are uniquely influenced in schizophrenia: (a) cognition, which includes those behaviors intimately related to the registration and processing of information and to the symbolic mediation and communication capacities of the person, and (b) those components of personality that determine the character of social contact with fellow humans.

While we have undoubtedly lost something of the complex clinical nature of schizophrenia in the primary concern with cognitive and social-relating behaviors, we hope to compensate for this loss by reducing the necessity for speculative patchwork within the circumscribed network of our theory. We have chosen to narrow our scope of explanation by staying as close as possible to the data of research and have foregone the temptation to present a clinically rich but ad hoc theory.

HISTORIC APPROACH TO CLASSIFYING SCHIZOPHRENIC BEHAVIOR

Beginning with Kraepelin's (1899) use of the term *dementia praecox* to designate schizophrenic behaviors as reflecting a disorder of adolescence or early adulthood, clinicians and researchers (somewhat later) have been faced with the problem of conceptualizing a vast array of symptoms as representative of a single disorder or disease. The response to this problem has been a variety of classificatory systems which have been imposed upon the heterogeneous collection of schizophrenic symptoms. The Kraepelinian classification schema, which has enjoyed the longest tenure, separated the schizophrenias into catatonic, hebephrenic, paranoid, and simple types. These classes are still represented today in the procedures for diagnosing mental patients, although additional classes have been added (e.g., "undifferentiated," "childhood," "residual") to relieve the burden of the diagnostician. The longevity of the Kraepelinian classification of schizophrenias has occurred despite its violation of every rule of classification. Its classes are not mutually exclusive; schizophrenics assigned to one category share defining attributes of schizophrenics assigned to others. The classification is not exhaustive in that persons designated as schizophrenics do not necessarily fit into any of the subtypes. Appending "wastebasket" categories such as "unclassified" continues the violation of classification procedures since different rules of assignment are introduced among the classes. Membership in some classes occurs because of the presence of particular symptoms; membership in other classes occurs because of the absence of defining symptoms.

Since readers might not be perturbed by the thought of violated rules of classification, the pragmatic limitations of the Kraepelinian system also should be reviewed. Classification, if it is to be useful, must serve at least one of two possible functions. It must either facilitate understanding of some area of human experience, or it must generate differential predictions about members of the various classes by virtue of class membership alone. There seems to be little basis for defending the traditional classification procedures for schizophrenics on either count. However, similar past protestations have not as yet resulted in much change in the clinical usage of Kraepelinian nomenclature.

Another widely applied procedure for subdividing schizophrenics is to group them according to the length of time which the identifying symptoms have been clinically manifest. Acute schizophrenia is used to designate the initial onset or early stage of schizophrenia, whereas chronic schizophrenia refers to the condition as it continues or reoccurs over time at a clinically evident level. This form of classification seems to offer the immediate advantage of greater objectivity than the Kraepelinian system in that time is a most palpable commodity—time since onset of symptoms can be reduced to numerical counts in terms of years or number of hospitalizations. It is not difficult to identify the limitations of this schema as a system of classification. It still depends upon the limited reliability of clinical judgment which establishes the presence of schizophrenia, compounded in this case by the lack of explicit guidelines as to what severity of symptoms shall be used to judge the time at which schizophrenia was initially clinically evident. The fact that this judgment must often be based upon information garnered from nonprofessionals, such as the parents or teachers, makes it even more difficult to establish the time of schizophrenic onset. Also, the time necessary to establish chronicity following the initial clinical manifestation of schizophrenia remains a matter of individual interpretation. Despite these difficulties, there is no doubt that gross categorizations can be effected which distinguish between long-term and short-term schizophrenics.

The distinction between acute and chronic schizophrenia has proven of some use for research as evidenced by group differences which have been reported in the literature. For example, acute and chronic schizophrenics have been found to differ in degree of overinclusive thinking (Payne, 1962) and in extent of stimulus scanning (Draguns, 1963). Broen (1968), in summarizing the evidence on the effects of chronicity in schizophrenia, suggests that the progression of change is toward increasing detachment from both external and internal stimulation to avoid the aversive effects of disorganization. Although differences in acute and chronic schizophrenics may be granted, suggesting that some differential predictions are possible based only on the knowledge of class membership, it is far from clear why acute and chronic schizophrenics differ. Johannsen and O'Connell (1965) concluded that the perceptual deficit of chronic schizophrenics is more closely related to progressive changes in the disorder itself than to environmental factors, but evidence supporting the importance of environmental effects comes from the finding that similar perceptual differences can be found between long-term and short-term prisoners (Silverman, Berg, and Kantor, 1965).

The third approach which has been taken to classifying schizophrenics has focused upon differences in premorbid adjustment. Phillips (1953) developed three scales upon which patients' case histories could be rated: (1) premorbid history including subscales on recent sexual adjustment, social aspects of recent sexual life, past history of personal relations and recent adjustment in personal relations; (2) precipitating factors; and (3) signs of the disorder itself. The best prognostic indicator of recoverability for the hospitalized schizophrenics studied was the premorbid history scale, the patients with a higher level of premorbid adjustment being more likely to show improvement. Schizophrenics demonstrating a poorer premorbid social-sexual competence have been termed "process," and those with better premorbid status are termed "reactive." Evidence to support the prognostic utility of a second premorbid rating instrument, the Elgin Prognostic Scale, has been reported (Chapman, Day, and Burstein, 1961), and the high similarity of the Elgin and Phillips premorbid adjustment scales is indicated by their correlation of .80 (Solomon and Zlotowski, 1964).

The importance of the process-reactive distinction has ranged far beyond its use as a prognostic indicator of recoverability. Grouping schizophrenics according to their level of premorbid adjustment has had a facilitative effect upon research with schizophrenics as well. The tremendous variability of performance that typically characterized unselected schizophrenic research samples has been markedly reduced by considering their process or reactive status—process schizophrenics or reactive schizophrenics are behaviorally more homogeneous groupings than schizophrenics-in-general.

One of the greatest potential gains from the use of a premorbidity approach to classification has rarely been exploited, since investigators have tended to ignore the origins of the process-reactive distinctions. The fact that the assignment to these classes is based upon premorbid social-sexual competence puts the researcher in a position to relate a given set of observed differences among schizophrenics to differences in social development history rather than to differences in current symptoms (Kraepelinian classes) or to duration of illness (acute versus chronic). The potential for clarifying the social antecedents of various forms of schizophrenic disorder appears considerably higher when process and reactive distinctions are maintained.

AGE OF ONSET IN SCHIZOPHRENIA

Establishing the age at which schizophrenia emerges as a clinical entity is of more than passing interest in any serious attempt to formulate a theory of its development. Time since birth will determine the range of experiences to which the person will have been exposed during the premorbid period. Breadth of experience has to be crucial to any theory of schizophrenic development that places social learning factors at the core. The stages of social and cognitive development through which the schizophrenic has passed, the succession of critical figures who may have influenced personality development (e.g., parents, peers, teachers, spouses), and the sheer time necessary to establish complex though maladaptive patterns of behavior all require the attention of the learning theorist. Others who contend that genetic transmission, chemical imbalance, or central nervous system anomaly are the critical pathological factors in schizophrenia need not be so vitally concerned with age of onset. At most, constitutional theorists depend upon experiential determinants as "triggers" which release the maladaptive behaviors contingent upon preexisting somatic flaw. Such triggers or stress provocations may occur at any age.

Wolman (1965), in his historical survey of the diagnostic precursors of schizophrenia, reports that adolescence was considered the stage of development during which "dementia" occurs almost a half century before Kraepelin (1899) proposed "dementia praecox" as a set of mental aberrations which appear in adolescence or early adulthood. Bleuler (1950), who coined the term "schizophrenia" around 1911, also believed the disturbance to be primarily associated with adolescence.

More recent review of the evidence regarding age of onset in schizophrenia leads Weiner (1970, p. 116) to conclude:

> . . . these observations indicate that a disturbed adolescent may be suffering the long-term effects of childhood schizophrenia, may be experiencing the initial onset of schizophrenia, or may be just beginning to display some prodromal indices that, if unchecked, will blossom into overt schizophrenia during his adult life.

Yet as one examines the evidence on psychotic children (whether these are labeled schizophrenia, autism, or psychosis of infancy or childhood), one is struck by such tremendous limitations in social development as to lend pessimism to any attempt to understand their pathology in complex social learning terms. The chronic limitations and culminating deterioration of childhood psychotics by the time they reach adolescence has been noted by Eisenberg (1956), Spivack, Haimes, and Spotts (1967), and Colbert and Koegler (1961). Other investigators, like Weiner, delineate the childhood psychotic as a schizophrenic pattern which should be distinguished from schizophrenic reactions which emerge at adolescence following a preadolescent development involving only limited or even an absence of psychological difficulties (Masterson, 1967; Neubauer and Steinert, 1952; Symonds and Herman, 1957).

The point to be emphasized here, as far as the present theoretical treatise is concerned, is that the earlier the onset of psychosis, the less the potential importance of social learning factors in the genesis of the disorder. Infantile autism, in which the child's prepsychotic social interactive capacities are negligible, cannot be sensibly explained as a learned life style influenced by and in response to sustained social stress. Genetic, chemical, or neurological deficit hypotheses appear far more tenable points of departure for explaining early childhood disorders. Similarly, the degree of imperviousness of the early childhood psychotic conditions to experiential or therapeutic modification would be consistent with a constitutional deficit theory of psychotic behavior.

On the other hand, the importance of experiential antecedents to psychotic disorders can be entertained when we identify premorbid life styles which reflect some degree of social development and social relationships of sufficient intensity and extensity to serve as important psychological influences. It will be schizophrenia in this sense to which the data presented in this book will be relevant and to which the theory of schizophrenic development will be addressed. This narrowed concern with schizophrenia as an adolescent or adult stage disorder in no way attempts to preclude infantile or childhood disorders from being called "schizophrenia" if it serves any clinical or theoretical purpose. It does signal the importance, however, of maintaining some nominal distinction between a schizophrenia in which constitutional factors are more likely to be paramount determinants and a schizophrenia in which learning antecedents are more likely to assume critical importance.

Perhaps the most fitting way to conclude a discussion about the nature of schizophrenia is to point out that schizophrenic behaviors are real and the proper subject of concern for the theorist or clinician. Vivid hallucinatory experiences, massive paranoid distortions of thought, bizarre motoric states, and incomprehensible language patterns offer little basis for questioning the reality of psychotic behavior, even for the most philosophically inclined. Schizophrenia, however, is a man-made construct devised to place the observable behaviors in some meaningful conceptual context. It is important to recall that the general context out of which schizophrenia emerged as a construct was a medical one and the specific context was the disease model. Thus, schizophrenia as a disease would be expected to show disease attributes—a singular disease-producing microbody which attacks the organism, a predictable course of development, a specific set of clinical symptoms, and a predictable course of recovery following particular forms of treatment. Despite the best efforts of geneticists, neuropathologists, and biochemists, no singular schizophrenia-producing somatic factor has been convincingly demonstrated. As has been stressed earlier in this chapter, a particular course of development and a specific pattern of symptoms defining schizophrenia have not been identified as yet. A specific treatment for schizophrenia does not exist and the various treatments offer rather unpredictable courses of recovery.

The simple truth is that "schizophrenic" makes a good adjective but "schizophrenia" makes a bad noun. We shall make the best of this situation by avoiding as far as possible any attempt to explain the genesis of a particular disease (or disorder). Rather we will concern ourselves with the behaviors which reach such nonadaptive proportions as to be considered schizophrenic. Among other things, this means that there is no need to defend our developmental theory as *the* causal explanation of schizophrenia. It need only be proposed as *one* of several possible explanations of how specified predispositional conditions can lead to the degeneration of behavior systems of such serious magnitude as to be termed schizophrenic.

REFERENCES

Bleuler, E. *Dementia praecox or the group of schizophrenias*. Translated by J. Zinkin. New York: International Universities Press, 1950.

Broen, W. E. *Schizophrenia: research and theory*. New York: Academic Press, 1968.

Chapman, L. J., Day, D., and Burstein, A. The process-reactive distinction and prognosis in schizophrenia. *Journal of Nervous and Mental Disease*, 1961, **133**, 383-391.

Colbert, E. G., and Koegler, R. R. The childhood schizophrenic in adolescence. *Psychiatric Quarterly*, 1961, **35**, 693-701.

Draguns, J. G. Responses to cognitive and perceptual ambiguity in chronic and acute schizophrenics. *Journal of Abnormal and Social Psychology*, 1963, **66**, 24-30.

Eisenberg, L. The autistic child in adolescence. *American Journal of Psychiatry*, 1956, **122**, 607-612.

Johannsen, W. J., and O'Connell, M. J. Institutionalization and perceptual decrement in chronic schizophrenia. *Perceptual and Motor Skills*, 1965, **21**, 244-246.

Kraepelin, E. (1899) Clinical psychiatry, 1st edition. Translated by A. R. Diefendorf from the 6th edition of *Lehrbuch der psychiatrie*. New York: Macmillan, 1902.

Masterson, J. F. *The psychiatric dilemma of adolescence*. Boston: Little, Brown, 1967.

Meehl, P. E. Schizotaxia, schizotypy, schizophrenia. *American Psychologist*, 1962, **17**, 827-838.

Neubauer, P. B., and Steinert, J. Schizophrenia in adolescence. *Nervous Child*, 1952, **10**, 128-134.

Payne, R. W. An object classification test as a measure of overinclusive thinking in schizophrenia. *British Journal of Social and Clinical Psychology*, 1962, **1**, 213-221.

Phillips, L. Case history data and prognosis in schizophrenia, *Journal of Nervous and Mental Disease*, 1953, **117**, 515-535.

Silverman, J., Berg, P. S. D., and Kantor, R. Some perceptual correlates of institutionalization. *Journal of Nervous and Mental Disease*, 1965, **138,** 32-37.

Solomon, L. and Zlotowski, M. The relationship between the Elgin and the Phillips measures of process-reactive schizophrenia. *Journal of Nervous and Mental Disease*, 1964, **138**, 32-37.

Spivack, G., Haimes, P. E., and Spotts, J. Adolescent symptomatology and its measurement. *American Journal of Mental Deficiency*, 1967, **72**, 74-95.

Symonds, A., and Herman, M. The patterns of schizophrenia in adolescence. *Psychiatric Quarterly*, 1957, **31**, 521-530.

Weiner, I. B. *Psychodiagnosis in schizophrenia*. New York: Wiley, 1966.

Weiner, I. B. *Psychological disturbance in adolescence*. New York: Wiley, 1970.

Wolman, B. B. Schizophrenia and related disorders. In B. B. Wolman (Ed.), *Handbook of clinical psychology*, New York: McGraw-Hill, 1965. Pp. 976-1029.

CHAPTER 2

The Mother as a Critical Source of Developmental Influence

While few would argue with the statement that the mother is an important influence upon the psychological development of her child, the almost exclusive attention paid to the mother in our research and in this book requires explanation.

The simplest reason why the mother garnered our attention is a practical one. It has been deemed more important to pursue the effects of a particular relationship upon the child's development in some depth than to extend our focus to other potentially important figures, such as the father. We would rather be narrow in our scope than to court superficiality by overextending the breadth of our inquiry.

Beyond scientific pragmatism, there is also reason to believe that the mother is *the* most important source of influence in the child's life. This assertion takes note of the facts that in the American culture (and almost all other cultures) the mother, not the father, assumes the major caretaking responsibility for the children and that by custom and legal discretion the mother will be the exclusive caretaker when a choice must be made between the mother and the father.

However, it is not the differential time commitment alone that argues for the unique importance of the mother's influence upon the child. The primacy of her relationship with the child must also be considered. Within the first year of life the mother almost invariably becomes an object of emotional attachment for the infant, whereas fathers attain this status far less frequently (Schaffer and Emerson, 1964). While the child's emotional bonds will multiply well beyond his initial attachment to his mother, the affectional mother-child tie within the first year is distinguished by the fact that it is a largely presymbolic-preverbal experience. This means that the infant's love and need for the mother early in life remains "unconscious" in the most reasonable sense of the word. The child cannot later recall, redintegrate, or understand the emotional experiences of that first year with his mother. Consequently, he may in later years be left with emotional responses and psychological needs stimulated by the mother which cannot be placed in any rational context or be tempered by cognitive controls.

The point to be made here is that the effects of maternal nurturance or its absence (if the mother rejects the child) would more likely include overreactions or other distortions on the part of the child than would the effects of any other socialization agent.

REVIEW OF THE EVIDENCE RELATING THE MOTHER TO THE SCHIZOPHRENIC DEVELOPMENT OF THE CHILD

The scientific enterprise, whether it be in psychology or any other science, is a continuous process having no clear beginning and no anticipated end. Each new set of evidence should take its place in the existing network of facts, laws, or theories which characterize the cumulative knowledge of that particular science. We have selected only a small sector of psychology within which to focus our research efforts so that it is possible to provide a fairly exhaustive review of the relevant research published within the past thirty years.

The research literature relating the mother's potential child-rearing contribution to the development of schizophrenia will be surveyed by dividing it into three spheres of influence—control, nurturance, and communication. While these categories are admittedly arbitrary, the organization of the evidence in this way will at least prepare the reader for the conceptual structure of the theory toward which we are building in this book. These categories also represent a framework which is comprehensive enough to subsume every published finding relevant to maternal influence upon schizophrenic development that we could find in the literature of the last three decades.

It also should be noted that our concern will be with clearly child-directed behaviors of the mother only, and research dealing with other attributes of schizophrenics (e.g., sex role, self-concept) which might be inferentially related to the behavior of the mother will not be reviewed. Similarly, studies concerned with demographic attributes of the mother which tempt one to look for filial effects, such as the mother's level of adjustment or her absence from the home, will not be covered.

Finally, the review of evidence will include reference to the father when this serves to clarify the role of the mother in the schizophrenic's family or when a study provides no basis for distinguishing between the roles played by the father and mother. In the latter case, the word "parents" will be routinely used.

Maternal Control of the Child in Schizophrenic Development

By child-rearing control we refer to the degree to which the mother provides cues serving to direct the child's behavior. Control may be effected by obvious means, such as verbal directive or environmental manipulation, or by more subtle strategies, such as control through guilt (martyrdom) or through feared loss of the mother's love or esteem. Control cues may be provided directly by the mother or may be indirectly supplied through the child's internally produced store of maternal expectations. It makes no difference whether the mother influences her son's behavior by telling him what he must do or the son elects to behave in a particular way because he anticipates she would want him to. In either case, the child behaves under maternal control. While a diversity of terms will be used by investigators cited in this section, each connotes the importance of maternal cues in mediating the schizophrenic's behavior.

Among the earliest investigators relating maternal control to schizophrenia in the child, Despert (1938) reported that about 50% of the mothers of schizophrenic children in her sample had been described in case records as aggressive and oversolicitous and as being the dominant parent. Clardy (1951), in a similar search of case records of schizophrenics, noted that about 50% of the parents were characterized as overprotective. Portrayal of the schizophrenic's parents as overprotective in case records has also been noted by Frazee (1953) and Wahl (1954, 1956).

Schofield and Balian (1959) detected maternal overprotection and domination in 24% of their schizophrenic cases and in less than 2% of the normals studied, while Donnelly's (1960) direct observations of mother-child interaction in the home presented the mother as more overprotective and controlling with the disturbed child than with the normal sib. Mothers of schizophrenics completed a child-rearing questionnaire for Mainord (1957) and more strongly endorsed attitudes indicating martyrdom, overprotection, and subtle domination than did the control mothers. Porro (1965) had schizophrenic sons, their normal brothers, and the normal brothers of nonpsychiatric hospitalized sons portray their mothers on a child-rearing attitude measure. The normal brothers of schizophrenics perceived their mothers as more martyred and subtly dominating than did the normal brothers of hospitalized normals. The schizophrenics' ratings fell in-between these two normal groups. Schizophrenics studied by McKeown (1950) had experienced their mothers as dominant, demanding, and protective. Dworin and Wyant (1957) depicted mothers of schizophrenics as emphasizing conformity, conventionality, and obedience in their sons. While his study is often cited as showing greater inconsistency in methods of control for mothers of schizophrenics, Mark (1953) found 33 questionnaire items which differentiated them from normal mothers to indicate greater restrictiveness and only 6 differentiating items to indicate less restrictiveness.

Possessiveness as an attribute of schizophrenics' mothers, based upon self-description, was reported by Freeman and Grayson (1955), a finding marginally replicated by Freeman and Simmons (1958). Waring and Ricks (1965), using a variety of data gathered in childhood clinic contacts, noted that those who subsequently became chronic schizophrenics came from prolonged symbiotic parent-child relationships relative to clinic controls.

The mothers of schizophrenics were considered controlling of their children according to the clinical observations of Jenkins (1952). Heilbrun (1960) found that schizophrenic daughters perceived their mothers as more controlling than did normal daughters. Using similar procedures McKinley (1964) demonstrated that schizophrenic sons viewed their mothers as more controlling than hospitalized nonpsychiatric males. Lane and Singer (1959), using a projective technique, found greater control attributed to parents, although they were concerned only with paranoid schizophrenics.

Karon (1963) proposed that the schizophrenogenic mother was one who, when the needs of mother and the child conflict, will indirectly satisfy her own needs by manipulating the child so that his behavior achieves this end. Several studies employing projective story-telling techniques with mothers and scored by relevant criteria have directly tested Karon's proposal. These studies (Meyer and Karon, 1967; Mitchell, 1968; Mitchell, 1969) all found that the mother of the schizophrenic and the mother of the normal could be distinguished by the former's inability (in the stories) to meet the needs of their children and instead to use their children to indirectly meet their own needs. An earlier investigation by Prout and White (1950) also presents evidence consistent with Karon's observations; schizophrenics' mothers were described as disinclined to let their sons be themselves as far as their futures were concerned and were prone to use their sons as substitutes for their own role satisfactions in life. More recently, Werner, Stabenau, and Pollin (1970) compared the projective stories of the parents of schizophrenics, delinquents, and normals. They found that the parents of schizophrenics provided more parent-child interaction themes reflecting overinvolved parental need rather than the child's need and more rigidly demanding interactions. A second study established that mothers of schizophrenics provided fewer personally involved, child-centered, flexible interactions in their stories than did the mothers of normals. The mothers of schizophrenics also emphasized an impersonal, autocratic submission-to-task rather than child-involved, flexible interactions. Rigidity and inflexibility have been reported by Perr (1958) to be descriptive of schizophrenics' parents.

Hotchkiss, Carmen, Ogilby, and Wiesenfeld (1955) collected observations of mothers as they visited their hospitalized schizophrenic sons. They suggest that there is no typical mother of a schizophrenic and, as an alternative, propose five types based upon their observations: (1) the oversolicitous, hovering, domineering mother, (2) the sweet, indulgent mother, (3) the seductive mother, (4) the intent, controlled, quietly purposeful mother, and (5) the removed, nonparticipating mother. It should be noted that the first four of these typologies could be subsumed under our broad definition of maternal control.

More equivocal evidence regarding the relationship between maternal or parental control and filial schizophrenia comes from two investigations which suggest the importance of interactive variables which may influence the nature of this relationship. Cheek (1964) recorded the interchanges between fathers and mothers and their schizophrenic sons or daughters and found that the male schizophrenic was characteristically submissive in dealing with his parents as evidenced by low rates of activity, dominance, and disagreement relative to normal males. However, female schizophrenics presented a marked contrast to the male by being more active and dominating with their parents. Cheek's findings suggest that sex of offspring makes a difference in the extent of parental control exerted over the schizophrenic. The level of education of the mother has been suggested by Zuckerman, Oltean, and Monashkin (1958) as a determinant of expressed maternal attitudes. While they did not limit their statement to maternal control attitudes, the particular attitude measure in question (the Parent Attitude Research Instrument) is comprised of about 70% control items. Zuckerman et al. caution that attitude deviance (e.g., higher child-rearing control) is to be expected with less educated mothers. However, Heilbrun (1961) found just the opposite to be true. The schizophrenics' mothers who had completed more formal schooling (finished high school or attended college) were more controlling in their expressed child-rearing attitudes than were the more highly educated mothers of normals. Less-educated mothers of schizophrenics were less controlling than their counterparts with normal daughters. The inconsistency between these two studies is further emphasized by the fact that the same child-rearing questionnaire was used in both.

There are yet additional studies which must be considered as presenting negative evidence relative to maternal control as a predisposing factor in schizophrenic development of children. Freeman, Simmons, and Bergen (1959) failed to find the indications of possessiveness in the mothers of schizophrenics that had been identified in the earlier Freeman and Simmons (1958) study. While the self-descriptions of the mothers of schizophrenics portrayed them as "over-possessive" relative to the mothers of normals, Klebanoff (1959) found that the schizophrenics' mothers did not differ in this regard from the mothers of brain-injured and retarded children. Singer (1954) reports that the recollection of maternal dominance and overprotection was prevalent in both his schizophrenic and control group. Two studies (Heilbrun, 1960; Zuckerman, Oltean, and Monashkin, 1958) that involved comparisons between the endorsed attitudes of schizophrenics' mothers and normals' mothers found no differences on a large cluster of child-rearing control scales. Comparison of interactions between the members of the schizophrenic's family and that of the normal family allowed little basis for distinguishing between them according to Meyers and Goldfarb (1961).

Many investigators have attempted to identify a more comprehensive pattern of parental behavior which could more effectively account for the establishment of schizophrenic behavior in children. This has led to the ubiquitous concept of the "schizophrenogenic" parental pattern in the clinical literature which is characterized by a dominant, overprotective, but basically rejecting mother and a passive, ineffectual father. Empirical support for this parental pattern as an historical antecedent to schizophrenia is plentiful. For example, Kohn and Clausen (1956) found that schizophrenics, when asked to recall their adolescence, depicted their mothers as stricter, more dominating, and more certain of themselves than their fathers. Normal controls more often recalled the opposite parental pattern. Jackson, Block, Block, and Patterson (1958) asked 20 psychiatrists to present their conceptions of the schizophrenogenic mother and father. Three types of mothers were described: (1) the controlled puritanical mother, (2) the dependent, helpless mother, and (3) the manipulating Machiavellian mother. Similarly, three father types emerged: (1) the defeated father, (2) the distant, autocratic father, and (3) the oscillating, chaotic father. These typologies are reasonably consistent with the schizophrenogenic parental pattern. Observations of the families of schizophrenics led Bowen, Dysinger, and Basamanie (1959) to depict the mothers as typically dominant and the fathers as being emotionally immature and unable to define their role in the family. Additional support for the schizophrenogenic parental pattern in schizophrenia can be gleaned from a host of studies in which the interview has been the most common medium of data collection (Behrens and Goldfarb, 1958; Despert, 1951; Gerald and Siegal, 1950; Guertin, 1961; Hadju-Gimes, 1940; Karon and Rosberg, 1958; Kasanin, Knight, and Sage, 1934; Lidz, Cornelison, Fleck, and Terry, 1957a; Lidz, Cornelison, Fleck, and Terry, 1957b; Lidz, Cornelison, Fleck, and Terry, 1957c; Lidz, Cornelison, Terry, and Fleck, 1958; Lidz and Lidz, 1949; Lidz, Parker and Cornelison, 1956; Tietz, 1949; Walters, 1939).

There are also several investigations which provide only partial support for the schizophrenogenic parent hypothesis because of additional variables which cut across the proposed parental roles. A study by Fleck, Lidz, and Cornelison (1963) reports a reasonable facsimile of the schizophrenogenic parental pattern for male schizophrenics with the mothers portrayed as engulfing and the fathers as passive and ineffectual. However, the pattern failed to emerge for female schizophrenics, introducing sex of the schizophrenic offspring as a moderating variable. Social class as an interactive factor was suggested by the findings of Roberts and Meyers (1955) who found the schizophrenogenic pattern in their lower-middle-class group. The schizophrenics' mothers were ambitious and domineering, whereas the fathers were unsuccessful in business and uninvolved in the family except as a harsh disciplinarian. This pattern did not obtain for the lower-class families. Sanua (1963) studied parent child-rearing patterns in the family of the schizophrenic as these may be influenced by social class and religious status. The passive and ineffectual character of the Jewish father was all that stood out for the lower-class families of schizophrenics. More salient patterns emerged for the middle-upper-class parents of schizophrenics: Jewish mothers tended to be overprotective with Jewish fathers dominant or rejecting and Protestant mothers tended toward dominance and rejection and the father toward rejection. In short, the maternal component of the schizophrenogenic pattern was observed in the middle-upper-class families independent of religion, whereas the paternal component appeared in only the lower-class Jewish families. Opler's (1957) study of the family backgrounds of schizophrenics differing in ethnic origin revealed that the schizophrenogenic pattern was characteristic of Irish families with a schizophrenic son. The family was dominated by the mother, and the father was a weak and shadowy figure. The opposite pattern was found in the parents of schizophrenics of Italian origin.

Negative evidence for the schizophrenogenic pattern hypothesis comes from a study by Caputo (1963) who failed to find maternal dominance-paternal passivity among the parents of schizophrenics.

An even more complex parent dominance-submission patterning was proposed for the families of schizophrenics by Rodnick and Garmezy (1957). Evidence accrued in their laboratory at Duke University led them to distinguish between the dynamics of parents whose schizophrenic sons presented a premorbid history of relatively adequate social-sexual adjustment ("goods" or reactive schizophrenics) or a premorbid history of inadequate adjustment in the social-sexual sphere ("poors" or process schizophrenics). They postulated that the roles played by the mother and father in the families of goods and poors are reversed. The mothers of poor premorbid patients assume the role of the more dominating, restrictive, and powerful parent, whereas the fathers of poors are easy-going and ineffectual. The reverse pattern was proposed for the families of good premorbid schizophrenics with the father assuming the authority role and the mother being more permissive and warm. Results of a reanalysis of an earlier study by Kohn and Clausen (1956) as well as data cited from one of their own preliminary studies (Rodnick and Garmezy, 1955) lent credence to their proposal of a reversal of authority roles in the parents of good and poor premorbid male schizophrenics. Both studies, it might be noted, proceeded methodologically by eliciting the description of the parents from the schizophrenic, not the parent.

Early support for the Rodnick-Garmezy proposal was reported by Farina (1960) and Farina and Dunham (1963). Observations of actual family interactions in both studies led to the conclusion that the mothers of poors were the dominant parent, whereas the father assumed dominant status in the family of the good schizophrenic. Using a similar family problem-solving procedure, Lerner (1965) noted disproportionate degrees of dominance and submissiveness in the parents of schizophrenics in line with the poor-good premorbid distinction drawn by Rodnick and Garmezy. Garmezy, Clark, and Stockner (1961) reported that male schizophrenics who present a good premorbid history attributed greater dominance to the father than the mother, and the opposite was true for poors.

Clark (1964) found conformity behavior to occur in poors in response to a cold, domineering mother figure depicted on a tape, but no goods were included in the investigation. More maternal dominance in the families of poors had been reported earlier by Bell, Garmezy, Farina, and Rodnick (1960). Firm and aggressive domination of the child was more frequent in the mothers of poor premorbid schizophrenics, whereas a warmer, more softly over-protective mother-child relationship was more common with good premorbid schizophrenics according to Alanen (1968).

Baxter and Becker (1962), reasoning that greater anxiety should be elicited by the dominant parent in the home, scored projective stories told by good and poor premorbid schizophrenics for anxiety in relationship to parental figures. The stories of poors included greater anxiety with mothers, whereas goods' stories included more anxiety with fathers. In an experiment by Goodman (1964), poors demonstrated greater pre-post digit symbol interference following an intervening mother-censure condition than when father censure was introduced. Goods presented the opposite pattern, showing greater sensitivity to father censure than mother censure.

Partial confirmation and partial disconfirmation of the Rodnick-Garmezy proposal is evident in several studies. Poors had a higher threshold for a tape-recorded "mother" voice than they did for a "father" voice in an experiment by Donovan and Webb (1965), but no difference in thresholds was found for goods. Bradford (1966) presented tape-recorded "interviews" to schizophrenics. In one, a mother subscribed to domineering-overprotective and subtly rejecting child-rearing practices and in the other the mother assumed the role of a warmly supportive, democratic figure. Poors differentiated their responses to these taped conditions, but goods did not differ in their responses to the maternal figures. (It is necessary to assume in both the Donovan and Webb and the Bradford studies that the significant effect of the female voice upon the behavior of the poors is an indicant of the dominant position of the actual mother before the authority-reversal proposal can be considered to have sustained even partial support.) Jackson (1970) had poor premorbid schizophrenics respond to a taped parental interaction involving a dominant mother and a passive father and found them to be more influenced by maternally related cues. Also in keeping with the Rodnick-Garmezy proposal, the goods when exposed to a father dominant-mother passive interaction were more affected by paternally related cues. However, when the dominance patterns were reversed, the poors continued to be influenced by the maternal figure but the goods continued to be influenced by the dominant figure.

Harris (1955), while finding no differences between poors and goods in the degree of dominance or overprotection attributed to the mother, did identify a tendency for poors to overestimate the size of mother-son pictures projected on a screen. The overestimation was nonselective, occurring to pictures depicting maternal dominance, acceptance, ignoring, or overprotection (also, unfortunately, to a picture of a large tree and a smaller bush). A modest tendency to underestimate the size of the mother-child pictures was observed among the goods. While interpreting their findings as generally disconfirming the parent-dominance reversal hypothesis for goods and poors, Fontana, Klein, and Cicchetti (1967) did indicate that poors saw both parents as more dominating than did the goods or normals and the mother as more dominating than did the normals. Further, mothers of poors were perceived as making important decisions for the child, not the father, while the opposite was true for goods. Becker and Siefkes (1969), in a rare study of female schizophrenics separated by premorbid adjustment, report that poor premorbid daughters ascribe stronger domineering or controlling tendencies to both parents relative to goods or controls. The trend which can be observed in these last five studies is for the poor premorbid schizophrenics to demonstrate the kind of behavior more or less consistent with theoretical expectation (maternal dominance and paternal passivity), but the goods' performance has failed to lend credence to any patterning in mother-father dominance in their parents.

The possibility of a confounding between good-poor parent dominance patterns and urban-rural differences was suggested by Query (1961). His study showed better premorbid adjustment in schizophrenics with overly strict or severe fathers to be more frequent in rural families, while urban families tended to evidence the schizophrenic's dependence on the mother.

There are about the same number of published studies that present evidence contrary to the Rodnick-Garmezy proposal as have been cited as being confirmatory or partially confirmatory. Farina and Holzberg (1967, 1968), basing their observations upon the schizophrenic's family interactions in an experimental setting, failed to find evidence of the reversal of authority patterns in the families of goods and poors. Poor and good premorbid male schizophrenics attributed equal dominance to their parents when the experimenter was a male and perceived the father as dominant when the experimenter was a female in a study conducted by Klein, Cicchetti, and Spohn (1967). They did note that their questionnaire was limited to the punitive aspects of dominance, however. Cicchetti (1967) reported that male schizophrenics in general viewed their parents as more dominant, overprotective, and rejecting on a questionnaire than did a group of normals; no distinction could be made between goods and poors. Again using the questionnaire method, Cicchetti, Klein, and Fontana (1967) found no difference in the perceptions of relative parental dominance between good and poor schizophrenics. They also failed to find any difference in the sensitivity of goods and poors to father-scolding and mother-scolding scenes in terms of the number of discrimination errors.

Goodman (1968) could identify no difference in the extent to which poors and goods were influenced by photographs of fathers and mothers. In a study by

Baxter, Williams, and Zerof (1965), the fathers of poors demonstrated more deviant attitudes than did the mothers of poors on a questionnaire which measured child-rearing dominance, overprotection, and ignoring. This pattern, which runs contrary to expectation within the Rodnick-Garmezy model, was not demonstrated by goods or by normals. Zahn (1956) attempted to replicate the earlier Harris (1955) findings suggesting the poors' tendency to overestimate the size of mother-son scenes projected on a screen. He failed to replicate the directional difference of the Harris experiment, although some procedural and subject differences between the two studies were noted. The literature contains still other studies which present disconfirmatory evidence for the parent dominance-reversal notion (Englehart, 1959; Geisinger, 1966; Kreinik, 1959).

Critique of the Research on Maternal Control

Consideration of the extensive body of research bearing upon the maternal control variable in the mothers of schizophrenics does not lend itself to any simple conclusion. If one presumes support for the etiological importance of maternal control in the history of schizophrenics from positive studies which have looked at the mother alone, at the mother and father in combination, or at the undifferentiated parents, including those studies which consider the premorbid adjustment of the schizophrenic offspring, the evidence of its importance is fairly impressive. Of the 84 studies that were cited in this section, 66 (or 79%) of them contain some indication of control as an attribute of the mother of the schizophrenic. Since this frequency count might easily distress a scientific purist, it should be added rather quickly that this hit rate does not assume that the father was any less controlling in a given study nor does it preclude the possibility that maternal control interacted with a variety of demographic variables or with filial attributes.

The conclusion that maternal control is an important social history variable in the development of schizophrenia is actually bolstered by the state of the research literature from which the conclusion emerges. The fact that anything positive could come out of such a heterogeneous array of research approaches to investigating such a varied nomenclature of maternal behavior attests to the importance of the control variable. Data was gathered from such diverse sources as interviews, clinical observations, laboratory family interactions, experimental situations, questionnaires, projective tests, case records, judgments of clinicians, and more. Data was gathered from the perspective of the parents, the schizophrenic children, or the investigating observer. The behaviors we have subsumed under our term, controlling, have been variously termed oversolicitous, overprotective, dominating, subtly dominating, martyring, demanding, protective, restrictive, possessive, symbiotic, using, overinvolved, autocratic, rigid and inflexible, seductive, strict, puritanical, Machiavellian, engulfing, powerful, authoritarian, and even controlling.

While the methodological issues surrounding our research program will receive major attention in the next chapter, it may not be premature to point out the tremendous potential scientific advantages inherent in accumulating a large body of data relevant to maternal child-rearing control using a standardized method of data collection, a single perspective, and one defining operation for maternal control.

Maternal Nurturance of the Child in Schizophrenic Development

Research usage of the term "nurturance" has not received the varied treatment we have already noted for "control." Maternal nurturance has been used largely to connote love or affection extended to the child. The opposite state of affairs in which these positive feelings are replaced by hostility or resentment toward the child has been commonly subsumed under the term "maternal rejection." However, in considering the nurturance-rejection dimension, we shall have a somewhat broader set of behaviors in mind beyond the expression of affection or hostility. Among these are generosity, sharing of personal feelings and experiences, encouragement, and trust.

Over twenty years ago Reichard and Tillman (1950) described two types of schizophrenia-producing mothers. One type, the overtly rejecting mother, was described in these terms:

> . . . Such a mother has usually conceived unwillingly and is rejecting of the child from birth onwards. She is cold and sadistically critical of her offspring, insists that the patient meet her excessive demands for neatness and cleanliness, and observance of social forms, or for fulfillment of her own unfulfilled ambitions. At the same time she destroys the patient's self-confidence by her constant nagging, disapproval, and complete nonacceptance of him—or her—as a person.

The second type for Reichard and Tillman was the covertly rejecting mother who:

> . . . exerts an equally malignant influence on her child's mental development, but in a much more subtle way. She is as dominating as the sadistically hostile mother, but her domination takes the form of overprotectiveness . . . This pattern is most frequently found in infantile, egocentric mothers who fatten parasitically on their children, through babying them, to prevent them from ever becoming independent. . . . The patient is not fooled, however, and when asked about his feelings never fails to indicate that he was not loved as a child. This is by far the most common pattern of parent-child relationships in schizophrenia (pp. 251-252).

Other early clinical investigators who emphasized the importance of low nurturance in the development of schizophrenia, either in terms of maternal rejection or a social history involving generalized feelings of rebuff, include Arieti (1955), Bolles, Metzger and Pitts (1941), Cholden (1956), and Hoskins (1946).

Schofield and Balian (1959) report that only about 65% of the schizophrenics studied "enjoyed the affection of their mothers" compared to 81% of the normals. Observations of mother-child interactions in the home led Donnelly (1960) to conclude that mothers directed less warmth and acceptance toward the psychotic child than his nonpsychotic sibling. Laxer (1967), using ratings of schizophrenic and nonschizophrenic patients, concluded that maternal rejection or ambivalence was a prime factor in schizophrenia.

Severe rejection (or overprotection) by one or both parents was found in the case records of 48% of a large number of schizophrenics admitted to a state hospital by Wahl (1954). A replication study (Wahl, 1956) placed this percentage figure at 50%. Cooper (1963) also noted that the parents of schizophrenic children displayed a lack of warmth and an emotional non-involvement relative to parents of nonschizophrenic psychiatric children or of normals. Among the variables distinguishing the parents of schizophrenics from control parents, according to Horner (1964), was a deficit in display of affection.

Lebow and Epstein (1963), using a story construction methodology with good premorbid schizophrenics, described the mother figure as particularly rejecting. The controls, under treatment for physical problems, depicted the mothers as highly nurturant. Nathanson (1967), using words and pictures, established an order of response to scolding and rejecting parental cues in which poor schizophrenics responded most, goods next, and normals the least.

There are a large number of studies, previously included in the section on maternal control, which also bear upon the role of maternal or parental nurturance in the family of the schizophrenic. Clardy (1951) and Frazee (1953), using case record approaches to assessing the schizophrenic's family, noted rejection of the child as a parental attribute. Clinic records obtained in childhood revealed clear parental rejection in 40% of those cases later hospitalized as schizophrenic but released (good premorbid schizophrenics?), in 15% of subsequent chronic schizophrenics, and in 10% of clinic control cases (Waring and Ricks, 1965). Caputo (1963) identified a pattern of bilateral parental hostility in the home toward the schizophrenic offspring. Schizophrenics attributed more rejection to their parents than did normals in an investigation by Cicchetti (1967). Parental rejection of the paranoid schizophrenic was inferred from the stories told by the son in a study by Lane and Singer (1959).

Bearing more focally upon mothers, Freeman and Grayson (1955) report that the mothers of schizophrenics reveal themselves to be inherently rejecting of their children in their self-descriptions. Fleck, Lidz, and Cornelison (1963) describe the mothers of female schizophrenics as maintaining an emotional distance from their daughters. The middle-upper-class Protestant mothers included in the study by Sanua (1963) invoked the description of being rejecting.

Three studies from the good-poor premorbid literature suggest that the mothers of poors may be especially rejecting. Harris (1955) found that poors assigned more rejecting attitudes to their mothers than did goods. Poors, in a study by Bradford (1966), differentiated their responses to a taped "interview" in which a mother subscribed to subtly rejecting child-rearing practices (among other attitudes) and to another taped counterpart in which the mother was warmly supportive. Goods did not differ in their responses to these two conditions. Baxter, Williams, and Zerof (1965), using a fantasy task, found that the mothers of poors and the fathers of goods were more prone to engage in verbal censure.

Critique of the Maternal Nurturance Research

The maternal nurturance evidence which our search was able to uncover certainly comes through as less impressive than the control literature as far as sheer number of studies is concerned. Yet if we consider maternal hostility and rejection to be the pathologic end of the nurturance child-rearing dimension, there is not a clear exception to the rule of greater pathology of the schizophrenic's mother. The tendency for schizophrenics' mothers to be rejecting of their disturbed offspring may be shared with the father, found only in poor premorbid schizophrenia, or even be a Protestant middle-upper-class phenomenon; the evidence is not sufficient to allow for specific conclusions. However, the general conclusion that maternal rejection, like maternal control, is sufficiently promising to merit systematic attention in research into the pathogenesis of schizophrenia appears warranted.

Maternal Communication in Schizophrenic Development

The manner in which the mother communicates with her child represents the third major division into which we have separated maternal child-rearing behaviors. We will be concerned with what the mother communicates but, more importantly, with the manner and the effectiveness of her communications to the schizophrenic child. While human communication in its broadest sense embraces any type of stimulus from which another human can infer meaning, our usage in this book will be restricted to formal verbal communication and the vocal or body cues which provide the stimulus context within which the spoken word is conveyed.

Lennard, Beaulieu, and Embry (1965) created father-mother-son discussion interactions and concluded that there was more communication between the mother and her schizophrenic son and less father-son communication than in the control families. They also observed more communication at the level of evaluation or interpretation of feelings and motives than at the level of nonevaluative reference in the families of schizophrenics. This difference was especially noticeable with the mothers of schizophrenics relative to their controls. The Lennard et al. study was one of only two pieces of research (as opposed to speculative clinical papers) that could be found in which an overall distinction was made between the attributes of maternal and paternal communication. The second will be reviewed later in a different context.

There are several family communication studies which have not attempted or, at least, have not been able to make a distinction between the parents of schizophrenics. Fisher, Boyd, Walker, and Sheer (1959) report more distant and less harmonious communication between the parents of schizophrenics, although they did not extend their observations to the parent-child level. Greater difficulties in conceptual thinking, including disturbances in the handling of attention and meaning, were noted among the parents of schizophrenics by Lidz, Wild, Schafer, Rosman, and Fleck (1962). The Fisher et al. and Lidz et al. studies, taken in combination, might lead one to expect pervasive problems in communication among the parents of schizophrenics which would extend to the parent-child level.

Wynne and Singer (1963a, 1963b) have taken the position that lack of clarity in parental patterns of communication is an etiological factor in schizophrenia. They have proposed that thought disorder in schizophrenia, particularly the inability to fix attention upon thematic material in a consistent and sustained manner, is learned by imitation of parental patterns of communication. Parental deficit in communication is evidenced by the blurring of meaning because of subtle shifts in attention to progressively tangential material. Projective test records have been used to successfully distinguish along these lines between the parents of schizophrenics and control parents (Singer and Wynne, 1963; 1965a; 1965b). Similarly, Morris and Wynne (1965) set up criteria for judging parental styles of handling attention, developing meaning, and expressing affect from recorded sessions of conjoint family therapy. Judges, using these criteria, made a perfect classification of the parents of schizophrenics, borderline schizophrenics, and nonschizophrenics.

Family group interviews as well as individual interviews with the mother, father, index sibling, and normal sibling provided the data for an investigation by Stabenau, Tupin, Werner, and Pollin (1965). Index siblings included schizophrenics, delinquents, and normals. The schizophrenic families showed blurred and unclear communication but this result was limited in its significance by the finding of wandering and unclear communication in the families of delinquents. Similarly, the parents of schizophrenics were found to have more idiosyncratic association and meaning responses relative to parents of normals by Ciarlo, Lidz, and Ricci (1967). However, the schizophrenics' parents did not differ from the parents of nonschizophrenic psychiatric patients. An even more negative experiment was reported by Haley (1968). He compared the clarity of communication among sets of parents with schizophrenic children, nonschizophrenic but abnormal children, and normal children by having them provide instructions for a task to be performed by children (not their own). No differences in task performance and, presumably, in clarity of task instructions were found.

Several special theories of communication deficit in the families of schizophrenics have been proposed. Wynne, Ryckoff, Day, and Hirsch (1958) proposed the concept of "pseudomutuality" in the parents of schizophrenics which has at its core the expression of support, agreement, and positive regard for the schizophrenic child which represent superficial rather than real dispositions of the parent and child. Differential expectations in the areas of dependency and responsibility communicated to the schizophrenic child and his nonschizophrenic sib (the "quadruple bind") was postulated to be of etiological significance by Lu (1962). As far as could be determined, neither of these clinical concepts has generated the research necessary to adequately evaluate its tenability.

The concepts of the "double bind" in the communication between the mother and her preschizophrenic child (Bateson, Jackson, Haley, and Weakland, 1956), in contrast, has elicited a substantial amount of research interest. Bateson et al., in their original proposal of double-binding communication, suggested that the mother of the preschizophrenic presents him with two orders of message: (1) hostile, withdrawing behavior is aroused in the mother on the approach of the child, and (2) simulated loving or approach behavior in the mother occurs when the child responds to her hostile and withdrawing cues. These conflicting communications from the mother in combination with injunctions against the child's questioning of the different orders of message (the metacommunication) were postulated to lead to an inability to exchange meaning in the child's social relationships.

Berger (1965) asked schizophrenics as well as several control groups to rate the statements on a questionnaire in terms of their similarity to statements made by their own mothers. The statements included samples of double-bind communication, and, in line with the double-bind hypothesis, the schizophrenics rated these samples as more similar to their mothers' verbal behavior.

However, the double-bind concept has not fared well when judged by the evidence from other investigations. Ciotola (1961) simulated double-bind conditions by setting up an impossible discrimination between two auditory tones. He failed to find schizophrenics to be any more affected by this experimental situation in terms of increased reaction times, greater concreteness, or increased tension than were nonpsychotic psychiatric controls. Again using experimental simulation of a double-bind situation, Potash (1965) presented his subjects with a two-person, three-choice game in which one of the choices was withdrawal, meaning that the player could neither win nor lose. This alternative was construed to be the counterpart of the postulated withdrawal of the preschizophrenic child to the mother's double-bind communication. Potash found that schizophrenics did not elect the withdrawal choice any more than did the hospital employee controls. Loeff (1966) presented metaphors to schizophrenics, delinquents, and normals; the double bind was simulated by having the content and affect of the metaphors in direct conflict. Both the schizophrenics and the delinquents differed from the normals in their ratings of the metaphors on the semantic differential. Both deviant groups also attended more to the metacommunication (i.e., communication about the communication) elements of the messages, which is contrary to expectation for the schizophrenics according to the double-bind hypothesis.

While the adequacy of these three experimental procedures in simulating the hypothesized double-bind situation between the mother and her preschizophrenic son is open to question, a study by Ringuette and Kennedy (1966) actually used letters written by parents of schizophrenics and controls to test for the presence of double-bind communication. These letters were presented to five sets of judges ranging from those trained on the double-bind concept to naive judges. None of these groups of judges could differentiate between the letters written by parents of schizophrenics and nonschizophrenics as far as double-bind communication was concerned. Schuham (1967), in summarizing the evidence on the double-bind hypothesis, concluded that: (1) the studies have provided no support for the double-bind hypothesis, (2) there is no evidence that double-bind communication is exclusive to pathological processes and is not represented in normal communication processes, and (3) there is no evidence that the double bind has an etiological connection with schizophrenic development.

Perhaps the most ambitious investigation of communication processes in the families of schizophrenics is that reported by Mishler and Waxler (1968). The taped interactions of parents and their schizophrenic sons or daughters were analyzed for communication styles, and these analyses were conducted separately for the families of good premorbid and poor premorbid schizophrenics. The good premorbid families of sons utilized a speech pattern which allowed for a high degree of predictability in the sequence of events and for minimizing uncertainty or ambiguity. This pattern was especially evident in the mothers of goods. Poor premorbid families were more similar to the families of normals as far as allowing for the disrupted, fragmental speech style characteristic of normals. The findings for the families of schizophrenic daughters, while described as less reliable, suggested that female good premorbid schizophrenics in interacting with their families contribute to a pattern of speech with the highest rate of disruption, just opposite to the findings for schizophrenic sons.

Becker and Finkel (1969) used raters to predict missing words in recorded free speech of the parents of female poors, goods, and normals. The highest speech predictability occurred with the parents of poor premorbid schizophrenics and the lowest with the parents of normals. These results appear to be inconsistent with those reported by Mishler and Waxler who found greater commonality than difference in the speech patterns of the parents of poor premorbid schizophrenics and of normals.

Critique of the Maternal Communication Research

It is most difficult to generate enthusiasm over the importance of maternal communication as an etiologic factor in schizophrenia based upon this survey of relevant research. However, it is necessary to point out that good communication research is more difficult to implement than studies of control or nurturance. The impressive amount of work which went into the small-sample study (32 schizophrenic families and 17 normal families) of Mishler and Waxler (1968) makes it clear why better communication research is out of reach except for those who have substantial research funding.

While there may be technical barriers to human communication research, the paucity of positive findings relevant to mother- or parent-schizophrenic child interactions certainly make this the sector of maternal behavior in which we can invest the least confidence as a source of influence in schizophrenic development. As we shall try to demonstrate later in this book, though, communication style of the mother can be profitably employed as an explanatory variable in schizophrenia despite the limited implications of the literature.

OVERVIEW OF THE RESEARCH RELATING THE MOTHER TO FILIAL SCHIZOPHRENIA

While it would be improper to take comfort in the rudimentary state of our knowledge about the family conditions that may be conducive to schizophrenic development, it must be admitted that it has lent a special enthusiasm to the task set before us in this book—that of building a mother-child social-learning theory of schizophrenia using only the information generated by research. The primary maternal variables which will form the fabric of the theory, maternal control and nurturance, have received sufficient documentation in the literature to qualify as at least correlates of schizophrenia in the child. Causal influence is another matter, and the task of presenting a convincing argument for maternal control-rejection patterns as antecedent dynamics of schizophrenia will consume several chapters.

There has been no attempt, as the reader may have noted, to include systematic critical evaluation of the scientific methodologies employed by the researchers cited in this chapter. This hardly means that the methods of investigation were above reproach, but it does underscore the fact that the family variables emerged as important *despite* the tremendous difficulties in implementing research into the development of schizophrenia. Such a noncritical stance is less charitable than pragmatic. It is almost axiomatic in our young science of psychology that the more rigorous our method and precise our data, the less important the implications of our findings for the human enterprise. In the context of discovery we should take what we can get in the way of "facts" and see what hangs together. When we get around to proof of our theoretical assertions, we should impose whatever greater rigor is at our disposal.

Other recent reviewers of the research into family variables in the etiology of schizophrenia have drawn much sterner conclusions about the state of our knowledge. Frank (1965, p. 201) summarizes his survey of forty years of research into the family's role in psychopathogenesis by stating:

> We end this survey by concluding that we have not been able to find any unique factors in the family of the schizophrenic which distinguishes it from the family of controls, who are ostensively free from evidence of patterns of gross psychopathology.

While Frank tends to dismiss the evidence from family studies in schizophrenia because of the absence of differential etiological factors, both Fontana (1966) and Mednick and McNeil (1968) reject the preponderance of family studies on methodological grounds. Fontana, in making the case for studies using direct observation of family interaction, rather pessimistically concludes:

> The greatest value of current studies of family interaction seems to lie in the guidelines the findings might provide for longitudinal research. Truly appropriate etiological conclusions can only be drawn from careful longitudinal studies. This reviewer doubts that sufficient knowledge is currently available to warrant the great expenditure involved in longitudinal research at the present time (p. 225).

A longitudinal approach to etiological factors in schizophrenia using a high-risk-for-schizophrenia group of children is recommended by Mednick and McNeil as a remedy for the serious flaws in methodologies usually employed in etiological research. A critical review of the major studies which claim support for the relationship between mother dominance and schizophrenia led Cicchetti (1969) to conclude that the concept of the "schizophrenogenic mother" was based upon misinterpretation of research findings rather than empirical fact.

Extended consideration of the methodological issues involved in the scientific investigation of the etiology of psychopathology shall concern us in the next chapter, especially as these are relevant to the procedures for data acquisition used in our own research program. We shall at that point take issue with many of the conclusions reached by other developmental researchers regarding the scientific strategies to be employed in discovering the effects of family influence upon the child.

REFERENCES

Alanen, Y. O. From the mothers of schizophrenic patients to interactional family dynamics. In D. Rosenthal and S. S. Kety (Eds.), *The transmission of schizophrenia.* New York: Pergamon Press, 1968.

Arieti, S. *Interpretation of schizophrenia.* New York: Brunner, 1955.

Bateson, G., Jackson, D. D., Haley, J., and Weakland, J. Towards a theory of schizophrenia. *Behavioral Science,* 1956, **1**, 251-264.

Baxter, J. C., Williams, J., and Zerof, S. Child-rearing attitudes and disciplinary fantasies of parents of schizophrenics and controls. *Journal of Nervous and Mental Disease,* 1965, **141**, 567-579.

Baxter, J. C., and Becker, J. Anxiety and avoidance behavior in schizophrenics in response to parental figures. *Journal of Abnormal and Social Psychology,* 1962, **64**, 432-437.

Becker, J., and Finkel, P. Predictability and anxiety in speech by parents of female schizophrenics. *Journal of Abnormal Psychology,* 1969, **74**, 517-523.

Becker, J., and Siefkes, H. Parental dominance, conflict, and disciplinary coerciveness in families of female schizophrenics. *Journal of Abnormal Psychology,* 1969, **74**, 193-198.

Behrens, M. L., and Goldfarb, W. A study of patterns of interaction of families of schizophrenic children in residential treatment. *American Journal of Orthopsychiatry,* 1958, **28**, 300-312.

Bell, R. Q., Garmezy, N., Farina, A., and Rodnick, E. H. Direct study of parent-child interaction. *American Journal of Orthopsychiatry,* 1960, **30**, 445-452.

Berger, A. A test of the double bind hypothesis of schizophrenia. *Family Process,* 1965, **4**, 198-205.

Bolles, M. M., Metzger, H. F., and Pitts, M. W. Early home background and personal adjustment. *American Journal of Orthopsychiatry* 1941, **11**, 530-534.

Bowen, M., Dysinger, R. H., and Basamanie, B. The role of the father in families with a schizophrenic patient. *American Journal of Psychiatry,* 1959, **115**, 1017-1020.

Bradford, N. H. Comparative perceptions of mothers and maternal roles of schizophrenic patients and their normal siblings. *Dissertation Abstracts,* 1966, **26**, 5545-5546.

Caputo, D. V. The parents of the schizophrenic. *Family Process,* 1963, **2**, 339-356.

Cheek, F. E. A serendipitous finding: sex roles and schizophrenia. *Journal of Abnormal and Social Psychology,* 1964, **69**, 392-400.

Cholden, L. Observations on psychotherapy of schizophrenia. In Frieda Fromm-Reichman and J. L. Moreno (Eds.), *Progress in psychotherapy.* New York: Grune and Stratton, 1956.

Ciarlo, D. D., Lidz, T., and Ricci, J. Word meanings in parents of schizophrenics. *Archives of General Psychiatry,* 1967, **17,** 470-477.

Cicchetti, D. V. Reported family dynamics and psychopathology: I. The reactions of schizophrenics and normals to parental dialogues. *Journal of Abnormal Psychology,* 1967, **72,** 282-289.

Cicchetti, D. V. Critical review of the research relating mother dominance to schizophrenia. *Proceedings of the 77th Annual Convention of the American Psychological Association,* 1969, **4,** 557-558.

Cicchetti, D. V., Klein, E. B., Fontana, A. F., and Spohn, H. E. A test of the censure-deficit model in schizophrenia, employing the Rodnick-Garmezy visual-discrimination task. *Journal of Abnormal Psychology,* 1967, **72,** 326-334.

Ciotola, P. V. The effect of two contradictory levels of reward and censure on schizophrenics. (Doctoral dissertation, University of Missouri) Ann Arbor: University Microfilms, 1961, No. 61-2278.

Clardy, E. R. A study of the development and course of schizophrenic children. *Psychiatric Quarterly,* 1951, **25,** 81-90.

Clark, A. R. Conformity behavior of schizophrenic subjects with maternal figures. *Journal of Abnormal and Social Psychology,* 1964, **68,** 45-53.

Cooper, B. Parents of schizophrenic children compared with parents of nonpsychotic emotionally disturbed and well children: a discriminant function analysis. *Dissertation Abstracts,* 1963, **24,** 1994-1995.

Despert, L. J. Schizophrenia in children. *Psychiatric Quarterly,* 1938, **12,** 366-371.

Despert, L. J. Some considerations relating to the genesis of autistic behavior in children. *American Journal of Orthopsychiatry,* 1951, **21,** 335-350.

Donnelly, M. The quantitative analysis of parent behavior toward psychotic children and their siblings. *Genetic Psychology Monographs,* 1960, **62,** 331-376.

Donovan, M. J., and Webb, W. W. Meaning dimensions and male-female voice perception in schizophrenics with good and poor premorbid adjustment. *Journal of Abnormal Psychology,* 1965, **70,** 426-431.

Dworin, J., and Wyant, O. Authoritarian patterns in the mothers of schizophrenics. *Journal of Clinical Psychology,* 1957, **13,** 332-338.

Englehart, R. S. Semantic correlates of interpersonal concepts and parental attributes in schizophrenia. Unpublished doctoral dissertation, Duke University, 1959.

Farina, A. Patterns of role dominance and conflict in parents of schizophrenic patients. *Journal of Abnormal and Social Psychology,* 1960, **61,** 31-38.

Farina, A., and Dunham, R. M. Measurement of family relationships and their effects. *Archives of General Psychiatry,* 1963, **9,** 64-73.

Farina, A., and Holzberg, J. D. Attitudes and behaviors of fathers and mothers of male schizophrenic patients. *Journal of Abnormal Psychology,* 1967, **72,** 381-387.

Farina, A., and Holzberg, J. D. Interaction patterns of parents and hospitalized sons diagnosed as schizophrenic or nonschizophrenic patients. *Journal of Abnormal Psychology,* 1968, **73**, 114-118.

Fisher, S., Boyd, I., Walker, D., and Sheer, D. Parents of schizophrenics, neurotics, and normals. *Archives of General Psychiatry,* 1959, **1**, 149-167.

Fleck, S., Lidz, T., and Cornelison, A. Comparison of parent-child relationships of male and female schizophrenic patients. *Archives of General Psychiatry,* 1963, **8**, 1-7.

Fontana, A. F. Familial etiology of schizophrenia: Is a scientific methodology possible? *Psychological Bulletin,* 1966, **66**, 214-227.

Fontana, A. F., Klein, E. B., and Cicchetti, D. V. Censure sensitivity in schizophrenia. *Journal of Abnormal Psychology,* 1967, **72**, 294-302.

Frank, G. H. The role of the family in the development of psychopathology. *Psychological Bulletin,* 1965, **64**, 191-205.

Frazee, H. E. Children who later became schizophrenic. *Smith College Studies in Social Work,* 1953, **23**, 125-149.

Freeman, H. E., and Simmons, O. G. Mental Patients in the community: Family settings and performance levels. *American Sociological Review,* 1958, **23**, 147-154.

Freeman, H. E., Simmons, O. G., and Bergen, B. J. Possessiveness as a characteristic of mothers of schizophrenics. *Journal of Abnormal and Social Psychology,* 1959, **58**, 271-273.

Freeman, R. V., and Grayson, M. H. Maternal attitudes in schizophrenia. *Journal of Abnormal and Social Psychology,* 1955, **50**, 45-52.

Garmezy, N., Clark, A. R., and Stockner, C. Childrearing attitudes of mothers and fathers as reported by schizophrenic and normal patients. *Journal of Abnormal and Social Psychology,* 1961, **63**, 176-182.

Geisinger, D. L. The effect of maternal versus paternal dominance on the performance of good and poor premorbid schizophrenics. Unpublished doctoral dissertation, Syracuse University, 1966.

Gerald, D. L., and Siegal, J. The family background of schizophrenia. *Psychiatric Quarterly,* 1950, **24**, 47-73.

Goodman, D. Performance of good and poor premorbid male schizophrenics as a function of paternal versus maternal censure. *Journal of Abnormal and Social Psychology,* 1964, **69**, 550-555.

Goodman, I. Z. Influence of parental figures on schizophrenic patients. *Journal of Abnormal Psychology,* 1968, **73**, 503-512.

Guertin, W. H. Are differences in schizophrenic symptoms related to the mother's avowed attitudes toward child rearing? *Journal of Abnormal and Social Psychology,* 1961, **63**, 440-442.

Hajdu-Gimes, L. Contributions to the etiology of schizophrenia. *Psychoanalytic Review,* 1940, **27**, 421-438.

Haley, J. Testing parental instructions to schizophrenic and normal children: A pilot study. *Journal of Abnormal Psychology,* 1968, **73**, 559-565.

Harris, J. G., Jr. A study of the mother-son relationship in schizophrenia. Unpublished doctoral dissertation, Duke University, 1955.

Heilbrun, A. B. Perception of maternal childrearing attitudes in schizophrenia. *Journal of Consulting Psychology,* 1960, **24**, 169-173.

Heilbrun, A. B. Maternal authoritarianism, social class, and filial schizophrenia. *Journal of General Psychology,* 1961, **65**, 235-241.

Horner, R. F. Important stimulus variables in the early family relationships of schizophrenic patients. *Journal of Clinical Psychology,* 1964, **20**, 344-3 6.

Hoskins, R. G. *The biology of schizophrenia.* New York: Norton, 1946.

Hotchkiss, G. D., Carmen, L., Ogilby, A., and Wiesenfeld, A. Mothers of young male single schizophrenic patients as visitors in a mental hospital. *Journal of Nervous and Mental Diseases,* 1955, **121**, 452.

Jackson, D. D., Block, J., Block, J., and Patterson, V. Psychiatrists' conceptions of the schizophrenogenic parents. *Archives of Neurology and Psychiatry,* 1958, **79**, 448-459.

Jackson, N. L. P., Jr. Sex and dominance cues in good-poor premorbid schizophrenia. *Journal of Abnormal Psychology,* 1970, **75**, 78-82.

Jenkins, R. L. The schizophrenic sequence: withdrawal, disorganization, psychotic reorganization. *American Journal of Orthopsychiatry,* 1952, **22**, 738-748.

Karon, B. P. The resolution of acute schizophrenic reactions: A contribution to the development of non-classical psychotherapeutic techniques. *Psychotherapy,* 1963, **1**, 27-43.

Karon, B. P., and Rosberg, J. Study of the mother-child relationship in a case of paranoid schizophrenia. *American Journal of Psychotherapy,* 1958, **12**, 522-533.

Kasanin, J., Knight, E., and Sage, P. The parent-child relationship in schizophrenia. *Journal of Nervous and Mental Disease,* 1934, **79**, 249-263.

Klebanoff, L. B. A comparison of parental attitudes of mothers of schizophrenics, brain injured, and normal children. *American Journal of Orthopsychiatry,* 1959, **24**, 445-454.

Klein, E. B., Cicchetti, D., and Spohn, H. A test of the censure-deficit model and its relation to premorbidity in the performance of schizophrenics. *Journal of Abnormal Psychology,* 1967, **72**, 174-181.

Kohn, M. L., and Clausen, J. A. Parental authority behavior and schizophrenia. *American Journal of Orthopsychiatry,* 1956, **25**, 297-313.

Kreinik, P. Parent-child themes and concept attainment in schizophrenia. Unpublished doctoral dissertation, Duke University, 1959.

Lane, R. C., and Singer, J. L. Familial attitudes in paranoid schizophrenia and normals from two socioeconomic classes. *Journal of Abnormal and Social Psychology,* 1959, **59**, 328-339.

Laxer, R. M. Schizophrenia and parental rejection or ambivalence. *Psychological Reports,* 1967, **20**, 987-993.

Lebow, K. E., and Epstein, S. Thematic and cognitive responses of good premorbid schizophrenics to cues of nurturance and rejection. *Journal of Consulting Psychology,* 1963, **27**, 24-33.

Lennard, H. L., Beaulieu, M. R., and Embrey, N. G. Interaction in families with a schizophrenic child. *Archives of General Psychiatry,* 1965, **12**, 166-183.

Lerner, P. M. Resolution of intrafamilial conflicts in families of schizophrenic patients. *Dissertation Abstracts,* 1965, **25**, 6761-6762.

Lidz, R., and Lidz, T. The family environment of schizophrenic patients. *American Journal of Psychiatry,* 1949, **106**, 332-345.

Lidz, T., Cornelison, A. R., Fleck, S., and Terry, D. The intrafamilial environment of schizophrenic patients: I. The father. *Psychiatry,* 1957, **20**, 329-342. (a)

Lidz, T., Cornelison, A. R., Fleck, S., and Terry, D. The intrafamilial environment of schizophrenic patients: II. Marital schism and marital skew. *American Journal of Psychiatry,* 1957, **114**, 241-248. (b)

Lidz, T., Cornelison, A. R., Fleck, S., and Terry, D. The intrafamilial environment of the schizophrenic patient. *Psychiatry,* 1957, **20**, 329-342. (c)

Lidz, T., Cornelison, A. R., Terry, D., and Fleck, S. Intrafamilial environment of the schizophrenic patient: VI. The transmission of irrationality. *Archives of Neurology and Psychiatry,* 1958, **79**, 305-316.

Lidz, T., Parker, N., and Cornelison, A. R. The role of the father in the family environment of the schizophrenic patient. *American Journal of Psychiatry,* 1956, **113**, 126-137.

Lidz, T., Wild, C., Schafer, S., Rosman, B., and Fleck, S. Thought disorders in the parents of schizophrenic patients: a study utilizing the object sorting test. *Journal of Psychiatric Research,* 1962, **1**, 193-200.

Loeff, R. G. Differential discrimination of conflicting emotional messages by normal, delinquent, and schizophrenic adolescents. (Doctoral dissertation, Indiana University) Ann Arbor: University Microfilms, 1966, No. 66-1470.

Lu, Y. Contradictory parental expectations in schizophrenia. *Archives of General Psychiatry,* 1962, **6**, 219-234.

Mainord, F. R. Parental attitudes in schizophrenics. *Dissertation Abstracts,* 1957, **17**, 896-897.

Mark, J. C. The attitudes of the mothers of male schizophrenics toward child behavior. *Journal of Abnormal and Social Psychology,* 1953, **48**, 185-189.

McKeown, J. E. The behavior of parents of schizophrenic, neurotic, and normal children. *American Journal of Sociology,* 1950, **56**, 175-179.

McKinley, R. A. Perceived parental attributes of schizophrenics as a function of premorbid social adjustment. *Dissertation Abstracts,* 1964, **24**, 4800.

Mednick, S. A., and McNeil, T. F. Current methodology in research on the etiology of schizophrenia: serious difficulties which suggest the use of the high-risk-group method. *Psychological Bulletin,* 1968, **70**, 681-693.

Meyer, R., and Karon, B. P. A study of the schizophrenogenic mother concept by means of the TAT. *Psychiatry,* 1967, **30,** 173-179.

Meyers, D. I., and Goldfarb, W. Studies of perplexity in mothers of schizophrenic children. *American Journal of Orthopsychiatry,* 1961, **31,** 551-564.

Mishler, E. G., and Waxler, N. E. *Interaction in families: An experimental study of family processes and schizophrenia.* New York: Wiley, 1968.

Mitchell, K. M. An analysis of the schizophrenogenic mother concept by means of the thematic apperception test. *Journal of Abnormal Psychology,* 1968, **73,** 571-574.

Mitchell, K. M. Concept of "pathogenesis" in parents of schizophrenic and normal children. *Journal of Abnormal Psychology,* 1969, **74,** 423-424.

Morris, G. O., and Wynne, L. C. Schizophrenic offspring and parental styles of communication. *Psychiatry,* 1965, **20,** 19-44.

Nathanson, I. A. A semantic differential analysis of parent-son relationships in schizophrenia. *Journal of Abnormal Psychology,* 1967, **72,** 277-281.

Opler, M. K. Schizophrenia and culture. *Scientific American,* 1957, **197,** 103-110.

Perr, H. M. Criteria distinguishing parents of schizophrenic and normal children. *Archives of Neurology and Psychiatry,* 1958, **79,** 217-224.

Porro, C. R. Perception of maternal child-rearing attitudes by schizophrenic males, their normal male siblings, and normal males whose siblings are normal. *Journal of Consulting Psychology,* 1965, **29,** 242-246.

Potash, H. M. Schizophrenic interaction and the concept of the double bind. (Doctoral dissertation, Michigan State University) Ann Arbor: University Microfilms, 1965, No. 65-2052.

Prout, C. T., and White, M. A. A controlled study of personality relationships in mothers of schizophrenic male patients. *American Journal of Psychiatry,* 1950, **107,** 251.

Query, J. M. N. Premorbid adjustment and family structure: a comparison of selected rural and urban schizophrenic men. *Journal of Nervous and Mental Disease,* 1961, **133,** 333-338.

Reichard, S., and Tillman, C. Patterns of parent-child relationships in schizophrenia. *Psychiatry,* 1950, **13,** 247-258.

Ringuette, E. L., and Kennedy, T. An experimental study of the double bind hypothesis. *Journal of Abnormal Psychology,* 1966, **71,** 136-141.

Roberts, B. H., and Meyers, J. K. Schizophrenia in the youngest male child of the lower middle class. *American Journal of Psychiatry,* 1955, **113,** 129-134.

Rodnick, E. H., and Garmezy, N. Motivational factors in the production of psychological deficit in schizophrenia. Unpublished progress report, 1955, Cited in Rodnick, E. H., and Garmezy, N. An experimental approach to the study of motivation in schizophrenia. In M. R. Jones (Ed.), *Nebraska symposium on motivation,* Lincoln: University of Nebraska Press, 1957. Pp. 109-184.

Rodnick, E. H., and Garmezy, N. An experimental approach to the study of motivation in schizophrenia. In M. R. Jones (Ed.), *Nebraska symposium on motivation.* Lincoln: University of Nebraska Press, 1957, pp. 109-184.

Sanua, V. D. The socio-cultural aspects of schizophrenia: a comparison of Protestant and Jewish schizophrenics. *International Journal of Social Psychiatry,* 1963, **9**, 27-35.

Schaffer, H. R., and Emerson, P. E. The development in social attachments in infancy. *Monographs of the Society for Research in Child Development,* 1964, **29,** No. 3.

Schofield, W., and Balian, L. A comparative study of the personal histories of schizophrenic and nonpsychiatric patients. *Journal of Abnormal and Social Psychology,* 1959, **59,** 216-225.

Schuham, A. I. The double-bind hypothesis a decade later. *Psychological Bulletin,* 1967, **68,** 409-416.

Singer, J. L. Projected familial attitudes as a function of socioeconomic status and psychopathology, *Journal of Consulting Psychology,* 1954, **18,** 99-104.

Singer, M. T., and Wynne, L. C. Differentiating characteristics of parents of childhood schizophrenics, childhood neurotics, and young adult schizophrenics. *American Journal of Psychiatry,* 1963, **120,** 234-243.

Singer, M. T., and Wynne, L. C. Thought disorder and family relations of schizophrenics: III. Methodology using projective techniques. *Archives of General Psychiatry,* 1965, **12,** 187-200. (a)

Singer, M. T., and Wynne, L. C. Thought disorder and family relations of schizophrenics: IV. Results and implications. *Archives of General Psychiatry,* 1965, **12,** 201-212. (b)

Stabenau, J. R., Tupin, J., Werner, M., and Pollin, W. A comparative study of schizophrenics, delinquents, and normals. *Psychiatry,* 1965, **28,** 45-49.

Tietz, T. A study of mothers of schizophrenic patients. *Psychiatry,* 1949, **12,** 55-65.

Wahl, C. W. Some antecedent factors in the family histories of 392 schizophrenics. *American Journal of Psychiatry,* 1954, **110,** 668-676.

Wahl, C. W. Some antecedent factors in the family histories of 568 male schizophrenics of the United States Navy. *American Journal of Psychiatry,* 1956, **113,** 201-210.

Walters, J. H. A study of family relationships of schizophrenic patients. *Smith College Studies in Social Work,* 1939, **9,** 189-191.

Waring, M., and Ricks, D. Family patterns of children who became adult schizophrenics. *Journal of Nervous and Mental Disease,* 1965, **140,** 351-364.

Werner, M., Stabenau, J. R., and Pollin, W. Thematic apperception test method for the differentiation of families of schizophrenics, delinquents, and "normals." *Journal of Abnormal Psychology,* 1970, **75**, 139-145.

Wynne, L. C., Ryckoff, I., Day, J., and Hirsch, S. Pseudomutuality in the family relations of schizophrenics. *Psychiatry,* 1958, **21**, 205-220.

Wynne, L. C., and Singer, M. T. Thought disorder and family relations of schizophrenics: I. A research strategy. *Archives of General Psychiatry,* 1963, **9**, 191-198. (a)

Wynne, L. C., and Singer, M. T. Thought disorder and the family relations of schizophrenics: II. Classification of forms of thinking. *Archives of General Psychiatry,* 1963, **9**, 199-206. (b)

Zahn, T. P. Acquired and symbolic affective value as determinants of size estimation in schizophrenic and normal subjects. Unpublished doctoral dissertation, Duke University, 1956.

Zuckerman, M., Oltean, M., and Monashkin, I. The parental attitudes of mothers of schizophrenics. *Journal of Consulting Psychology,* 1958, **22**, 307-310.

CHAPTER 3

Procedures of the Research Program

It is difficult to imagine a type of human research replete with more problems and issues than are inherent in the study of developmental psychopathology. Many of these problems are shared with all behavioral research which contends with complex human social behavior, others are intrinsic to the study of behavior change over lengthy periods of time, while still others are generated by a concern with abnormal behavior. We believe that a consideration of the most salient issues relevant to our research program and an understanding of the rationale behind our resolution of the problems are necessary to reasonably weigh our results and conclusions.

ISSUES RELATED TO INVESTIGATING THE DEVELOPMENT OF SCHIZOPHRENIC PSYCHOPATHOLOGY

Establishing the Independence of Genetic versus Environmental Contributions

There is no more fertile ground for continuation of a debate than the inability of either side to be explicit. The question of whether schizophrenia is to be considered a genetically transmitted condition or a disorder produced by environmental stress has defied resolution because as yet no one has satisfactorily elaborated how either genetic factors or environmental factors could cause schizophrenic behaviors. This has required antagonists in either camp to base their arguments on evidence of such ambiguity as to be nonpersuasive. For example, consanguinity studies and twin studies have repeatedly demonstrated higher incidence rates of schizophrenia as a function of closer family ties and a more similar genetic endowment to the index schizophrenic. However, the same studies have left themselves open to environmentalist contention that the social conditions under which children are reared are considerably more pathological when the index schizophrenic is their parent or that twins also share environmental commonalities as well as genetic similarities.

A recent publication, the *Proceedings of the Second Research Conference of the Foundations' Fund for Research in Psychiatry* (Rosenthal and Kety, 1968), reports the contributions of specialists from around the world in the area of schizophrenic development. Certainly, this compendium of opinion should present us with an authoritative set of conclusions regarding the relative importance of hereditary and environmental influences in the genesis of schizophrenia. Indeed, Rosenthal's (1968) summary of the conference concludes with some confidence that a general consensus finally appears to have been reached among experts that heredity is implicated in the development of schizophrenia. He proceeds, however, to point out that acknowledgment of the contribution of heredity still leaves a wide latitude for interpreting the relative importance of genetic and environmental factors in the etiology of schizophrenia. He notes at one extreme:

> In the strictest sense, it is clearly not schizophrenia that is inherited. The genes that are implicated produce an effect whose nature we have not yet been able to fathom. It is clear that not everybody who harbors the genes develops schizophrenia. . . . It is for such reasons, and perhaps others, that many people have maintained and may continue to maintain that schizophrenia is *not* an inherited disease. They might nevertheless acknowledge a contribution of heredity but would be inclined to minimize its importance (p. 416).

Others will approach the question of the importance of heredity from the opposite pole:

> They say that it is a secondary matter whether any particular individual does or does not develop clinical schizophrenia. What is primary is that if he has the implicated hereditary factors, he is either basically or potentially schizophrenic. . . . the belief is that no one will develop true schizophrenia if he does not harbor the implicated gene(s). People who interpret the question in this way will assert that schizophrenia *is* an inherited disease, and they will minimize the importance of environmental factors (p. 416).

Yet another position regarding heredity would be:

> . . . whether or not a potentially identifiable genotype eventually leads to a clinically schizophrenic illness depends primarily on environmental factors, among them the kinds of life experiences the gene carrier encounters. However, individuals with this genotype may develop many other phenotypical patterns as well, not all of them bad. . . . Moreover, those who develop clinical schizophrenia may constitute only a fraction of the total number of individuals who harbor the genotype. . . . Proponents of this view would be inclined to say that schizophrenia is *not* an inherited disease (p. 417).

In contrast, a polygenic view would contend that the qualitatively different outcomes noted immediately above "are the results of different combinations of genes, none of which by itself would necessarily be clinically pathogenic, and that schizophrenia must therefore be considered an inherited disease" (p. 417).

These divergent conceptual approaches to the heredity-environment issue in schizophrenia, summarized by Rosenthal, have been presented in some detail to emphasize his own conclusion that despite their variance, these views all assume that heredity *and* environment are implicated in schizophrenia. However, accepting this general conclusion regarding the etiology of schizophrenia does not lead us much closer to the specifics of schizophrenic development. Neither does the unanimous admonition of the specialists which urges us to consider the interaction of heredity and environment as a major goal of the future.

Meehl (1962) several years ago considered the reasons why psychologists were so reluctant to accept the implications of twin studies for hereditary contribution to schizophrenia. He suggested this to be so because to accept heredity seemed tantamount to denying the importance of such psychodynamics as family social learning. He denies the necessity for such concern by invoking essentially the same arguments as emerged from the conference on schizophrenia. Even if a genetic flaw were a necessary precondition for schizophrenia, it fails to be a sufficient basis for understanding its occurrence or its formal attributes. Meehl did take a strong genetic position as far as the "necessary but not sufficient" dictum was concerned. He proposed a state, schizotaxia, involving a neural integrative defect produced by genetic mutation, as the necessary condition for the occurrence of schizophrenia.

The critical feature of the heredity-environment issue for our purpose is that environmental stressors must be assumed no matter how avidly one adheres to a genetic model. This is true whether the external stress is thought of as merely a trigger mechanism which releases the genetically induced schizophrenia or as a more instrumental influence which must be considered in order to understand the schizophreniform behavior itself. The fact should not be ignored, however, that either of these levels at which an interaction between heredity and environment may be considered in the genesis of schizophrenia fails to make the strongest case for the importance of environmental circumstances. This would come from the demonstration that schizophrenia may develop in the absence of faulty genes. However, the apparent difficulties in devising a more exact test for the presence of a schizophrenia-producing gene other than the presence or absence of schizophrenia in a parent or sibling makes it just as difficult to rule out a genetic contribution as to prove one.

The necessity to proceed cautiously when considering the etiology of schizophrenia certainly emerges as a conservative ethic from this discussion, but this holds only insofar as we are unable to establish with any confidence the relative contributions of heredity and experience. We will pretend to no such caution in our formulation of the way in which a particular segment of experience, with the mother, may serve as an important environmental contributor to this interaction. Our private assumption, which remains blissfully protected from the data of our research, is that schizophrenic behaviors may be learned in the absence of genetic flaw, a point-of-view shared by Leon Eisenberg (1968), who was called upon to act as a discussant at the conference on schizophrenic development. In sounding a note of caution for researchers interested in teasing apart the contributions of heredity and environment, he suggests that given extreme family trauma the risk of schizophrenia in the children would be almost as high among those with normal genetic status as among those who are carriers of the schizophrenic gene.

The Use of Normal Subjects in Seeking the Origins of Psychopathology

It has been commonly observed that man's supraordinate position on the planet earth has not evolved from superior physical skills or sensory acuity but can be explained exclusively in terms of higher order capacities of the central nervous system, especially the cerebral cortex. One may speculate that it is one of these higher order functions, man's rational nature, which has been largely responsible for the lingering tendency even among professionals to set schizophrenic behavior apart categorically from normal behavior. The difficulties experienced by the individual observer in understanding the often bizarre behavior of schizophrenics stems in large measure from the loss of one of our primary guides to understanding others–asking ourselves why we would behave in a particular manner under particular conditions. If what is observed is beyond our own experience, our empathic guide to understanding (whether we are right or wrong) is gone. The inability to incorporate the schizophrenic's behavior into our rational experience has led to the assumption–implicit or explicit–that such behavior must be governed by laws different from those determining normal behavior. Over the centuries the sophistication of the assumptions underlying the presumed uniqueness of abnormal behavior has progressed far from its demonic origins, but this type of thinking is still subtly represented in the present day search for an exclusive constitutional agent, genetic, chemical, or neural, to explain deviant behavior.

At this point we are not concerned about specific causal determinants, constitutional versus learning, but rather how we should view whatever aspect of schizophrenia is learned. There are two questions here. For one, are the behaviors we agree are schizophrenic to be considered different from the behavior of normals only in degree or are these behaviors to be considered different in kind from those of normals? The other question relates to whether the schizophrenic has responded to the same dimensions of experience as the normal so that the laws of human behavior as they emerge will be able to explain the development of both. Or do we need two sets of laws?

Those few theorists who have been responsible for truly landmark contributions in the application of learning theory to psychopathology have taken very explicit stands with regard to the continuity between normal and abnormal behavior. Dollard and Miller (1950), whose influential treatise on psychopathology and psychotherapy attempted a coalescence of psychoanalytic and learning theories, remark:

> The notion of "abnormal" behavior misleads many people. They think it to be the study of persons entirely different from the rest of mankind. Practically all specialists agree now that such is not the case. The very same variables which are operating in an extreme degree in mentally ill people are present in people who are not ill. . . . Important variables which are hard to see in mild degrees become very clear when presented in extreme degrees (p. 5).

Thirteen years later, Bandura and Walters (1963) reaffirmed the principle of continuity.

> Our social-learning principles seek to explain deviant behavior in terms of classes of events that appear to be equally important for the establishing of nondeviant patterns of response. The approach carries the implication that the distinction between deviant and nondeviant behavior represents a value judgment and that categorical value judgments of this nature, though important for determining the decisions and actions of agents of social control, are of little theoretical significance (p. 44).

Acceptance of the premise that all behavior, normal or abnormal, can be explained in terms of a common set of principles holds important implications for investigation of schizophrenia and its development. Much of this importance stems from the various sources of bias which the schizophrenic disorder itself may introduce into the data of research and which may argue, interestingly enough, against the use of schizophrenics in investigating the origins of their own disorder.

One source of bias introduced by using schizophrenic subjects stems from the number of years which intervene between the period when critical experiences are influencing the development of the child and the period when the symptoms of schizophrenia reach clinical proportions (usually during adulthood). The years spanning these periods may be expected to distort our research data if for no other reason than people forget or selectively remember the experiences of the earlier developmental period by the time they are adults. The same can be said of the aging parents of these schizophrenic offspring whose vintage retrospections regarding the family share the same problems.

Since the presence of schizophrenia must be authenticated before we know whose life history is relevant to study, the nature of the schizophrenic condition becomes a possible source of bias to any investigation which includes the schizophrenic as a source of data. Thought disturbance, social aversiveness, and limited cooperation may make the usual assumptions about subject understanding of instructions and motivation or ability to follow directives rather tenuous. To these limitations as subjects imposed by behavioral pathology, we may add those factors which are introduced by the social control and treatment of schizophrenia. The effects of institutionalization, various drug regimes, electroconvulsive or insulin shock, and various psychological therapies introduce their own brands of bias into the performance of the schizophrenic as a subject.

Even if we attempt to circumvent the biasing effects of the schizophrenic disorder itself by basing our familial observations upon the information or performance of nonafflicted members, this is no safeguard against the schizophrenic condition exerting an indirect influence upon our attempts to reconstruct the developmental history. Many of the ways in which family members relate to the schizophrenic may be better understood as a consequence of the disorder than as an antecedent to it. The prodromal behaviors that precede the clinical manifestation of schizophrenia may exert their own kind of controls upon those close to the person. Of even greater impact are the strange to bizarre actions of the full-blown schizophrenic and the realization that a family member has been afflicted with the most serious of mental disorders. Just as families mobilize different ways of dealing with the social implications of having a schizophrenic member, there are a myriad of ways in which the guilt, shame, fear, anger, or pity generated could introduce bias into reconstructions of earlier developmental data or current modes of relating to the schizophrenic. These disorder-induced behaviors may bear no resemblance to premorbid styles of relating.

It is not difficult to identify prior research into the family antecedents of schizophrenia vulnerable to these sources of bias. Essentially all studies of this nature which have involved either the schizophrenic or the parents of the schizophrenic have risked the distortions introduced by these sources of bias. Reexamination of the research cited in Chapter 2 would show that this would pertain to essentially every study which we were able to find bearing upon maternal or parental variables in schizophrenia. Yet another reason why even clearer commonalities have not emerged from the general body of research on schizophrenic development!

One procedure for life history research that seems to get around the distortions introduced by time and the effects of schizophrenia itself involves the comparison of the childhood records of adults who subsequently become schizophrenic with the records of adults whose development has run a more normal course. Lane and Albee (1970) used this approach to investigate the early intellectual characteristics of schizophrenics by referring back to the Cleveland public school records of adult patients in state and federal mental hospitals in the area. The use of childhood records to seek the developmental antecedents of schizophrenia has enjoyed use by other investigators as well

(Birren, 1944; Nameche, Waring, and Ricks, 1964; O'Neal and Robins, 1958). While avoiding the pitfalls of bias associated with the use of adult schizophrenic patients or their families as subjects, the childhood-record method introduces methodological problems all its own. Mednick and Schulsinger (1970) have pointed out that when the researcher is working with twenty- to thirty-year-old records, he is forced to take what he finds. For example, differences in terminology from one record to the next must remain unresolved. An even greater limitation of static record data is that the researcher must deal with whatever variables happen to be treated systematically in the records, and these variables may or may not be relevant to the hypotheses which appear worthy of testing years after the records were obtained. While such recorded data as childhood IQ scores (Albee, Lane, Corcoran, and Wernecke, 1963) and birth weight (Lane and Albee, 1966) of schizophrenics may hold some circumscribed importance, they are certainly not the raw materials from which complex developmental theories are built.

If the continuity betwen normal and abnormal behavior is taken seriously, as we believe it must, then yet another methodology can be utilized to avoid the difficulties we have been discussing. Given the same principles governing the development of people who subsequently become schizophrenic and those who do not, we should be able to investigate these principles in people who do not demonstrate clinically evident psychopathology at the time of investigation and who may never do so. The utilization of normals in researching the possible social antecedents to schizophrenia allows rather obvious ways of circumventing the problems of time lag and contaminating effects of the disorder implicit in studying adult subjects already suffering from schizophrenia. Normals can be studied cross-sectionally as children, adolescents, or adults or longitudinally across levels. Variables chosen for study are those deemed relevant by the researcher, and the focus of measurement is upon the current behavior of subjects who are at an age selected as appropriate to the researcher's interest. By dealing with normals as research subjects, no problems exist as far as the intrusion of aberrant behaviors into subject performance or as far as the influence of relating to a schizophrenic upon nonschizophrenic research participants.

The use of normal subjects to study phenomena relevant to the understanding of psychopathology is certainly not new or rare. It is not difficult to find studies of cognitive or perceptual behavior in normals which intend to clarify the mechanisms of defense, the effects of stress or anxiety upon performance, etc. One less commonly observes a researcher who explicitly contends that he is investigating a schizophrenic behavior by analyzing its more muted form in normals. One reason for this is the fact that schizophrenics represent a far more reasonable or even necessary subject population if we are interested in some aspect of schizophrenic functioning per se. For example, if our interest is in the effects of failure upon the achievement motivation of schizophrenics, we have little reason not to direct our research attention to schizophrenics. If we were interested in the developmental antecedents of achievement motivation problems in schizophrenics, our choice of subjects might well be normal children.

A recent laboratory experiment by Norbert (1971) demonstrates the possibility of even clarifying the nature of symptomatic schizophrenic behavior by investigating the performance of normals. An interest in hallucinations led her to test the hypothesis that people are more likely to attribute meaning to meaningless visual displays if the sensory stimulation requires them to use their nonpreferred imaginal mode. Norbert found that normals who preferred visual imagination tended to erroneously hear meaningful sounds, whereas preference for auditory imagination resulted in greater misrepresentation of visual cues.

As we have stressed, the type of research into schizophrenia in which the use of normal subjects presents the greatest promise is that which seeks its developmental origins. Social influences can be assessed at any stage of development without introducing the confounding effects of the disorder. Our research program has been largely predicated upon the assumption of continuity–that those principles which can account for the development of schizophreniform behaviors in normal late adolescents can be generalized to the acquisition of more extreme schizophrenic behaviors of adults.

Working with normals in seeking developmental principles which will enhance our knowledge of psychopathogenesis does require further assumption, however. It is necessary to contend with the question of why some normals who experience the conditions found to be etiologically significant to some disorder end up suffering from the disorder while others, perhaps most, do not. There are two assumptions that we consider reasonable. One, we assume that the antecedent factors which have come to be considered relevant to schizophrenic development have been studied at less intense levels than would have been the case if we had been able to focus our measures only on those who would subsequently become schizophrenic. More extreme levels should breed more extreme subsequent reactions. A second assumption accepts the possibility of some interactive variable(s) which, given certain conditions, will tip the scale one way or the other as far as the manifestation of the disorder is concerned. Genetic endowment has already been considered as such an interactive variable. Current limitations of knowledge make it likely that many yet unidentified psychological variables also may contribute to the ultimate shift of the scale either toward schizophrenia or a more effective adjustment.

The Use of Retrospective Report in Developmental Research

The strategy of life history research must assume one of two general approaches to the timing of its data. Either the data will be contemporaneous with the events in question or the data will be retrospective in character, following the events by some variable period. Longitudinal research which follows the same individuals over time remains the most venerable procedure for working systematically with contemporaneous data, although it is not the only way by any means. Cross-sectional research, which studies different individuals at successive developmental periods, represents one alternative approach to the collection of temporally current data.

Retrospective methods which seek to study life history variables by having people recall prior events offers both convenience as well as the problems which go with symbolic reinstatement of experience following the passage of time. Critiques of retrospective approaches to developmental research, especially those which compare them with longitudinal study, are unanimous in disclaiming the use of retrospection. Kagan and Moss (1962), in considering the study of normal psychological development, remark:

> There has always been, however, an explicit and rather dogmatic conviction that selected adult motives, attitudes, and behaviors begin their growth during the first 10 years of life. Once established during the childhood years, these responses are likely to remain permanent aspects of the individual's behavior repertoire. Retrospective impressions of childhood gathered from psychotherapy sessions, anecdotal reports, and private introspections support this belief, but more substantial evidence has been difficult to obtain. Only systematic longitudinal observations can discover those behaviors that are marked for future use and those that will be lost along the way (p. 1).

Information about the first five years of life was elicited from mothers and their normal children with an elapsed period of up to 30 years in a study of the retrospective methods conducted by Yarrow, Campbell, and Burton (1970). Their conclusion was:

> Our findings, and those of previous researchers into retrospective reports, do demonstrate consistently a statistically significant amount of overlap between baseline and recall, even though the amount in common is low. Therefore, when other possibilities are not available to investigate an important question, retrospective data may reflect to some extent what relations exist. The employment of such information, however, should be contingent on the recognition of its serious limitations (p. 69).

Burton (1970), working with the same data, reports that baseline data, maternal retrospective data, and child retrospective data failed to reveal evidence of either convergent or discriminant validity.

Frank (1965), whose pessimistic review of research into the role of the family in psychopathology has already received our attention, addressed himself to the methodology problem by pointing out the dangers of selectivity and distortion in retrospection. An even sterner conclusion was rendered by Fontana (1966) who lumps clinical observation and retrospection as unsuitable bases for a scientific body of etiological facts relevant to schizophrenia. For Fontana, only longitudinal research can establish appropriate etiological conclusions. Ricks (1970) has recently observed that retrospection is a short-cut method of data collection offering but a first approximation to concurrent data.

Perhaps the point that retrospective methods in developmental research are open to criticism has received sufficient emphasis. What is rarely found in critiques of retrospection, however, is consideration of the most basic determinants of error in recalled data. Since we are dealing with a memory function, two basic determinants of how faithfully recall will represent prior experience are (1) the degree to which the original experience was learned and (2) the amount of elapsed time between learning and recall. If, in a verbal learning and memory experiment, one group of subjects was presented with a paired-associate list for one trial and tested for retention the following day, it would surprise no one to find less accurate "retrospection" than in a group presented with twenty trials on the same list the previous day. Similarly, given an equal and reasonable number of learning trials, the superiority in recall of a group tested the following day to one called back after a 30-day lapse is entirely predictable. It must be equally obvious that if we are trying to reinstate previous developmental experience through our subjects, the same questions must be considered. Was the object of retrospection initially well learned and does the time interval between experience and recall challenge the limits of human information storage? If our interests lead us to be concerned with information relevant to the first five years of life and our sources, mothers or children, must contend with an elapsed time of up to 30 years as in the Yarrow, Campbell, and Burton study, retrospection would seem to be a poor choice indeed.

There seems to be no special reason why retrospection needs to be singled out as far as motivated distortions of information are concerned. A subject at any age, whether the data being sought are current or retrospective, and whether experimental manipulation, observation, self-report, or test is used, can distort to gain some end. This is a general problem of personal data acquisition with which the investigator must contend no matter which procedure is chosen for developmental investigation.

There is one methodological consideration that distinguishes traditional developmental research, which seeks to understand the development of normal children who are expected to become normal adults, and research into the development of children whose adult status is likely to be schizophrenic. In the former case, longitudinal study of the same individuals is usually considered to be the best method of research despite the inevitable problems of nonrepresentative sampling and selective attrition. However, when the investigator is specifically interested in the development of schizophrenia, longitudinal study requires his identification of the subjects long before they manifest the symptoms which mark them as schizophrenic. Since schizophrenia has a low probability outcome (about 1 in 100) in the general population, it is not feasible to investigate its developmental origins by blind sampling.

While the latent recognition and low incidence factors argue against the longitudinal method of studying the development of schizophrenia, there are those who consider it possible to circumvent these problems and so retain the advantages of longitudinal study. Mednick and his associates (Mednick and McNeil, 1968; Mednick and Schulsinger, 1970) have suggested the identification of a sample of children who show a high risk for schizophrenia and to follow them longitudinally. This method, which allows for the eventual appearance of sufficient numbers of schizophrenics to lend some degree of reliability to the data, has other intrinsic advantages. The early premorbid characteristics and their interactions with life circumstances which distinguish those who eventually demonstrate schizophrenic behavior can be compared not only with those who emerge as normal but also those who become deviant-but-nonschizophrenic.

The attempt to modify longitudinal procedures for use with schizophrenics may introduce new problems which limit the degree to which the results can be generalized. The most obvious problem is introduced by the criteria for selection which are required in order to increase the risk for schizophrenia in the children to be followed longitudinally. For Mednick, the basis for inferring high risk was the presence of process schizophrenia in the mother of the child which was projected to increase the incidence of filial schizophrenia from about 1% to 15%. One verified consequence of increasing the risk for schizophrenia in children turned out to be the selection of families in which the mother was absent a substantial portion of the child's life (Mednick and Schulsinger, 1970). This raises the question of whether any factors found to be associated with the development of children subsequently diagnosed as schizophrenic can be generalized to the development of schizophrenia in the person reared under family circumstances in which the mother is not absented from the home nor rendered functionally incompetent by schizophrenia when she is in the home.

One further limitation of longitudinal study is its failure to coordinate effectively with experimental efforts to garner knowledge. Often the participation in one experiment may preclude a subject's being used in another, because he has learned something in the first which may influence his behavior in the second. If our total investment were in a static sample of subjects followed over time, repeated experimental probes would most likely be impossible.

Working with the Subjective Experience of the Child

Observation and measurement of any social behavior, including that which the mother directs toward the child, can proceed from three different vantage points. The social behavior may be considered (a) from the point of view of the behaving social agent, (b) through the eyes of the person on the receiving end of the behavior, or (c) as the behavior registers upon someone who is in a position to be a nonparticipant observer. If we consider the mother as the social agent in question, we can approach the assessment of maternal behavior by directing our inquiry toward the mother herself, by eliciting the perceptions of the recipient child, or by collecting the observations of a neutral observer. Each approach offers a range of specific methods. Mothers may be asked how they rear their children by means of interview or questionnaire, or this may be indirectly inferred from the mother's responses to psychological tests. Children's views of their mothers' behavior have been commonly tapped by the same procedures. Nonparticipant observation of maternal behavior can subsume such techniques as review of case records, listening to taped interactions, or direct observation of mother-child interaction.

While the distinction drawn among these approaches to systematic observation of social behavior is not new, there are some implications of each approach which have received little, if any, attention from researchers. These have to do with what the investigator really wants to garner from his data. If his basic interest is in the psychological systems of the mother—her attitudes, motives, needs, affect, or cognitive styles—then inquiry directed to the mother is the reasonable choice. If objective determination of manifest material behavior is the goal, nonparticipant (i.e., "scientific") observation represents the clear preference. However, if we are interested in the impact of maternal behavior upon the child, there is no substitute for drawing our inferences about the mother's behaviors as they are experienced by the child. At the risk of redundancy, methodological choice comes down to this. Given the goals of understanding and predicting maternal behavior, the mother represents the most relevant source of data. When the goal is objective recording of maternal behavior (as in establishing norms), the scientist-observer's data are preferable. Interest in understanding and predicting the influence of maternal behavior upon the child is best facilitated by tapping the experience of the child.

Clearly, research into family influences on the development of psychopathology in the child falls into the third category, placing priority on relating the ways in which children have experienced family members with subsequent development of pathological behavior. It seems so reasonable to expect more lawful relationships to emerge from investigation of two sets of responses within the same organism (i.e., the perceptual responses as related to the pathological responses) that one wonders why this approach has not achieved greater favor among researchers. The fact that psychology in its short history as a science has chosen to emulate the established natural sciences by rejecting subjectivism in its scientific operations can be offered as one explanation. Those behavioral events that achieve scientific credence are those that are open to impartial observation and free from subjective impression. If this is true, it means that in the study of human social behavior we have confounded subjectivism in the subject and subjectivism in the scientist. Introduction of impression and bias into research data by the scientist is unacceptable. Allowance for the subjective character of human social experience is in many cases a necessity.

Frank (1965), following his extensive survey of the literature and conclusion that no unique factors could be identified in the family of the schizophrenic, presaged our stress on the subjective experience of the child when he noted:

> It might well be that the reality of the family is not the important dimension in determining the child's reactions; rather, it might be the perception of the family members, and this might often have little or no relation to the people as they really are. This would mean, then, that in many instances the important variables in the development of psychopathology might be factors which the child brings to the family, the functioning of the nervous and metabolic systems and the cognitive capacity to integrate stimuli into meaningful perceptual and conceptual schema. Indeed, we are left to wonder, as do the psychoanalysts, whether the proclivity towards fantasy distortion of reality might not be *the* factor in the determination of psychopathology, and this proclivity might not be always determined by the child's experiences per se (p. 201).

Summary of Research Issues in Developmental Psychopathology

It must be rather obvious at this juncture what methodological orientation guided the research program which is reported in subsequent chapters. We did not concern ourselves with genetic causation but rather with social influences that could be theoretically linked to schizophreniform behavior in individuals whatever the genetic endowment might be. Normal subjects were our major source of evidence in the attempt to derive principles of development that could help us understand how people become schizophrenic. Retrospective report provided our access to earlier developmental experience of the child with added safeguards of bringing the reference period (adolescence) close to the time of retrospection and making the object of recall (perceived maternal behavior) a highly learned experience. The child's subjective experience of the mother has attracted our exclusive attention.

The reasons behind these methodological choices have been discussed in some detail. We remain aware that our approach to data acquisition is not without problems and limitations, some of which it shares with all research into human social behavior, especially as it is considered from a developmental perspective. We do contend that our approach is a most pragmatic and effective way to go about the formulation of a theory of developmental psychopathology based exclusively upon research, much of it involving experimental manipulation. The nature of the evidence we shall present and the theory which it generated shall be the ultimate test of our contention.

The availability of the circumplex maternal child-rearing model, the essential agreement of this model with alternate child-rearing schemas, and the evidence on schizophrenic development directed us to a quadrant approach for conceptualizing maternal child-rearing experience in our own research program. The working assumption was that the impact of maternal behavior upon the child could be meaningfully summarized by locating her along two independent axes, one ranging from high to low control and the second from high to low nurturance. A further simplification reduced the positioning on each axis to only two categories, high versus low, leaving all subjects assignable to one of four quadrants of child-rearing experience. Each quadrant invoked a particular maternal typology, again following the lead of Schaefer's circumplex model, presumably better allowing our research results to tie in with the terminology of other investigations. The quadrant labels seen in Table 1 actually proved to be disadvantageous in the long run, since they invited surplus meanings which created more confusion than they resolved. Accordingly, our research quadrant model returned to the safer procedure of distinguishing among subjects by the high or low status of perceived maternal control and nurturance and allowing the accumulated evidence to determine whether any given quadrant corresponds to some preestablished typology.

What came to replace the original quadrant approach, which invested equal interest in all combinations of high and low control and nurturance, was a more singular interest in one particular combination of experience for the child—high control and low nurturance. This combination of experience or quadrant has

Table 1. Control-Nurturance Quadrants and Attributed Maternal Child-Rearing Typologies

	Control-Nurturance Quadrant			
Investigator	High Control-High Nurturance	High Control-Low Nurturance	Low Control-Low Nurturance	Low Control-High Nurturance
Heilbrun	Over protective	Rejecting	Ignoring	Accepting
Schaefer	Accepting Over indulgent Protective indulgent Over protective Possessive	Possessive Authoritarian dictorial Demanding antagonistic Rejecting	Rejecting Neglecting Indifferent Detached Freedom	Freedom Democratic Cooperative Accepting
Becker	Over protective Organized effective	Rigid controlling Authoritarian (hostile-neurotic)	Neglecting Anxious neurotic	Indulgent Democratic

been given the shorthand label of "aversive maternal control" and will assume a central position in our attempt to present a social developmental theory of schizophrenia. While we believe the remaining three quadrants, taken individually, to be of potential importance in understanding other phenomena relevant to social behavior, the narrowing of our scope of inquiry since 1968 has led us to combine them to form a general comparison group for the aversive-control quadrant.

THE MATERNAL CHILD-REARING MEASURES

The Measurement of Maternal Child-Rearing Control

The original selection of the Parent Attitude Research Instrument (PARI), a child-rearing questionnaire developed by Schaefer and Bell (1958), was based upon our need for an efficient way of assessing a broad base of maternal behavior. The format of the PARI was patterned after earlier questionnaires by Shoben (1949) and Mark (1953), being comprised of generalized third-person statements about child rearing. These items, which are reproduced in Appendix A, were selected by Schaefer and Bell so as to constitute 23 five-item scales. Each scale, in turn, was tested for internal consistency among the contained items. Of even greater importance for our purposes, as it turned out, it was quickly established that the factor structure of the PARI included a major loading of 16 scales on what Zuckerman, Ribback, Monashkin, and Norton (1958) termed "authoritarian control" and what Schaefer (1961), after independent factor analysis, labeled "approval of maternal control of the child." Additional three-scale minor factors ("hostility-rejection of the homemaking role," "democratic attitudes") were also identified but have proven to be of little significance for our research. Table 2 presents the names of the 23 PARI scales and their factor organization.

A general review of the PARI as a means of assessing maternal attitudes by Becker and Krug (1965) offered strenuous criticism of its effectiveness despite its popularity as a research tool. In their words, "The PARI has stimulated research and raised a few interesting questions. It has served as an important stepping-stone, but it appears to be the time to move on" (p. 361). Since their review and conclusions were directed toward the customary use of the PARI as directly administered to mothers, it is of interest that these reviewers at least took fleeting stock of our work and the potential of the PARI as a means of getting at the child's perceived experience of the mother. They note that:

In a series of studies, Heilbrun (1960a; 1960b) and Heilbrun and McKinley (1962) have used the PARI to assess daughters' perception of their mothers'

Table 2. PARI Scales and their Factor Structure

Scale Number and Description		Primary Factor Loading[a]
2	Fostering dependency	AC
3	Seclusion of mother	AC
4	Breaking the will	AC
5	Martyrdom	AC
6	Fear of harming baby	AC
10	Excluding outside influences	AC
11	Deification	AC
12	Suppression of aggression	AC
15	Approval of activity	AC
16	Avoidance of communication	AC
17	Inconsiderateness of husband	AC
18	Suppression of sex	AC
19	Ascendance of mother	AC
20	Intrusiveness of mother	AC
22	Acceleration of development	AC
23	Dependency of mother	AC
7	Marital conflict	HR
9	Irritability	HR
13	Rejecting homemaking role	HR
1	Encouraging verbalization	DA
14	Equalitarianism	DA
21	Comradeship and sharing	DA
8	Strictness	

[a] AC = Authoritarian-control, HR = hostility-rejection of homemaking role, DA = democratic attitudes.

child-rearing attitudes. The findings indicate interesting differences in the perception of mother by normal and by abnormal groups and suggest another possible use for the PARI. However, since these findings are not directly relevant to the validity of the PARI, they are given only passing mention (p. 346)."

The question of what validity means with regard to a questionnaire of maternal child-rearing attitudes is complicated by the issue of what represents an adequate criterion. In light of our earlier discussion of the differing vantage points from which maternal behaviors may be observed—self, experimenter, or child—it is far from clear whether one can justify relating observations taken from one vantage point with those gathered from another and consider this a test of validity. Perhaps before we concern ourselves with the validity of the PARI, used as a measure of the child's perception of maternal behavior, it would be profitable to review the explicit conditions under which we have administered the questionnaire and the implicit assumptions which are made about the responses which we obtain.

The PARI is administered with instructions to the subject to read each statement of attitude and to "answer it as you think your mother would." The subject proceeds to assign one of four responses to the 115 statements—"strongly agree," "mildly agree," "mildly disagree," or "strongly disagree." In keeping with the instructional set, the son or daughter must in each case, we assume, reinstate some explicit statement made by the mother or some related form of behavior demonstrated by the mother. It is expected that such reinstatement would be in keeping with the biases learned by the child in his multiplicity of experiences with the mother. Thus, our measure of perceived maternal control is based upon 80 probes (16 five-item scales) into the child's subjective experience of the mother as an agent of influence.

There was no particular reason to believe that the use of the PARI under the perceptual instructions which were initially adopted was any better or even as good as a dozen other ways in which the maternal experience could have been assessed. For example, the mere substitution of "should" for "would" in the directive to "answer as you think your mother would" might have made a difference. Similarly, rewording the PARI statements to get more directly at the child's experience might have facilitated our work. The simple truth of the matter is that we were fortunate in our selection of measures so that our initial choice of operations for quadrant assignment of maternal experience has continued to retain its heuristic value.

This brings us back to the topic of validity. It seems futile to search for the commonly accepted index of validity when considering a measure of subjective experience. What is the criterion of subjective experience other than some other measure of subjective experience, and what makes one measure a predictor and the other a criterion? One can more profitably evaluate a measure like the experienced control items on the PARI by determining the extent to which it serves to facilitate discovery, its heuristic value. Or one can consider the extent to which it generates empirical relationships that form an interlocking nomological network that lays the groundwork for sound theory construction. The latter tactic has been proposed as a form of validation without a criterion (see Cronbach and Meehl, 1955, for their formulation of "construct validity"). Our contention is that the PARI, as we have used it, has amply demonstrated its heuristic value and construct validity as a measure of perceived maternal control.

The reliability of the PARI control measure has been assessed by the split-half method using alternate items to constitute two separate control scores based upon 40 items each. The reliability coefficient (corrected for doubled length) was a substantial .88 for the PARI control scores of 100 college males.

Norms for the PARI perceived control scores for both college-age males and females (modal age of 19 years) are made available in Appendix B. The male normative table converts the total raw scores on the 80 control items to T-score equivalents with the T-score distribution having a mean of 50 and a standard deviation of 10. Raw scores, it might be pointed out, are based upon the assignment of 4 to all "strongly agree" responses, 3 to "mildly agree," 2 to "mildly disagree," and 1 to "strongly disagree." Thus, raw scores for males have a potential range from 80 to 320 with college males averaging about in the middle of the range at 193. Three scales have been eliminated from the control measure for females, since they failed to discriminate between females differing in level of adjustment (Heilbrun and McKinley, 1962). Thus, the female raw score can range from 65 to 260; female college student norms place the raw score mean at about 152. The use of these normative tables can free the experimenter from depending upon gradually emerging sampling statistics for quadrant assignment during the course of an experiment and also allow for better comparisons across experiments by using the same defining operation for high or low control.

The Measurement of Maternal Child-Rearing Nurturance

Since no objective measure of maternal child-rearing nurturance appropriate for our use was available to us, it was decided to construct our own (Heilbrun, 1964). A series of eight rating scales were developed to tap various aspects of maternal and paternal giving or affection from the perspective of the child. The modes of nurturance experience included felt affection, physically expressed affection, felt approval, sharing of personal feeling and experience, concrete giving, encouragement, trust, and security. Each nurturance variable was reduced to a five-point scale with each point accompanied by a descriptive anchoring statement of degree. Scores on these scales can vary from 1 (low nurturance) to 5 (high nurturance) so that the total score can range from 8 to 40. Appendix C includes these Parent-Child Interaction Rating Scales, and the attributed maternal nurturance norms for college students can be found in Appendix D.

While the Parent-Child Interaction Rating Scales, like the PARI, are better evaluated on the basis of their heuristic contributions to our theory, some initial data relevant to their validity has been presented by Heilbrun (1964). One common observation (Burchinal, 1958; Emmerich, 1959b; Kagan and Lemkin, 1960) regarding nurturant behavior in parents is that mothers offer more of this commodity to their children than do fathers. Ratings of both parents by 124 college subjects on the Parent-Child Scales resulted in greater experienced nurturance from the mother in 87 cases, greater nurturance from the father in 17, and 20 equal scores. This disproportionality, tested by chi square, was highly significant statistically ($p < .001$). The split-half reliability for the Parent-Child Scales was .74 based upon the records of 100 males.

REFERENCES

Albee, G. W., Lane, Ellen A., Corcoran, C., and Wernecke, A. Childhood and intercurrent intellectual performances of adult schizophrenics. *Journal of Consulting Psychology,* 1963, **27**, 364-366.

Bandura, A., and Walters, R. H. *Social learning and personality development.* New York: Holt, Rinehart and Winston, 1963.

Becker, W. C. Consequences of different kinds of parental discipline. In M. L. Hoffman and Lois W. Hoffman (Eds.), *Review of child development research.* New York: Russell Sage Foundation, 1964. Pp. 169-208.

Becker, W. C., and Krug, R. S. The Parent Attitude Research Instrument—a research review. *Child Development,* 1965, **36**, 329-365.

Birren, J. E. Psychological examinations of children who later became psychotic. *Journal of Abnormal and Social Psychology,* 1944, **39**, 84-96.

Burchinal, L. G. Mothers' and fathers' differences in parental acceptance of children for controlled comparisons based on parental and family characteristics. *Journal of Genetic Psychology,* 1958, **92**, 103-110.

Burton, R. V. Validity of retrospective reports assessed by the multitrait-multimethod analysis. *Developmental Psychology Monograph,* 1970, **3** (No. 3, Part 2).

Cronbach, L. J., and Meehl, P. E. Construct validity in psychological tests. *Psychological Bulletin,* 1955, **52**, 281-302.

Dollard, J., and Miller, N. E. *Personality and psychotherapy.* New York: McGraw-Hill, 1950.

Eisenberg, L. The interaction of biological and experiential factors in schizophrenia. In D. Rosenthal and S. S. Kety (Eds.), *The transmission of schizophrenia.* New York: Pergamon Press, 1968. Pp. 403-409.

Emmerich, W. Parental identification in young children. *Genetic Psychology Monographs,* 1959, **60**, 257-308. (a)

Emmerich, W. Young children's discrimination of parent and child roles. *Child Development,* 1959, **30**, 403-419. (b)

Fontana, A. F. Familial etiology of schizophrenia: is a scientific methodology possible? *Psychological Bulletin,* 1966, **66**, 214-227.

Frank, G. H. The role of the family in the development of psychopathology. *Psychological Bulletin,* 1965, **64**, 191-205.

Goldin, P. C. A review of children's reports of parent behaviors. *Psychological Bulletin,* 1969, **71**, 222-236.

Heilbrun, A. B. Perception of maternal child rearing attitudes in schizophrenics. *Journal of Consulting Psychology,* 1960, **24**, 169-173. (a)

Heilbrun, A. B. Perceptual distortion and schizophrenia. *American Journal of Orthopsychiatry,* 1960, **30**, 412-418. (b)

Heilbrun, A. B. Parent model attributes, nurturant reinforcement, and consistency of behavior in adolescents. *Child Development,* 1964, **35,** 151-167.

Heilbrun, A. B., and McKinley, R. Perception of maternal child-rearing attitudes, personality of the perceiver, and incipient psychopathology. *Child Development,* 1962, **33,** 73-83.

Kagan, J., and Lemkin, J. The child's differential perception of parental attributes. *Journal of Abnormal and Social Psychology,* 1960, **61,** 440-447.

Kagan, J., and Moss, H. A. *Birth to maturity: a study in psychological development.* New York: Wiley, 1962.

Lane, E. A., and Albee, G. W. The comparative birth weights of adult schizophrenics and their siblings. *Journal of Psychology,* 1966, **64,** 227-231.

Lane, E. A., and Albee, G. W. Intellectual antecedents of schizophrenia. In M. Roff and D. F. Ricks (Eds.), *Life history research in psychopathology.* Minneapolis: University of Minnesota Press, 1970. Pp. 189-207.

Mark, J. C. The attitudes of the mothers of male schizophrenics toward child behavior. *Journal of Abnormal and Social Psychology,* 1953, **48,** 185-189.

Mednick, S. A., and McNeil, T. F. Current methodology in research on the etiology of schizophrenia: serious difficulties which suggest the use of high-risk group method. *Psychological Bulletin*, 1968, **70**, 681-693.

Mednick, S. A., and Schulsinger, F. Factors related to breakdown in children at high risk for schizophrenia. In M. Roff and D. F. Ricks (Eds.), *Life history research in psychopathology*. Minneapolis: University of Minnesota Press, 1970. Pp. 51-93.

Meehl, P. E. Schizotaxia, schizotypy, schizophrenia. *American Psychologist*, 1962, **17**, 827-838.

Nameche, G., Waring, M., and Ricks, D. Early indicators of outcome in schizophrenia. *Journal of Nervous and Mental Disease*, 1964, **139**, 232-240.

Norbert, N. An inquiry into the nature of hallucinations. Unpublished master's thesis, Emory University, 1971.

O'Neal, P., and Robins, L. N. Childhood patterns predictive of adult schizophrenia. *American Journal of Psychiatry*, 1958, **115**, 385-391.

Ricks, D. F. Life history research in psychopathology: retrospect and prospect. In M. Roff and D. F. Ricks (Eds.), *Life history research in psychopathology*. Minneapolis: University of Minnesota Press, 1970. Pp. 288-307.

Roe, A. Early determinants of vocational choice. *Journal of Counseling Psychology*, 1957, **4**, 212-217.

Rosenthal, D. The heredity-environment issue in schizophrenia: summary of the conference and present status of our knowledge. In D. Rosenthal and S. S.

Kety (Eds.), *The transmission of schizophrenia.* New York: Pergamon Press, 1968. Pp. 413-427.

Rosenthal, D., and Kety, S. S. (Eds.) *The transmission of schizophrenia.* New York: Pergamon Press, 1968.

Schaefer, E. S. A circumplex model for maternal behavior. *Journal of Abnormal and Social Psychology*, 1959, **59**, 226-235.

Schaefer, E. S. Converging conceptual models for maternal behavior and for child behavior. In J. C. Glidewell (Ed.), *Parental attitudes and child behavior*. Springfield, Ill.: Thomas, 1961.

Schaefer, E. S., and Bell, R. Q. Development of a parental attitude research instrument. *Child Development*, 1958, **29**, 339-361.

Shoben, J. R., Jr. The assessment of parental attitudes in relation to child adjustment. *Genetic Psychology Monographs*, 1949, **39**, 101-148.

Slater, P. E. Parent behavior and the personality of the child. *Journal of Genetic Psychology*, 1962, **101**, 53-68.

Yarrow, M. R., Campbell, J. D., and Burton, R. V. Recollections of childhood: a study of the retrospective method. *Monographs of the Society for Research in Child Development*, 1970, **35** (5, Serial No. 138).

Zuckerman, M., Ribback, B. B., Monashkin, I., and Norton, J. A. Normative data and factor analysis on the Parental Attitude Research Instrument. *Journal of Consulting Psychology*, 1958, **22**, 165-171.

CHAPTER 4

The Research (Phase I): Maternal Control and Filial Maladjustment

The initial programmatic research bearing upon the mother's child-rearing influence included several correlational studies designed to answer a host of exploratory questions about experienced maternal control and its measurement. Does maternal control as perceived by the child relate to psychopathology of the child any differently than maternal control as perceived by the mother? Is the sex of the child a factor in the effects of maternal control upon the child's development? Will maternal control be a differentiating factor between levels of adjustment within normal samples as well as between schizophrenics and their adult controls? Can the relationship between maternal control and filial deviance be demonstrated regardless of the age of the children?

Initial investigation focused upon the perceived maternal child-rearing attitudes of schizophrenic daughters (Heilbrun, 1960a). Twenty-six females, admitted into a large midwestern state hospital within a given year and who carried uncontested diagnoses of schizophrenia, were included in the study because they met the additional requirements of being sufficiently cooperative and lucid as subjects and of having a living mother also willing to participate. The schizophrenic daughters were themselves about 37 years of age on the average at the time of the study and had an average education in excess of 11 grades. The PARI was administered individually to each schizophrenic (by some member of the hospital staff known to the patient) under the instructional set to provide the answers she believed her mother would. Special care was taken to insure that the instructions were clear to the schizophrenic. Mothers of the hospitalized females were contacted by mail and requested (over the hospital chief of staff's signature) to cooperate by using the PARI to describe their child-rearing attitudes.

Control daughters and their mothers were obtained as subjects through civic organizations or from medical wards of a general hospital using both personal contact and the mail to obtain the completed PARI's. Crude screening for psychological disturbance within the normal daughter group was based upon her answering "no" to the question of whether she had ever used a mental health facility. The 26 normal daughters presented a mean age of about 33 years and a mean education of approximately 12 years.

A preliminary comparison of the PARI's, as completed by the mothers of schizophrenic and the mothers of normal daughters, failed to uncover any difference in child-rearing attitudes between them. This finding substantiated an earlier negative report by Zuckerman, Oltean, and Monashkin (1958) who compared the endorsed child-rearing attitudes of mothers of male schizophrenics to those obtained from mothers of normal sons.

When the daughters were asked to consider their mothers' child rearing via the PARI, quite a different picture emerged. Table 3 clearly portrays the greater deviance of the mother as viewed by the schizophrenic daughter. A closer look at the perceptual patterning, furthermore, leaves little doubt that control is the domain of experience within which the schizophrenic daughter identifies her

Table 3. Comparisons of Mothers' Mean Attitude Scale Scores as Attributed by Schizophrenic and Normal Daughters

Scale Number and Description		Primary Factor Loading[a]	Schizophrenic ($N = 26$)	Normal ($N = 27$)	p Value
2.	Fostering dependency	AC	14.10	11.25	.01
3.	Seclusion of mother	AC	14.55	12.45	.01
4.	Breaking the will	AC	13.60	11.25	.01
5.	Martyrdom	AC	13.75	10.80	.01
6.	Fear of harming baby	AC	14.80	14.00	
10.	Excluding outside influences	AC	13.00	11.45	.01
11.	Deification	AC	15.35	13.40	.05
12.	Suppression of aggression	AC	13.50	11.15	.01
15.	Approval of activity	AC	14.65	13.60	
16.	Avoidance of communication	AC	12.90	10.60	.05
17.	Inconsiderateness of husband	AC	13.85	12.60	
18.	Suppression of sex	AC	13.25	10.65	.01
19.	Ascendance of mother	AC	14.85	11.80	.01
20.	Intrusiveness	AC	12.85	10.60	.05
22.	Acceleration of development	AC	15.35	12.45	.01
23.	Dependency of mother	AC	14.20	12.85	
7.	Marital conflict	HR	14.80	15.80	
9.	Irritability	HR	13.25	14.80	.05
13.	Rejecting homemaking role	HR	12.00	11.60	
1.	Encouraging verbalization	DA	16.55	16.75	
14.	Equalitarianism	DA	16.50	16.40	
21.	Comradeship and sharing	DA	17.85	18.35	
8.	Strictness		14.45	13.75	

[a]Taken from Zuckerman, Ribback, Monashkin, and Norton, 1958. AC = control factor, HR = hostility-rejection of role factor, DA = democratic attitudes factor.

mother as deviant. All 12 scales upon which significant t-test differences were found are included in the control factor of 16 scales on the PARI, and each difference reflected the schizophrenic's view of her mother as more controlling.

It is interesting to note that the one significant finding outside of the control factor is on scale 9 ("Irritability") and represents a reversal relative to the control scale differences. Rather than showing the schizophrenic attributing greater deviance to her mother as had been the case for control scales, the normal daughter viewed her mother as more deviant on scale 9. This is of importance in that it argues against a position (simply checking the left columns) or acquiescence (simply agreeing with whatever is said) response set among schizophrenics as the basis for the control score difference. A response set explanation of the control factor differences would be contraindicated not only by the scale 9 reversal, but also by the fact that all 12 of the higher perceived scores for the schizophrenics fell within a unitary factor-analytic cluster of 16 scales and no differences appeared among the 7 noncontrol scales. The concentration of perceived differences within control scales alone suggests that the subjects are responding to substantive meaning of the items and not to some test-taking set.

McKinley (1963) extended the use of the PARI as a measure of perceived maternal child-rearing experience to state hospital male schizophrenics (mean age of 33 years and about 11 years of schooling) and to general hospital controls of approximately the same age and education. He was further interested in whether the level of premorbid adjustment of the schizophrenic would interact with the PARI scores. This interest stemmed from the persuasion of Rodnick, Garmezy, and their associates that the parental dominance-submission patterns were reversed in the families of process and reactive schizophrenics. As pointed out in Chapter 2, research has failed to verify the process-reactive distinction in parent dominance patterns. McKinley's perception data similarly failed to suggest any clearcut differences between the mothers (or the fathers) of schizophrenics in keeping with premorbid status. However, as Table 4 indicates, the schizophrenic sons, taken as a whole, established the same picture of their mothers as had the schizophrenic daughters. They were viewed as more controlling than the mothers of the control males with 9 of the 16 scale comparisons achieving statistically significant F values. Similarly for sons as for daughters, no scale comparisons outside of the control factor suggested group differences in perception of the mother.

Among the problems inherent in interpreting the results of the two studies of schizophrenic perception of maternal child rearing, two loomed as particularly troublesome. One of these problems centered about the extent to which the use of schizophrenics as subjects might be introducing distortions into the data which were more related to the experience of being schizophrenic than the actual experiences with the mother. Perhaps the most compelling concern was

Table 4. Mean Maternal PARI Scale Scores for Poor Premorbid Schizophrenics, Good Premorbid Schizophrenics, and Hospitalized Controls (McKinley Data)

Scale Number and Description		Factor Loading	Poors (N=18)	Goods (N=17)	Controls (N=18)	p Value
2.	Fostering dependency	AC	14.89	13.71	11.78	.05
3.	Seclusion of the mother	AC	14.05	14.76	13.94	
4.	Breaking the will	AC	12.83	14.06	11.61	.05
5.	Martyrdom	AC	13.94	15.12	12.22	.05
6.	Fear of harming the baby	AC	13.17	14.65	14.33	
10.	Excluding outside influences	AC	14.05	15.00	12.22	.05
11.	Deification	AC	15.39	16.23	14.55	
12.	Suppression of aggression	AC	12.83	13.82	11.05	
15.	Approval of activity	AC	14.89	14.00	13.44	
16.	Avoidance of communication	AC	13.78	13.06	10.94	.05
17.	Inconsiderateness of husband	AC	14.17	15.53	11.28	.01
18.	Suppression of sexuality	AC	13.83	12.41	11.22	.05
19.	Ascendance of the mother	AC	14.33	13.35	10.83	.05
20.	Intrusiveness	AC	13.33	14.41	10.50	.01
22.	Acceleration of development	AC	15.83	14.94	14.78	
23.	Dependency of the mother	AC	13.94	13.59	13.33	
7.	Marital conflict	HR	15.44	15.29	15.83	
9.	Irritability	HR	14.67	13.12	13.44	
13.	Rejecting the homemaking role	HR	13.05	12.71	10.94	
1.	Encouraging verbalization	DA	14.33	14.53	14.22	
14.	Equalitarianism	DA	13.83	14.35	13.94	
21.	Comradeship and sharing	DA	15.94	16.59	17.17	
8.	Strictness		14.22	15.29	14.17	
	Factor AC (cumulative score)		225.28	228.65	198.05	.01
	Factor HR (cumulative score)		43.17	41.12	40.22	
	Factor DA (cumulative score)		44.11	45.47	45.33	

the possibility that the common perception of the mother as more controlling by the schizophrenic could be attributed to a generalized response to the institutionalized restraints of the hospital or the other forms of social control commonly imposed upon deviant behavior. In other words, the schizophrenic offspring could be attributing more child-rearing control to the mother as a function of his failure to distinguish in his own thinking between societal controls imposed on the disturbed and disturbing behavior of schizophrenia and the interactional experience with his mother during his premorbid years.

One way of testing the hypothesis that the PARI results with schizophrenics should be interpreted as systematic distortions of thought would be to compare the schizophrenics' perceived PARI responses and their mother's actual endorsements on the same items. If the schizophrenic had been responding to the PARI with generalized feelings of being controlled, induced by his experience as a schizophrenic, we would expect a difference between the two PARI scores. Heilbrun (1960b) analyzed the mother and daughter PARI scores from his earlier study and did find a difference in congruence between the schizophrenic and normal mother-daughter pairings on the control scores. However, it turned out that the schizophrenic daughters were significantly more *accurate* in predicting their mothers' responses to the control factor items than were the normal daughters. Subsequent work has substantiated this finding with male schizophrenics. Porro (1965) and Farina and Holzberg (1967) found no tendency for schizophrenic sons to introduce any special bias into their child-rearing perceptions of the mother. Porro used the normal sibling of the schizophrenic son as his basis for comparison, while Farina and Holzberg compared the schizophrenics to hospitalized psychiatric (but nonschizophrenic) patient controls.

Even if we accept the fact that the schizophrenics in our initial studies were just as capable of developing a perceptual schema of child-rearing behavior for their mothers as the kinds of people used for controls, this still left us with the problem of whether these contemporary perceptions have historical relevance. Is anyone in his fourth decade of life capable of the quality of retrospection that allows researchers to reliably sample earlier family experience? Perhaps what we were obtaining from the adult, schizophrenic or normal, when we asked him to reinstate his experienced interaction with his mother had more to do with general stereotypes about how mothers behave than specific relevance to his own development.

The decision at this point was to consider the same questions regarding perceived maternal control and filial psychopathology in a younger population of subjects for whom the mother is still a vivid and influential social agent. The late-adolescent college student became our object of study and remains so to the present. Heilbrun and McKinley (1962) began by comparing the attitudes attributed to their mothers by girls who gave evidence of being psychologically deviant and by girls who did not. Both groups averaged about 19 years of age. Deviance was inferred from scores on the Minnesota Multiphasic Personality Inventory (MMPI) (Hathaway and McKinley, 1951), a well-established objective questionnaire whose scales were derived empirically by their ability to separate the performance of various classes of psychiatric patients and normals. The MMPI had been given to two successive freshman classes at the University of Iowa and the deviant girls were selected from among the 7% most elevated and thus most maladjusted scale profiles. Normal control girls as defined by the MMPI were those whose scores on the clinical scales did not deviate more than one standard deviation from college female norms.

The patterns of PARI scores for these late-adolescent females, reported in

Table 5, presented some similarities to the attitudes attributed by older schizophrenic and normal daughters to their mothers. The mother emerged as more controlling in the eyes of the deviant late-adolescent girls, with 6 of the 16 control factor scale differences tested by analysis of variance reaching statistical significance within at least the 10% confidence interval. In contrast to the female schizophrenic findings, the younger deviant female presented their mothers as more hostile and rejecting of their homemaking role. This particular percept, later replicated with another sample of deviant late-adolescent girls, has not received the research attention necessary to clarify its developmental implications.

Daniel (1963) rounded out the investigation of perceived maternal control and filial deviance by exploring this contingency in late-adolescent college males. This was accomplished, in part, by following the same procedure as Heilbrun and McKinley. The MMPI, administered as part of the freshman entrance battery at the University of Iowa, was used to identify males with highly deviant profiles and those with profiles which provided reasonable approximations of the male

Table 5. Comparison of Mothers' Mean Attitudes as Perceived by Deviant and Normal Late-Adolescent Daughters

Scale Number and Description	Factor Loading	Deviant Group ($N = 56$)	Normal Group ($N = 52$)	p Value
2. Fostering dependency	AC	10.4	10.6	
3. Seclusion of mother	AC	12.4	11.2	.05
4. Breaking the will	AC	11.5	10.5	.05
5. Martyrdom	AC	13.0	12.1	
6. Fear of harming baby	AC	14.0	13.0	.10
10. Excluding outside influences	AC	11.2	10.8	
11. Deification	AC	13.3	14.1	
12. Suppression of aggression	AC	11.6	12.3	
15. Approval of activity	AC	14.4	14.2	
16. Avoidance of communication	AC	10.2	9.4	
17. Inconsiderateness of husband	AC	11.4	9.9	.05
18. Suppression of sex	AC	10.4	9.3	.10
19. Ascendance of mother	AC	11.3	10.5	
20. Intrusiveness	AC	11.2	10.7	
22. Acceleration of development	AC	13.5	11.9	.01
23. Dependency of mother	AC	12.4	11.6	
7. Marital conflict	HR	16.0	14.8	.05
9. Irritability	HR	13.4	11.9	.05
13. Rejecting homemaking role	HR	11.6	10.4	.05
1. Encouraging verbalization	DA	17.5	17.8	
14. Equalitarianism	DA	16.1	16.9	
21. Comradeship and sharing	DA	15.5	15.1	

college norms. A replication sample of females was also included to establish the reliability of the Heilbrun and McKinley results. As can be observed in Table 6, Daniel chose to score the PARI somewhat differently from the prior three studies by focusing only upon the factor scores rather than the individual scales. The control factor score in his study, for example, would represent the cumulative score over the 16 control scales. His results, tested by the *t* statistic, corresponded to those reported by McKinley for male schizophrenics; deviant male adolescents perceived their mothers as more controlling than their normal controls. No difference for the hostility-maternal role rejection factor was observed, again in keeping with the male schizophrenic findings. Daniel also replicated the Heilbrun and McKinley attributed control differences between deviant and normal adolescent females, the former group representing their mothers as more controlling. The higher attributed hostility-rejection of role for the deviant girls also corresponded to earlier results.

The question of whether the usual technical requirements of test validity can be meaningfully applied to a measure which intends to get at the subjective experience of the person is a moot one. What is to be the criterion of validity used in such a case other than another procedure for tapping the same subjective behavior? Daniel approached this problem by including a second method of assessing perceived control in his study in order to gain information about the convergent validity of the PARI control score. Selected cards from the Thematic Apperception Test (TAT) (Murray, 1943), which depicted an adult female figure or which frequently elicit stories introducing adult females, comprised the experimental series. Buffer cards, which included no female figure and which rarely elicit themes of female pressure, served to mask the nature of the task. The experimental cards were scored for themes of female pressure directed

Table 6. Comparison of Mothers' Attitudes on the Control (AC) and Hostility-Rejection (HR) Factors of the PARI as Perceived by Deviant and Normal Late-Adolescents

Factor		Deviant Group		Normal Control Group		
		N	Mean	*N*	Mean	*p* Value[a]
Males	AC	23	198.61	21	183.19	.05
	HR	23	39.78	21	38.24	
Females	AC	22	193.32	19	178.11	.05
	HR	22	42.46	19	38.05	.05

[a] One-tailed tests were used for female comparisons.

toward the central character using Eron's (1950) scoring system (pressure was the closest available approximation to the meaning of control). Theme scores were separated into maternal pressure, nonmaternal female pressure, and a combined female pressure score.

Daniel's results revealed a tendency for the deviant male subjects to introduce more pressure themes than normal controls when stories involved either mother figures or other nonmaternal adult females, but statistical significance ($p < .05$) was achieved only after these two scores were combined. Daniel also evaluated the responses of the central characters to maternal pressure in the TAT stories using Eron's scoring system. Deviant males supplied more passive responses to maternal pressure, whereas normal controls introduced more aggressiveness into the responses to pressure for their central characters.

While these findings cannot be regarded as robust evidence for convergent validity of the PARI control factor scores, it should be borne in mind that Daniel's approach to relating the PARI and TAT was indirect and undoubtedly underestimates the relationship between control factor scores and pressure themes. He established that subjects differing in level of adjustment also demonstrated the same differences in attribution of control and pressure. A direct comparison between the PARI and the TAT was not made, such as comparing the maternal pressure scores for subjects falling high or low on the distribution of PARI control scores.

A review of where we stood in the research program by this time underscored some promising beginnings. The control factor scores on the PARI, when used to assess the maternal experience for both the male and female schizophrenic, revealed the elevated maternal control which the preponderance of the family research in schizophrenia would lead us to expect. When the focus of research was switched to late adolescents, both sons and daughters, a relationship between psychological deviance and higher maternal control could still be identified. This encouraged the alternative of continuing the research with younger age populations for whom the maternal experience was still vivid and with whom fewer problems of research methodology presented themselves.

REFERENCES

Daniel, J. L. Perception, generalization and reaction to maternal authoritarian-control attitudes for college students varying in level of adjustment. Unpublished master's thesis, University of Iowa, 1963.

Eron, L. D. A normative study of the Thematic Apperception Test. *Psychological Monographs*, 1950, **64**, No. 9 (Whole No. 315).

Farina, A., and Holzberg, J. D. Attitudes and behaviors of fathers and mothers of male schizophrenic patients. *Journal of Abnormal Psychology*, 1967, **73**, 381-387.

Hathaway, S. R., and McKinley, J. C. *The Minnesota Multiphasic Personality Inventory Manual* (Rev.). New York: Psychological Corporation, 1951.

Heilbrun, A. B. Perceptions of maternal child-rearing attitudes in schizophrenics. *Journal of Consulting Psychology*, 1960, **24**, 169-173. (a)

Heilbrun, A. B. Perceptual distortion and schizophrenia. *American Journal of Orthopsychiatry*, 1960, **30**, 412-418. (b)

Heilbrun, A. B., and McKinley, R. Perception of maternal child-rearing attitudes, personality of the perceiver, and incipient psychopathology. *Child Development*, 1962, **33**, 73-83.

McKinley, R. A. Perceived parental attributes of schizophrenics as a function of premorbid adjustment. Unpublished doctoral dissertation, University of Iowa, 1963.

Murray, H. A. *Thematic Apperception Test Manual.* Cambridge, Mass.: Harvard University Press, 1943.

Porro, C. R. Perception of maternal child-rearing attitudes by schizophrenic males, their normal male siblings, and normal males whose siblings are normal. *Journal of Consulting Psychology*, 1965, **29**, 242-246.

Zuckerman, M., Oltean, M., and Monashkin, I. The parental attitudes of the mothers of schizophrenics. *Journal of Consulting Psychology*, 1958, **22**, 307-310.

Zuckerman, M., Ribback, B. B., Monashkin, I., and Norton, J. A. Normative data and factor analysis on the Parental Attitude Research Instrument. *Journal of Consulting Psychology*, 1958, **22**, 165-171.

CHAPTER 5

The Research (Phase II): Perceived Maternal Control-Nurturance Patterns, Personality Deviation, and Censure-Induced Cognitive Deficit

Progress beyond the knowledge garnered from the initial correlational studies of perceived maternal control and deviant outcome in sons and daughters required that we make several changes in our research strategy. It was necessary first to gain a more satisfactory representation of the maternal child-rearing experience. The addition of the perceived maternal nurturance variable to the previously studied control dimension allowed us to represent the full scope of maternal child rearing in keeping with Schaefer's circumplex model. We proceeded from this point forward to organize our data according to quadrants of maternal control-nurturance experience—high control and high nurturance (HC-HN), high control and low nurturance (HC-LN), low control and high nurturance (LC-HN), low control and low nurturance (LC-LN).

We also saw progress as contingent upon moving our research into the laboratory where we might capitalize on the increased precision of experimental investigation. To do this we switched procedurally from the use of the child-rearing measure as the dependent variable, the object of study, to the combined usage of control-nurturance measures as independent variables, the basis for defining our experimental groups.

The major influence in determining the initial direction the experimentation should follow came from some of the early research of Rodnick and Garmezy (1957) in the Duke University laboratories. Their work was based upon the premise of a heightened sensitivity to social censure in schizophrenia, a condition learned in the context of the child's relationship with a controlling and rejecting mother. They proposed that the schizophrenic responds to censure, implied or real, with a variety of task-irrelevant responses such as avoidance, rumination, or emotional arousal. These task-irrelevant responses serve to interfere with appropriate responses, and they postulate this interference as the source of cognitive deficit (Meehl's "cognitive slippage") consistently observed in schizophrenics.

While Rodnick and Garmezy (and their students) deserve credit for developing a censure-induced, response-interference theory of cognitive deficit within a research context, it would not be accurate to consider them the sole proponents of a response-interference theory of schizophrenic thinking or even its originators. Years before, Cameron (1938) concluded that the schizophrenic was left with unorganized, competing thoughts because of the absence of organizing factors that are inherent in the need to communicate with others. The schizophrenic's lack of desire to make himself understood by others, then, was proposed by Cameron as the key to his lack of thought organization.

Shakow (1950) also placed early emphasis upon response competition as the basis for thought disorganization in schizophrenia. He stressed the importance of attentional dispositions so that schizophrenia, for Shakow, was characterized by intrusion of inappropriate responses which occur because the schizophrenic is searching among stimuli and alternate responses to stimuli for those which are related to his unfulfilled needs.

At least two additional response-interference theories of cognitive deficit in schizophrenia have been proposed since the influential Rodnick-Garmezy paper. Both the Mednick (1958) and the Broen and Storms (1967) proposals subscribe to the basic axioms of Hull-Spence behavior theory (Spence, 1956; 1960) including the following ways of conceptualizing human behavior:

1. Whether a given response will be manifested in performance depends upon the strength of that response and the drive or arousal state of the person at the particular moment. Response and drive strength combine multiplicatively to determine performance.

2. A person usually maintains the potential for several alternative responses (the response hierarchy) in a given situation. One of these is likely to be dominant or most likely to occur.

3. A response cannot occur, whether it is dominant or nondominant, unless its momentary strength (i.e., response × drive strength) is above some minimum value, its threshold.

4. The momentary strength of a given response cannot rise above some maximum value, its ceiling.

Put in simplest terms, Mednick proposed that schizophrenics are especially anxiety prone. Anxiety, acting as a source of drive, tends to energize both appropriate and competing responses in a given situation, pushing many competing responses above evocation threshold. Thus, under conditions of high anxiety associations that are relatively weak and remote under low levels of arousal are raised above threshold to act as potential sources of interference with appropriate associations.

Broen and Storms present a theory similar to Mednick's. They conceive of greater equivalence of appropriate and competing responses which increases the likelihood of disorganized response patterns in schizophrenia. Disorganization (primarily cognitive disorganization) comes in the form of a partial collapse of response hierarchies under conditions of arousal or high drive. They contend that dominant (appropriate) responses lose out to responses ordinarily lower in the hierarchy of response alternatives (inappropriate responses) because of a ceiling effect which prohibits dominant responses from being energized by high drive conditions like anxiety as much as subordinate responses.

It would not be difficult to translate the Rodnick-Garmezy theory into either the Mednick or Broen-Storms proposals. The major distinction is the selective attention paid by Rodnick and Garmezy to social censure as a primary source of anxiety in schizophrenia as well as a potent cue in organizing an associated hierarchy of responses.

The facts that high control-low nurturance had been identified as a critical maternal child-rearing pattern in schizophrenia (see Chapter 2) and, within the Rodnick and Garmezy schema, had been linked with censure sensitivity and cognitive deficit in schizophrenics offered us a clear research direction. The principle of continuity between normal and abnormal behaviors led us to expect late adolescents who have experienced high maternal control and low maternal nurturance also to show cognitive deficit in response to negative evaluation. Evidence in support of this developmental linkage in late adolescents would act circularly to lend greater confidence to the etiological importance of aversive maternal control in schizophrenia.

In essence, the purpose of this chapter (and the next) is to present all of the research accomplished to date that examines the possible schizophreniform character of late adolescents who considered their mothers to exert high control and to offer low nurturance. Evidence to substantiate this relationship will be drawn in small part from psychometric findings but in larger measure from experimental investigations that probed the effects of negative evaluation upon the HC-LN offspring. The possibility that studies of evaluative cue effects could be used to explore self-conceptual differences among groups gained belated recognition in this phase of our research and will be considered as a further schizophreniform index.

MATERNAL CONTROL-NURTURANCE PATTERNS AND PSYCHOMETRIC INDICES OF SCHIZOID BEHAVIOR

There has been only a limited amount of correlative psychometric data collected in our research because of the scientific skepticism that attends relating one set of questionnaires with another set. Hall (1963) did obtain MMPI scores for the four child-rearing groups on two scales which he felt should be most relevant to the detection of schizoid characteristics in a nonclinical population. The Schizophrenia Scale, derived empirically by identifying questionnaire items with some success as a schizoid barometer with college students. Dahlstrom and Welsh (1960) report that "... terms chosen by college-level peers to describe the high 8 (Schizophrenia Scale) girls ... suggest the schizoid personality pattern present in the criterion group for this scale" (p. 202). In addition, they conclude from published research that:

> ... the analysis of the records of college students seen in counseling found that the group who showed peak scores on scale 8 presented problems in peer relationships and group acceptance. Sexual preoccupation was frequent along with sexual confusion, nymphomaniac tendencies, and bizarre fantasies (p. 203).

The second MMPI scale used by Hall was Social Introversion, included as an indication of social aversiveness. Dahlstrom and Welsh in discussing evidence relating to high and low scores on this scale present the picture of a dimension whose correlates range from modest, shy, self-effacing, sensitive, cold, and distant at the high end to versatile, sociable, enthusiastic, talkative, assertive, and adventurous at the low end.

The Hall MMPI findings and partial replication data (Heilbrun, 1968) are shown in Table 7. The HC-LN males in the Hall study did emerge as more schizoid than any other group as far as elevations on the two MMPI scales, and this was partially replicated by the Heilbrun data which included only the LC-HN group for comparison purposes. Statistical analyses reported by Heilbrun revealed the differences to be significant ($p < .05$) for both the Schizophrenia and Social Introversion Scales. A parallel statistical reanalysis of Hall's data gave identical results. Hall's HC-LN males were significantly higher on Schizophrenia

Table 7. MMPI Indices of Schizoid Tendencies in Late-Adolescent Males

	Perceived Maternal Child-Rearing Pattern							
	High Control-Low Nurturance		High Control-High Nurturance		Low Control-Low Nurturance		Low Control-High Nurturance	
MMPI	*N*	Mean	*N*	Mean	*N*	Mean	*N*	Mean
Hall data[a]								
Schizophrenia	35	12.7	29	9.9	32	10.2	31	8.2
Social Introversion	35	26.0	29	23.9	32	24.1	31	19.2
Heilbrun data[a]								
Schizophrenia	20	63.6					20	55.6
Social Introversion	20	53.4					20	44.6

[a]The Hall data was reported in raw score units, whereas the Heilbrun study used the more conventional T-scoring system with the general population mean set at 50 and standard

($p < .01$) and on Social Introversion ($p < .001$) than the LC-HN males.

While these psychometric differences support the contention that HC-LN males are more schizoid than those falling in the orthogonal LC-HN quadrant, they nevertheless represent only relative comparisons. This leaves open the question of whether the HC-LN subjects would appear schizoid if looked at in more absolute terms as, for example, if compared to general college norms. Normative standards published by Fowler and Coyle (1969), based upon incoming freshmen at the University of Alabama in 1965 (intermediate in time between the Hall and Heilbrun investigations), provide stable points of reference to infer *how* schizoid the groups represented on Table 7 really are. College raw score means of 11.3 for Schizophrenia and 23.3 for Social Introversion suggest only a modest elevation on these two scales for the HC-LN males in the Hall study; the between-group difference is mediated mostly by the lower (and healthier) scores of the LC-HN males. However, the college T-score means of 58.1 and 48.6 reported by Fowler and Coyle for the same scales indicate an average departure from the norm of about a half standard deviation for the HC-LN subjects in the Heilbrun investigation, suggesting both relative and absolute elevations for the Schizophrenia and Social Introversion scores.

A personological comparison of college males and females falling within the four quadrants of maternal child-rearing experience was included in an investigation by Heilbrun and Orr (1965). The psychometric instrument used was the Adjective Check List (Gough and Heilbrun, 1965) which measures a number of personality variables having relevance to normal personality functioning. Table 8 incorporates the group means on those scales for which statistical tests established significant differences. The major trend of differences for late-adolescent college males on the six significant personality scales has the HC-LN and LC-LN presenting similar scores which, in turn, differ from the two high nurturance groupings. The females provided a completely different array of significant personality variables from the males with the two low nurturance groups most readily distinguished from HC-HN girls.

Post hoc consideration of the personality findings for the late-adolescent males identified two distinguishable clusters of traits. For one, the HC-LN and LC-LN male adolescents appear to be deficient on "ego control" type behaviors—achievement, endurance, and order. This suggested some type of impairment in those behavior-maintaining systems which allow for the sustaining of goal-directed activity and for the delay of gratification in achieving goals. Later experimentation amply documented this interpretation. The second cluster of personality variables which distinguished the low nurturance male groupings was considered to bear upon degree of interpersonal warmth. Their low scores on intraception and nurturance indicate a lack of concern and regard for others and little empathic understanding. High autonomy suggests a disregard for social convention and an independence in interpersonal contact. It seems

Table 8. Personality Differences among Late-Adolescent Males and Females Differing in Perceived Maternal Child-Rearing Experience

Personality Variables	Perceived Maternal Child-Rearing Pattern							
	High Control-Low Nurturance		High Control-High Nurturance		Low Control-Low Nurturance		Low Control-High Nurturance	
	Males ($N = 53$)	Females ($N = 39$)	Males ($N = 31$)	Females ($N = 21$)	Males ($N = 31$)	Females ($N = 18$)	Males ($N = 58$)	Females ($N = 38$)
Achievement	46.8		51.5		44.6		51.4	
Endurance	45.3		50.1		41.0		49.8	
Order	46.0		50.3		41.7		49.7	
Intraception	46.3		50.9		48.6		53.4	
Nurturance	44.0		47.7		41.1		48.5	
Autonomy	56.8		52.6		60.5		52.9	
Affiliation		49.4		52.8		43.4		59.3
Heterosexuality		52.2		58.0		48.3		53.0
Succorance		53.1		47.1		55.9		50.2

NOTE. The data reported in this table are group means for those scales upon which significant ($p < .05$) personality differences were found. The college norm is set at a score of 50 with a standard deviation of 10 on these scales.

reasonable to conclude that the first "ego control" cluster of traits ties in with the cognitive deficit factor and the second trait cluster relates to the social aversiveness factor of schizophreniform behavior. The HC-LN male was identified as more schizoid within both clusters. The meaning of the covariation of the HC-LN group with LC-LN, which was occasionally observed in subsequent research, will be considered later in this chapter.

The somewhat less robust personality findings for girls suggested an emotional dependency (i.e., succorance) for the HC-LN group but whatever differences emerged were contributed in most part by the LC-LN and HC-HN groups.

MATERNAL CONTROL-NURTURANCE PATTERNS AND THE EFFECTS OF CENSURE ON COGNITION

Hall (1963) initiated the experimentation relating effects of negative evaluation to maternal child-rearing control-nurturance patterns in his doctoral research. The experimental part of Hall's investigation began with the administration of the Wisconsin Card Sorting Test (Grant, Jones, and Tallantis, 1949). This concept identification task required the male college subjects to sort cards containing geometric figures varying in color, shape, and form under one of four stimulus cards as they tried to establish which of these was the correct concept. After selecting what was to be correct, the male experimenter proceeded to say "wrong" whenever the match between the sort and the stimulus card did not involve the correct concept. Ten consecutive correct sorts was the criterion for having learned the solution to the concept identification problem. At that point the correct concept was shifted, and it became necessary for the subject to identify the new concept.

Following completion of the concept task, Hall presented the subject with one form of the Verbal Reasoning subtest of the Employee Aptitude Survey (Grimsley, Ruch, Warren, and Ford, 1957) which requires the subject to decide whether or not the available facts provide sufficient information to support a definite conclusion. It was necessary to complete this 30-item test within a five-minute period. The first form of the reasoning task was administered with minimal experimenter involvement. When the subject had completed this form, his paper was collected and presumably scored by the experimenter who placed a punched scoring key over the answer sheet and quickly scanned the answers with a disapproving expression. All subjects at this point received a standard set of censuring comments from the experimenter: "Mr. ________ , you have done worse than would be expected of someone at the college level. Apparently you weren't keeping your mind on what you were doing. I think you had better do the test again, and this time we will do it together to be sure you read *all* the facts and *all* the conclusions." In the course of administering the second form of the Verbal Reasoning subtest, the experimenter involved himself as much as possible by pointing to each conclusion as the subject read it aloud and recording the answer given by the subject on the answer sheet.

Expectations were that a sensitivity to censure would elicit responses which interfere with the conceptual and verbal reasoning performances of the subject on the two experimental tasks. The results found in Table 9 were far from definitive, although they could be considered encouraging. The HC-LN males did not emerge as the group showing the greatest impairment on the Wisconsin Card Sorting Test, although along with the HC-HN group they contributed to the significant ($p < .05$) "main effect" of control reported by Hall—high control males were more disrupted than low control males.

Intervening censure appeared to have its most detrimental effect on verbal reasoning for the HC-LN males; their group was the only one of the four which failed to improve in performance from the first verbal reasoning task to the second. However, none of the mean change effects was of much magnitude and the differences in change scores were not reliable.

Whenever results do not fall neatly into place in keeping with an hypothesis under investigation, the two most obvious alternatives are to scrap the hypothesis or the methodology. In our case there were some rather obvious changes to be effected in the methodology before we could consider the censure

Table 9. Effects of Aversive Reinforcement upon Cognitive Performance of Late-Adolescent Males from Varying Perceived Maternal Control-Nurturance Pattern Groups (Hall Data)

	Perceived Maternal Child-Rearing Pattern			
	High Control-Low Nurturance (N = 34)	High Control-High Nurturance (N = 29)	Low Control-Low Nurturance (N = 30)	Low Control-High Nurturance (N = 30)
Mean concept identification error scores	5.7	7.7	3.8	4.2
Mean verbal reasoning difference scores[a]	–.4	.5	.9	.2

[a] A plus score indicates improvement from test 1 to test 2; a minus score indicates a decrement in performance.

sensitivity of the HC-LN late adolescent to have been critically assessed. Foremost in this regard were the stimulus attributes of the source of censure in the experimental situation. In the Hall investigation the experimenter was a male, not too discrepant in age from the late-adolescent male subjects. If the HC-LN mother-child relationship is the primary learning source for extreme discomfort in the face of censure, then, according to principles of stimulus generalization, we should be able to demonstrate sensitivity to censure more readily if we increased the similarity between the source of censure cues in the laboratory and those experienced previously by the subjects.

Olsen (1965) approached the methodology problem in two ways. She introduced a female experimenter (herself) within the experimental setting to increase the similarity to the mother at least as far as gender was concerned. Probably of more importance, Olsen incorporated a taped representation of a mother censuring her son as part of her procedure.

More specifically, two tape recordings were made of five-minute conversations between: (1) a mother and son in which the mother is engaging in continuous control and censure of the son (aversive scene) and (2) a mother and son in which the mother is noncontrolling and nonevaluative toward the son (neutral scene). The mother was portrayed by a professional, middle-aged actress and her son by a 12-year-old boy with acting experience. Both worked from prepared scripts (see Appendix E). The topics were similar in both recordings with the conversations centered around the areas of academics, athletics, extracurricular activities, and peer relationships. In the aversive scene the mother presented a clear and consistent manner of control and hostile rejection toward the son with regard to each topical area, whereas the neutral scene represented the mother as noncontrolling and nonevaluative in all of her comments directed toward the son. Sound intensity of the tapes was approximately equal.

Olsen's experimental procedure involved initial group testing of 314 male college subjects with the child-rearing questionnaires to allow their assignment to maternal child-rearing experience groups. At a later date each subject was recalled individually to the laboratory where the effects of the maternal censure cues and of success and failure instructions upon cognition were studied.

Cognitive performance was measured by a modification of the Stroop Color-Naming Test (1935). Two alternate-form lists of 144 color words printed in another color were used, e.g., the word "green" was printed in brown, the word "brown" in red, the word "red" in blue. Five different words and colors were used: red, brown, blue, green, and yellow. The colors were arranged so that any regularity of occurrence would be avoided and so that no color (or word) immediately succeeded itself in either column or row. No word was printed in the color it named but approximately an equal number of times in each of the other four colors. An alternate form of the Stroop was constituted by imposing different orders of the words and colors involved in the original form. Instructions to the subject directed him to name the color in which each word was printed, not the color the word named. This can be recognized as a reversal of the highly habituated reading response.

Olsen chose the Stroop for her experiment for two reasons:

1. Performance on the task, which calls for a nondominant response, is especially susceptible to interfering responses.

2. Since it was quite unlikely that the subjects had any past experience with this task or tasks like it, it would be difficult for them to evaluate the quality of their own performance. Arbitrary reinforcement by the experimenter, which was to be part of the experimental methodology, would stand a better chance of being effective.

Parenthetically, more detailed attention has been accorded the aversive-maternal-control tape and the Stroop Color-Naming tasks because both subsequently became standard components of the laboratory method by which our theory of schizophrenic development was amplified and tested.

Olsen's laboratory procedure began by introducing the experiment as bearing upon susceptibility to distraction. The subject was told that not being distractible was closely linked to good academic performance and creativity in order to increase his motivation to perform well. After first screening for color blindness and explaining what was expected on the Stroop, the subject put on earphones and listened to one minute of the aversive or neutral tape, depending upon the condition to which he was assigned. At the end of this period, he began the Stroop as the auditory input continued. The entire five-minute scene was heard whether the subject completed the task earlier or not.

Upon completion of the tape, differential reinforcement conditions were imposed randomly among the subjects by the female experimenter. Success instructions communicated that the subject had done extremely well, even better than what would be expected of someone at his college level. He was told that he was to go through the task again and urged to do as well as he had done the first time. In contrast, failure instructions indicated that the subject had done rather badly, worse than would be expected of someone at the college level. After expressing the opinion that he was either not keeping his mind on what he was doing (i.e., he was distractible) or the instructions were not clear to him (i.e., he was uncomprehending), the experimenter urged him to try to improve on the next trial. A third set of neutral instructions was used which refrained from any evaluation of performance but simply informed the subject of the next trial coming up.

The second trial involved performance on the alternate form of the Stroop with no auditory input. Success, failure, or neutral instructions were again imposed after Stroop #2, consistent with those given to the subject after the first trial. A third Stroop trial was then run followed by success instructions to all subjects.

This experiment gives us two categories of data relevant to our interests. For one, the data from the first trial are concerned with whether response interference induced by maternal censure cues will be more prevalent within the HC-LN group. For the other, cognitive performance on the second and third trials provides information about the persistence of disruption introduced by the aversive scene and about the effects upon cognition of experimenter evaluation, including the censure implicit in failure instructions. Olsen's method of statistical analysis, examined in the light of hindsight, was not the one which would best clarify the functional properties of HC-LN membership. Accordingly, her results were interpreted as equivocal in nature when, in fact, more recent reanalysis of her findings suggests a far clearer picture of specific responsivity to censure of HC-LN males. Unfortunately, statistical tests were not possible because all of the data necessary for this purpose were not available for the reanalysis.

The response to taped maternal stimulation on Stroop #1 for the four child-rearing groups is represented in Table 10 by the number of errors observed given either aversive input or neutral input. The HC-LN males were the most disrupted by the aversive maternal cues and actually made fewer errors than some groups when the competing cues were of a neutral nature. These observations are best summarized by the error difference score which clearly suggests the greater disruption of the HC-LN group when exposed to maternal censure cues using neutral input performance as a group baseline for disruption.

Table 10. Errors in Cognitive Performance Given Competing Aversive and Neutral Maternal Stimulation for Males from Varying Perceived Maternal Control-Nurturance Pattern Groups (Olsen Data)

	Perceived Maternal Child-Rearing Pattern			
Type of Input	High Control-Low Nurturance (1)	High Control-High Nurturance (2)	Low Control-Low Nurturance (3)	Low Control-High Nurturance (4)
Aversive				
Mean errors	9.60	6.79	5.38	8.20
N	45	38	29	45
Neutral				
Mean errors	6.20	6.61	5.04	6.22
N	45	39	28	45
Mean difference (Aversive-Neutral)	3.40	.18	.34	1.98

	Combined Reference Group (Groups 2-4)
Aversive input	
Mean errors	6.99
N	112
Neutral input	
Mean errors	6.07
N	112
Mean difference (Aversive-Neutral)	.92

Considering that Olsen used only the LC-HN subjects as a basis for comparison with the HC-LN group, it is clear why the results of her analyses were somewhat equivocal. We have come to favor a reference grouping in our more recent research which combines all subjects who do not appear in the HC-LN quadrant in what can be considered a non-"aversive maternal control" reference group (i.e., membership is defined by the *absence* of experienced aversive maternal control). Looking at the bottom of Table 10 allows us this more stable basis for comparison; while groups of subjects who have not experienced aversive maternal control perform similarly given input of aversive versus neutral maternal stimulation (difference = .92), the HC-LN subjects were noticeably deficient in the presence of maternal censure cues (difference = 3.40). In light of the levels of intersubject variability reported by Olsen, there is little doubt that this difference in patterning would be statistically significant.

Table 11 summarizes the combined error scores on the Stroop for trials two and three which followed the exposure of subjects to the aversive or neutral tapes. Each group includes equal proportions of subjects who received praise, criticism, or neutral feedback following each trial. These figures allow us to assess the effects of the taped censure cues in yet another way, the extent to which disruption persists over time. A tendency for all groups to perform more poorly after having been initially exposed to the aversive tape can be observed. Yet the data indicate that just as the HC-LN group demonstrated greater cognitive interference in the presence of maternal censure cues, the disruptive effect of these cues most distinctly persists for the HC-LN group over time and in the absence of the instigating cues.

Table 11. Errors in Cognitive Performance Following Aversive and Neutral-Maternal Stimulation for Males from Varying Perceived Maternal Control-Nurturance Pattern Groups (Olsen Data)

Prior Tape Condition	Perceived Maternal Child-Rearing Pattern: High Control-Low Nurturance (1)	High Control-High Nurturance (2)	Low Control-Low Nurturance (3)	Low Control-High Nurturance (4)
Aversive				
Mean errors	12.64	10.33	10.01	10.84
N	45	38	29	45
Neutral				
Mean errors	8.60	8.75	8.68	7.82
N	45	39	28	45
Mean difference (Aversive-Neutral)	4.04	1.58	1.33	3.02

	Combined Reference Group (Groups 2-4)
Prior aversive tape	
Mean errors	10.47
N	112
Prior neutral tape	
Mean errors	8.34
N	112
Mean difference (Aversive-Neutral)	2.13

The performances on the second and third trials considered another way allow us to examine the effects of positive and negative evaluation by the female experimenter. In this comparison each group includes an equal proportion of subjects who had been initially exposed to the aversive and the neutral tape. Error scores combined over these two trials (Table 12) suggest a somewhat more disruptive effect of negative feedback from the experimenter upon the HC-LN subject (12.00 errors) than neutral (10.53 errors) feedback. The remainder of the subjects demonstrated essentially equal numbers of errors (10.06 versus 9.94) following failure and neutral feedback. However, this differential effect could probably not be demonstrated statistically.

Table 12. Errors in Cognitive Performance Following Success, Failure, and Neutral Feedback for Males Varying in Perceived Maternal Control-Nurturance Pattern Groups (Olsen Data)

Feedback Condition	Perceived Maternal Child-Rearing Patterns			
	High Control-Low Nurturance (1)	High Control-High Nurturance (2)	Low Control-Low Nurturance (3)	Low Control-High Nurturance (4)
Success				
Mean errors	9.33	8.58	7.97	7.82
N	30	24	21	30
Failure				
Mean errors	12.00	9.50	11.43	9.90
N	30	26	14	30
Neutral				
Mean errors	10.53	10.40	9.05	10.27
N	30	27	25	30

	Combined Reference Group (Groups 2-4)
Success feedback	
Mean errors	8.17
N	72
Failure feedback	
Mean errors	10.06
N	70
Neutral feedback	
Mean errors	9.94
N	82

In summary, Olsen's data even without statistical tests argue for the special sensitivity of the HC-LN male late-adolescent to maternal censure cues as would be expected from the application of the Rodnick-Garmezy model to schizoid normals. The somewhat less robust findings when censure was administered live by the female experimenter seems most reasonably explained by the failure to achieve sufficient similarity between the mother and the experimenter (a young and attractive female graduate student) as censuring agents. The clearest group cognitive impairment effect over the final two trials (14.33 errors) was observed in the 15 HC-LN adolescents censured by the experimenter but "primed" by previous exposure to the maternal censure cues. Her failure instructions did register with relative impact for the sensitized HC-LN subject.

While Olsen introduced the taped maternal censure scene and a female experimenter as means of increasing cue similarity to prior interactions with the mother, Heilbrun, Orr, and Harrell (1966) accomplished the same end by using a female experimenter who was approximately the same age as the mothers of the male college subjects. This investigation of the effects of critical evaluation upon cognitive performance employed the Wisconsin Card Sorting Test as the laboratory task, as had Hall, but with modifications. The task was increased in difficulty by using Gormezano's revised decks (Gormezano and Abraham, 1961; Gormezano and Grant, 1958), constructed so that an incorrect dimension (e.g., form) is intermittently reinforced for a specified percentage of the cards when the subject's performance with respect to the correct sorting category (e.g., number) is reinforced. Intermittent reinforcement of the wrong concept would have the effect of increasing the difficulty of discrimination and enhancing task difficulty. This change was effected on the premise that the concept identification problems presented to the college subjects by Hall were not of sufficient difficulty to allow for a failure experience and, thus, to demonstrate the expected unique deficit of the HC-LN males. A second change called for the delivery of reinforcement on every sort (either "right" or "wrong"), whereas Hall had only reinforced on sorts that were incorrect.

The 63 male subjects were paid volunteers obtained on the University of California (Berkeley) campus; their mean age was 20.0 years. (Data from a second sample of males bearing upon paternal control-nurturance patterns were included in the Heilbrun, Orr, and Harrell report, but these results will not be discussed until the final chapter.) Control and nurturance measures were administered in small groups while subjects were seen individually for the laboratory session.

The effectiveness of socially reinforced conceptual performance for the four child-rearing groups (Table 13), as evidenced by the commission of sorting errors, is highly reminiscent of the Hall results. Statistical analysis involved group by group comparisons with the LC-HN subjects, presumably the most adjustive of the child-rearing groupings. (Analysis of variance was precluded because of the failure to meet the requirement of homogeneity of variance.) Both the HC-LN ($p < .025$) and HC-HN ($p < .05$) males committed more errors than the LC-HN reference group. Like the Hall error findings with the Wisconsin Card Sorting Test, a "main effect" of perceived maternal control can be identified; both high control groups demonstrated a conceptual impairment relative to LC-HN.

The second score reported on Table 13, the total correct score, was suggested by the Gormezano et al. studies and introduced into our scoring since it provides a second way of assessing congnitive effectiveness which is relatively independent of actual errors. The total correct score represented the cumulative number of correct sortings made by the subject before he began sequences of 10 successive correct responses on both decks, the criterion of correct solution of the concept problems. Although the total score appears to be more an accuracy than an error score, it actually represents the complement to the total error score in a trials-to-learning type measure. The total correct score is based upon the number of positively reinforced ("right") trials necessary for the subject to reach the criterion sequence just as total errors gives the number of negatively reinforced ("wrong") trials required to reach the same level of learning. Accordingly, total correct, like total errors, provides an index of learning efficiency. This can be illustrated by considering two hypothetical subjects who gave the following records of right (R) and wrong (W) sorts in reaching the learning criterion:

Subject No. 1 . . . WWWWRRRRRRRRRR
Subject No. 2 . . . WRRRWRRRRWRRRRRWRRRRRRRRRR

Both subjects have the same total error score of 4, but the first subject with a total correct score of 0 is a more effective learner than the second subject with a total correct score of 12.

Table 13. Concept Identification Performance of Males Varying in Maternal Control-Nurturance Child-Rearing Experience

	Perceived Maternal Child-Rearing Pattern			
Score[a]	High Control-Low Nurturance ($N = 16$)	High Control-High Nurturance ($N = 16$)	Low Control-Low Nurturance ($N = 16$)	Low Control-High Nurturance ($N = 15$)
Mean total error	3.29	3.35	2.91	2.05
Mean total correct	3.45	1.72	2.32	2.00

[a] A square-root transformation ($\sqrt{\text{score} + .5}$) was applied to all individual scores to reduce the skewness of the frequency data and to make them more amenable to parametric tests of significance.

Returning to Table 13 makes it clear that the HC-LN males were singularly impaired in their cognitive behavior using the total correct score as the index. Not only were the HC-LN subjects the only ones inferior to the LC-HN group ($p < .025$), but they were substantially deficient ($p < .002$) to all other groups combined (mean total correct score = 2.01). One final point about this particular index of cognitive inefficiency before moving on. The failure to retain an idea after being repeatedly informed it is the correct solution may represent the clearest indication of cognitive slippage available from this concept identification procedure.

Replication of the concept identification study with daughters rather than sons (Heilbrun and Orr, 1965) again employed a "mother-figure" experimenter and University of California subjects like the Heilbrun et al. (1966) investigation. A comparison of Table 14 with prior Table 13 indicates similar but not identical results. The HC-LN girls, when compared with the LC-HN reference group, committed significantly ($p < .05$) more errors in solving the concept problems under continuous right-wrong reinforcement. However, they shared this deficit status with the LC-LN group which also differed reliably ($p < .05$) from the reference group. The total correct score analysis revealed that only the LC-LN girls deviated ($p < .05$) from LC-HN females.

Yet another approach to assessing the effects of evaluative stress (including censure) on cognition was taken in a more naturalistic study by Heilbrun, Gillard, and Harrell (1965). The initial experiment involved 45 males and 60 females while the replication experiment included 54 males and 62 females; all were volunteers obtained on the University of Iowa campus.

The procedures for the initial and replication experiments were the same except for some unimportant differences in subject procurement. Subjects were

Table 14. Concept Identification Performance of Females Varying in Maternal Control-Nurturance Child-Rearing Experience

	Perceived Maternal Child-Rearing Pattern			
Score[a]	High Control-Low Nurturance ($N = 21$)	High Control-High Nurturance ($N = 7$)	Low Control-Low Nurturance ($N = 10$)	Low Control-High Nurturance ($N = 20$)
Mean total error	3.54	1.99	4.36	2.40
Mean total correct	2.79	1.70	3.68	2.07

[a] A square-root transformation ($\sqrt{\text{score} + .5}$) was applied to all individual scores to reduce the skewness of the frequency data and to make them more amenable to parametric tests of significance.

informed that we were investigating the question of whether males or females were more distractible and that the experiment was to be conducted in the form of a contest. To encourage maximum effort, a cash prize (a pre-inflation $25.00) was promised to the best performer. The instructions specified, however, that to be qualified to win the prize the subject had to be on the winning male or female side. These instructions were delivered at the time of group testing on the two child-rearing questionnaires.

From one to four weeks later, the subjects were recalled in same-sex groups of from two to five for the experimental session. A female experimenter met with the male groups and a male experimenter met with the female groups. Each boy or girl was required to perform on the Stroop Color-Naming Test (understood by the subjects to be the distractibility task) before the experimenter and the audience of same-sex peers. Instructions at this time stressed speed of performance but placed special emphasis upon the avoidance of errors. The subject was informed that each time an error was made the experimenter would say "wrong," and it would be necessary to correct the error. After completing his turn, the subject returned to his seat and was replaced by someone else from the audience. Order of performance was left to vary unsystematically by child-rearing group, since neither experimenter was aware of the group assignment of the subjects.

In summary, the experimental procedure was intended to place the subject under considerable evaluative stress and create high task motivation. These ends were hopefully to be accomplished by appealing to competition between the sexes, by offering a substantial monetary incentive for outstanding individual performance, and by requiring the subject to perform before an audience whose own opportunity to win the money was dependent upon the subject's level of performance.

Results (Table 15) of the initial and replication studies identified the HC-LN group as having experienced the greatest difficulty under evaluative stress in three of the four comparisons of the child-rearing groups. The male HC-LN subjects in the first experiment made more errors on the Stroop than any group including the LC-HN subjects ($p < .05$) who served as the reference group. Replication failed to produce any differences among male groups, however. Female HC-LN groups in both studies demonstrated the least cognitive efficiency among the four groups, although comparisons of their mean error scores with those of the LC-HN females failed to achieve significance.

Interestingly enough, the LC-LN girls who had been the poorest performers on the reinforced concept identification task in the Heilbrun and Orr study emerged as the most effective performers in both sets of data within the Heilbrun, Gillard and Harrell study, significantly ($p < .05$) superior to the HC-LN girls in each case. Variable performance of the LC-LN females was

Table 15. Stroop Performance of Males and Females Varying in Maternal Control-Nurturance Child-Rearing Experience

	Perceived Maternal Child-Rearing Pattern							
	High Control-Low Nurturance		High Control-High Nurturance		Low Control-Low Nuturance		Low Control-High Nurturance	
Experiment	*N*	Mean[a]	*N*	Mean[a]	*N*	Mean[a]	*N*	Mean[a]
Initial								
Males	13	2.24	10	2.14	9	1.90	13	1.64
Females	19	1.72	11	1.47	9	1.22	21	1.56
Replication								
Males	15	2.36	12	1.99	12	2.48	15	2.51
Females	20	1.64	11	1.20	13	1.12	18	1.37

[a] A square-root transformation ($\sqrt{\text{score} + .5}$) was applied to all individual scores to reduce the skewness of the frequency data and to make them more amenable to parametric tests of significance.

attributed to an indifference to social evaluation which, in turn, would have a tangible effect upon task motivation. Given a relatively low-incentive experiment like that of Heilbrun and Orr, LC-LN performance would be expected to suffer. However, given a relatively high-incentive procedure as that involved in the Heilbrun, Gillard, and Harrell experiment, task motivation could be brought up to the point of generating superior performance.

A somewhat different tack was taken in investigating the effects of censure cues upon cognition in a study conducted by Heilbrun and Tiemeyer (1968). The Rodnick-Garmezy (1957) explanation of cognitive deficit for schizophrenics on socially reinforced tasks proposes that "environmental stimuli possessing properties of censure or rebuff may have served as signals for the arousal of personal ruminations, preoccupations, anxiety, and withdrawal responses or fantasied behavior" (p. 131). Heilbrun and Tiemeyer hoped to establish whether the HC-LN male manifests competing responses like these in the presence of censure cues. In other words, they pursued the question of whether a parallelism existed in the censure-mediated sources of cognitive interference between those proposed for schizophrenics and those which appear important for HC-LN sons.

The methodology employed in this study involved the collection of fantasy responses to selected cards from the Thematic Apperception Test (Murray, 1943). Nine cards were selected as portraying appropriate scenes, meaning that they included a male central figure and at least one adult social agent to provide the censuring (and controlling) cues. Social agent-male figure combinations included mother and son (cards 1, 6BM, 13B), father and son (cards 3BM, 9BM, 7BM), wife and husband (card 4), female peer and male lover (card 13MF), and two male peers and male friend (card 18BM).

Subjects in this investigation (Emory University males) were told that they were to take an empathy test. Specific instructions were:

> Empathy represents the ability to put yourself in the place of another person and accurately experience what he is feeling.
>
> You will be shown a number of cards with scenes printed upon them. In each scene you will be given a remark made by one person and be asked to put yourself in the place of the other person and to imagine how he would feel.
>
> Write your description of these feelings in the box labelled "feelings." After you have done this, try to predict what the person with these feelings would do, what action he would take. Write this in the box labelled "actions." Try to complete each scene in about five minutes.
>
> Respond to the cards in the order in which you find them. As soon as you have responded to the scene on one card, go on to the next.

Interpretation of responses to projective techniques like the TAT depends upon the assumption that when the subject attributes a covert or overt behavior to the "hero" in a given story, under general instructions to tell what is going on, that behavior will represent a relatively characteristic mode of response for the subject under similar social stimulus conditions. By introducing the TAT in the guise of an empathy test and under the specific instructions given above, Heilbrun and Tiemeyer sought to go beyond the "projective assumption." Their goals were to achieve greater certainty that the subject was identifying with the appropriate male figure in his story development, that he was using his own feelings and experience to guide his responses, and that the stories would be directed toward explicit themes (i.e., covert and overt response to censure and control).

A pilot study using 19 college males was necessary in order to establish the final form of the "empathy test." About half of these subjects were administered the 9 TAT cards with one set of censuring remarks made by the social agents serving as cues for their stories, whereas the remaining number produced stories for the 9 cards with a second set of censure remarks serving as cues. The story stem chosen for each card was the one which elicited the most variable feeling and action responses.

The main study included 44 additional college males and involved the usual group-testing procedures for the child-rearing questionnaires and, later, individual administration of the TAT cards. Five categories of feeling and action responses were maintained for statistical analysis. These categories were identified in the pilot study and met the criterion of appearing at least once on the average within the stories of the subjects in the main study. These response categories included two relating to feeling and three relating to action. Strong emotionality (shame, guilt, hostility, fear) and resentment (without strong affect) were feeling categories. Overt withdrawal, conformity, and inaction (i.e., socially ineffectual behavior) represented action categories.

The mean frequencies of feeling and action themes in the nine stories for the child-rearing groups are presented in Table 16. Analysis of variance revealed three significant effects within the data. The first of these was a main effect of nurturance on the strong emotionality dimension ($p < .05$). This means that a higher incidence of strong emotional responses to censure were detected among the HC-LN and LC-LN males relative to the two HN groups. While the effect was not restricted exclusively to the HC-LN adolescent, he was found disposed in fantasy toward affective responses to censure which could disrupt ongoing cognition.

A second significant ($p < .025$) main effect of nurturance reflected the greater frequency of socially ineffectual behavior in response to censure for the two LN groups. Understanding of this finding requires further elaboration of the inaction category. Inaction as socially ineffectual behavior was scored when the type of action taken in response to censure cues failed to deal effectively with (1) the person who was the source of censure, (2) the control directive presented concomitantly with the censure, or (3) the discomforting effects of the aversive social stimulation. As illustrations of responses scored as inaction, Heilbrun and Tiemeyer give us the following:

> He simply staggers to the floor, falling into a stupor, and is carried home by his friends. He later has no recollection of how he got home (card 18BM).
>
> He is very sullen for a little while and then forgets (card 13B).
>
> He recovers for awhile then lapses back into a state of frustration (card 3BM) (p. 11).

The incompetent situational responses of the HC-LN (and LC-LN) male following censure recalls the earlier finding of Daniel (1963) based upon fantasy materials. He found that psychologically deviant late adolescents supplied more "passive" responses to maternal pressure in their TAT stories.

Table 16. Response to Censure Cues in Stories Told by Males from Varying Perceived Maternal Child-Rearing Groups

	Perceived Maternal Child-Rearing Pattern			
Response	High Control-Low Nurturance ($N = 12$)	High Control-High Nurturance ($N = 10$)	Low Control-Low Nurturance ($N = 11$)	Low Control-High Nurturance ($N = 11$)
Strong emotionality	4.58	3.60	4.91	3.55
Resentment	1.92	2.20	2.18	1.91
Withdrawal	.50	1.50	1.27	1.18
Conformity[a]	.92	.70	1.18	.18
Inaction	2.08	1.40	2.36	1.18

[a] This type of action theme was more prevalent than would be suggested by these means. The conformity score was obtained by subtracting the number of nonconformity responses from the number of conformity responses for each subject.

The third effect noted by Heilbrun and Tiemeyer was a suggestive ($p < .10$) interaction for the withdrawal response. Examination of the means for withdrawal action themes on Table 16 indicated a primary contribution of the deviant and low HC-LN group mean to this effect in contrast to the similar and higher means of the three remaining groups. This observation was tested by comparing the mean withdrawal score for HC-LN subjects with the combined mean for the remaining subjects (1.31); the difference was statistically reliable ($p < .05$).

Heilbrun and Tiemeyer concluded that the low incidence of overt withdrawal responses to censure for the HC-LN male was tied to the greater availability of implicit withdrawal (a type of attentional "turning off") as a means of defending against social censure. They proposed that:

> If (HC-LN) males employ implicit withdrawal responses as a generalized means of immediate adaptation to social censure, this mechanism is accompanied by the opposite tendency to avoid use of overt withdrawal responses to the same cues. Two reasons can be suggested why these opposite tendencies should be found in the HC-LN male. Hypothetically, this is the only maternal child-rearing class in which the child has the concomitant experience of being psychologically bound to the mother via her control while having to face her censure and rejection. Maternal control mitigates against the child's demonstrating overt withdrawal from contact with the source of censure. Implicit withdrawal remains as the more available mechanism for neutralizing aversive cues from the mother. The second reason follows directly from the first—the more effective implicit withdrawal responses become in neutralizing aversive stimulation, the less the instigation to engage in overt withdrawal behaviors (p. 12).

The possibility of a differential pattern of overt-covert withdrawal habits for HC-LN males relative to other late adolescents actually had gone unnoticed among the findings of an earlier investigation in our program (Barker, 1965). Barker was concerned with the possible linkage between the maternal child-rearing experience and shame induction in response to censure cues. Theoretical formulations of White (1960) and Erikson (1950) as well as the experimental literature (Baldwin and Levin, 1958; Levin and Baldwin, 1958; Levin, Baldwin, Gallwey, and Paivio, 1960; Paivio, 1961, 1963, 1964; Paivio, Baldwin, and Berger, 1961; Paivio and Lambert, 1959) combined to suggest that the shame response leads to overt avoidance or withdrawal types of behavior. Thus, Barker proposed that the HC-LN son (whom he thought would be the most vulnerable to shame induction) would demonstrate the strongest avoidance-withdrawal response in an experimental situation involving censure by a mother figure.

Barker's subjects, male undergraduates at the University of Iowa, were initially assigned to child-rearing quadrants by group testing procedures and later chose to volunteer for the experiment proper. When each subject came to the laboratory individually, he was introduced to an investigation of "natural acting ability." He was asked to perform a rather dramatic section of Hamlet in a simulated theatrical situation. The setting was designed to create the impression that the subject's performance was being evaluated by an expert audience in an adjoining room behind a one-way vision window. The illusion of an audience was produced by means of prerecorded tape segments consisting of conversation between a simulated dramatic arts instructor (portrayed by a middle-age actress) and, presumably, several of her graduate students in dramatic arts. The tape segments, activated without knowledge of the subject by the experimenter at appropriate times, also created the illusion of conversation between the experimenter and the expert woman judge and allowed for the delivery of censure for incompetent performance.

Following recitation of the Hamlet soliloquy and the evaluation of his performance as wooden and inept, the subject was asked to set the stage for a second acting effort by establishing the preferred volume for his voice and the intensity of a spotlight in an otherwise darkened room which would be used for the next recitation. These preferred settings gave Barker his two primary dependent variables—physical withdrawal as gauged by lowering voice volume or by lowering light intensity. Presentation of the second recitation was followed by positive remarks from the female judge to alleviate any distress created by the censure cues.

A neutral condition was imposed for half the subjects, designed to minimize the possibility of eliciting any shame response. The subject performed in the same room used for the shame condition but with drapes drawn across the one-way vision window. Neutral condition procedures involved the same reading of dramatic passages, but the subject was left alone in the room as he recited into a tape recorder. Anonymity of the recorded performance was assured, the subject being told that his name would not be affixed to the tape and that the interest of the study was normative rather than individual. Light and voice volume intensity settings were taken after the subject had completed the first reading and had recalled the experimenter.

The mean illumination settings (Table 17), while enigmatic to Barker's hypothesis, provide a measure of consistency with the overt withdrawal response findings reported by Heilbrun and Tiemeyer. Only the HC-LN and LC-HN data were used for statistical comparison and resulted in a significant ($p < .05$) interaction. LC-HN males behaved in keeping with shame-induction expectations; following censure they selected a level of illumination less than their neutral condition counterparts. HC-LN males, however, chose an intensity of light considerably higher than their neutral condition controls. The failure to select a reduced level of illumination clearly contraindicates the use of overt withdrawal in response to censure by the HC-LN subjects, just as the overt withdrawal response rarely achieved thematic representation in the HC-LN stories within the Heilbrun and Tiemeyer study. The decreased sensitivity to sensory

Table 17. Illumination Preferences under Shame and Neutral Conditions for Males from Varying Perceived Child-Rearing Groups (Barker Data)

	Perceived Maternal Child-Rearing Pattern			
Condition	High Control-Low Nurturance	High Control-High Nurturance	Low Control-Low Nurturance	Low Control-High Nurturance
Shame				
N	15	15	10	15
Mean[a]	58.20	54.43	48.60	44.80
Neutral				
N	15	15	10	15
Mean[a]	44.20	49.27	51.50	50.40

[a] Illumination scores could range from 0 (low) to 100 (high).

stimulation which accompanies the withdrawal of attention from his surroundings, proposed as the basis for the projective findings, could also serve to explain why the HC-LN subject selected as high an absolute level of illumination as he did.

A summary of the cognitive research reviewed in this section is included in Table 18 to underscore our conclusion that the HC-LN maternal child-rearing experience does foster a sensitivity to censure which is often marked by deviant, usually impaired, cognitive performance. The fact that such deviance was consistently but not exclusively found in the HC-LN group made it clear that greater conceptual and experimental sophistication was necessary to tease apart the effects of the varying child-rearing experiences.

PROCEDURAL PROBLEMS RELATED TO THE CENSURE-COGNITION RESEARCH

Variable Schedules of Reinforcement

The series of investigations into censure effects on cognition reported in this chapter brought to light several methodological problems. The first of these problems will only be mentioned in passing, since it will serve as a starting point for discussing the line of programmatic research to be presented in the next chapter. In brief, the first problem evolves from variable schedules of reinforcement imposed on subjects within groups; "right-wrong" evaluations of performance on the Wisconsin Card Sorting Test and "wrong" reinforcements on the Stroop Color-Naming Test are contingent upon the skill of each individual subject. This means that in a frequency sense (i.e., number of "wrong") the degree of censure is left to vary from subject to subject depending on how well

Table 18. Presence or Absence (Yes or No) of Exceptional Effects of Censure Cues on Cognition for the HC-LN Perceived Maternal Child-Rearing Pattern Group

Investigation	Performance Variable	Perceived Maternal Child-Rearing Pattern[a] HC-LN	HC-HN	LC-LN	LC-HN
			(Same Effect Present in Other Groups?)		
Hall (1963)	Concept identification	Yes	No	No	No
Olsen (1965)	Stroop color-naming	Yes	No	No	Yes
Heilbrun, Orr, and Harrell (1966)	Concept identification	Yes	Yes	No	No
Heilbrun and Orr (1965)	Concept identification	Yes	No	Yes	No
Heilbrun, Gillard, and Harrell (1965)	Stroop color-naming	Yes	No	No	No
Heilbrun and Tiemeyer (1968)	TAT stories	Yes	No	Yes	No
Barker (1965)	Light intensity preference	Yes	No	No	No

[a]HC-LN = high control-low nurturance, HC-HN = high control-high nurturance, LC-LN = low control-low nurturance, LC-HN = low control-high nurturance.

he performs. Such individual variability must introduce imprecision into the search for group differences.

Pre-experimental Differences among Groups

Magaro (1970) raised two methodological questions about the experiments employing the concept identification task reported by Heilbrun and his associates. The first of these had to do with the lack of evidence that pre-experimental differences did not exist among the child-rearing groups in subject variables related to Wisconsin Card-Sorting Test performance (e.g., conceptual ability, test taking skills, tolerance for the ambiguity inherent in the task). Magaro's concern was that should such subject differences exist, they, rather than the censure, could be responsible for the HC-LN group deficit. If we accept the fact that concept identification is an intelligence-related behavior, there is some recent evidence in a study of ninth-grade girls by Gaetz (1970) which goes a long way in answering this criticism by Magaro. Using our procedures for defining child-rearing groups, Gaetz reports evidence that the HC-LN girls (along with HC-HN girls) in his investigation were significantly brighter than the two LC groups in both verbal ($p < .004$) and nonverbal ($p < .001$) intelligence. The intelligence measure was the Canadian Lorge-Thorndike

Intelligence Tests considered by their developers to be tests of abstract intelligence, the ability to work with ideas and the relationships among ideas (Lorge, Thorndike, Hagen, and Wright, 1967). Thus, when required to take tests of abstract intelligence which do not involve evaluative cues, the HC-LN subject was among the better performers relative to the other child-rearing groups. While indirect, such evidence certainly encourages us to look at the effects of the censure cues rather than at preexisting intelligence differences as the critical mediators of impaired concept performance for HC-LN subjects.

Heilbrun, Orr, and Harrell (1966) earlier had considered the possibility that intelligence should be considered as a control variable for the concept task. They decided against this after correlating scores on the freshman intellectual ability test at the University of Iowa (the American College Testing Battery) with error scores on the Wisconsin Card Sorting Test. None of the 20 product-moment correlations generated for the male child-rearing groups separately and for all subjects combined achieved statistical significance. Here we have direct evidence that pre-experimental intelligence differences among college students fail to assume any importance in accounting for the subject variability in concept performance on the Wisconsin Card Sorting Test.

Overreaction to Censure versus Underreaction to Praise

Another methodological problem identified by Magaro related to our assumption that it was the differential response to censure ("wrong") which was primary rather than differences in how the groups responded to praise ("right"). He was quite correct, of course, in that poorer performance on the concept task could be attributed to the lack of response to positive reinforcement for HC-LN subjects just as well as to an overreaction to negative cues. As Magaro points out, an even stronger a priori case might be made for the primacy of the positive cue effect based on sheer number, since almost all subjects received more "rights" than "wrongs." Magaro's own study produced evidence which helped answer his methodological question. He separated 60 male college subjects into the 4 child-rearing groups by the usual technique and followed with individual administration of the Semantic Differential (Osgood, Suci, and Tannenbaum, 1957) as a basis for rating subjective response to a series of stimulus scenes. The rating technique provides scores on three dimensions: evaluative (nice-awful, kind-cruel, fair-unfair); potency (hard-soft, large-small, strong-weak); activity (sharp-dull, fast-slow, hot-cold).

Each subject was shown four scenes including a neutral scene containing two trees, a positive affect scene in which a mother is feeding her son, a censure scene with a mother scolding her son, and a similar father-son scolding scene. Magaro found the HC-LN and LC-LN groups placed more negative evaluations ($P < .05$) on the censure scenes than did the two high nurturance groups. However, no differences among the four groups in evaluative response to the tree or positive feeding scene were identified. Activity or potency ratings also failed to demonstrate any significant effects. He concluded from finding differential negative connotations on the censure scenes but none on the positive feeding scene that the effect in the continuously reinforced concept task used by Heilbrun et al. was probably induced by censure rather than praise cues.

Even more compelling evidence that the HC-LN offspring does not underrespond to positive evaluation of his performance has been reported by Heilbrun and Gillard (1966). The 66 female college subjects in this experiment, assigned to child-rearing groups by our standard procedures, were given a uniform success experience on a visual discrimination task which was devised in such a way as to allow apparent performance level to be under experimenter control. All of the girls had been presented with a block-design construction test prior to any motivational manipulations so as to establish baseline performance. Following the positive evaluation of performance on the interim task, an alternate form of the block-design procedure was administered.

Each form of the block-design test included 15 four-block designs collected from the two forms of the Wechsler-Bellevue Intelligence Scale, the Kohs designs, and some that Heilbrun (1959) had constructed for an earlier study. The procedure involved the presentation of a block-design pattern for one second by means of a lantern slide projector with the subject allowed 30 seconds to construct the design immediately thereafter. Credit was given for correct placement of each block within the time limit (total credits per block = 4, total possible credits = 60). No evaluation of performance was given to the subject during the block-design tasks, although all subjects were urged to complete the designs as accurately and quickly as possible.

The motivational effects of the success experience should be reflected in the change in performance from the initial administration of the task to the second administration which immediately followed the success instructions. A gain score, given by the formula was used:

$$\frac{\text{score block design No. 2 minus score block design No. 1}}{\text{60 minus score block design No. 1}}$$

Put into words, this ratio score represents the amount of gain from the first to the second test out of the total possible that a given subject could gain. For example, if a girl scored 50 on test No. 1 and 55 on test No. 2, she would have gained 5 points out of the maximum of 10 that she could gain. This particular formula was used to compensate for a ceiling effect brought about by the low task difficulty. Even though the block-design task is included as a standard component of intelligence tests, the change score did not correlate (r = .00) with freshman intelligence scores derived from the American College Testing Program.

This fact lends credence to the assumption that individual differences in change from the first block-design test to the second are related to motivational rather than intellectual factors.

If the initial (pre-success) performance levels on the cognitive-motor task are examined in Table 19, the similarity among the four child-rearing groups can be noted. Parenthetically, this represents yet another piece of evidence to alleviate Magaro's concern about pre-experimental cognitive or test-taking subject differences among the child-rearing groups.

In contrast to the absence of statistically meaningful differences among the child-rearing groups in baseline performance, a significant ($p < .05$) main effect for control was identified in the analysis of variance for the gain scores. HC-LN and HC-HN females improved their design scores more following positive evaluation of performance on another task than did the two LC groups.

Relevance of Task Difficulty

The fourth and final procedural problem evolving from our research at this stage on which some evidence may be brought to bear is the possible importance of task difficulty in understanding our results. Let us illustrate the problem by some results which appear paradoxical in light of cognitive research findings discussed in this chapter. Heilbrun and Gillard (1966), in addition to the block design procedures, included an angle discrimination task in their experiment. The discrimination was an easy one, requiring an error of at least 15 degrees in angle matching to produce an error. An error count taken over 60 discriminative choices (see Table 20) indicated that the HC-LN females, again in combination with those in the HC-HN group, were superior performers to LC females.

Table 19. Changes in Cognitive-Motor Performance Following Success for Females Varying in Perceived Maternal Child-Rearing Experience

	Perceived Maternal Child-Rearing Pattern			
Score	High Control-Low Nurturance ($N = 16$)	High Control-High Nurturance ($N = 17$)	Low Control-Low Nurturance ($N = 16$)	Low Control-High Nurturance ($N = 17$)
Initial block-design				
mean score	48.94	50.47	47.24	47.75
Gain score[a]	.61	.47	.18	.34

[a]Gain score = $\frac{\text{score block-design test No. 2 minus score block-design test No. 1}}{\text{60 minus score block-design test No. 1}}$.

Table 20. Discrimination Accuracy for Females Varying in Perceived Maternal Child-Rearing Experience.

	Perceived Maternal Child-Rearing Pattern			
	High Control-Low Nurturance ($N = 16$)	High Control-High Nurturance ($N = 17$)	Low Control-Low Nurturance ($N = 16$)	Low Control-High Nurturance ($N = 17$)
Mean number discrimination errors[a]	2.94	2.76	5.00	5.47

[a]Out of a total possible of 60.

Analysis of variance confirmed the significance ($p < .01$) of this effect. The surprising thing about the superiority of the HC-LN girls, at least, is that most of the discriminative choices were made under conditions involving rather massive negative reinforcement. In contrast, then, to all of the research summarized in Table 18, HC-LN subjects performed relatively well when exposed to censure cues. The gross angle discrimination procedure would certainly qualify as an easier task than either the Wisconsin Card Sorting Test or the Stroop Color-Naming Task, leaving open the possibility that the appearance of censure-induced cognitive deficit for HC-LN subjects would depend on whether the task was easy or difficult.

The importance of task difficulty in predicting the performance of humans experiencing different levels of emotionality comes directly out of Hull-Spence behavior theory. For example, a set of experiments reported over 16 years ago (Spence, Farber, and McFann, 1956) led to the conclusion that high-anxious subjects were superior performers when the intrinsic nature of the paired-associate task minimized competing responses to those which were to be learned (i.e., the task was an easy one). However, when the paired-associate task was constructed so that incorrect responses would stand to compete with the correct ones, the results were reversed: low-anxious subjects were superior performers. Hull-Spence theory accounts for this interaction between task difficulty and level of emotionality by assuming that emotional responses contribute to the general drive level of the organism with the dominant response being energized most by the increased drive. In a difficult learning situation in which the correct response is not initially dominant, it can be seen why the higher drive level would be expected to lead to less effective performance.

The proposed interaction between level of emotionality and task difficulty presents a tempting explanation for the reversal in performance for HC-LN subjects on the angle-discrimination task in the Heilbrun and Gillard investigation. If censure cues arouse strong emotionality in the HC-LN offspring (and the Heilbrun and Tiemeyer results indicate that they do), then the ease of the visual discrimination procedure would lead us to expect better performance from HC-LN subjects just as more difficult cognitive tasks had proven to be more difficult for them.

Fortunately, a recent experiment by Betty Jo (Gillard) Ehlert (1970) provides a direct test of the role played by task difficulty in determining whether censure will facilitate performance or produce cognitive impairment. Hull-Spence drive theory provided the theoretical base for her prediction relating to task difficulty. This particular research, conducted with male schizophrenics, had a second purpose of considerable relevance to the thrust of our research program. Earlier, Heilbrun, Gillard, and Harrell (1965) had addressed themselves to the inconsistency of evidence relevant to the Rodnick-Garmezy theory of cognitive deficit in schizophrenia by stating:

> Rodnick and Garmezy . . . have proposed an interference hypothesis to account for the deficit cognitive behaviors of schizophrenics when exposed to socially aversive cues. They reason that the schizophrenic has become extremely sensitive to social censure, primarily because of his experience with a rejecting mother. Social cues denoting censure elicit response sets of a withdrawal-avoidance nature, which are usually incompatible with effective cognitive performance. Although the Rodnick-Garmezy hypothesis has not received consistent support from the studies of schizophrenic performance under conditions of social reinforcement (Buss and Lang, 1965), the more basic and complete proposition, that *given maternal rejection* the schizophrenic offspring will subsequently demonstrate cognitive impairment when exposed to social censure, has not been adequately tested. To do so would require a more rigorous attempt to distinguish between schizophrenics who have experienced maternal rejection and those who have not (p. 233).

Ehlert tested the proposal that censure would more likely elicit cognitive deficit in schizophrenics who had experienced a "rejecting" (i.e., high control-low nurturant) mother than in schizophrenics perceiving their mothers as "accepting" (i.e., low control-high nurturant). She also included a praise condition to compare its effects with those of censure. Her predictions were: (1) censure would result in poorer performance for HC-LN schizophrenics than LC-HN schizophrenics; (2) there will be an interaction between child-rearing experience, censure and praise, and task difficulty. HC-LN schizophrenics will be inferior to LC-HN schizophrenics on a hard task after censure, but this inferiority will disappear on an easy task; the differential change from hard to easy task will not be noted for these groups after praise.

Ehlert attempted to gather an acute sample of schizophrenics by including only those with less than a total of three years of hospitalization. The average length of hospitalization turned out to be 14 months. All subjects lived at home with both parents until at least 14 years of age. HC-LN and LC-HN status were defined by the same questionnaires administered under the same instructional sets as in all of our programmatic research.

Within two weeks of the small-group questionnaire session, the subjects were recalled for the individual experimental session. At this time the schizophrenic was presented with a series of tasks including a pre-test of the Stroop Color-Naming Test, an angle-matching task on which he was either praised or censured for his performance, and both a high-interference (difficult) and low-interference (easy) form of the Stroop.

The praise condition involved telling the subject "You did exceptionally well on this task . . . You were able to get 15 correct out of the twenty and the average is only 10. This is a hard task and your performance was extremely good." Censure was mediated by having the female experimenter say "You have done very poorly on this task. You got only 5 out of the twenty angles correct and the average is 10. I would have expected you to do much better. You'll just have to concentrate harder" (p. 16).

Following either praise or censure, the schizophrenic was next administered the hard form of the Stroop; the easy form was given to the subject upon completion of the difficult Stroop. These cognitive tasks represented modifications of the standard Stroop procedures reported by Hochman (1967) in which the word stimuli are exposed serially in a memory drum so that exposure rate can be more carefully controlled. The difficult (high interference) Stroop procedure was one in which the words were the names of colors printed in incongruent colors (e.g., the word "blue" printed in green ink). The easy (low interference) procedure involved the presentation of words unrelated to color (run, hold, put, take) printed in the same colors. Instructions in either case directed the schizophrenic to name the color in which each word was printed as it appeared in the window of the drum. Hochman had reported clear differences in level of performance given lists comprised of nominal color and noncolor words.

Cognitive performance of schizophrenics as a function of the several independent variables in the Ehlert experiment is represented in the data of Table 21. Statistical tests reported in her dissertation which achieved significance included a main effect ($p < .05$) for child-rearing experience; HC-LN schizophrenics made more cognitive errors on the high interference Stroop (26.56) than did the LC-HN schizophrenics (17.94). There was also a significant interaction ($p < .05$) between child-rearing experience and task difficulty; whereas LC-HN subjects performed almost identically on the hard (17.94) and easy (17.13) Stroop, HC-LN subjects were markedly inferior on the hard (26.56) relative to the easy (14.07) Stroop.

The rather heroic prediction of a triple interaction among child rearing, type of evaluation, and task difficulty did not receive statistical support. Considering the small number of subjects and the kind of performance variability inherent in using schizophrenics as subjects, it is no surprise that her theoretically elegant

Table 21. Cognitive Performance of Male Schizophrenics as a Function of Praise and Censure, Task Ease or Difficulty, and Perceived Child-Rearing Experience (Ehlert Data)

	Perceived Maternal Child-Rearing Pattern					
	High Control-Low Nurturance			Low Control-High Nurturance		
Reinforcement Condition	Easy Task	Difficult Task	Total	Easy Task	Difficult Task	Total
Censure						
Mean number of errors	16.13	28.87	22.50	18.13	14.50	16.32
Praise						
Mean number of errors	12.00	24.25	18.13	16.13	21.38	18.76
Total	14.07	26.56	20.32	17.13	17.94	17.54

NOTE: Number of errors possible on each task = 60. Number of subjects per cell = 8.

prediction was not confirmed. Yet if we keep in mind what Ehlert was looking for and what she obtained, it is difficult to accept the verdict of the particular statistical test employed in her study. Specifically, her prediction of a third-order interaction would have required, in essence, that the two anticipated second-order interactions would have to differ significantly from each other. One of these predicted interactions, between child rearing and task difficulty following censure, was clearly present in her data. HC-LN schizophrenics, following censure, were impaired in their performance on the difficult task (28.87) whereas LC-HN schizophrenics performed remarkably well (14.50) on the same task. In contrast, HC-LN schizophrenics, following censure, actually performed slightly better on the easy task (16.13) than did the LC-HN schizophrenics (18.13). While an analysis of this second-order interaction was not reported in her study, it is hard to imagine that it would fail to achieve significance. It is entirely consistent with her expectations concerning the effects of censure on HC-LN schizophrenics when the task is susceptible to response interference.

Ehlert anticipated that the differential effects of praise on HC-LN and LC-HN schizophrenics would be considerably less than those of censure, so she expected no child rearing by task difficulty interaction effect following praise. Again, this is exactly what was found. HC-LN schizophrenics, following praise, made only slightly more errors on the difficult Stroop (24.25) than were committed by LC-HN schizophrenics (21.38). HC-LN schizophrenics, following praise, made slightly fewer errors on the easy Stroop (12.00) than did the LC-HN schizophrenics (16.13). The schizophrenic child-rearing experience groups perform in much the same way following praise, as Ehlert had anticipated they would, and a statistical test would certainly convey nonsignificance.

These comments regarding the manner in which Ehlert chose to analyze her results are not intended to be critical. Hers was the more rigorous test of a complex prediction, a wise course to chart when a dissertation committee must be satisfied. All that is being asserted here is that her conservative statistics may well have caused a type II error of inference—the retention of the null hypothesis and the failure to identify a relationship that exists in fact.

To summarize this important study, Ehlert demonstrated that:

1. HC-LN schizophrenics demonstrated greater cognitive deficit on the high-interference Stroop than did LC-HN schizophrenics. (This replicates our repeated findings that HC-LN adolescents have a special difficulty with the card form of the high-interference Stroop.)

2. HC-LN schizophrenics (as we interpret her data) show a distinct reaction to censure which has the effect of disrupting their performance on more difficult tasks which are susceptible to interference but has much less of an effect on performance of easy tasks. The censure of LC-HN schizophrenics does not result in any difference in performance as a function of task difficulty.

3. The effect of praise upon subsequent performance (as we interpret her data) is to facilitate the performance of HC-LN subjects if the task is easy. (We also found this to be the case following praise for the HC-LN subjects on a simple angle-discrimination task.) Praise mediated similar facilitative effects in the LC-HN schizophrenic group.

SOME POSTULATES OF THE SYSTEM

Certain sets of assumptions, either derived from the earlier Rodnick-Garmezy proposals or evolved during the second phase of our research, helped to provide us with a frame of reference for understanding our results. Not surprisingly, subsequent evidence illuminated the limitations of these first approximations, although we would still maintain that they were more incomplete than inaccurate. In any case, these postulates are presented here for the sake of completeness and to serve as a reference for the research to be covered in the next chapter. This set of assumptions relate to the HC-LN child and set forth the basis for social aversiveness and cognitive disturbances (Heilbrun, 1966):

1. HC-LN mothers inhibit the development of personal initiative and a sense of competence in the child.

2. The child's inability to act independently binds him to the mother as a critical agent.

3. The child comes to anticipate critical and rejecting responses from the mother.

4. The most likely adaptive responses of the child to anticipatory failure or to actual maternal criticism are of an avoidance or withdrawal nature.

5. Avoidance may take the form of the child's avoiding commitment to a potentially evaluated act or, given commission of the act, evading the source of evaluation. Withdrawal may take the form of terminating the act once initiated or placing physical or psychological distance between himself and the evaluator during the course of the evaluative interaction.

6. In addition to anticipatory failure response and learned adaptive avoidance-withdrawal response, emotional responses such as fear, anger, shame, or frustration will become conditioned to cues associated with real or anticipated evaluation.

7. This chain of responses will be most readily aroused and strongest (i.e., capable of competing with other responses) when the mother herself serves as a cue for its elicitation.

8. Generalization principles would suggest that the greater the similarity between the critical agent (real or potential) and the mother or between the act to be evaluated and those responded to aversively by the mother, the greater the probability that the response chain will be elicited and the more vigorous the response elicited.

These postulations, looked at from the point of view of enduring attributes, assumed the HC-LN child would lack a sense of competence, be highly sensitized to social reinforcement (especially negative) and would use avoidance behaviors to avert the distress associated with anticipated rebuff and criticism. In addition, this child was expected to behave in ways which would make his sensed incompetence and his anticipation of failure a self-fulfilling prophecy. His avoidance of social participation would deter the development of social skills, further decreasing his social stimulus value. Reduced levels of aspiration would inhibit the achievement of significant goals. Even his ability to think effectively would be reduced at times through occurrence of obtrusive, irrelevant, and competing symbolic and emotional responses linked to his anticipation of failure or rejection of his behavior.

Insertion of these sequential postulates at this point may serve two purposes. Their emphasis upon the associations between censure-rejection cues and responses which may disrupt cognitive behavior in the case of the HC-LN child gives us the rationale for understanding the research included in this chapter. Since cognition had to be studied by examination of what was available to us, the person's performance, it was necessary to *assume* that performance differences were contingent in some important way upon the occurrence of nonobserved interfering responses. Inference was made somewhat less vulnerable in this regard through our choice of cognitive tasks which increased the likelihood that response interference would occur. Yet a motivational explanation for the pattern of results in these studies of cognition remains a viable alternative; cognitive deficit of the HC-LN adolescent also could have resulted from his tendency to give up in the face of censure or failure cues. In fact, the postulates assert that both associative and motivational explanations are correct.

Reduction in effectiveness is expected to result from both the intrusion of disruptive responses and the avoidance of failure by not striving after goals which may be beyond certain reach, a motivational dimension.

In order to effectively disentangle the contributions of associative and motivational factors to behavioral deficit in HC-LN subjects, a new experimental approach clearly was necessary. It is to this set of studies that we shall turn our attention in the next chapter.

REFERENCES

Baldwin, A. L. and Levin, H. Effects of public and private success or failure on children's repetitive motor behavior. *Child Development*, 1958, **29**, 363-372.

Barker, C. L. Maternal childrearing history and subsequent sensitivity to shame in college males. Unpublished doctoral dissertation, University of Iowa, 1965.

Broen, W. E., Jr., and Storms, L. H. A theory of response interference in schizophrenia. In B. A. Maher (Ed.) *Progress in experimental personality research.* Vol. IV. New York: Academic Press, 1967. Pp. 269-312.

Buss, A. H., and Lang, P. J. Psychological deficit in schizophrenia: I. Affect, reinforcement, and concept attainment. *Journal of Abnormal Psychology*, 1965, **70**, 2-24.

Cameron, N. Reasoning, regression and communication in schizophrenics, *Psychological Monographs*, 1938, **50**, No. 1 (Whole No. 221).

Dahlstrom, W. G., and Welsh, G. S. *An MMPI handbook: a guide to use in clinical practice and research*. Minneapolis: University of Minnesota Press, 1960.

Daniel, J. L. Perception, generalization and reaction to maternal authoritarian-control attitudes for college students varying in level of adjustment. Unpublished master's thesis, University of Iowa, 1963.

Ehlert, B.J. Attributed maternal childrearing histories of adult male schizophrenics and performance under task-irrelevant censure. Unpublished doctoral dissertation, University of Iowa, 1970.

Erikson, E. H. *Childhood and society*. New York: W. W. Norton, 1950.

Fowler, F. D., Jr., and Coyle, F. A., Jr. MMPI characteristics of freshmen entering college. *The Psychological Record,* 1969, **19**, 263-271.

Gaetz, E. L. Perceived childrearing practices in relationship to intelligence. Unpublished master's thesis, University of Calgary, 1970.

Gormezano, I., and Abraham, F. D. Intermittent reinforcement, nonreversal shifts, and neutralizing in concept formation. *Journal of Experimental Psychology*, 1961, **61**, 1-6.

Gormezano, I., and Grant, D. A. Progressive ambiguity in the attainment of concepts in a Weigl-type card sorting problem. *Journal of Experimental Psychology*, 1958, **55**, 621-627.

Gough, H. G., and Heilbrun, A. B. *Joint manual for the Adjective Check List and the need scales for the ACL*. Stanford, California: Consulting Psychologists Press, 1965.

Grant, D. A., Jones, O. R., Tallantis, B. The relative difficulty of the number, form, and color concepts of a Weigl-type thinking and reasoning problem. *Journal of Experimental Psychology*, 1949, **39**, 552-557.

Grimsley, G., Ruch, F. L., Warren, N. D., and Ford, J. S. *The Employee Aptitude Survey Test: Test 7, Verbal Reasoning*. Los Angeles: Psychological Services, 1957.

Hall, C. L., Jr. Patterns of parental identification as related to schizoid behaviors in grossly normal males. Unpublished doctoral dissertation, University of Iowa, 1963.

Heilbrun, A. B. An immediate memory modification of the block design task: relative performances of brain-damaged and control subjects. *Journal of Consulting Psychology*, 1959, **23**, 390-394.

Heilbrun, A. B. Perceived maternal childrearing patterns and subsequent deviance in adolescence. *Adolescence*, 1966, **1**, 152-178.

Heilbrun, A. B. Cognitive sensitivity to aversive maternal stimulation in late-adolescent males. *Journal of Consulting and Clinical Psychology*, 1968, **32**, 326-332.

Heilbrun, A. B., and Gillard, B. J. Perceived maternal childrearing behavior and motivational effects of social reinforcement in females. *Perceptual and Motor Skills*, 1966, **23**, 439-446.

Heilbrun, A. B., Gillard, B. J., and Harrell, S. N. Perceived maternal rejection and cognitive inference. *Journal of Child Psychology and Psychiatry*, 1965, **6**, 233-242.

Heilbrun, A. B., and Orr, Helen K. Maternal childrearing control history and subsequent cognitive and personality functioning of the offspring. *Psychological Reports*, 1965, **17**, 259-272.

Heilbrun, A. B., Orr, H. K., and Harrell, S. N. Patterns of parental childrearing and subsequent vulnerability to cognitive disturbance. *Journal of Consulting Psychology*, 1966, **30**, 51-59.

Heilbrun, A. B., and Tiemeyer, E. B. Relationships between perceived maternal child-rearing experiences and projective responses to censure-control cues in normal males. *The Journal of Genetic Psychology*, 1968, **112**, 3-14.

Hochman, S. H. The effects of stress on Stroop color-word performance. *Psychonomic Science*, 1967, **9**, 475-476.

Levin, H., and Baldwin, A. L. The choice to exhibit. *Child Development*, 1958, **29**, 373-380.

Levin, H., Baldwin, A. L., Gallwey, M., and Paivio, A. Audience stress, personality, and speech. *Journal of Abnormal and Social Psychology*, 1960, **61**, 469-473.

Lorge, I., Thorndike, R. L., Hagen, E., and Wright, E. N. *Manual for administration, Canadian Lorge-Thorndike Intelligence Tests.* Canada: Thomas Nelson and Sons (Canada), 1967.

Magaro, P. A. The connotative meaning of parent-child relationships as related to perceived maternal warmth and control. *The Journal of Genetic Psychology*, 1970, **117**, 25-35.

Mednick, S. A. A learning theory approach to research in schizophrenia. *Psychological Bulletin*, 1958, **55**, 316-327.

Murray, H. A. *Thematic Apperception Test manual.* Cambridge, Mass.: Harvard University Press, 1943.

Olsen, S. P. Response interference as a function of social evaluation and maternal childrearing experience. Unpublished doctoral dissertation, University of Iowa, 1965.

Osgood, C. E., Suci, G. J., and Tannenbaum, P. H. *The measurement of meaning.* Urbana, Ill.: University of Illinois Press, 1957.

Paivio, A. Personality, success and failure, and preferred degree of public exposure. *Bulletin of the Maritime Psychological Association*, 1961, **10**, 50-58. (*Psychological Abstracts*, 37:889).

Paivio, A. Audience influence, social isolation, and speech. *Journal of Abnormal and Social Psychology*, 1963, **67**, 247-253.

Paivio, A. Childrearing antecedents of audience sensitivity. *Child Development*, 1964, **35**, 397-416.

Paivio, A., Baldwin, A. L., and Berger, S. Measurement of children's sensitivity to audiences. *Child Development*, 1961, **32**, 721-730.

Paivio, A., and Lambert, W. E. Measures and correlates of audience anxiety ("stage fright"). *Journal of Personality*, 1959, **27**, 1-17.

Rodnick, E. H., and Garmezy, N. An experimental approach to the study of motivation in schizophrenia. In M. R. Jones (Ed.), *Nebraska symposium on motivation*. Lincoln: University of Nebraska Press, 1957. Pp. 109-184.

Shakow, D. Some psychological features of schizophrenia. In M. L. Reymert (Ed.), *Feelings and emotions*. New York: McGraw-Hill, 1950. Pp. 283-290.

Spence, K. W. *Behavior theory and conditioning.* New Haven: Yale University Press, 1956.

Spence, K. W. *Behavior theory and learning.* Englewood Cliffs, N. J.: Prentice Hall, 1960.

Spence, K. W., Farber, I. E., and McFann, H. The relation of anxiety (drive) level to performance in competitional and noncompetitional paired-associates learning. *Journal of Experimental Psychology*, 1956, **52**, 296-310.

Stroop, J. R. Studies of interference in serial verbal reactions. *Journal of Experimental Psychology*, 1935, **18**, 643-662.

White, R. W. Competence and the psychosexual stages of development. In M. R. Jones (Ed.), *Nebraska symposium on motivation*. Lincoln: University of Nebraska Press, 1960. Pp. 97-141.

CHAPTER 6

The Research (Phase II): Perceived Maternal Control-Nurturance Patterns, Motivational Deficit, and Self-Esteem

PERCEIVED MATERNAL CONTROL-NURTURANCE PATTERNS AND MOTIVATION

The methodological and, to some extent, conceptual problem of separating associative and motivational contributions to observed performance differences in our subjects has already been acknowledged. A second methodological problem has commanded our attention as well. Tasks such as the Stroop Color-Naming Test and the Wisconsin Card Sorting Test, within which social reinforcement is contingent upon the actual effectiveness of the subject, introduced different schedules of reinforcement for each person. This served to create differences in the experimental conditions to which each person was exposed and to introduce an additional source of imprecision as we compared the cognitive performances of our groups. A new type of experimental procedure was called for which could resolve both problems, one which could clearly delineate the effects of socially induced failure upon motivation and also could be expected to present a more uniform failure experience across all subjects.

An achievement motivation task, originally devised by James (1957) and subsequently used with children by Crandall (1963), offered promise of satisfying these methodological needs. The procedures, which were incorporated into several of the studies to be discussed in this chapter, will be described here in some detail. The task involved the visual discrimination of angular size. Subjects were seated in a laboratory room about eight feet away and facing a wall upon which was mounted a row of five white disks, each six inches in diameter. Centered on each of these disks was a clearly defined angle, varying by 10° steps from 45° to 85°. In addition, the lower legs of the angles differed by 5° steps from each other relative to the horizontal, differing from 10° below the horizontal to 10° above. The embedding of the angles within a circular frame of reference (rather than the more natural horizontal-vertical context) and the variable rotation of the angles were intended to increase the difficulty of the discrimination task.

The subject was instructed that he was to be tested for his ability to make spatial discriminations and that he would be shown angles like those mounted on the wall. His task was to match each test angle with its "identical" counterpart among the five standard angles on the wall. He was told that the average high school student gets 10 out of 20 correct, and the subject was asked at this point to estimate the number he expected to match correctly out of 20.

Included within the 20 test angles were five each of four different angle sizes (50°, 60°, 70°, and 80°). Since each angle size fell midway between two of the standard angles, there were no correct matching responses possible. Test angles were presented in a fixed order so that the subject would not be presented the same-size angle or the same lower-leg angle slope on two consecutive cards. The discrimination task was sufficiently difficult so that a priori schedules of "right-wrong" reinforcement could be presented to the subject by the experimenter without arousing suspicion regarding the bogus nature of the task. Thus, subjects could be given a more uniform failure experience by reinforcing everyone at only, say, 5 correct out of 20, or, in similar fashion, uniformity of success on the task could be approximated by effecting a high hit rate for the subjects. It is true that equating failure or success experience on an objective basis such as this does not allow you to assume equivalent subjective experience—that all subjects will feel the same impact of the failure or success. In fact, the opposite was assumed, since we were pursuing the theoretical notion of disproportionate subjective sensitivity to censure or failure among the child-rearing groups.

The visual discrimination procedure allowed us to examine the effect of past failure upon the goals which our late adolescent subjects set for subsequent performance. Goal-setting, as an aspect of motivational behavior, seemed well suited to the investigation of avoidance or withdrawal behaviors as responses to censure or failure cues, since goal reduction represents a way of avoiding the same degree of failure by minimizing the discrepancy between aspiration and prior outcome.

The Motivational Effects of Failure

The initial investigation of the effects of induced failure upon achievement motivation was conducted by Heilbrun and Orr (1966). A sample of 61 males was collected from among University of California undergraduates. Their mean age was 20.8 years. Grouping of the subjects by perceived maternal child rearing was achieved by our usual questionnaire procedures. Subjects were seen individually for the laboratory aspects of the study by the female experimenter who was approximately the same age the subjects' mothers were expected to be.

The individual experimental procedures involved the presentation of the angle discrimination task as described. On trial 1 (the first time through the 20 test items) each subject was given five positive reinforcements ("right") and 15 negative reinforcements ("wrong"). This provided a clear failure experience, falling from 1 to 15 below the initial goals set by the subjects and 5 below the bogus high school norm. Subjects were again asked to state the number they would get correct upon repetition of the task. Following rearrangement of the standard disks on the wall to avoid memory effects, the subjects were exposed to a second failure experience of only 6 correct out of 20 on trial 2. A third set of goals were then obtained and a relatively successful schedule of reinforcement was presented on trial 3 to allay the effects of imposed failure. The child-rearing group comparisons presented in Table 22 portray the same effects of negative social evaluation and failure upon achievement motivation as we consistently observed in our studies of cognitive performance reported in Chapter 5. HC-LN males reduced their levels of aspiration more than any other group following failure on trial 1; their decrement in goals was significantly ($p < .01$) greater than that shown by the LC-HN males who served as the reference group for statistical comparisons in this investigation. Neither the HC-HN nor LC-LN decrement was distinguishable from that of the reference group when the same comparison was made.

The greater drop in achievement level for the HC-LN males conceivably could have been produced by an artifact—an initially higher set of expectations than the other groups prior to the trial 1 failure experience. If so, the alternate interpretation could be made that the greater drop for HC-LN subjects merely represented their way of correcting a uniquely unrealistic set of expectations. Even though there were no statistical differences among the mean pre-trial 1 achievement levels (HC-LN = 14.25, HC-HN = 13.11, LC-LN = 13.18, LC-HN = 13.47), the arithmetic differences were in the direction we have described. Accordingly, a second score was examined which compared the post-failure goals with the actual number of "correct" responses permitted on trial 1, five; all subjects' achievement levels were compared to a common score they thought they obtained on the first trial. Analysis of this score again disclosed that the HC-LN group alone differed reliably ($p < .05$) from LC-HN males. Thus, the drop in achievement motivation for the HC-LN subjects following failure also reflected a reduction of goals to an absolutely lower level than the reference group.

After the subjects in the Heilbrun and Orr experiment had completed the final angle discrimination trial, on which they were given a relatively successful schedule of reinforcement of 13 correct, a second experimental procedure was introduced. The subject was given 100 poker chips and told that he was to engage in a guessing game in which he was to bet on the outcome of his guesses. The experimenter informed him that she was going to think of a number and that he was to guess whether it was odd or even, with a 50-50 chance of being correct. Before each of 10 guesses the subject was required to bet from a

Table 22. Effects of Failure on Achievement Motivation for Late-Adolescent Males Varying in Perceived Maternal Child-Rearing Experience

	Perceived Maternal Child-Rearing Pattern			
Motivational Change Score	High Control-Low Nurturance ($N = 20$)	High Control-High Nurturance ($N = 9$)	Low Control-Low Nurturance ($N = 11$)	Low Control-High Nurturance ($N = 21$)
Mean difference between post-failure and pre-failure goal[a]	–6.25	–4.89	–4.45	–4.05
Mean difference between post-failure goal and and level of reinforcement on trial 1[b]	3.00	3.22	3.73	4.52

[a]Minus scores indicate a decrease in anticipated performance as a function of the intervening failure experience on trial 1.

[b]This score reflects the extent to which subjects maintained goals in excess of the number "correct" they obtained in trial 1 (i.e., 5).

minimum of one chip up to a maximum of half those in his possession at the time. If wrong, he would lose the number of chips bet; if right, he would be paid an equal number. Instructions ended with the information that whichever subject had the largest number of chips in his possession at the completion of the tenth trial would be awarded a prize of $20.00 following termination of the entire experiment. A fixed and losing schedule of reinforcement was imposed for all subjects with the experimenter saying "right" after the third, seventh, and tenth guesses and "wrong" after the remaining seven guesses.

It seemed a reasonable assumption that if the subject took this kind of guessing contest seriously (and the monetary incentive was added to be more certain of this), he would adopt some type of betting strategy. For examples, he might adopt a conservative strategy of minimizing losses by betting only small numbers of chips each time or take the opposite tack and bet the maximum allowed on each guess. Whatever the strategy adopted, however, he could scarcely succeed, since his guess was treated as wrong most of the time. (One subject defied probability and ended up with more than 100 chips and the $20.00 prize.) Our interest was in seeing if we could detect differences in the relinquishing of risk-taking strategies in the face of failure. The assumption was that failure-sensitive persons would more quickly give up on their approach(es) to winning if they experienced failure.

The tendency to change betting strategies was inferred from how variable the percent of chips bet by the subject turned out to be—vacillating between betting many and betting very few chips was taken to mean he was unable to commit himself to an approach. Variability of the seven bets following being told "wrong" by the experimenter was scored by using the standard deviation for each subject's betting performance around his own average. Inspection of these scores suggested bimodality—the subjects either varied very little in percent of chips bet or varied a great deal in their betting patterns. Accordingly, the data was treated both parametrically (see Table 23) and nonparametrically (see Table 24). The mean variability scores contained in Table 23 were analyzed by using the LC-HN as a reference group. Looked at this way, the HC-LN group turned out to be the only one which was significantly more variable than the reference group ($p <$ .05, one tail), although the LC-LN subjects were indistinguishable from those in the HC-LN group in terms of their average variability. However, the non-parametric chi square analysis of the data in Table 24 (which tells us whether the proportion of persons falling above and below a common median level of betting variability in two groups can be considered to be different) draws a clearer picture. Seventy percent of the HC-LN males were highly variable and 67 percent of the LC-HN males showed low variability when these two groups were compared. The chi square value of 4.14 was significant ($p < .05$). Neither of the remaining two comparisons approached significance.

The general conclusion drawn from the Heilbrun and Orr investigation again stressed the familiar sensitivity of HC-LN subjects to evaluative cues of a negative nature. Given more systematic control over the presentation of aversive cues than we had before, we continued to find that the HC-LN subject

Table 23. Variability of Percent Bet Scores for Males Varying in Perceived Maternal Child-Rearing Experience

	Perceived Maternal Child-Rearing Pattern			
	High Control-Low Nurturance ($N = 20$)	High Control-High Nurturance ($N = 8$)	Low Control-Low Nurturance ($N = 11$)	Low Control-High Nurturance ($N = 21$)
Mean variability score[a]	11.15	7.84	11.21	8.10

[a] Based on each subject's standard deviation of percent bet after seven negatively reinforced guesses.

Table 24. Chi Square Comparison[a] of Betting Variability Scores

	Groups Compared					
	HC-LN versus	LC-HN	HC-HN versus	LC-HN	LC-LN versus	LC-HN
Subjects above combined median score	14	7	12	3	7	9
Subjects below combined median score	6	14	9	5	4	12
	$X^2 = 4.14$		$X^2 = .28$		$X^2 = .55$	

[a]With Yates' correction.

responded most strenuously to their negative implications. He dropped his achievement levels further following failure on a task when he presumed that his perceptual skills were called into play. Beyond this, he appeared least able to commit himself to self-devised risk-taking strategies when he was failed even though the task called for no particular skill, unless the subject believed in mind reading.

A replication of the Heilbrun and Orr study was run to test the effects of failure for late-adolescent girls on the visual discrimination task. Heilbrun and Gillard (1966), collecting their female subjects (mean age = 19.0 years) on the University of Iowa campus, found similar but not identical results (Table 25). Following a failure experience of only 5 correct out of 20, a significantly greater drop in achievement levels was found for both high-control groups relative to the two low-control groups ($p < .05$). Nothing other than this main effect of control was significant among these tabled data.

One of the theoretical concerns that we had encountered by this point in our research had to do with the contributed effects upon motivation of experienced maternal control and maternal nurturance considered independently. Virginia Crandall (1963) had defined the child's perceived reinforcement history in her research in terms of his ratings of the positive or negative character of parental response to his behavior. This seemed to offer a reasonable interpretation of perceived maternal nurturance—a score that summarizes the positive or negative character of the mother's response to the child's behavior. Our reasoning suggested that this reinforcement experience, when generalized, would shape the child's anticipations of reinforcement in other situations in which he would expect to be judged.

Table 25. Effects of Failure on Achievement Motivation for Late-Adolescent Girls Varying in Perceived Maternal Child-Rearing Experience

	Perceived Maternal Child-Rearing Pattern			
Motivational Change Score	High Control-Low Nurturance ($N = 16$)	High Control-High Nurturance ($N = 17$)	Low Control-Low Nurturance ($N = 16$)	Low Control-High Nurturance ($N = 17$)
Mean pre-failure goal	11.44	11.59	10.88	10.71
Mean difference between post-failure and pre-failure goal[a]	–4.19	–5.12	–3.38	–3.35
Mean difference between post-failure goal and and level of reinforcement on trial 1[b]	2.25	1.47	2.50	2.35

[a]Minus scores indicate a decrease in anticipated performance as a function of the intervening failure experience on trial 1.

[b]This score reflects the extent to which subjects maintained goals in excess of the number "correct" they obtained in trial 1 (i.e., 5).

It was conjectured (Heilbrun, Harrell, and Gillard, 1967) that the primary mediated effect of perceived maternal control was to establish the sensitivity of the child to evaluative stimuli. High maternal control would be associated with heightened sensitivity to evaluation, whereas low maternal control would mediate lowered responsiveness to evaluative cues. The combination of these two mediated motivational dispositions, anticipation of positive or negative outcome in goal-directed activity and sensitivity to evaluative cues, seemed to offer reasonable explanations for many of the research results which have been described in the previous and present chapters. Furthermore, our major expository goal in this book is to point up progressively the unique effects of the HC-LN developmental experience. Identification of two motivational dimensions for control-nurturance patterns offers a basis for understanding why the HC-LN group had not emerged consistently as unique in the results of our research. In studies that clearly emphasize motivational variables, as ours have, some procedures may place greater priority upon reinforcement cue sensitivity while other procedures may capitalize more on anticipated outcome. If so, performance commonalities between HC-LN and HC-HN adolescents or between HC-LN and LC-LN adolescents could be understood in terms of the shared properties of heightened cue sensitivity in the former case or anticipated negative outcome in the latter case.

The experiment to be considered next, conducted by Heilbrun, Harrell, and Gillard (1967), accomplished two things. First, it extended the experimental analysis of motivation beyond the effects of failure and success upon the four child-rearing groups to the effects of nonreinforcement. Given no evaluative cues, what happens to the goal striving of the late adolescent? Second, the mode of data analysis allowed a more refined look at the proposed control-related and nurturance-related motivation effects.

The 237 subjects in this experiment were volunteers from a large undergraduate class at the University of Iowa and were split into approximately half of each sex. After group testing to establish child-rearing experience, each subject was recalled individually for the laboratory session. The angle-discrimination task was employed with some modifications. Some subjects were given an initial success experience on trial 1 (13-15 correct), some were presented with failure on trial 1 (5-7 correct), and still others performed on trial 1 without any evaluative feedback as to correctness or incorrectness (nonreaction). After the subjects were informed of their scores on trial 1 (except for the nonreaction group), they were asked to set a goal for trial 2. No reinforcement was given to any subject on trial 2, and following completion of the trial yet another achievement level was requested of the subjects, this time without feedback of scores. Having obtained this final level of aspiration, the subject was told that the third trial would not actually be run and that his score on trial 2 had actually been either 12, 13, or 14. This latter score was given to avert undue reactions to the experiment by those who were initially failed.

The effects of social nonreaction are given in Tables 26-28. The data for males and females have been combined, since statistical analysis failed to suggest any sex differences. The effects of nonreaction upon achievement level were analyzed by comparing the two high-control groups with each other and, similarly, the two low-control groups. It was predicted that the subjects with positive (high nurturance) and negative (low nurturance) reinforcement histories would impose their characteristic anticipations of outcome in the absence of evaluative cues; low-nurturance subjects would respond to nonreaction by a greater curtailment of achievement levels than high-nurturance subjects. However, it was further predicted that this effect would be observed only in the reinforcement sensitive high-control adolescents.

Analysis of the achievement scores separately by level of perceived control provided ample support for the predictions. HC-LN subjects reduced their aspiration levels more than HC-HN subjects after the nonevaluated trial when

Table 26. Effects of Social Nonreaction upon Achievement Motivation Following Prior Success for Late Adolescents Varying in Perceived Maternal Child-Rearing Experience

	Perceived Maternal Child-Rearing Pattern			
Motivational Change Score	High Control-Low Nurturance (N = 26)	High Control-High Nurturance (N = 25)	Low Control-Low Nurturance (N = 25)	Low Control-High Nurturance (N = 22)
Mean difference between post-success and post-nonreaction goals[a]	1.88	.48	1.48	1.09
Mean difference between post-nonreaction and level of reinforcement on trial 1[b]	−2.85	−.16	−1.24	−1.45

[a] A plus score indicates a decrease in goals following nonreaction.

[b] A minus score indicates that the goals following nonreaction were lower than the bogus success on trial 1.

they had been given a preliminary success experience ($p < .005$), and the absolute level of their goals fell further below the previous reinforcement level they had "attained" on the success trial ($p < .001$). Those HC-LN adolescents who were initially failed did not increase their goals as much as the HC-HN adolescents following nonevaluation ($p < .005$), although the absolute difference between these goals and the scores given them on the failure trial did not differentiate these groups. The predominant effect of the absence of evaluative feedback, then, was to restrict the HC-LN subject's anticipated performance more whether he had a prior experience of success or failure on the same task.

No differences in response to nonreaction were found between LC-LN and LC-HN subjects following success or failure. Nor were any significant differences identified within either the high or low control levels for the nonreaction-nonreaction condition (see Table 28), although the HC-LN subjects were, characteristically, the most conservative in their goal-setting among the four groups.

An even clearer demonstration of the unique motivational response of the

Table 27. Effects of Social Nonreaction upon Achievement Motivation Following Prior Failure for Late Adolescents Varying in Perceived Maternal Child-Rearing Experience

	Perceived Maternal Child-Rearing Pattern			
Motivational Change Score	High Control-Low Nurturance (N = 24)	High Control-High Nurturance (N = 22)	Low Control-Low Nurturance (N = 21)	Low Control-High Nurturance (N = 24)
Mean difference between post-failure and post-nonreaction goals[a]	–.08	–1.50	–1.19	–.54
Mean difference between post-nonreaction and level of reinforcement on trial 1[b]	3.13	3.64	3.29	2.96

[a] A minus score indicates an increase in goals following nonreaction.

[b] A plus score indicates that the goals following nonreaction were higher than the bogus failure scores on trial 1.

Table 28. Effects of Social Nonreaction upon Achievement Motivation Following Prior Nonreaction for Late Adolescents Varying in Perceived Maternal Child-Rearing Experience

	Perceived Maternal Child-Rearing Pattern			
Motivational Change Score	High Control-Low Nurturance (N = 11)	High Control-High Nurturance (N = 11)	Low Control-Low Nurturance (N = 12)	Low Control-High Nurturance (N = 14)
Mean difference between initial post-nonreaction and final post nonreaction goals[a]	.00	–.82	–1.00	–.21

[a] A minus score indicates an increase in goals following the final nonreaction trial.

HC-LN group in this experiment can be made if it is compared to the other three groups combined, a procedure that we have favored in more recent research. Looked at in this way, the aversive-maternal-control subjects: (1) dropped their achievement levels more (1.88) in the success-nonreaction condition than the reference group (1.01); (2) failed to elevate their achievement levels as much (–.08) in the failure-nonreaction condition as the reference group (–1.06); and (3) failed to raise their achievement levels as much (.00) as the reference group (–.65) in the nonreaction-nonreaction condition. The t values for the success and failure condition comparisons were significant ($p < .025$; $p < .01$, respectively). The nonreaction-nonreaction condition comparison did not reach significance ($p < .25$). We can conclude from this mode of analysis that the HC-LN subject responds to nonreinforcement with a singular curtailment in achievement strivings relative to the remaining child-rearing groups.

The two-step proposal (differences in anticipated outcome to be found in reinforcement-sensitive groups only) which received support in the nonreaction experiment was again tested using delay of reinforcement procedures (Heilbrun, 1969). Terrell's (1965) review of research into delayed reinforcement effects emphasized the decreasing predictability of these effects upon learning as one moves from experiments with animals to those employing children and, finally, to research with adult human subjects. The time interval between responses and contingent reward, which is inversely related to learning in animals, has been investigated with contradictory results when children have been used as subjects. Research on delay of reinforcement at the adult human level was summarized by Terrell as failing to support conclusions or theories derived from animal work.

Spence's (1956, 1960) inhibition theory of delayed reinforcement in instrumental reward conditioning, based upon animal research, is one such case in point. He proposed that delay of reward, given expectancy of reward on the part of the animal, produces frustration. The frustration, in turn, competes with the task-relevant instrumental response through task-irrelevant responses elicited by frustration cues. While this theory holds some logical appeal for understanding delay of reinforcement with humans, Terrell concludes that evidence extracted from research with humans fails to support predictions from the theory.

Coming back to the two-step proposal, the Heilbrun experiment sought to establish whether the inhibition theory of delayed reinforcement would prove more predictive with humans if we considered reinforcement sensitivity as mediated by experienced maternal control and anticipated reinforcement outcome as mediated by experienced maternal nurturance. One basis for expecting enhanced prediction from the theory was the identification of a subset of children (low control) who appear less susceptible to the influence of social reinforcement and whose behavior would be less predictable under any condition of reinforcement, delayed or otherwise. Accordingly, predictions from

Spence's delay-of-reinforcement theory should stand a better chance of being supported within a high-control group of children.

It was further reasoned that the induction of frustration in human subjects during the delay period should be related to the subjective probability held by the subject that reward will follow from his goal response. Spence (1960) made this explicit in his theory by requiring that ". . . the subject had to learn to expect or anticipate a reward upon responding to a stimulus before there would be any inhibition or frustration effect" (p. 97). Although animal behavior in a delayed reinforcement experiment might be reasonably predictable from knowledge of the immediate experimental conditions, the specific effect of delay upon human subjects might be expected to vary with the life history experiences of the person. The particular manner in which the person comes to anticipate outcome in reinforced situations, which we have related to perceived maternal nurturance, would be especially important. It would be expected that delay of reinforcement will prove more frustrating to the human subject whose anticipation is that of reward compared to the subject who anticipated social reward less and aversive social evaluation more.

Thus, the two-step proposal led to these predictions:

1. HN adolescents who tend to anticipate positive outcome in socially reinforced situations will experience greater frustration with delay of reinforcement than LN subjects with less positive or more negative anticipation of outcome. Given an experimental task that is susceptible to interference from frustration-induced responses and involving delay of reinforcement, HN group performance will be inferior to LN group performance.

2. The differential performance predicted for groups differing in level of perceived maternal nurturance will be found for reinforcement-sensitive adolescents (HC) but not for those who are less responsive to reinforcement (LC).

A prior experiment (Heilbrun and Orr, 1965), employing the same task and type of female subjects included in the experiment under discussion, had found HC-HN girls to be superior in performance to HC-LN girls when reinforcement was given immediately following the subject's response. Since this is exactly the opposite of the effect being predicted under a delay of reinforcement paradigm, the actual experimental prediction was for a reinforcement condition by level of nurturance interaction for HC females. HC-HN subjects should be superior to HC-LN subjects when reinforcement is immediate but HC-LN subjects should perform more effectively than HC-HN subjects when reinforcement is delayed. The expectation that LC females would be less predictable allowed no basis for predicting a similar interaction within this group as the temporal conditions of reinforcement changed.

The 74 female subjects who participated in this experiment were Emory University undergraduates. Their average age was 19.3 years. Small-group testing procedures to establish maternal child-rearing experience proceeded in the usual manner. Individual procedures, imposed upon recall of the subjects, entailed the presentation of the Wisconsin Card Sorting Test under one of two reinforcement conditions. The immediate reinforcement condition involved the female experimenter's saying "right" or "wrong" immediately following the subject's placement of the response cards under one of the four stimulus cards. As described earlier in the book, reinforcement continued until the girl made 10 consecutive correct sorts, signaling solution of the concept-identification task. At that point, a new card deck was introduced (unknown to the subject) and a second concept became the object of problem solving until 10 consecutive correct sorts again indicated a successful solution. In this immediate reinforcement condition, the sorted card was left in position for 30 seconds following reinforcement of the response, was then removed from the table, and the next card in the deck was handed to the subject.

The delayed-reinforcement condition introduced a 30-second delay following the subject's placement of the response card. After her delayed positive or negative response, the experimenter removed the card immediately and handed the subject the next card from the deck.

These experimental procedures kept the time for each trial (i.e., sorting and reinforcement of an individual sort) relatively constant across subjects except for the variable time taken by subjects to decide upon placement of the card. No subject required more than 15 minutes to correctly solve both concept problems.

Performance on the concept task was measured in terms of number of trials taken to reach the criterion run of 10 consecutive correct responses on each deck. The trials-to-learning counts for both decks were summed so that the performance score which was the basis of analysis represented how effectively the girl solved both concept problems. Neither the first trial on the first or second deck was counted in the trials-to-learn score. Parenthetically, this score represents the sum of the total error score and the "total correct" score which were previously analyzed separately. Since we derived similar implications from these scores considered independently, there seemed to be no basis for continuing to treat them separately.

Trials-to-learn means, based on scores corrected for negative skewness by a square-root transformation, are included in Table 29. Analysis of variance performed for the HC groups disclosed no effect of either nurturance level or reinforcement condition. A significant interaction effect ($p < .05$) was found, however, and it confirmed the experimental prediction. HC-LN females demonstrated inferior performance to HC-HN females given immediate evaluative feedback, as they had in the previous experiment (Heilbrun and Orr, 1965). When a 30-second delay period was inserted between the girl's response and the experimenter's reinforcement, the reverse was found; HC-LN females

Table 29. Trials-to-Learning on a Concept Task Under Conditions of Immediate and Delayed Reinforcement for Girls Varying in Perceived Maternal Child-Rearing Experience

Reinforcement Conditions	Perceived Maternal Child-Rearing Pattern							
	High Control-Low Nurturance		High Control-High Nurturance		Low Control-Low Nurturance		Low Control-High Nurturance	
	N	Mean[a]	*N*	Mean[a]	*N*	Mean[a]	*N*	Mean[a]
Immediate	9	3.91	11	2.91	9	2.93	9	3.30
Delayed	8	2.50	9	4.81	10	3.68	9	3.08

[a]Based upon a square-root transformation of the number of trials to reach criterion runs for two concept problems.

were superior to HC-HN females on the concept task. Parallel analysis for the LC groups failed to reveal any main or interaction effects.

A complication arose in the analysis of HC groups which required nonparametric treatment of the same data. Imposition of reinforcement delay resulted in highly variable performance among HC-HN girls and very similar performances among the HC-LN girls to the point where the variance of the former group was more than 30 times as great as the variance of the latter group. Since the significant interaction which was obtained might have been attributable to heterogeneous variances rather than the pattern of mean differences, a nonparametric statistic (insensitive to differences in variability) was called upon to clarify the issue.

The trials-to-learn scores for all HC subjects were distributed separately for the immediate and delayed reinforcement conditions, and each distribution was cut as near its median score as possible. Faster learning was defined as 6 or less trials to criterion runs under immediate reinforcement ($N = 11$) and seven or more trials as slower learning ($N = 9$). With delayed reinforcement, faster learning was defined as 10 or less trials ($N = 9$) and slower learning as 11 or more ($N = 8$). To test for the previously obtained interaction by the chi square analysis, a procedure that considered two learning patterns was employed. Pattern 1, which included faster learning with immediate reinforcement or slower learning with delayed reinforcement, should characterize a large proportion of HC-HN subjects and a small proportion of HC-LN subjects. Pattern 2 (slower learning with immediate reinforcement or faster learning with delayed reinforcement) should be demonstrated by a small proportion of HC-HN girls and a large proportion of HC-LN girls. These expectations were met when 16 HC-HN females and 5 HC-LN females manifested pattern 1 performances and 4 HC-HN and 12 HC-LN females fell in the pattern 2 category; chi square analysis found these proportions to differ reliably ($p < .01$). The predicted interaction obtained with analysis of variance was clearly attributable to the pattern of mean performance scores and not to heterogeneity of variance.

While the delayed reinforcement results, as originally published, were interpreted primarily as offering a basis for understanding the equivocal nature of delay effects with children, our present purposes are better served by pointing out the concordance between the nonreaction and the delay of reinforcement studies. Both accrued evidence which supports the proposed relationships between maternal control experience and sensitivity to evaluative cues and between experienced maternal nurturance and expectancies of reinforcement. These combine in the HC-LN adolescent to present us with the picture of a youngster overconcerned with how others will respond to him and forced to contend with his own expectations of not meeting their standards.

As has already been pointed out, considering the control and nurturance dimensions separately for the moment also offers a basis for understanding why the HC-LN group in many experiments discussed to this point did not always emerge as uniquely deviant in their performance. They share the property of reinforcement sensitivity with the HC-HN group and more negative expectancies with the LC-LN group; either property may have assumed greater importance depending upon the procedures specific to a given investigation.

Educational Applications

Implications of the motivational research reported thus far in the chapter for continuing educational performance are not difficult to derive. If we accept the reasonable assumption that how well the student performs is a positive function of the level of achievement motivation he maintains, special problems would be expected for reinforcement-sensitive HC-LN youngsters who relinquish goals most readily following failure or even following the absence of evaluation.

Heilbrun and Waters (1968) investigated underachievement in college as it might be related to maternal child-rearing experience. College underachievement appeared to be an especially promising avenue of investigation, since the higher educational experience would most likely introduce the naturalistic conditions similar to the failure induction and nonevaluation conditions of our research. We would expect that the greater educational competition at the college level would increase the proportion of failure experiences for previously successful high school students. It also seems evident that there is a diminished amount of reinforcement available to the college student contingent upon his performance. The pattern of education changes from a system in high school in which grade reinforcements on examinations and other assignments are frequently made available to the student to a system in college where formal evaluation of performance is drastically reduced in frequency. The parents also become far less accessible as sources of reinforcement because of the physical distance from home.

Motivational implications of the earlier laboratory research led Heilbrun and Waters to predict that a deficit in achievement motivation would occur in HC-LN college males, whereas the opposite effect would be observed in HC-HN counterparts. However, it was expected that the two LC groups would not be distinguishable from each other in college achievement motivation. The motive to achieve was not directly measured in this study; rather it was assumed that quality of college classroom performance relative to expectation based upon aptitude test scores and high school performance was a reasonable barometer of motivation.

The 102 male subjects in this study volunteered for participation from undergraduate classes at Emory. Their modal age was about 19 years. Questionnaires for assessing maternal child-rearing experience were administered in small groups, as usual, and the information necessary to establish level of college achievement was obtained through the cooperation of the registrar's office.

Predicted grade-point averages for the subjects were generated by the regression equation used by Emory University to predict undergraduate performance, a formula based upon high school grades and the verbal and mathematics scores of the Scholastic Aptitude Test. Quality of academic achievement (and underlying achievement motivation) for a given student was defined by the difference between his obtained and his predicted grade-point averages. If the student's grades exceed prediction, he would be considered a high achiever. Failure to reach predicted average would indicate underachievement. (The Emory formula is known systematically to overpredict grades, so the obtained minus predicted scores will be negative considering the sample taken as a whole.)

Table 30 includes the indices of college achievement for the male child-rearing groups. The achievement patterns which were predicted from the notivational implications of our laboratory evidence were found. HC-LN males were clearly underachieving relative to the HC-HN males whether the first quarter only was considered ($p < .05$ one tail) or the entire freshman year ($p < .025$ one tail). The LC-HN and LC-LN group discrepancy scores fell intermediate to the two HC group scores and gave no hint of differing from each other for either academic period. The predictable nature of these findings is rather remarkable when it is considered that (1) the elapsed time between the freshman year and the participation of our subjects in this study ranged up to three years, and (2) that the most serious underachievers would have left school before coming to our attention. Both factors would serve to attenuate the relationships that were found.

A replication of the underachievement study for females was included in the

Table 30. Differences in Obtained and Predicted Freshman Grade-Point Averages of Male College Students Differing in Perceived Maternal Child-Rearing Experience

	Perceived Maternal Child-Rearing Pattern			
Academic Period	High Control-Low Nurturance ($N = 24$)	High Control-High Nurturance ($N = 27$)	Low Control-Low Nurturance ($N = 28$)	Low Control-High Nurturance ($N = 26$)
First quarter mean discrepancy[a]	−.38	−.03	−.19	−.21
First academic year mean discrepancy[a]	−.25	.04	−.10	−.18

[a]Means represent the average discrepancy between obtained grades and predicted grades, with plus scores indicating overachievement and minus scores indicating underachievement.

investigation of delayed reinforcement (Heilbrun, 1969) which was discussed earlier in this chapter. The Emory first-quarter and first-year grades were available for 46 of the 74 girls included in the experimental sample, and the same prophecy formula was applied to determine predicted grade-point average. When the mean obtained minus predicted grade-point averages are compared for the child-rearing groups (Table 31), the results generally confirm what we have previously found. Female HC-LN students are underachievers in their first quarter of college relative to HC-HN girls ($p < .01$ one tail), and this difference holds up when the entire freshman year is considered ($p < .05$ one tail). The two female LC groups did not differ reliably in their discrepancy scores for either period. However, it was not until the more stable grades from the entire freshman year were considered that the obtained minus predicted values provided a good fit to the male results. That is, the two LC groups became essentially equal and assumed intermediate status between the underachievement of the HC-LN group and the high achievement of the HC-HN group.

Still another educationally related application of our child-rearing findings was suggested by the evidence on social influences in the development of creativity. Barron (1965), in discussing factors influencing creativity in children, points to "... a developing body of testimony from educators and from psychologists in the school system (which) suggests that much potential creativity is made to wither by an unfavorable climate both in the classroom and in society at large (pp. 96-97)." Several studies are cited which support the conclusion that divergent creative behavior is either negatively reinforced by teachers or peers

Table 31. Differences in Obtained and Predicted Freshman Grade-Point Averages of Female College Students Differing in Perceived Maternal Child-Rearing Experience

	Perceived Maternal Child-Rearing Pattern			
Academic Period	High Control-Low Nurturance (N = 14)	High Control-High Nurturance (N = 12)	Low Control-Low Nurturance (N = 8)	Low Control-High Nurturance (N = 12)
First quarter mean discrepancy[a]	–.79	–.11	–.81	–.31
First academic year mean discrepancy[a]	–.55	–.13	–.35	–.37

[a]Means represent the average discrepancy between obtained grades and predicted grades, with minus scores indicating underachievement.

(Drews, 1960; Getzels and Jackson, 1962; Torrance, 1962) or that the creative child is less influenced by what other people think of him (Hammer, 1961; Helson, 1961). Barron's review of the creativity research at the University of California's Institute for Personality Assessment and Research also clearly implies that creative architects, mathematicians, and writers share a common attribute of independence and autonomy which make them less sensitive to social evaluative cues.

The high susceptibility to influence of the HC-LN adolescent, especially when negative evaluation is concerned, would suggest that he would be an unlikely candidate for creative behavior. This hypothesis was tested in a study (Heilbrun, 1971) which capitalized upon a carefully devised scale of creativity developed by Smith and Schaefer (1969). The Creativity Scale was constructed from items on the Adjective Check List. Derivation of the 27-item scale proceeded by identifying achieving high school students who were nominated by their teachers as creative and who also scored above a cut-off point on two Guilford creativity tests. This creative group was compared with other achieving high school students nominated by the same teachers as showing no evidence of creativity and who scored below a cutting point on the Guilford tests. Evidence of either artistic or scientific creativity was used for boys, whereas artistic and creative writing originality was used for girls. The Creativity Scale includes the 27 self-descriptive adjectives which differentiated creative boys and girls of all types from the noncreative high-achieving controls and which held up after four cross validations.

Two studies were conducted which tested the predicted deficit in creativity for the HC-LN male. The 96 subjects included in the two studies had an average age of 18.9 years and were obtained as volunteers from among Emory students. In the first study the 42 participants were administered the child-rearing questionnaires in our standard fashion and the Adjective Check List under the usual self-descriptive set. The 54 subjects in the second study were treated procedurally in the same way with one exception. The Adjective Check List was administered to the subject under an instructional set to describe himself as he thought others viewed him. As it turned out, the two instructional sets for the personality measure produced the same results.

Creativity Scale norms were developed for this study from raw to T-score conversions for the scientifically and artistically creative high school male groups which Smith and Schaefer generously made available to the investigator. The T-scale norms set the average expected score at 50 and the standard deviation at 10. Since these norms represent the average of the conversions for both types of creative groups, we would expect them to be relevant to a more general creativity factor in college males. It also should be kept in mind that the norms are selectively based upon artistically and scientifically creative high school boys only and not upon high school boys in general.

Reference to Table 32 suggests a rather clear confirmation of our expectations. In the first study which presented standard self-descriptive instructions for the Adjective Check List, the HC-LN males fell significantly below the creativity level of the LC-HN reference group ($p < .01$ one tail). The same HC-LN deficit in creativity is suggested by the findings of the second study in which we were dealing with the behavioral conception which the adolescent considered others to hold of him; HC-LN Creativity Scale scores were lower than those of their reference group ($p < .05$ one tail).

Table 32. Creativity Scale Scores for Late-Adolescent Males Differing in Perceived Maternal Child-Rearing Experience

	Perceived Maternal Child-Rearing Pattern			
	High Control-Low Nurturance		Reference Group[a]	
Study	*N*	Mean	*N*	Mean
Study 1	21	43.24	21	51.44
Study 2	15	44.33	39	49.56

[a]The comparison group in Study 1 were LC-HN males only. A more general comparison group was constituted for Study 2 including all males who did not fall in the HC-LN quadrant.

It is reasonably safe to ignore intelligence restrictions as the source of problems in educational attainment or creative potential for the HC-LN adolescent within the studies reviewed in this section. There was a control for intelligence within the predictive formula in the two underachievement studies. One can also point to the Gaetz (1970) findings that HC youngsters were actually brighter in verbal and nonverbal intelligence than LC youngsters and that this held independently of level of perceived nurturance (i.e., HC-LN children were as bright as HC-HN children). Reluctance to maintain loftier goals which challenge capabilities but expose the adolescent to failure appears to be the basis for the academic underachievement. A similar reluctance to risk censure contingent upon divergence has been suggested as an explanation of low creativity in children. In either case, the restraining motivational influence of aversive social stimulation upon the HC-LN late adolescent can be readily inferred.

PERCEIVED MATERNAL CONTROL-NURTURANCE PATTERNS AND SELF-ESTEEM

Arieti (1970), in considering the concept of schizophrenia, attributes major importance to prepsychotic problems with the self-image. Even at the childhood stage of development the self and self-image are already abnormal. Low self-esteem is not a direct reproduction of negative appraisal from others; the young child tends to integrate disproportionately into his self-image those elements that hurt him more, and, in some cases, satisfy him more, and, by their extreme nature, stand out. Thus, the self, although related to external evaluation, is not for Arieti a simple reproduction but rather a "grotesque representation" of it.

Arieti proposes that with time the inadequate self and self-image bring about complications so that:

> . . . the patient—adolescent, young adult or adult—will believe that his future has no hope and the promise of life will not be fulfilled. More than that he feels threatened from all sides, as if he were in a jungle . . . where the threat is not to survival, but to the self-image. The dangers are concept-feelings such as that of being unwanted, unloved, unlovable, inadequate, unacceptable, inferior, awkward, clumsy, not belonging, peculiar, different, rejected, humiliated, guilty, unable to find his own way among the different paths of life, disgraced, discriminated, kept at a distance, suspected . . . (p. 35).

Since even this chaotic level of self-esteem is considered prepsychotic in Arieti's view of schizophrenic development, an even more massive level of self-conceptual degeneration is expected within the schizophrenic condition itself:

> The ineluctable conceptual conclusions reached recently by the patient and their emotional accompaniment reactivate the early inner experiences of childhood, not just because of their strength but also because of their fundamental similarity. These resurging experiences reinforce the recent ones as they are in agreement with them, and the result is of dire proportions and consequences. It is this concordance, or the unification of early and late experiences which first reawakens the early experiences and secondly completes and magnifies in terrifying ways the horrendous vision of the self. In the totality of his human existence, and through the depth of all his feelings, the individual now sees himself as totally defeated, without any worth or possibility of redemption (p. 36).

If progressive deterioration of the self-image is as salient in schizophrenic development as Arieti so graphically describes, it should be possible for us to demonstrate some impairment in self-esteem for the HC-LN adolescent if aversive maternal control is to be considered a relevant antecedent in schizophrenia.

The simple truth is that we did not plan any studies in our research program specifically designed to investigate self-esteem differences among the four child-rearing groups. The description of two experiments has been reserved to this point in the chapter, however, since their results turned out to have some clear implications for self-esteem. The first of these experiments (Heilbrun, 1970) was directed primarily toward the remaining category of extrinsic reinforcement experience which had not been investigated in the programmatic research to that point. We had considered the effects of reinforcement delivered directly to the subject in a number of ways and had additionally investigated the effects upon the subject of nonreinforcement from another person. What remained was the effect of social reinforcement directed toward one person upon the behavior of another person who is in the role of observer.

Vicarious reinforcement, as this type of indirect reinforcement experience is called, assumes a surprisingly important role in explaining various child development phenomena. As one example, various attempts to develop a modeling explanation of parent identification in children more often than not require an assumption of vicarious reward for behavior matching if any thought at all is given to the specifics of behavior acquisition. As a second example, socialization practices often require the assumption that the behavior of an observer may be influenced without direct reinforcement of that observer. Bandura and Walters (1963, pp. 181-182) suggest that this assumption is implicit in the socialization activities of parents, teachers, and representatives of authority in society when they use exemplary models or directly administer rewards or punishments to a child in front of others.

Heilbrun's experiment into the effects of vicarious reinforcement upon the late-adolescent child-rearing groups involved 176 Emory University males. Their mean age was 18.7 years. The collection of questionnaire data proceeded as in all prior research. Within two weeks of the questionnaire session, the subjects were recalled to the laboratory by the female experimenter in groups of two or three.

When three subjects participated, all were seated around a large table upon arrival at the experimental room. They were informed that our interest was in measuring performance on a perceptual-motor task which required the reproduction of spatial designs. Subjects were given one 100-item form of a digit-symbol task devised especially for this study, using the digit-symbol subtest of the Wechsler Adult Intelligence Scale (Wechsler, 1955) as a model. This task, which emphasizes speed, presents the person with numbers 1 through 9 paired with 9 different symbols at the top of a sheet and 100 empty squares with numbers 1 through 9 appearing at random above each. The subject is directed to fill as many of the squares as possible with paired symbols within the 90-second limit.

After 90 seconds the sheets were collected, and the experimenter quickly scored the performances for number correct out of view of the subjects. Positioning of the participants in the experiment made it difficult for the subjects to know what the others' performance levels were. At this point the experimenter instructed the subjects that one of them would be chosen for subsequent training on a visual discrimination task and that this training should influence his ability to perform on the digit-symbol task. These instructions, then, were couched in such a way that given positive reinforcement and a success experience on the training, the trainee should expect to perform better on the digit-symbol assignment. Given negative reinforcement and a failure experience in training, no improvement should be expected.

The bogus training procedure made use of the angle discrimination task described in some detail earlier in this chapter. The subject who was to receive the training was seated facing the wall upon which the 5 standard disks were mounted. Half of the subjects were negatively reinforced (given only 6 of 20 correct). The experimenter also provided standard failure instructions after the tenth and twentieth responses to the effect that the person was not concentrating and was experiencing more difficulty than most. The positive reinforcement subcondition for the remaining half of the subjects involved a 14 of 20 correct reinforcement schedule and induction of a success experience through remarks indicating that the subject had done very well.

Vicarious reinforcement effects were instrumented by selecting the second of the three subjects, informing him that he would not receive the training and that he should move to a designated chair in the room. The chair was positioned so that this subject could look directly at the trainee but could not see the angles mounted on the wall. The positive or negative verbalizations of the experimenter directed to the trainee were, of course, clearly audible to the observer.

The third subject was told to take a seat outside the experimental room in the hallway while the training was being conducted. From this position he could neither see nor hear anything that was going on within the room. When only two subjects appeared for the experimental session, this nonreinforcement condition was omitted.

Upon completion of the training procedure, the subjects were reassembled about the table and given an alternate 100-item form of the digit-symbol task. Before starting, however, the experimenter gave each subject a slip of paper upon which was printed the number of designs he reproduced on the first test. Each person was asked to write the number which he believed he would get correct upon second testing. Completion of the second digit-symbol task marked the end of the experiment. These procedures gave us the opportunity to explore the effects of positive and negative vicarious reinforcement on both perceptual-motor performance and achievement motivation. In addition, direct reinforcement and nonreinforcement effects on the child-rearing groups could be assessed.

The scores which served as dependent variables in this experiment reflected: (1) the extent to which the achievement level set for the second trial differed from the number correct that the subject actually obtained on trial 1($LOA\text{-}DS_1$); and (2) the extent to which performance on trial 2 differed from that on trial 1 ($DS_2\text{-}DS_1$). Two preliminary analyses of variance indicated that there were no reliable differences among the four child-rearing groups on either score given no intervening reinforcement. These mean scores are included in Table 33 and do suggest a general tendency for the nonreinforced controls to improve their performance as they gain experience with the task. The average gain anticipated by the subjects was 3.5 symbols in the 90-second period, whereas the average actual improvement was 4.1 symbols.

The major statistical analyses were performed independently for each of the four child-rearing groups with locus of reinforcement (direct versus vicarious)

Table 33. Change in Achievement Level and Digit-Symbol Performance for Nonreinforced Control Males Varying in Perceived Maternal Child-Rearing Experience

	Perceived Maternal Child-Rearing Pattern			
Score[a]	High Control-Low Nurturance ($N = 10$)	High Control-High Nurturance ($N = 9$)	Low Control-Low Nurturance ($N = 11$)	Low Control-High Nurturance ($N = 13$)
$LOA\text{-}DS_1$	1.1	2.2	2.6	6.9
$DS_2\text{-}DS_1$	4.9	3.3	4.7	3.5

[a] $LOA\text{-}DS_1$ = difference between level of aspiration for trial 2 and performance on trial 1; $DS_2\text{-}DS_1$ = difference between performance on trial 2 and performance on trial 1.

and type of reinforcement (positive versus negative) being the two factors considered in each analysis. Looking at the effects on achievement motivation first (Table 34), locus of reinforcement emerged as significant for the LC-LN group ($p < .05$) and approached significance for HC-LN ($p < .10$). Both groups set more conservative goals when positive or negative reinforcement was experienced vicariously rather than directly. This means that positive reinforcement facilitated performance more when it was received directly (as part of the training) by the two LN groups, but negative reinforcement had a more suppressive effect when experienced vicariously.

Looking at achievement motivation from the vantage point of *type* of reinforcement, significant effects were again identified for the two LN groups. Both the HC-LN ($p < .05$) and LC-LN ($p < .05$) males clearly articulated their response to the two types of reinforcement; they set higher achievement goals following the "successful" training condition relative to the "unsuccessful," whether they were receiving the evaluative cues directly or experiencing them vicariously. Again, the highest goals for these groups were set following direct positive reinforcement and the lowest goals came after the vicarious negative reinforcement condition.

Two significant ($p < .05$) interaction effects emerged from the analysis of digit-symbol performance change (Table 35). HC-LN subjects, when they were the ones receiving the training, showed essentially no improvement in performance following "success" (.8) and marked improvement after "failure"

Table 34. Change in Achievement Level[a] as a Function of Reinforcement Conditions and Perceived Maternal Child-Rearing Experience

	Perceived Maternal Child-Rearing Pattern							
Reinforcement Condition	High Control-Low Nurturance *N*	Mean	High Control-High Nurturance *N*	Mean	Low Control-Low Nurturance *N*	Mean	Low Control-High Nurturance *N*	Mean
Direct Reinforcement								
Positive	8	8.1	8	6.0	10	10.7	9	6.4
Negative	10	4.4	8	4.8	7	5.6	7	4.9
Vicarious Reinforcement								
Positive	13	5.2	6	6.2	8	5.8	7	3.4
Negative	8	1.6	9	4.3	7	–1.1	8	5.6

[a]Difference between post-reinforcement level of aspiration for trial 2 and performance on trial 1; positive scores indicate that levels of anticipated achievement are higher than previous performance.

Table 35. Change in Digit-Symbol Performance[a] as a Function of Reinforcement Conditions and Perceived Maternal Child-Rearing Experience

Reinforcement Condition	Perceived Maternal Child-Rearing Pattern: High Control-Low Nurturance *N*	Mean	High Control-High Nurturance *N*	Mean	Low Control-Low Nurturance *N*	Mean	Low Control-High Nurturance *N*	Mean
Direct reinforcement								
Positive	8	.8	8	3.0	10	4.1	9	7.2
Negative	10	7.4	8	6.8	7	5.4	7	3.4
Vicarious reinforcement								
Positive	13	5.2	6	6.8	8	6.8	7	.3
Negative	8	2.6	9	2.6	7	7.6	8	8.6

[a]Difference between post-reinforcement performance on trial 2 and prereinforcement performance on trial 1; the higher the score, the greater the improvement following reinforcement.

(7.4); when HC-LN males were observers, they improved more following "successful" training of the other subject (5.2) than after "failure" (2.6).

LC-HN subjects behaved in a fashion opposite to that found for the HC-LN group. When directly reinforced as the trainee, positive reinforcement mediated a greater improvement in performance (7.2) than did negative reinforcement (3.4); observing another person receive positive reinforcement produced minimal change (.3), whereas vicarious negative reinforcement resulted in a substantial improvement in performance (8.6) ($p < .05$).

Heilbrun centered the interpretation of these results around self-conceptual differences in effectiveness of transaction with the environment (White's [1960] "sense of competence"), a dimension not unlike Rotter's internal-external control of reinforcement (1966). The goals of the two LN groups were most readily influenced by another person. They elevated their goals substantially more with "successful" training than if exposed to "unsuccessful" training, whether they were the ones receiving the training or the ones merely observing others being trained. The interpretation placed upon these findings by Heilbrun was that the less the individual feels he can control his environment, the more readily his aspirations are shaped by reinforcement contingencies imposed directly by outside social agents or vicariously influenced by the reinforcement experiences of those about him. This conclusion emphasizes what our earlier research also has shown; the HC-LN adolescent is highly responsive to evaluative directives from his social environment and, inferentially, less responsive to himself as a source of influence.

While the achievement motivation data are suggestive of self-esteem problems in the HC-LN male, reflecting as they do his susceptibility to influence, it is the perceptual-motor performance change that appears to set him off in this experiment as uniquely ill-equipped to engage in self-direction. Reference back to Table 35 allows us to abstract a rather strange fact about the HC-LN subject. When he was put in the role of being the person undergoing the presumed training and was positively reinforced, no performance change occurred despite the fact that he was led to believe that he was in a better position to perform. In fact, the earlier Table 33 indicates that there is a practice effect on this digit-symbol task of over 4 points so that the mean change score of .8 for the HC-LN group receiving "successful" training is even suggestive of a suppression effect. Yet when this group is failed in training so that they have no basis for assuming themselves to be better equipped for the task, they improve markedly (7.4). In contrast and significantly ($p < .05$) interacting with this HC-LN group effect, directly reinforced LC-HN males, informed that they have been given a facilitative experience, improve on repeated testing (7.2) more than their LC-HN counterparts who are led to believe that they have not been helped by training (3.4).

The interpretation offered by Heilbrun to account for the HC-LN and LC-HN differences was predicated upon the expectation that these two groups should represent the low and high polar extremes along a dimension of self-esteem and self-confidence. He states:

> The one aspect of the significant results which does not seem to fit (the self-conceptual model) is the effect of direct reinforcement upon digit-symbol performance. The LC-HN *S*s demonstrated more improvement following (direct) positive than negative reinforcement despite their presumed sense of competence. Perhaps one further point may be made apropos of this seeming contradiction. The direct reinforcement condition explicitly directed *S* to himself as a gauge for subsequent behavior. As far as he knew, *he* had either been successful in "training" and should expect subsequent performance to improve or *he* had done poorly and should not expect such improvement. The more confidence *S* has in himself as a reliable gauge, the more his subsequent behavior should fall in line with his own expectations. Conceptualized in this way, the direct reinforcement DS_2-DS_1 results fall into place (pp. 260-261).

Within this interpretive framework we can see that self-esteem is being weighed in terms of the relative importance being assigned by a person to external social agents and to himself as sources of influence on his own behavior. The weight for the HC-LN adolescent would be heavily toward reinforcement from others and the LC-HN adolescent should be more responsive to self-reinforcement.

Since the results direct our attention again to the polar positions assumed by HC-LN and LC-HN adolescents on the self-esteem dimension, reexamination of the nonreinforcement control data (Table 33) is in order. Recall that analysis of variance established that no significant differences among the four child-rearing groups were in evidence when their expected performances were compared. This condition, in which the subject was sent into the hall, required that he depend exclusively on his own self-evaluation as he predicted the level of his next performance. Under these circumstances we would expect that self-esteem differences would be especially important in mediating differences in projected performance so that the absence of differences becomes difficult to explain. In fact, reanalysis of the LOA data on Table 33 in which only the extreme groups are compared did establish that the HC-LN males were more conservative ($p <$ .05 one tail) than LC-HN males.

A more explicit test of differences among the child-rearing groups in self-esteem, considered in terms of sources of influence, was incorporated in an investigation of self-reinforcement effectiveness (Heilbrun and Norbert, 1970). One hundred and nine Emory undergraduates (85 males and 24 females) volunteered for this experiment; their average age was 18.8 years. Data collection procedures for the questionnaires followed our standard format with the subjects being assigned to individual laboratory sessions within two weeks following the small-group testing.

The experimental methodology for investigating self-reinforcement and social reinforcement made use again of the ubiquitous angle discrimination task. The subject was told that the interest of the study was in spatial discrimination ability. Instructions by the female experimenter for the self-reinforcement condition, besides explaining the nature of the task, included directives to the subject to make his angle-matching choice within 15 seconds, to record his choice on a special sheet, and, finally, to indicate by "R" for "right" if he was relatively certain of the correctness of his choice or by "W" for "wrong" if he was relatively uncertain.

Before beginning the task, the subject was asked to predict the number he thought he would get correct out of 20 after being given a fictitious norm of 10 out of 20 correct for the average high school student. The subject was asked to count and record the number of responses he had judged to be right when he had finished the task. The experimenter at this point told the subject to compare the number he judged to be correct (his self-reinforcement) with the number he thought he would get right before he started. Another level of aspiration was requested of the subject with his attention specifically directed to the first estimate and his self-reinforcement. To this point the experimenter had remained uninvolved in either the goal-setting or reinforcement operations of the subject. A second trial was conducted for the subject at this point (under social reinforcement conditions) with the level of reinforcement being the same as the subject set for himself in trial 1.

The social-reinforcement condition involved the instructions and procedures as used in the self-reinforcement condition except the subject was not allowed to set goals independently of the experimenter or to provide his own reinforcement. Rather than this, the goals were recorded by the experimenter and "right-wrong" reinforcement was delivered by her as well.

Each person in the social-reinforcement condition was paired with another person in the self-reinforcement condition of the same sex and from the same child-rearing group. The schedule of reinforcement selected for the member of the pair to be socially reinforced was such as to expose him to the same algebraic difference between his initial goal and subsequent achievement (level of reinforcement) as obtained for the paired subject who was self-reinforced. As an example, the self-reinforced subject had chosen 12 as his initial goal and judged 14 discriminations as correct. The paired subject, having stated his initial goal as, say, 14 correct, would be reinforced by the experimenter at 16 correct. Both would be reinforced at two correct above their goal previous to trial 1. Prearranged right-wrong schedules which allowed anywhere from 0-20 correct were available to the experimenter. The pairing assignments were made by the senior investigator. In the second reinforcement condition, subjects were allowed a second trial under self-reinforcement instructions.

The dependent variable representing reinforcement effectiveness in the Heilbrun and Norbert experiment reflected the correspondence between change in achievement level from pre-trial 1 to pre-trial 2 and the level of intervening reinforcement. The score was derived by taking the absolute difference between initial and subsequent levels of aspiration. A plus or minus sign was assigned depending on whether the change was in the direction assumed by reinforcement level relative to initial aspiration level (plus) or opposite to the direction taken by reinforcement level relative to initial aspiration level (minus). Heilbrun and Norbert cite, as an example, that if the subject set 13 correct as his initial goal, was reinforced (by self or experimenter) at 15 correct, and chose 16 as his next goal, his change score would be +3. On the other hand, if he selected 13 correct initially, was reinforced at 15 correct, and then adopted 10 correct as his post-reinforcement goal, his score would be −3. These change scores, which ranged from −3 to +9, were corrected by square-root transformation for positive skewness.

The shift in goals following reinforcement, included in Table 36, was analyzed independently by source of reinforcement (self versus social). A predicted main effect of nurturance was identified in the self-reinforcement effects. The two LN groups (combined mean = .77) were significantly less effective self-reinforcers than the HN groups (combined mean = 1.36) ($p < .03$ one tail). The finding that LN subjects were least responsive to intrinsic reinforcement dovetailed nicely with the vicarious reinforcement results previously discussed which found the two LN groups to be most influenced in selecting achievement levels by extrinsic reinforcement.

Table 36. Change in Achievement Level Following Self-Reinforcement and Social Reinforcement for Late Adolescents Varying in Perceived Maternal Child-Rearing Experience

	Perceived Maternal Child-Rearing Pattern							
	High Control-Low Nurturance		High Control-High Nurturance		Low Control-Low Nurturance		Low Control-High Nurturance	
Source of Reinforcement	*N*	Mean	*N*	Mean	*N*	Mean	*N*	Mean
Self	12	.93	9	1.01	15	.64	12	1.62
Experimenter	12	1.56	9	1.30	15	.93	12	1.47
Difference (self minus experimenter)		–.63		–.29		–.29		+.15

The expectation that the LC-HN adolescents would be the most effective self-reinforcers was confirmed by comparing their mean (1.62) with that of the remaining groups combined (.83); the difference in means was significant ($p <$ .02 one tail). A nonparametric chi square reanalysis of these data was required because of heterogeneous variance, with the median change score for the 48 subjects used to define effective and ineffective self-reinforcers. The 12 LC-HN subjects split into 11 effective and one ineffective self-reinforcer; the remaining 36 subjects split into 18 effective and 18 ineffective self-reinforcers. The significant ($p < .025$) results of the nonparametric test confirmed the significance of the previous difference between means and the greater ability to engage in self-reinforcement by LC-HN late adolescents.

There were some predictions which did not receive support in this experiment. The HC-LN group did not demonstrate the unique self-reinforcement deficit that was expected but shared this property with LC-LN subjects. The two LN groups also did not show higher responsiveness to direct reinforcement than did the HN groups as we expected.

Perhaps the most compelling comparison to be made in establishing a hierarchy of self-esteem among our child-rearing groups is to compare directly the extent to which achievement level was influenced by self-reinforcement and by social reinforcement within matched pairs of subjects. The expectation was that low self-esteem would be coupled with a pattern of lower responsiveness to self-reinforcement and higher responsiveness to social reinforcement, with the reverse being true for high self-esteem. Looking back at Table 36 reveals just such a self-esteem patterning effect in the same two groups that the vicarious reinforcement study also cast at the extremes. HC-LN adolescents demonstrated the low self-esteem pattern; those who engaged in self-reinforcement influenced their own achievement levels considerably less (−.63) than their paired counterparts who were reinforced by the experimenter. LC-HN adolescents presented the high self-esteem pattern; self-reinforcers were more influential (+.15) than the paired LC-HN subjects who were reinforced by the experimenter. These two mean difference scores varied significantly ($p < .05$) from one another. Again, as in the previous vicarious reinforcement investigation, HC-HN and LC-LN group means were intermediate in value, suggesting that self-esteem in these types of child-rearing experience groups tends to fall somewhere between the level expected of HC-LN and LC-HN adolescents.

It would not seem complete if a discussion of the self-concept did not include some reference to language. The self-concept is, if nothing else, a compendium of linguistic responses which reflect the person's attitudes toward his own behavior, character, level of skill, and so on. Self-esteem should be represented in the qualitative nature of the language which the person uses to describe himself. Accordingly, we would expect to be able at the least to demonstrate that the LC-HN and HC-LN groups, which have been identified as being at the high and low extremes of self-esteem in the vicarious reinforcement and self-reinforcement experiments, will demonstrate the appropriate qualitative language differences in self-reference.

Some unanalyzed data collected in the course of an earlier investigation (Heilbrun, 1968) present the opportunity to compare the behavioral adjectives endorsed by HC-LN and LC-HN late-adolescent males when asked for a candid description of themselves. The 40 subjects were Emory students with an average age of 18.6 years. The Adjective Check List was administered under standard self-descriptive instructions. This instrument includes 300 words and the subject is free to endorse as many or as few as he wishes.

Analysis of performance on the Adjective Check List for our present purposes proceeded by comparing the frequency of endorsement for each adjective among the 20 HC-LN males and among the 20 LC-HN males. Table 37 includes the distinguishing self-conceptual items which achieved significance at or beyond the 10% confidence level. While the number of differentiating adjectives was not great, their qualitative distinctiveness is clear. Those descriptive words which proved to be correlates of HC-LN group membership convey poor self-esteem, whereas positive self-regard characterized the distinctive LC-HN self-conceptual features.

A summary of the programmatic research covered in this chapter (Table 38) clearly portrays the HC-LN late-adolescent as motivationally sensitive to evaluative cues having their origin in the social environment. The same consistency of effect can be noted for the HC-LN groups as when the cognitive research was summarized in the previous chapter (Table 18). Restriction in self-esteem for the aversive-maternal-control subject can also be identified

Table 37. Self-Conceptual Differences between Late-Adolescent Males Varying in Perceived Maternal Child-Rearing Experience

Perceived Maternal Child-Rearing Pattern	
High Control- Low Nurturance (N = 20)	Low Control- High Nurturance (N = 20)
More frequently endorse:	More frequently endorse:
anxious (.05)	attractive (.05)
cynical (.10)	cheerful (.10)
defensive (.05)	clever (.10)
hard-headed (.10)	confident (.05)
irritable (.10)	daring (.05)
nervous (.05)	handsome (.05)
obliging (.05)	initiative (.10)
restless (.01)	patient (.01)
sarcastic (.05)	polished (.10)
self-punishing (.05)	realistic (.10)
shy (.10)	self-confident (.05)
silent (.01)	sharp-witted (.05)
slow (.10)	thorough (.10)
withdrawn (.05)	unselfish (.01)
worrying (.01)	

NOTE: Chi square probability levels included in parentheses. All chi square values received Yates' correction for continuity.

on Table 38 by reference to the last three studies listed.

It is by review of the two summary tables at the end of the present and preceding chapters that one can best grasp the substantial empirical underpinnings upon which we shall proceed to build a theory of schizophrenic development in the next chapter. Of the 19 performance comparisons cited in these two tables, the HC-LN group behaved in keeping with the hypothesized effects of the aversive-maternal-control experience in every case. It also can be observed that HC-LN adolescents were much more likely to emerge as behaviorally unique in the motivational studies than was the case in the earlier cognitive research. This is most likely attributable to the better methodological controls which were introduced as we gained experience.

THINKING, MOTIVATION, AND SELF-ESTEEM DEFICIT IN THE HC-LN LATE-ADOLESCENT

The burden of the last two chapters has been to demonstrate that when the adolescent's phenomenal experience has been that of aversive maternal control, he is more likely to demonstrate schizophreniform behaviors than when this has

Table 38. Presence or Absence (Yes or No) of Exceptional Motivational Effects for the HC-LN Perceived Maternal Child-Rearing Group

Investigation	Performance Variable	Perceived Maternal Child-Rearing Pattern[a] HC-LN	HC-HN	LC-LN (Same Effect Present in Other Groups?)	LC-HN
Heilbrun and Orr (1966)	Achievement level	Yes	No	No	No
	Risk-taking	Yes	No	Yes	No
Heilbrun and Gillard (1966)	Achievement level	Yes	Yes	No	No
Heilbrun, Harrell and Gillard (1967)	Achievement level	Yes	No	No	No
Heilbrun (1969)	Concept identification and delay of reinforcement	Yes	No	No	No
	Academic underachievement	Yes	No	No	No
Heilbrun and Waters (1968)	Academic underachievement	Yes	No	No	No
Heilbrun (in press)	Creativity	Yes		No	
Heilbrun (1970)	Achievement level	Yes	No	Yes	No
	Digit symbol performance	Yes	No	No	No
Heilbrun and Norbert (1970)	Achievement level	Yes	No	Yes	No
Heilbrun (1968)	Self-concept	Yes			No

[a]HC-LN = high control-low nurturance; HC-HN = high control-high nurturance; LC-LN = low control-low nurturance; LC-HN = low control-high nurturance.

not been the case. Beyond the general confirmation achieved from psychometric signs of schizoid behavior for the HC-LN group, the body of cognitive and motivational evidence portrays the HC-LN son or daughter as vulnerable to his social environment in ways that are conceptually compatible with what is known about the premorbid development or clinical manifestations of schizophrenia.

The most compelling conclusion to be drawn from the research covered to this point is that the HC-LN adolescent maintains a keen sensitivity to social evaluative responses and that when these assume a negative character (real, implied, or anticipated), he is vulnerable to self-defeating cognitive or motivational consequences. Responses associated with negative reinforcement interfere with ongoing thought or memory processes and cognitive deficit results. Goals are readily relinquished to avoid the upsetting discrepancy between aspiration and attainment. The convergence between these behavioral attributes of the HC-LN offspring and some commonly observed properties of schizophrenics (e.g., censure sensitivity, thought disturbance, avoidance-withdrawal as self-protective behaviors) is clear.

The second broad conclusion emerging from the research is that the HC-LN adolescent suffers from a deficit in self-esteem. Studies have identified the more specific deficits of restricted ability to use his own experience as a frame of reference for subsequent activity, a marked discrepancy between his self-influence and his susceptibility to influence by others, and a more negative self-conceptual catalogue of verbal self-statements available for mediation of effective action. Commonality in self-esteem level between our HC-LN subject and the schizophrenic is identifiable in kind, if not degree.

Finally, we would note that our two empirically based conclusions enter into a congenial logical relationship with one another; a deficit in self-esteem is consistent with the self-defeating nature of the HC-LN subject's response to criticism. Even though failure is noxious to the HC-LN adolescent, his thinking becomes more ineffective and his goals more limited in the face of aversive cues. His concern with failing brings with it the very behaviors that are most likely to create failure. Habituated self-defeating behaviors generate little opportunity for the positive growth of self-esteem.

REFERENCES

Arieti, S. The concept of schizophrenia. In R. Cancro (Ed.), *The schizophrenic reactions: a critique of the concept, hospital treatment, and current research.* New York: Brunner-Mazel, 1970. Pp. 25-40.

Bandura, A., and Walters, R. H. *Social learning and personality development.* New York: Holt, Rinehart, and Winston, 1963.

Barron, F. The psychology of creativity. In *New directions in Psychology II.* New York: Holt, Rinehart, and Winston, 1965. Pp. 3-134.

Crandall, V. R. Reinforcement effects of adult reactions and nonreactions on children's achievement expectations. *Child Development,* 1963, **34,** 335-354.

Drews, E. *Freedom to grow.* N.E.A. Journal, 1960, **49,** 20-22.

Gaetz, E. L. Perceived childrearing practices in relation to intelligence. Unpublished master's thesis, University of Calgary, 1970.

Getzels, J. W., and Jackson, P. D. *Creativity and intelligence.* New York: Wiley, 1962.

Hammer, E. F. *Creativity.* New York: Random House, 1961.

Heilbrun, A. B. Cognitive sensitivity to aversive maternal stimulation in late-adolescent males. *Journal of Consulting and Clinical Psychology,* 1968, **32**, 326-332.

Heilbrun, A. B. Perceived maternal childrearing and effects of delayed reinforcement upon concept acquisition. *Developmental Psychology,* 1969, **1**, 605-612.

Heilbrun, A. B. Perceived maternal child-rearing experience and the effects of vicarious and direct reinforcement on males. *Child Development,* 1970, **41**, 253-262.

Heilbrun, A. B. Maternal child rearing and creativity in sons. *Journal of Genetic Psychology,* 1971, **119**, 175-179.

Heilbrun A. B., and Gillard, B. J. Perceived maternal childrearing behavior and motivational effects of social reinforcement in females. *Perceptual and Motor Skills,* 1966, **23**, 439-446.

Heilbrun, A. B., Harrell, S. N., and Gillard, B. J. Perceived maternal childrearing patterns and the effects of social nonreaction upon achievement motivation. *Child Development,* 1967, **38**, 267-281.

Heilbrun, A. B., and Norbert, N. Maternal child-rearing experience and self-reinforcement effectiveness. *Developmental Psychology,* 1970, **3**, 81-87.

Heilbrun, A. B., and Orr, H. K. Maternal control childrearing history and subsequent cognitive and personality functioning of offspring. *Psychological Reports,* 1965, **17**, 259-272.

Heilbrun, A. B., and Orr, H. K. Perceived maternal childrearing history and subsequent motivational effects of failure. *Journal of Genetic Psychology,* 1966, **109**, 75-89.

Heilbrun, A. B., and Waters, D. B. Underachievement as related to perceived maternal child rearing and academic conditions of reinforcement. *Child Development,* 1968, **39**, 913-921.

Helson, R. Creativity, sex and mathematics. In D. W. MacKinnon (Ed.), *The creative person.* Berkeley: University of California Extension, 1961.

James, W. Internal vs. external control of reinforcement as a basic variable in learning theory. Unpublished doctoral dissertation, Ohio State University, 1957.

Rotter, J. B. Generalized expectancies for internal versus external control of reinforcement. *Psychological Monographs,* 1966, **80** (28, Whole No. 609).

Smith, J. M., and Schaefer, C. E. Development of a creativity scale for the Adjective Check List. *Psychological Reports,* 1969, **25**, 87-92.

Spence, K. W. *Behavior theory and conditioning.* New Haven: Yale University Press, 1956.

Spence, K.W. *Behavior theory and learning.* Englewood Cliffs, N. J.: Prentice-Hall, 1960.

Terrell, G. Delayed reinforcement effects. In L. P. Lipsett and C. C. Spiker (Eds.), *Advances in child development and behavior.* New York: Academic Press, 1965.

Torrance, E. P. *Guiding creative talent.* Englewood Cliffs, N J.: Prentice-Hall, 1962.

Wechsler, D. *Wechsler Adult Intelligence Scale.* New York: Psychological Corporation, 1955.

White, R. W. Competence and the psychosexual stages of development. In M. R. Jones (Ed.), *Nebraska symposium on motivation.* Lincoln: University of Nebraska Press, 1960. Pp. 97-141.

CHAPTER 7

Aversive Maternal Control and Schizophrenic Development: the Theory

While the weight of the evidence reviewed to this point encouraged us to believe that a functional tie existed between the aversive maternal control experience and the development of schizophreniform behaviors, little headway had been made toward building a comprehensive social-learning theory of schizophrenic development. As it turned out, progress along these lines hinged on a belated recognition of an eccentricity in some old data which, in turn, fostered an experiment having importance to us far beyond our expectations.

Olsen's (1965) dissertation research, which was discussed at some length in Chapter 5, left in its wake the unanswered question of why HC-LN males, exposed to maternal censure-control cues, failed to show significantly more cognitive disruption than the LC-HN control subjects which she used as the reference group. Her suggestion was that the tape-recorded scene between a mother and her son presented maternal verbal behavior so discrepant from the prior experience of the LC-HN son that it assumed high curiosity value. It was reasoned that HC-LN subjects made a substantial number of errors on the Stroop because the censure-control cues, relevant to their life history, elicited potent associated and interfering responses. LC-HN subjects, on the other hand, made similar numbers of errors because they were diverted from the cognitive task by the experientially unique properties of the mother's verbal behavior which aroused their curiosity. However, there were subtle indications in her error data that the HC-LN subjects were more variable in cognitive disruption than the other groups, although this could not be demonstrated statistically. The possibility occurred to us that HC-LN subjects, considered collectively, did not demonstrate a more distinct susceptibility to disruption because this predisposition is peculiarly represented within the group. If so, two possible explanations stood out.

The less exciting possibility was that the HC-LN group included two classes of subjects: (1) those for whom the questionnaire-based representation of the maternal child-rearing experience was accurate (true positives) and who made a substantial number of errors in line with expectation; and (2) those for whom the questionnaires provided inaccurate representation of maternal experience (false positives) and who made relatively few errors. If so, increased intragroup variability for the HC-LN males in the Olsen investigation would stem from either a skewed or a bimodal distribution of error scores with the true positives performing in a similarly disrupted way and the false positives presenting a homogeneous and more effective picture of cognitive functioning. This line of reasoning would assume that false negatives, true aversive-control subjects misclassified by the questionnaires, would tend to be found in relatively small numbers within the other three quadrant groups, probably somewhat more often in HC-HN and LC-LN. Thus, the influence of misclassification would be most salient in the HC-LN group who would be more "watered down" in the disruptive effects of censure-control cues than the other three groups would be spuriously increased in their apparent susceptibility to disruption.

An alternative and more intriguing explanation for the less-than-expected effect of maternal censure cues upon the HC-LN subjects and the increased variance of these effects in the Olsen study also assumes that the HC-LN child-rearing quadrant is comprised of two homogeneous subgroupings. However, this counter-explanation contends that these subgroupings are functionally linked to developmental dynamics and not to misclassification. A posteriori reasoning suggested that the presentation of maternal censure-control cues relevant to the family experience of the adolescent (as would be the case with the HC-LN subject) elicited life-history-relevant patterns of response to aversive maternal stimulation. Since the nature of the eliciting stimulus was negative, it was further assumed that the evoked response patterns would be related to the presence of adaptive or coping mechanisms. If any universal psychological motives can be posited for living organisms, it would be their tendency to reduce or avoid the effects of impinging aversive stimulation by whatever innate or learned response mechanisms they have at their disposal.

The hypothesis that the HC-LN cognitive performance in the Olsen investigation was related to the presence of subsets of subjects who have adapted differentially to the experienced maternal aversive stimulation did not require the additional assumption that subjects from the remaining child-rearing quadrants were responding haphazardly to the censure-control cues. It was only to be assumed that whatever the effects of these aversive cues, they could not be explained in terms of learned coping patterns relevant to their maternal history.

THE THEORETICALLY PIVOTAL EXPERIMENT

The trains of thought which have just been discussed culminated in an experiment (Heilbrun, 1968) that sought to place the weight of evidence on the side of one explanation or the other. The child-rearing experience groups were ascertained for about 100 Emory undergraduate males by the standard questionnaire procedures but only the 20 who appeared in the HC-LN and the 20 who emerged as LC-HN were included in the experiment. LC-HN males were selected as experimental controls for two reasons. Their quadrant placement denotes a maternal child-rearing experience which most distinctly differs from that of the HC-LN son; accordingly, they represent the group for which we could most safely infer the historical irrelevance of the maternal behaviors depicted on the maternal control-censure tape. They also demonstrated a level of disruption in the Olsen study most similar to the HC-LN group. It seemed especially important to demonstrate with this particular control group that despite a similar impact of censure cues upon cognition, distillation into two subgroups based upon degree of cognitive disruption did not have the same psychological significance as it did within the HC-LN group. The average age of the 40 male volunteers in this experiment was 18.6 years.

Within a few weeks of the group testing, subjects were recalled individually and given the Minnesota Multiphasic Personality Inventory (MMPI) (Hathaway and McKinley, 1951). This particular questionnaire was to provide the basis for comparing the experimentally identified subgroupings within the child-rearing groups and was chosen for two reasons. First, it includes 10 basic clinical scales covering a broad range of psychopathology. Considering the broadside rather than pinpoint character of our hypothesis at this stage, it seemed important to allow the breadth of possibilities which a multiscale comparison allowed. Then too, the MMPI had received such extended usage over the years that it had accumulated a considerable backlog of behavioral correlates for nonclinical samples scoring high or low on the clinical scales. This meant that there were two categories of information available from the MMPI scores obtained from presumably normal subjects: (1) their similarity to clinical groups such as schizophrenics, hysterics, or obsessive-compulsives which can be inferred by the commonality between the test-taker's responses and those characterizing the clinical groups (i.e., high scores on specific clinical scales); and (2) behavioral correlates of nonclinical subjects scoring high (or, less frequently, low) on these scales which have been identified empirically over the years.

Following administration of the MMPI to the subject, he was asked to participate in an experimental procedure similar to that we had employed three years earlier in the Olsen investigation. The subject was instructed to complete the 144 items on the Stroop Color-Naming Test as accurately and rapidly as possible. While performing on the Stroop he was required to listen to a taperecorded scene in which a mother is engaging in a hostile and controlling diatribe with her son. (The dialogue of this aversive mother-son scene along with the neutral scene originally used in the Olsen experiment are reproduced in Appendix E.) Both errors and time to completion on the Stroop task were recorded. Preliminary inspection of error and time scores for the HC-LN and LC-HN groups verified the observation made from the Olsen data. Considering only an index of central tendency, these two groups did not differ statistically in susceptibility to disruption by maternal censure cues. In fact, the HC-LN males made fewer errors on the average (3.75) than did the LC-HN males (5.10).

The primary analysis proceeded by first subdividing the late adolescents in each child-rearing group into cognitively disrupted and cognitively nondisrupted subgroupings by a method which placed equal weight upon accuracy and speed of Stroop performance. Subjects were rank ordered independently within each child-rearing group by accuracy and time scores and the two ranks for each subject were summed. The 10 subjects within each group with the lowest sum-rank scores were defined as better performers (nondisrupted) and the 10 subjects with the highest sum-rank scores were defined as poorer performers (disrupted). The next step in the analysis was to compare the MMPI scores for the two child-rearing groups (i.e., main effects) and for the disrupted-nondisrupted subgroups within each child-rearing group (i.e., simple effects) by analysis of variance. Table 39 includes the mean MMPI clinical scale scores for the HC-LN versus LC-HN groupings and disrupted-nondisrupted subgroupings.

Comparison of HC-LN and LC-HN groups resulted in four significant main effects among the 10 scales. HC-LN males were higher than LC-HN males on Depression ($p < .01$), Psychasthenia ($p < .05$), Schizophrenia ($p < .05$), and

Table 39. MMPI Clinical Scale Mean Scores for Late-Adolescent Males Varying in Perceived Maternal Child-Rearing Experience and Degree of Disruption by Maternal Censure-Control Cues

	Perceived Maternal Child-Rearing Pattern					
	High Control-Low Nurturance			Low Control-High Nurturance		
MMPI Scale[a]	Disrupted (N = 10)	Nondisrupted (N = 10)	Total Group (N = 20)	Disrupted (N = 10)	Nondisrupted (N = 10)	Total Group (N = 20)
Hs	51.3	57.8	54.6	53.6	47.9	50.8
D	53.5	69.3	61.4	54.3	47.5	50.9
Hy	56.2	58.5	57.4	57.9	54.5	56.2
Pd	62.9	58.7	60.8	54.2	54.8	54.5
Mf	60.9	64.8	62.8	65.9	57.9	61.9
Pa	62.3	53.3	57.8	53.6	55.4	54.5
Pt	61.5	64.8	63.2	55.7	55.5	55.6
Sc	65.8	61.5	63.6	55.4	55.9	55.6
Ma	71.7	54.8	63.2	58.1	59.4	58.8
Si	52.4	54.4	53.4	43.8	45.3	44.6

[a]MMPI scale abbreviations: Hs = Hypochrondriasis, D = Depression, Hy = Hysteria, Pd = Psychopathic Deviate, Mf = Masculinity-Femininity, Pa = Paranoia, Pt = Psychasthenia, Sc = Schizophrenia, Ma = Hypomania, Si = Social Introversion.

Social Introversion ($p < .05$). Heilbrun pointed to three primary maladjustive trends which could be inferred from these main effects: (1) social withdrawal or alienation (D, Sc, Si); (2) thinking difficulties (Pt, Sc); and (3) high anxiety (D, Pt). The behavioral commonality between the HC-LN late adolescent and the schizophrenic suggested by these psychometric differences has already received comment earlier in the book.

Our central interest was in detecting MMPI differences between disrupted and nondisrupted HC-LN subjects which would not be replicated in the similarly separated LC-HN subgroups. Two scales presented strong evidence for this pattern of effects. The Depression (D) Scale analysis identified a significant child rearing by level of disruption interaction ($p < .01$) which tells us that the difference between the disruption subgroups of HC-LN males differs in turn from the difference between subgroups of LC-HN males. Further analysis of these subgroupings revealed a significant difference ($p < .01$) between nondisrupted (69.3) and disrupted (53.3) HC-LN subjects, whereas nondisrupted (47.5) and disrupted (54.3) LC-HN subjects did not differ reliably. The uniquely high elevation of nondisrupted HC-LN males on the Depression Scale is evident. Not only is the mean elevation some 22 T-score points higher than was found for the nondisrupted reference group, but it is over 17 points higher than recent freshman male college norms reported by Fowler and Coyle (1969) for the Depression Scale. They found that some 1500 males averaged about 52.1 (standard deviation of 10.4) on this scale.

Hypomania (Ma) was the second scale for which a significant interaction ($p < .05$) and an isolated simple effect within the HC-LN group ($p < .01$) were found. Here the reverse relationship was found between disrupted and nondisrupted HC-LN subgroups; disrupted males evidenced a remarkably high mean score (71.7) which was over 13 points higher than the disrupted LC-HN group and 12 points higher than the Fowler and Coyle norm of 59.4 (standard deviation of 11.1). Comparison of the subgroupings within the LC-HN sample revealed almost identical Hypomania Scale means for disrupted (58.1) and nondisrupted (59.4) subjects.

The next inferential step was to translate the unique MMPI psychometric attributes of high D for nondisrupted HC-LN males and high Ma for disrupted HC-LN males into the personality correlates established by research for these peak scores among normals. Personality correlates of absolutely high or relative high-point D-Scale scores among normals (as reviewed in Dahlstrom and Welsh, 1960) can be drawn from four studies. Two studies of normal college-age women (Black, 1953; Hovey, 1953) report that high-D girls were rated as *shy* and *nonaggressive*. Hathaway and Meehl (1960), focusing upon general population adult males, found high-D males to be described by their acquaintances as *modest, sensitive,* and *individualistic* and as *having general aesthetic interests. Dissatisfaction,* particularly *self-dissatisfaction,* were noted as well as ratings of *emotional, high strung,* and *worrisome.* The descriptive terms *serious, prone to drink, verbal, generous,* and *sentimental* also emerged.

Assessment staff ratings of adult males made at the University of California's Institute for Personality Assessment and Research (Block and Bailey, 1955; Gough, McKee, and Yandell, 1955) identified the following adjectives as characterizing high-D males: *aloof, apathetic, cautious, conventional, dull, evasive, indifferent, leisurely, modest, moody, painstaking, patient, peaceable, quiet, retiring, silent, simple, slow, submissive, timid, unassuming, unexcitable,* and *withdrawn.* Other observations of the staff on these men took cognizance of their *typical overcontrol, slow personal tempo,* and their *vacillating, hesitant manner of making decisions.* They were viewed as *conforming, conscientious,* and *responsible* but *lacking self-confidence* and *pessimistic about their professional futures.* While described as *permissive* and *accepting* and *showing respect for others,* the high-D male was also thought to *avoid involvement in things* and to maintain *cold* and *distant relationships with others.* When difficult situations arise, they were expected to *sidestep trouble* and *to make concessions to circumvent unpleasantness.*

Self-rating obtained from the high-D subjects in the same studies tended to coincide with the ratings of judges. Hathaway and Meehl found males more frequently endorsed *individualistic, high-strung* and *likes drinking,* whereas females identified themselves as more *frank, modest, high-strung, sensitive, shy, naive, self-dissatisfied,* and *prone to worry.* Black's study revealed self-descriptions for his high-D college girls which included these terms: *affected, aloof, indecisive, moody, neurotic, quiet, secretive, self-dissatisfied,* and *self-distrusting, shy, not self-controlled,* and *worrying.* These girls by selectively avoiding certain self-descriptive terms also characterized themselves as *nonaggressive, not cheerful, not contented, uncourageous, indecisive, not energetic, unfriendly, not independent, not laughter-ful, not lively, unpoised, impractical, not self-confident,* and *untalkative.*

Since the terms describing the high-D normal are gathered from such diverse sources—males and females, college normals and general population normals, judges' ratings and self-ratings—a cohesive behavioral picture should not be expected. Yet it is not difficult to abstract some common threads among all the studies. Dahlstrom and Welsh lend assistance here by their capsule statements relating to the four sets of data. Typical are statements that the personality processes correlated with high-D normals "seem to act against familiarity and closeness" with peers (Hovey and Black studies), that "social distance and reserve" were seen (Hathaway and Meehl data), and that the Institute for Personality Assessment and Research results added "further insight into their social alienation" (p. 173).

The nucleus of the high-D personality pattern observed in normals was clearly social withdrawal or alienation, but other attributes also emerged with some consistency. Especially noteworthy among these would be self-dissatisfaction, worry, and a reticence to commit themselves to things, decisions, or ideas.

A similar review of the normal personality correlate research for the MMPI Hypomania Scale by Dahlstrom and Welsh drew its findings from the same studies as for the Depression Scale. High or high-point Ma Scale correlates as judged by others presented a generally more favorable picture. Hathaway and Meehl's high-Ma males were viewed in terms suggestive of *sociability, energy,* and *openness.* Specifically, their acquaintances described them as *forward, talkative* and *verbal, individualistic, impulsive, enthusiastic, adventurous, curious,* with *wide interests.* They *liked drinking* and were considered *generous, softhearted, affectionate,* and *sentimental.* The high-Ma females in this study were described as *frank, courageous, idealistic, talkative, enthusiastic,* and *versatile.*

Hovey's group of high-Ma student nurses were rated by their superiors as *poised* around others, *not reserved or shy, self-confident,* and *facile in oral expression.* They were perceived as likely to show *initiative* and *ingenuity, efficient* and *responsible,* but *not as conscientious. Leadership* qualities were observed but so was *immaturity.*

Less favorable ratings were rendered for the high-Ma males in the University of California assessment program. While they were viewed as *expressive* and *exciting* persons, they also impressed the staff as *guileful* and possibly *deceitful. Actions* appeared to be considerably *influenced by subjective feelings* which were *diffuse* and *highly personal.* While described as *sensitive, thoughtful,* and *imaginative,* they also came through as *anxious* and *nervous* and as *unfriendly.*

Peer's observations of the high-Ma college females in the Black study depicted them as *enterprising, energetic, persevering,* and *idealistic* but, in a less positive vein, as *awkward* and *infantile, boastful* and *showoffs, selfish, self-centered,* and *inflexible.* These girls were not considered to be *mature, loyal, popular, honest,* or *peaceable.* Peers were also less likely to view them as *not self-controlled* and *seclusive.*

Self-ratings for the high-Ma person were obtained in two of the studies. Hathaway and Meehl report their males to endorse *impulsive, talkative, adventurous, liking to drink,* and *frank* but also *seclusive. Worrying* and *high-strung* appeared as well. Females in the same study looked upon themselves as *enterprising, sociable, grateful* and *idealistic.*

Black compiled a long list of terms which the high-Ma females used to identify themselves. On the negative side of the ledger, they described themselves as *jealous, aggressive,* and *flattering.* They also failed to use such terms as *reliable, generous,* and *clear-thinking.* More positively, they considered themselves to be *enterprising, energetic, enthusiastic, decisive, self-confident, sociable, polished, sophisticated, poised, worldly, independent, individualistic, unconventional, relaxed, peaceable, contented, not indecisive or sensitive, affectionate, good-tempered, laughter-ful, natural, self-controlled, popular, curious, not quiet, shy* or *seclusive, adaptable, versatile, courageous, practical,* and *not unrealistic* or *given to partiality.*

Liberally sprinkled throughout these descriptive terms relating to the high-Ma normal is the clear implication of a socially extraverted orientation, just the opposite social orientation to that observed for the high-D normal. Beyond this we are struck with the inconsistencies not only between studies but also between self-observation and the observations of others. Sociable stands in contrast with seclusive and unfriendly; frank with guileful, deceitful, and flattering; self-confident with worrying, self-dissatisfied, anxious, nervous, and high-strung; poised and sophisticated with infantile and immature; and idealistic and affectionate with selfish and self-centered. Inconsistent, at times incompatible, behavioral observations such as these argue for a personality pattern in which the person's social motives and his manifest social impression and attainment fail to achieve proper synthesis.

Heilbrun, considering the meaning of the two HC-LN subgroupings in his 1968 paper, combined the perceptual implications of the differential tape-induced cognitive disruption and the social differences between high-D and high-Ma normals to hypothesize two styles of adaptation to the sustained aversive qualities of the HC-LN mother's behavior. One mode of adaptation to aversive maternal stimulation would involve avoidance behaviors which place the child at least temporarily beyond reach of the aversive cues. The combination of low cognitive disruption and high-D MMPI scores was interpreted to mean that the defended behavior of this coping style manifests itself on the perceptual level by the ability to screen out aversive maternal stimulation that occur in his proximal environment. Defense would be mediated on the social level by avoidance or withdrawal behaviors which remove him from situations involving possible maternal censure or from the mother herself.

This closed style of adaptation to experienced aversive maternal control, generalized to all situations involving or implying evaluation, would account not only for the social alienation, overcontrol, and hesitancy of the high-D person but even the more adjustive attributes of conformity, conscientiousness, and responsibility. Heilbrun construed these individuals as committed to reducing risks as far as social evaluation is concerned. He further noted that their defending style, which reduces the aversive qualities of the mother and other social agents through diminishment of the input of social reinforcers, contributes to the self-doubt, worry, and pessimism regarding the future observed in the high-D person. The defense, in short, serves to curtail any increments to their self-esteem.

The contrasting style of adaptation to aversive maternal control, inferred from the combination of disrupted cognition and high-Ma scores, was hypothesized to involve an orientation toward the mother and the social environment as potential sources of social approval. This open-style adapter employs his behavior as a calculated means of eliciting the positive regard denied him by his mother. However, inadequate self-monitoring, the intrusion of strategem, and his egocentric concern with eliciting positive responses make it unlikely that his behavior will be of such a quality as to sustain the social rewards necessary to enhance his low self-esteem. Since his method of coping with negative evaluation is to offer behavior which will change the nature of the evaluative cues, the open-style person must remain alert to the evaluative meaning of behavior. Thus, his functioning will reflect a vigilance to social reinforcement at the perceptual level.

Despite the proposed contrasts in the two styles of adaptation to aversive maternal control—social withdrawal and perceptual defense for the closed style and calculated social approach and perceptual vigilance for the open style—it was emphasized by Heilbrun that both modes of adaptation by the HC-LN child lead to a common adjustive impasse. Neither allows him to modify through experience the damage to his self-esteem mediated by the maternal control-rejection experience.

The analogy has been drawn between these learned styles of reducing the psychological discomfort of aversive maternal stimulation and the options which are available to persons exposed to aversive physical conditions such as intense visual or auditory stimuli (Heilbrun, 1971). Under such conditions the person may attempt to: (1) remove the aversive stimulation at its source (e.g., a switch); (2) reduce the aversiveness of the stimulation by defensive perceptual tactics (e.g., closing the eyes or placing hands over the ears); or (3) introduce physical distance between the stimulation and the sensory receptors (e.g., running away). The open-style HC-LN adolescent, to continue the analogy, is viewed as the youngster in active search of interpersonal switches which he can throw in order to turn off or avoid the anguish of censure or rejection. His closed-style HC-LN counterpart, in turn, assumes a more passive character with regard to influencing aversive stimulation at its interpersonal source, but rather diverts his efforts to protecting himself from experiencing the brunt of its impact.

At the time these two distinct behavioral styles were sketched from the implications of our findings, a parallel was drawn between the styles and premorbid schizophrenic development:

> The finding that HC-LN males, who as a group show schizoid features, tend to split into introverted adapters and extraverted nonadapters to aversive maternal stimulation lends itself to one very interesting possibility. Considerable interest has been generated in the classification of schizophrenics into types based upon premorbid history . . . . Male poor premorbid (process) schizophrenics, who have a more guarded prognosis for recovery, are distinguished

by: "the patient who has exhibited a poorly integrated prepsychotic personality characterized by marked sexual, social and occupational inadequacy, a lack of emotional responsiveness and social isolation" [Garmezy and Rodnick, 1959, p. 451]. Good premorbid males have a far more successful history of social and heterosexual competence. The present results raise the possibility that *one* source of premorbid differences in schizophrenics is the adaptive style developed by the child in response to aversive maternal stimulation. Reduction of aversive stimulation by avoidance and insulation would represent a more frequent dynamic of the poor premorbid schizophrenic: generalized social avoidance behavior, especially with figures similar to the mother (i.e., females), would help account for the social incompetence in general and heterosexual inadequacy in particular.

Response to aversive maternal stimulation by poorly monitored strategem-based social approach behaviors should be encountered more frequently among good premorbid schizophrenics. Although this style of adaptation apparently fails to reduce the disruptive effects of the aversive maternal stimulation, it does enhance the possibilities of establishing social relationships in which the male can temporarily compensate for the psychological damage mediated by the mother-child interaction (Heilbrun, 1968, 330-331).

In the next section we will treat the extended theory of schizophrenic development which has evolved from this nucleus over the past four years.

The identification of subsets of late adolescents within the HC-LN group which appear to differ in social orientation and in their perceptual styles of contending with evaluative cues also adds a clarifying postscript to the programmatic research cited in the previous two chapters. These studies, which regularly exposed the subjects to a variety of evaluative conditions, were able to identify systematic effects upon the HC-LN group. However, the effects were sometimes commonly shared with subjects from another child-rearing experience quadrant. Consequently, our inferences could not be as sharply hewn as we would have liked. The existence of HC-LN subgroupings which share a sensitivity to evaluative cues but which attend to them in different ways could only add to the heterogeneity of the HC-LN group performance. Research subsequent to 1968 has clearly affirmed the heterogeneous character of the HC-LN group; the fact that despite this we were consistently able to demonstrate effects involving HC-LN subjects taken as a whole attests to the potency of the relationships. Interestingly enough, the same problem of behavioral heterogeneity was partially resolved in research using schizophrenic subjects by introducing the process-reactive distinction (Higgins, 1969; Garmezy and Rodnick, 1959). It finally dawned on us that in our quest to establish the schizoid properties of the HC-LN quadrant, we apparently had been contending with "process" and "reactive" adolescents.

PROCESS AND REACTIVE CONTINUUM IN SCHIZOPHRENIA

A parallel has been drawn between the open-style and closed-style of adaptation to aversive maternal control and the premorbid behavioral patterns which define reactive and process schizophrenia. It will become increasingly evident that this parallelism assumes a central position in our theory of schizophrenic development. Process-reactive differences will also play a key role in the validational evidence which will command our attention in the next chapter. The importance of the process-reactive distinction to the task of theory building and validation makes it necessary to examine the origin and nature of the process-reactive continuum in greater depth.

The historic origins of a process-reactive schizophrenic distinction reside in the longstanding clinical observation that some schizophrenics respond favorably to treatment whereas others appear to be noncurable. Kantor and Herron (1966), in their discussion of the evolution of the process and reactive constructs, cite workers who almost a half-century ago hypothesized that schizophrenics could be usefully separated into a more malignant group of process schizophrenics and a reactive group with a more benign prognosis (Kretschmer, 1925; Mauz, 1930).

More recently, several techniques have been developed by which prognosis in schizophrenia presumably could be established along with the process and reactive status of the schizophrenic. Higgins' (1969) review of the process-reactive literature identifies four major sets of criteria which have received extensive use in reaching such a prognostic decision. The Phillips Scale (1953) evolved from the case histories of schizophrenic patients who ultimately ended up in a shock treatment program. The scale, as originally derived, included three parts: premorbid history, possible precipitating factors, and signs of the disorder. Greater success in predicting the outcome of treatment established the premorbid history items as the critical section of the Phillips Scale, and these have become the exclusive criterion of process-reactive classification for those who have used this scale. The premorbid history items, reproduced in Appendix F, include information on recent sexual adjustment, social aspects of sexual life during and immediately after adolescence, social aspects of recent sexual life, history of personal relations, and recent personal relations. It is evident that the exclusive focus of the case history search necessary to complete the Phillips Scale ratings is the social-sexual competence of the patient.

A second method of assessing process and reactive status in schizophrenia, and the oldest of the four techniques, is the Elgin Prognostic Scale (Wittman, 1941). This prognostic device was constructed to predict recoverability in schizophrenia from 20 rating scales which evaluate prepsychotic personality, nature of onset, and typicality of psychosis. A similar method drawing upon case history material, developed by Kantor, Wallner, and Winder (1953), has enjoyed its share of use in process-reactive differentiation.

An entirely different approach to prediction of outcome in schizophrenia can be credited to Meadow and Funkenstein (1952) who proposed that the combination of physiological and psychological test measures would distinguish three categories of patients. Type I schizophrenics were identified physiologically by a marked response in systolic blood pressure to adrenergic stimulation, low blood pressure, and failure of the blood pressure to rise under most stress conditions; this physiological pattern was accompanied by a loss of abstract thinking ability, inappropriate affect, and a poor prognosis. Type II was characterized by a distinctly different autonomic pattern, a more intact ability for abstraction, anxiety, or depression, and a good prognosis. Type III showed no autonomic disturbance, little loss of abstraction ability, paranoid delusions, and a fair prognosis.

Higgins (1969), in reviewing the evidence regarding the efficacy of these four techniques for determining process-reactive status, concludes that:

> . . . all but the Phillips scale have suffered a decline in popularity. In the case of the Elgin and Kantor and associates scales this subsidence is probably due to the relatively ambiguous and abstruse nature of their items as compared to the greater simplicity and specificity of the Phillips. As for the mecholyl test which is used for determining autonomic patternings, inherent difficulties in administration in combination with questionable reliability . . . have doubtlessly contributed to its demise (pp. 450-451).

Higgins continues by citing a substantial number of studies which suggest that the Phillips Scale, more than any other technique, holds a common correlational bond with the remaining criteria of process-reaction status.

Since the Phillips Scale undoubtedly represents the most extensively used instrument for drawing process-reactive distinctions in schizophrenia and, apparently, has been more successful than any other, we will narrow our attention to that scale alone. First, it is important for our purpose to draw attention to a conclusion about the Phillips Scale which Higgins underscores by his citation of more recent evidence. While the items included in the scale are those which were empirically identified as offering the best basis for predicting response to hospital treatment (shock treatment to be specific), subsequent usage has suggested that Phillips scores may be less related to improvement than to initial level of functioning (Lewinsohn, 1967). In line with this conclusion, we find that high Phillips Scale scores (indicating process schizophrenia) relate to poorer premorbid occupational adjustment (Cicchetti and Ornston, 1968), earlier first neuropsychiatric hospitalization (Cicchetti and Ornston, 1968; Nuttall and Solomon, cited in Higgins, 1969), and more insidious onset of the disorder (Cancro and Sugarman, 1968).

The conclusion drawn from examining the empirical correlates of the Phillips Scale, that those schizophrenics which it classifies as process are clearly less adequate in their premorbid development than those which it classifies as reactive, also could have been reached rationally by inspection of the items (see Appendix F). The rater's use of the Phillips Scale requires that he seize upon facts from the case history of the schizophrenic from which he assigns scores reflecting earlier social and sexual competence. The less effective the behavior in either sphere, the higher the score and greater the probability that the schizophrenic will be classed as process.

From the convergence of empirical and logical inference, we draw one simple conclusion. The most effective basis for assignment of schizophrenics to process and reactive classes is to establish their level of social-sexual competence during the developmental period extending from adolescence through young adulthood. Zigler and Phillips (1962) arrived at a similar conclusion in their view that Phillips Scale scores identify degrees of social competence. They further concluded that the process-reactive distinction is not only reducible to the social maturity dimension but also cite considerable evidence indicating that process and reactive status represent different points on a developmental continuum which is relevant not only to schizophrenics but to all forms of psychopathology as well as to normally functioning children, adolescents, and adults (Grace, 1956; Hurwitz, 1954; Lane, 1955; Levine, 1959; Phillips and Zigler, 1961; Smith and Phillips, 1959; Zigler and Phillips, 1960).

In summary, the process-reactive distinction has emerged as a set of orthogonal points on a continuum representing degrees of competence in the social-sexual sphere. The distinction seems applicable not only to schizophrenia but to other types of psychopathology and to persons functioning within the normal range of behavior. Process and reactive differences, especially when they are based upon the Phillips Scale, have developmental relevance with a special focus upon the span of years ranging from adolescence through the early adult years.

Thus, our postulation of etiologic applicability of the adaptive-style dynamics to process and reactive schizophrenic development did not involve any new assumptions about the process-reactive continuum. We were contending only that the hypothesized parent-child dynamics which could promote process and reactive types of schizoid late adolescents might be usefully applied to understanding the process and reactive premorbid development of schizophrenics. This contention will assume paramount importance in the effort to validate our theory in the next chapter. At that point we will consider in some detail the rather extensive research literature bearing upon the behavioral differences between process and reactive schizophrenics (for reviews see Herron, 1962; Higgins, 1964; Higgins, 1969; Higgins and Peterson, 1966; Kantor and Herron, 1966; Schooler and Feldman, 1967).

A THEORY OF SCHIZOPHRENIC DEVELOPMENT

Despite the vast amount of research into schizophrenia that has been reported, it is difficult to grasp any sense of progress in the construction of theories which serve to explain the genesis of this form of psychopathology. As an illustration, a relatively recent book, *Theories of Schizophrenia* (Buss and Buss, 1969), reports seven independent approaches to explaining schizophrenic behavior. These were chosen, we presume, as the best theories available. Yet the dates at which these theoretical papers first made their appearance ranged from 1934 to 1962. The vacuum surrounding major theoretical development in the decade of the 1960's, despite the increasing sophistication of the concerned professions, is not only a sobering commentary on our progress but also a testimonial to how difficult the job really is. It is with the hazards of the undertaking clearly understood that we set about the articulation of a new theory of schizophreniform development.

The Aversive Maternal Control Experience

As the child develops from the completely dependent stage of infancy to the relatively independent adult stage, the mother comes to represent the critical socialization agent. The child's habituated patterns of responding socially, perceptually, and emotionally to his social environment and to himself will be influenced in a major way by his interpersonal dealings with the female parent. This will be more the case with some configurations of maternal behavior than with others. If the child feels free to assume increasing autonomy while continuing to experience the nurturant qualities of affection, respect, and trust as he grows, the way is clear to transact effectively with his expanding social environment. In contrast, the failure on the part of the child to emerge in his own way of thinking from the controlled, dependent status of early childhood to a more autonomous relationship with the mother by adolescence deters the establishment of a sense of interpersonal competence. His sense of worth is further reduced by his perception of maternal rejection; if this parent who knows him best cannot communicate love and esteem, then he indeed must be unlovable and unworthy of esteem. Thus, the combined experience of sustained maternal control and maternal rejection act in common to shape a self-conceptual system which mirrors the disparagement and doubt he has identified in his mother's behavior toward him.

The aversive maternal control experience introduces a type of pathological circularity into the child's development. Initiation of new relationships within which he could experience greater independence and positive regard is deterred by his poor self-image and expectations of further rejection, and he remains firmly entrenched in the very relationship which instigated his problems. The mother, for her part, comes to regard the child with even greater disapproval as he reaches the stage where more autonomous functioning is expected (adolescence). The child's fear or clumsiness in establishing more profitable interpersonal contacts is magnified, in turn, by the mother's more obvious control and rejection which derive from her growing realization that the aging child is psychologically deviant. Control and rejection, which at one time may have been as much a figment of the child's imagination as of the mother's intent, become increasingly real properties of the mother's behavior.

The aspects of the child's make-up which are directly mediated by the aversive maternal control experience, then, are: (1) a continuing instigation to respond in keeping with maternal expectation and an anticipation of failure to meet maternal standards and, thereby, to elicit censure or more subtle rejection; (2) a self-conceptual deficit; and (3) the establishing of generalization gradients with the mother serving as the prototypic stimulus for interpersonal transactions.

Adaptation to the Mother as an Aversive Stimulus

Encapsulation of the child within the aversive-control relationship with his mother, without the benefit of some compensatory relationship (as with his father), makes it necessary that he devise some way of adapting in situ to the discomforting qualities he perceives in his mother. The most primitive coping mechanisms for dealing with a painful stimulus available to the child are tactics of avoidance and withdrawal which place physical or psychological distance between the child and the source of pain. This style of adapting to the mother as an aversive stimulus involves a range of behaviors from noninvolvement and disengagement on the psychological side to motoric flight and hiding on the physical side. The child also learns to deploy his attention in such a way as to reduce the input of potentially upsetting cues which, by and large, are those with evaluative connotations. This social-perceptual style of coping with potentially distressing cues from the mother, or some other figure to whom the child has generalized his expectations of failure, is functionally geared to close out the source of aversiveness. It has been identified, accordingly, as the closed adaptive style.

The second set of behaviors which may serve to reduce the aversive qualities of the child's relationship with his mother involves the diametrically opposite tack. It becomes necessary for this child to clearly identify what is expected of him interpersonally which will elicit positive responses from significant others. Thus, he continues to relate as closely to the mother as she will allow, attempting to behave in such ways as to replace his sense of rejection by her with hoped-for attitudes of love, pride, and trust. This mode of adapting requires that the child engage himself in game-like attempts to please and impress not only the mother but also the extended generalized gradient of individuals whose evaluative responses hold the key to reducing his insecurity. This mode of coping with the mother as an aversive stimulus requires the child's continuing orientation toward his social environment and close attention to interpersonal cues relevant to social expectations and evaluative judgments. Accordingly, it is referred to as the open style of adapting.

Choice of Adaptive Styles

The question of why some children would learn to reduce the aversiveness of maternal control-rejection cues by open and some by closed patterns of behavior is a critical one. The major determinant of coping style according to theory is the clarity of meaning characterizing the mother's communication to the child. The messages coming from the mother which the child responds to as control may be clearly communicated by the dominating mother or indirectly and vaguely communicated by the subtly manipulating mother. The dominating mother not only is likely to openly exert control over the child's behavior but also to be the dominant figure in the family, extending her control to the father as well. In contrast, the manipulative mother influences the child (and the husband) by innuendo, with martydom and guilt induction representing the primary modus operandi.

The child will either learn to orient toward the mother or away from the mother depending upon how clearly she communicates her control and rejection messages. Clear aversive communication mediates avoidance behavior in the child; his certainty of meaning lends itself to social-perceptual tactics which orient him away from aversive social stimuli and thwart stimulus input. Unclear communication elicits approach behavior which has as its goal the clarification of maternal messages; uncertainty of meaning for the child facilitates social-perceptual behaviors which orient him toward social stimuli and enhance stimulus input.

The closed-style mother, whose clearly communicated control directives have instituted her child's orientation away from his social environment, also discourages the disclosure of personal concerns on the part of the child. Her disinterest in being exposed to any expression of his difficulties further solidifies his behavioral style by which he seeks to insulate himself from his social environment. The open-style mother, on the other hand, reinforces the child's orientation toward her by an intrusive need to know everything that is going on within the realm of the child's thoughts and feelings.

Adaptive Style and Personality Development

As the child comes to learn one or the other mode of adaptation to the mother and to generalize these adaptive styles to other interpersonal transactions, certain personality traits will be necessarily influenced and the styles will assume an increasingly pervasive role in the child's total functioning.

The subjective manner in which the person responds to failure or transgression will differ for the two styles. Guilt would be the correlate of the open adaptive style. The open-style child has already incorporated the two ingredients which distinguish guilt as a unique response to failure to meet some standard. Voluntary initiation of social contact for purposes of confession and expiation, the hallmark of guilt, follows directly from two established response dispositions. The open-style child has already learned to move toward the mother (and others) to alleviate distress states by social reward-seeking strategies; he also has a lower threshold for self-disclosure which has been facilitated by the mother's intrusive needs. Confession, while it might elicit punishment earlier than would otherwise be the case, is also likely to decrease its intensity and shorten the duration of subsequent disfavor. Accordingly, it is in keeping with strategies which promise to evoke positive esteem.

Closed-style children have not learned to seek alleviation of distress by approaching others nor to disclose what is troubling them. Rather, they would be expected to respond in the opposite fashion to failure or transgression, to avoid the proximity of people and the disclosure of the source of their distress. Therefore, shame would be the dominant response to failure to achieve a standard for the closed-style child with withdrawal as its goal response.

Open-style and closed-style patterns also would include a different hierarchical ordering of available mechanisms of defense against intolerable communications relevant to the self. While some more benign defense mechanisms such as rationalization and intellectualization could just as likely be available within either pattern, dominant and more pathogenic modes of neutralizing anxiety will differ. The open-style child, who diverts a major share of his attention to his social environment as he weighs social expectation and evaluative outcome, will use an externalizing defense already molded by his incessant concern about his worth in relationship to those constituting his social milieu. Projection, the attribution of an undesirable trait to others as a way of denying its presence in oneself, would be the major pathological mechanism of defense within the open adaptive style. The projective defense can be recognized as a reversal in the continuing flow of self-relevant information being processed by the open-style child in which input repugnant to the self is turned back upon its source.

The closed adaptive style, which serves a generally protective function by diverting the child away from his social environment, would foster an internalized mode of defense, one that does not require redirecting his attention outward. Repression, the diversion of anxiety-arousing material from awareness, would be the primary pathological mechanism of defense within the closed adaptive style. It not only is consistent with the habitual inward attentional flow of the open-style child but also with his perceptual habits. Having learned to diminish or preclude the registration of social evaluative cues upon the exteroceptors to defend against devaluating communication, the closed-style child would be in a favorable position to utilize a defense which precludes threatening communications from registering upon the interoceptors.

Still another dimension of personality which distinguishes the two styles of adaptation is the child's tolerance for ambiguity, particularly as this pertains to the meaning of social stimulation. The open style, having grown out of the child's need to clarify maternal communication and subsisting on a continuing need to identify social expectations and evaluative cues, will bring with it an intolerance for uncertainty in the meaning of socially related stimulation. Decisions regarding self-relevant meanings, reached prematurely, will suffer from an under-representation of fact and an over-representation of subjectively tinged assumption.

The closed adaptive style not only allows a tolerance for ambiguity in stimulus meaning but in one sense actually functions to induce ambiguity. The attempt to escape aversive social cues by avoidance or blocking responses serves to create gaps in understanding self-relevant social meanings and, thus, to create ambiguity. This style substitutes ambiguity of meaning for the expected (and feared) clear communication of aversive meaning.

Adaptive Style and Emotional Arousal

The defended nature of the closed style will reduce the amount of emotional arousal experienced by the child, since it requires the avoidance of extrinsic evaluative cues having the potential for eliciting strong affective states such as anxiety, frustration, or anger. However, if the situation is such as to render the social or perceptual defenses ineffective, the closed-style child will be emotionally responsive to extrinsic cues. His protection against heightened (aversive) emotional states generated by internally produced cues (thoughts, memories) will be determined largely by the effectiveness of his repressive mechanism.

Open-style children will be more emotionally responsive to the external environment or to internally produced cues, especially when they are engaging a situation or its symbolic representation within which the question of their meaning to others is at stake. Emotional controls are imposed only indirectly by the open-style child's ability to maintain a continuing input of reassuring messages regarding his worth.

Adaptive Style and Heterosexual Adjustment

Adolescence, bringing with it increasing pressures to channel sexual drive to members of the opposite sex, will reveal a broadening difference between children who have assumed the two adaptive styles. For males, increasing similarity between female peers (i.e., as these girls approach womanhood) and their mothers will evoke characteristic modes of responding to their mothers. Their adaptive styles should be generalized in clear form. This means that the closed-style male will alleviate the threat of control and rejection by another woman through avoiding heterosexual entanglements.

The open-style male, in contrast, will be drawn to heterosexual relationships because they offer the best source of compensation for the unsuccessful relationship with the mother. However, several factors mitigate against a lasting, mutually satisfying heterosexual relationship for the open-style male even when the relationship consummates in marriage. First, the open-style male in the last analysis will demonstrate a unilateral concern with his own need for assurance and esteem and will engage in style-determined strategies to achieve this end. Mutuality will be missing in the relationship. Second, the heterosexual relationship will be more compensatory than important in its own right and obviously cannot serve to restore what is past. Third, active competition between the subtly controlling mother (if still alive) and the female partner would be expected. Fourth, generalization of needs from a frustrating mother-son relationship to a wife-husband relationship is likely to expose the wife to the husband's role expectations of the "good mother" in which she may find little reward, particularly after real children make similar demands. Finally, the similarity of the wife to the mother, imposed by the open-style husband's common responses to both, threatens the introduction of taboo responses to sexual contact within the marriage.

Although the closed-style male will avoid heterosexual relationships, just as he restricts social contact in general, he maintains the capacity for sexual arousal to the same or even greater degree than the open-style male. There is, however, a clearer differentiation of heterosexual and homosexual cues as sources of arousal in the case of the open-style male than in his closed-style counterpart. Autoerotic behavior is the likely goal response for the closed-style male whatever the source of arousal because of his generalized avoidance of close social contacts.

While the theoretical expectations relevant to heterosexual adjustment for open-style and closed-style females would be somewhat similar to those proposed for males, some differences must certainly be entertained. Expectations regarding social introversion-extraversion and their overriding effects upon heterosexual relationships would be common to both sexes and would lead us to predict greater restraint in heterosexual (or homosexual) contact for closed-style females. It seems likely though that heterosexual adjustment will be a less important distinction between females who have adopted different coping styles than it is for males. This follows in part from the fact that the female traditionally does not assume the initiative in heterosexual relationships; the closed-style female need not be so seriously penalized by her lack of initiative in establishing or maintaining peer contact. Parenthetically, the conclusion that heterosexual development should be a less salient discriminating variable for closed-style and open-style girls is consistent with our impression that the Phillips Scale has proved less useful for separating female schizophrenics into process and reactive categories.

Attention Deployment and Disorders of Thinking

Attention, that process which ". . . enables organisms to respond selectively to important features of their environments while ignoring features which are of little or no importance" (Egeth, 1967, p. 41), assumes a central explanatory position within the present theory. Initial instigation of differences in attention deployment among children of aversive-control mothers, as we have already pointed out, rests in the levels of clarity with which the mother communicates her control and rejection directives. Given clear directives, the most available (and perhaps only) escape route is to place physical or psychological barriers between the source of the aversive cues and their registration in awareness. The closed-style child learns to deflect social stimulation which threatens to confront him with repugnant meaning about himself. This requires that he learn to deploy his attention either to nonthreatening features of his external environment or to turn his attention inward to his internal environment (e.g., thoughts, images, memory, bodily sensations). The more successful the child becomes at diverting his attention from noxious but central external cues to benign but peripheral stimuli, the more he will have to contend with meaning gaps in his social experience—the more effective the adaptation, the more ineffective his social adjustment.

The open-style originates in the required concentration of attention upon the mother in order to extract meaning from her unclear communication. Instigation to orient attention to the external environment based upon the open-style child's need to ferret out expectation, is complemented by his pursuit of self-relevant evaluative meanings in social situations. The demands of sustained vigilance to external happenings or their immediate representation in consciousness will restrict the amount of internal attentional focus. The open-style child will spend a less-than-expected amount of time attending to thoughts, memories, images, or other intrinsic cues, especially as these might be considered in terms of extended or alternate meanings.

The disproportionate displacement of attention either inward or outward introduces its own special blend of problems in thinking. The closed adaptive style and its attendant diversion of attentional scanning to only selective aspects of the external environment or to the safer confines of intrinsic cues will often require that thinking proceed without relevant, often vital, information from the social environment. (It would be similar to the student whose thoughts "drift away" during a lecture and who later finds an informational gap in his classroom notes.) Hence, the thinking of the closed-style child will suffer from a loss of information filtering in from his social surroundings. His thoughts, especially as they represent the child's understanding of the social environment, will become less effective as mediators of transaction with other humans as they are guided by less extrinsic information. This will be a special problem for the closed-style child, since his general tendency to withdraw socially will place its own limits upon his understanding of fellow humans; lacking even the normal degree of "common sense," he will be in a poor position to fill the informational gaps created by his perceptual defenses.

The thinking problems which would accompany the predisposition to external scanning would be quite different in origin and form. The broad attention to cues emanating from his social environment would bring with it an information overload based upon a failure to selectively attend to cues according to an effective hierarchy of importance. Restricted internal scanning which results from the major deployment of attention outward by the open-style child denies him the cognitive habits by which he could compensate for the flooding of information. Instead of logical filtering of alternatives, adoption of hierarchies of importance, or retrieval of past experience from memory store for establishing points of reference, open-style children will process informational input without due regard for logic, importance, or past experience.

The open-style child's intolerance for ambiguity adds motivational fuel to his thinking problems. Not only has this child failed to develop internal scanning habits which allow him to effectively compensate for the information overload from his social environment, but it is difficult for him to delay the imposition of meaning on this input. The greater opportunity for error which accompanies premature conclusions makes it even less likely that the open-style child will maintain modes of thinking about himself in relation to others which correspond to social realities.

Transition from a Closed Premorbid Style of Adaptation to Process Schizophrenia

In explicating the theory we have to this point made reference to the "child" who develops one or the other behavioral style of coping with aversive maternal control. By remaining indefinite we have been spared the necessity of specifying age (or sex, with one exception, for that matter). Some chronological vagueness is required by current lack of evidence, but the assumption is made that whatever the timing of onset of the style, the critical phase for deterioration from schizophreniform childhood eccentricities to psychotic schizophrenic symptoms extends from adolescence through young adulthood (perhaps 15 to 25 years of age).

The transition from a closed adaptive style to process schizophrenia would be a slow, insidious process. What began as a tension-reducing mechanism, avoidance of persons or situations which portend censure-failure-rejection experiences, creates an early identification of the child as "different" or "strange." An unfortunate circularity will make these increasing realities over time. As the child moves away from social contact to protect himself, he has less opportunity to develop the skills of social interchange which eventually form the basis for effective interpersonal dealings as adults. His retreat from people, which began as a way of protecting himself from the *feeling* of being inadequate, deprives him of the opportunity to be anything else. As those about him come to respond to him as deviant, he will be driven to even more extensive use of his withdrawal defenses to avoid their evaluative responses. As the style and the social incompetence continue to feed on one another, what started out as selective social withdrawal will blend into a social alienation within which the person maintains continuous instigation to withdraw from social contact from which he indiscriminantly anticipates rejection.

The selection of social avoidance-withdrawal tactics by the closed-style child to maintain the fragile integrity of his self-concept contributes to the long and insidious character of schizophreniform development in another way. The tokens of achievement by which "healthy" development is judged in most contemporary cultures almost without exception require not only a modicum of ability to relate interpersonally but a willingness to risk losing in some competitional arena. Thus, opportunities to engage in the critical psychological growth experiences in adolescence or early adulthood—academic, athletic, heterosexual, or occupational—are vitiated by his mode of self-protection.

The tenacity of the closed adaptive style, once it becomes established, may be further determined by the same factors which contribute to the persistence of fear-motivated avoidance behavior in animals and humans. Baum (1970), in considering phenomena ranging from laboratory-produced avoidance responses in animals conditioned by electric shock to phobic behaviors in humans, points out that when the subject has been successful in avoiding pain by some instrumental act, the onset of extinction does not introduce any discriminable change. As long as the avoidance response removes the animal from danger (and thereby reduces the fear), it cannot learn that the painful stimulus no longer follows the warning stimulus.

The avoidance behavior of the closed-style child would persist for much the same reasons. Interpersonal situations involving the threat of failure signal avoidance or withdrawal responses. These serve to provide immediate reduction of fear because the danger of failure has been averted; fear reduction functions to reinforce the avoidance response. If avoidance is successful in any given situation, the person does not have the opportunity to learn that his anticipations were wrong. With time and with the spiraling effects of increased fear and more extensive social withdrawal, the frequency and amount of reinforcement increase. As we have pointed out, the withdrawal mechanism inhibits the development of social competence and denies corrective experiences to the child. Thus, the use of social avoidance breeds incompetence; incompetence increases the extensity of danger signals and the intensity of fear; increased frequency and extent of fear reduction increase the reinforcement value of avoidance. As in a science fiction novel, the social-avoidance mechanism grows by feeding on itself.

The thinking of the closed-style child would be expected to show progressive changes of two types if clinical schizophrenic proportions are to be reached. First, autism, the absorption in internally generated fantasy material rather than externally responsive reality material, would follow from his lasting and increasing detachment from his social environment. Second, discontinuities in thought would result from the loss of informational input inherent in the selectivity of his external scanning. We would expect the clearest examples of thought disturbance to be produced by coalescence of autism and discontinuity—when gaps in the continuity of thought linked to external cues come to be filled by autistic bridges. This blend would have neither transactional value as it would appear in the form of language nor mediational value for the person's own behavior, at least as far as effective social adjustment would be concerned.

The theoretical transition we have proposed from closed-style adaptation to process schizophrenia must as a minimal requirement be consonant with the commonly identified developmental features of this form of schizophrenia. The review of prognostic criteria by Kantor and Herron (1966, pp. 17-21) points most often to five antecedent characteristics in the premorbid history of (process) schizophrenics who respond poorly to treatment: (1) social introversion; (2) heterosexual inadequacy; (3) gradual and insidious onset of symptoms; (4) earlier age of symptom onset; (5) absence of a clear event precipitating symptom onset. The specifications of our theory which link process development and a closed style of adaptation to the mother seem entirely compatible with these defining premorbid attributes of process schizophrenia.

Transition from an Open Premorbid Style of Adaptation to Reactive Schizophrenia

The compensatory orientation of the open-style child to his social environment as a source of esteem-building experiences does not set him apart from the mainstream of normal development to anywhere near the extent as would the closed adaptive style. His divergence would reside initially not so much in his manifest interpersonal behaviors but in private cognitive machination directed to achieving his social goals and in agonizing over the meaning of social cues. While his relationships may be lacking in durability, emotional depth, and mutuality, they do place him in a position of achieving sufficient satisfactions as to sustain a reasonably normal social development. The weak link is the failure of successful developmental experiences to register in any indelible way upon the self-conceptual system. One accomplishment does not leave him any less insecure when he again infers a need to prove his worth. It is to be expected that despite his singular need to prove himself, however, his rather shallow mode of thinking will lead him to some unfortunate decisions about social tactics or goals. Failure experiences or social rebuffs, while of even incidental significance to the casual observer, would be extremely aversive to the open-style person and would instigate compensatory interpersonal activities.

With time, the increasing weight and complexity of the institutionalized demands of our culture—marriage, parenthood, and work—place the open-style adapter under special stress, since success in each case is not to be a product of simple stràtegy but will require sustained commitment. The importance of mutuality in marriage will create particular problems for the open-style person because of his egocentric concern for meeting his own needs. However, marriage will represent a critical requirement, at least for the male, since it would be within the context of this close relationship with an adult female that he will seek compensation for the earlier frustrations experienced with his mother.

The threat of deterioration from the behavioral pattern of the open style to a reactive schizophrenia is posed by any major event which can be interpreted by the person as signifying his failure or as a threat to his security (e.g., loss of work, separation or divorce, death of someone looked to for need fulfillment) and for which no coping strategy is available. The rapid onset of symptoms would take one of two predominant forms—a serious depression or a paranoid reaction. Both symptom patterns relate dynamically to guilt fostered by the critical event. The projection and delusional embellishment of a paranoid reaction can serve the defensive function of displacing the origins of failure onto an outside agent or agency, thereby relieving guilt. Depression would follow from the full-blown impact of the critical event without the protective paranoid reaction to buffer the person from guilt and intrapunitive behavior.

Open Adaptive Style and Paranoid Behavior

Anyone, normal or mentally ill, may show delusional behavior if he acts upon some faulty premise or misrepresents evidence. These erroneous constructions can be readily corrected in the case of normals by factual restructuring of the premise or the evidence. Dramatic delusional distortions also can be understood as the by-products of bizarre mentation frequently reached in schizophrenia. We would contend that neither of these should be confused etiologically with the lucid, systematic, and complex misinterpretations of interpersonal meaning which evolve from the exposure of a paranoid character structure to severe interpersonal stress. As examples, the antecedents and functional significance to be attributed to a chronic schizophrenic's unelaborated conviction that he is being eaten from the inside by worms should be considered separately from an elaborate persecutory delusion which pervades and colors the entire range of the schizophrenic's social perceptions and interpersonal transactions.

We postulate that children who have assumed an open style of adapting to aversive maternal control would be predisposed to qualities which, taken together, introduce a high risk for paranoia. There are seven behavioral properties of the open style, already proposed or derivable as corollary to our proposals, which conjointly form this etiologic predisposition to paranoid behavior.

1. *Low Self-Esteem.* The basic fabric from which paranoid reactions will eventually be cut is a self-conceptual system that reflects low estimate of the self, chiefly in the person's assessment of his competence and worth within the interpersonal sphere.

2. *Sensitivity to Social Evaluation (especially critical).* The person must care about the regard others hold for him. This directs the attempts of the person either toward defending against social response or toward rectifying his low self-esteem through social objects who are in a position to respond to him with signs of approval, trust, or affection.

3. *Broad External Scanning.* If the alternative of orienting to the social environment as a means of alleviating the distress of low self-esteem is followed, an attentional readiness to respond to external social cues is required. It is within the context of interpersonal transactions that the critical cues signifying self-relevant expectations or evaluations are to be found. Broad external scanning serves to funnel a large amount of information into the cognitive mechanisms through which new information is processed and collated with information held in storage to form a suitable basis for interpretation of meaning.

4. *Low Interpersonal Trust.* The continuing conviction of one's lack of worth (as opposed to an unstable self-conceptual system which may periodically generate low self-esteem) and a commitment to seeking social approbation manufacture a self-defeating by-product. The more successful the social strategies are in eliciting favorable responses, the more the person is confronted with evaluative meanings that are in conflict with those he holds to be true. He is also at least partially aware of the game-like character of his behavior through which he seeks approval. These factors combine to divest positive responses,

which he actively solicits from others, of impact and, more importantly, of credibility. In short, he cannot trust the meanings or intentions of those he forces into a position to judge him.

5. *Defensive Projection.* An overriding orientation toward his social environment rather than direction of his attention inward shapes the mode of defense that will be most available. Under continuing self-assessment he will make important use of other people as a yardstick of merit. The mechanism for denial of intolerable material which follows from this orientation would most likely be projection—the denial of an unfavorable trait in oneself by attributing it to another person.

6. *Intolerance of Ambiguity.* The inability to delay imposition of meaning upon extrinsic stimulation combines with the extensive flow of information from the outside extracted by the broad external scanner. This serves to increase the probability of premature and erroneous conclusions about the meaning of social cues.

7. *Inflexible Social Ideation.* Informational flooding introduces its own brand of aversiveness for the external scanner—the cognitive overload creates disorganization in his thinking. The person senses that he is going "crazy" in the most generally understood sense of the term; he cannot order his perceptions and thoughts and feels that he is losing control. The delusion offers a method of structuring his thinking and perception around some organizing though faulty premise (e.g., persecution, control) thereby reducing the anxiety generated by not being able to order one's thoughts. Thus, delusional thinking derives its inflexible property not only from its defensive character but also from its self-reinforcing organizing function. The delusion, which offers a simplifying frame of reference within which otherwise unrelated stimulus meanings can be conveniently ordered, allows the paranoid to reduce the mounting anxiety which is generated each time his vigilant external scanning pours in more information than he can effectively organize. Asking the paranoid to give up his delusion, as is so often implicit in treatment, is tantamount *in his terms* to asking him to give up his sanity.

Adaptive Style, Response to Treatment, and Chronicity in Schizophrenia

The theoretical proposal which we have presented is intended to specify a set of developmental conditions that could account for the emergence of process and reactive schizophrenias in the late adolescent or early adult years. Although the responsibility of our developmental theory rightly ends at the point where behavior reaches psychotic proportions, there are two relevant points to be made regarding the post-psychotic period.

First, the fact that the process and reactive schizophrenic distinctions arose out of the differences in response to hospital treatment is consistent with projections from the adaptive-style theory. Treatment of the acute schizophrenic, usually within a hospital setting, places him in a strange ward situation and hopefully involves strenuous treatment attempts by the staff to intervene in the course of his disorder. The schizophrenic, whose long-standing defenses have led him to pull away from social relationships no matter how well intended they may be, will introduce these defenses between himself and those who would provide therapy. Accordingly, closed-style premorbid development would bode poorly for response to treatment (as in process schizophrenia). In contrast, the open-style premorbid development, which has directed the person toward others for his own need fulfillment, makes him in one sense an ideal candidate for patient-oriented hospital treatment. Better prognosis for a patient with treatment-compatible needs (as in reactive schizophrenia) is to be expected.

The second and final point to be made is that the effects of chronicity of the schizophrenic disorder, process or reactive, would serve to erode whatever differences existed between the groups in their premorbid development or their acute psychotic stages. Broen (1968) has written an excellent source book for the reader who would be interested in pursuing the effects of chronicity in schizophrenia at great length. The reason for raising the point here is to emphasize that the trends of evidence from which we will attempt to seek verification for our developmental theory (the goal in the next chapter) may not be in keeping with data gathered exclusively from chronic schizophrenic patients.

REFERENCES

Baum, M. Extinction of avoidance responding through response prevention (flooding). *Psychological Bulletin,* 1970, **74**, 276-284.

Black, J. D. The interpretation of MMPI profiles of college women. Ph.D. dissertation, University of Minnesota, 1953. *(Dissertation Abstracts*, 1953, **13**, 870-871.)

Block, J., and Bailey, D. Q-sort item analysis of a number of MMPI scales. Officer Education Research Laboratory, Technical Memorandum, OERL-TM-55-7, May, 1955.

Broen, W. E., Jr. *Schizophrenia: research and theory.* New York: Academic Press, 1968.

Buss, A. H., and Buss, E. H. *Theories of schizophrenia.* New York: Atherton Press, 1969.

Cancro, R., and Sugarman, A. A. Classification and outcome in process-reactive schizophrenia. *Comprehensive Psychiatry,* 1968, **9**, 227-232.

Cicchetti, D.V., and Ornston, P.S. Reported family dynamics and psychopathology: II. The reactions of mental patients to a disturbed family in psychotherapy. *Journal of Abnormal Psychology,* 1968, **73**, 156-161.

Dahlstrom, W. G., and Welsh, G. S. *An MMPI handbook: A guide to use in clinical practice and research.* Minneapolis: University of Minnesota Press, 1960.

Egeth, H. Selective attention. *Psychological Bulletin,* 1967, **67**, 41-57.

Fowler, R. D., Jr. and Coyle, F. A., Jr. MMPI characteristics of freshmen entering college. *The Psychological Record,* 1969, **19**, 263-271.

Garmezy, N., and Rodnick, E. H. Premorbid adjustment and performance in schizophrenia: Implications for interpreting heterogeneity in schizophrenia. *Journal of Nervous and Mental Disease,* 1959, **129**, 450-466.

Gough, H. E., McKee, M. G., and Yandell, R. J. Adjective check list analyses of a number of selected psychometric and assessment variables. Officer Education Research Laboratory, Technical Memorandum, OERL-TM-55-10, May, 1955.

Grace, N. A developmental comparison of word usage with structural aspects of perception and social adjustment. Unpublished doctoral dissertation, Duke University, Durham, North Carolina, 1956.

Hathaway, S. R., and McKinley, J. C. *The Minnesota Multiphasic Personality Inventory manual.* (Rev. Ed.) New York: Psychological Corporation, 1951.

Hathaway, S. R., and Meehl, P. E. Adjective check list correlates of MMPI scores. Cited in W. G. Dahlstrom and G. S. Welsh, *An MMPI handbook: A guide to use in clinical practice and research.* Minneapolis: University of Minnesota Press, 1960.

Heilbrun, A. B. Cognitive sensitivity to aversive maternal stimulation in late-adolescent males. *Journal of Consulting and Clinical Psychology,* 1968, **32**, 326-332.

Heilbrun, A. B. Style of adaptation to perceived aversive maternal stimulation and selective attention to evaluative cues. *Journal of Abnormal Psychology,* 1971, **77**, 340-344.

Herron, W. G. The process-reactive classification of schizophrenia. *Psychological Bulletin,* 1962, **59**, 329-343.

Higgins, J. The concept of process-reactive schizophrenia: Criteria and related research. *Journal of Nervous and Mental Disease,* 1964, **138**, 9-25.

Higgins, J. Process-reactive schizophrenia. *Journal of Nervous and Mental Disease,* 1969, **149**, 450-472.

Higgins, J., and Peterson, J. C. Concept of process-reactive schizophrenia: A critique. *Psychological Bulletin,* 1966, **66**, 201-206.

Hovey, H. B. MMPI profiles and personality characteristics. *Journal of Consulting Psychology,* 1953, **17**, 142-146.

Hurwitz, I. A. A developmental study of the relationships between motor activity and perceptual processes as measured by the Rorschach test. Unpublished doctoral dissertation, Clark University, 1954.

Kantor, R. E., and Herron, W. G. *Reactive and process schizophrenia.* Palo Alto, Calif.: Science and Behavior Books, 1966.

Kantor, R., Wallner, J., and Winder, C. Process and reactive schizophrenia. *Journal of Consulting Psychology,* 1953, **17**, 157-162.

Kretschmer, E. *Physique and character.* New York: Harcourt Brace, 1925.

Lane, J. Social effectiveness and developmental level. *Journal of Personality,* 1955, **23**, 274-284.

Levine, D. Rorschach genetic level and mental disturbance. *Journal of Projective Techniques,* 1959, **23**, 436-439.

Lewinsohn, P. M. Does the Phillips Scale of Premorbid Adjustment predict improvement of initial status? *Proceedings of the 75th Annual Convention of the American Psychological Association,* 1967, **2**, 225-226.

Mauz, F. *Die prognostick der endogenen psychosen.* Leipzig: Georg Thieme, 1930.

Meadow, A., and Funkenstein, D. H. The relationship of abstract thinking to the autonomic nervous system in schizophrenia. In P. H. Hoch and J. Zubin (Eds.), *Relation of psychological tests to psychiatry.* New York: Grune and Stratton, 1952. Pp. 131-144.

Nuttall, R. L., and Solomon, L. F. Prognosis in schizophrenia: The role of premorbid, social class, and demographic factors. Unpublished manuscript, Boston College, Boston, no date. (Cited in Higgins, J., Process-reactive schizophrenia. *Journal of Nervous and Mental Disease,* 1969, **149**, 450-472.)

Olsen, S. P. Response interference as a function of social evaluation and maternal child-rearing experience. Unpublished doctoral dissertation, University of Iowa, 1965.

Phillips, L. Case history data and prognosis in schizophrenia. *Journal of Nervous and Mental Disease,* 1953, **117**, 515-525.

Phillips, L., and Zigler, E. Social competence: The action-thought parameter and vicariousness in normal and pathological behaviors. *Journal of Abnormal and Social Psychology,* 1961, **63**, 137-146.

Schooler, C., and Feldman, S. E. *Experimental studies of schizophrenia.* Goleta, Calif.: Psychonomic Press, 1967.

Smith, L., and Phillips, L. Social effectiveness and developmental level in adolescence. *Journal of Personality,* 1959, **27**, 239-249.

Wittman, P. A scale for measuring prognosis in schizophrenic patients. *Elgin State Hospital Paper,* 1941, **4**, 20-23. (Cited in Herron, W. G. The process-reactive classification in schizophrenia. *Psychological Bulletin,* 1962, **59**, 329-343.)

Zigler, E., and Phillips, L. Social effectiveness and symptomatic behaviors. *Journal of Abnormal and Social Psychology,* 1960, **61**, 231-238.

Zigler, E., and Phillips, L. Social competence and the process-reactive distinction in psychopathology. *Journal of Abnormal and Social Psychology,* 1962, **65**, 215-222.

CHAPTER 8

The Research (Phase III): Validation of the Adaptive-Style Theory of Schizophrenic Development

There are two cardinal rules to observe in clinical theory construction if the product of one's labor is to create a ripple of excitement and even claim some degree of permanence. The first is to make the theory broad enough and flexible enough to offer something for everybody. The second is to place sufficient buffers between the postulates of the theory and research data as to make them resistent, if not immune, to critical test. Behavioral constructs that are vaguely defined or that by their very nature introduce open-ended systems of thought are especially useful as protective buffers. Examples of such constructs which are prominent in clinical parlance include "minimal brain dysfunction," "unconscious," "reaction formation," and "spontaneous remission."

The theory of schizophrenic development presented in the previous chapter, perhaps because it had its origins in research rather than clinical observation, did not offer any serious obstacles as far as scientific verification was concerned. However, the approach required to test the theory was a unique one, as far as we know, introduced to meet the special problems of conducting experimental developmental research into the origins of a low incidence behavioral outcome. It is necessary that the strategy of research which guided the testing of the adaptive-style theory be made clear to the reader at this juncture, since comprehension of the strategy is requisite to understanding the relevance of the evidence.

The theory, in brief, proposes that children exposed to a sustained aversive-maternal-control experience try to protect themselves by one of two primary coping styles. The adoption of a closed style produces schizophreniform behaviors characteristic of the process schizophrenic, whereas the adoption of an open style brings about behaviors of formal similarity to reactive schizophrenics. Since longitudinal research strategies were not open to us, for reasons discussed earlier in the book, a strategy of research capitalizing on cross-sectional data acquisition was necessary. A procedure was followed within which two bands of evidence became critical to establishing the validity of the adaptive-style theory.

The first band of evidence included the behavioral differences between process and reactive schizophrenics for which supporting research evidence garnered by other investigators was available. The second band of evidence was derived from the experiments conducted in our own laboratory using nonclinical samples of late-adolescent males for whom we could infer both the quality of maternal child-rearing experience, and (if relevant) the nature of adaptive style. It was always possible to derive directional predictions for our studies from the concordance between first-band evidence and postulates of the adaptive-style theory. The degree to which the results of the second-band studies, in turn, confirmed directional predictions provides the verification of theory. This method whereby we sought parallel differences between process and reactive schizophrenics and closed-style and open-style adolescents allows us to answer this basic question; do closed-style males display process schizophreniform behaviors and open-style males manifest reactive schizophreniform behaviors? If these parallels can be demonstrated, we would have succeeded in linking explicit family developmental experiences to behavior having the formal characteristics of reactive or process schizophrenia.

The format which will be followed for the remainder of this chapter will be to identify some discrete aspect of the theory which will be the target for verification, to review the process versus reactive schizophrenic research literature relevant to this behavior, and then to describe the closed-style versus open-style adolescent research which is to serve as a test of the theory.

CLARITY OF MATERNAL COMMUNICATION

The supposition that two distinct patterns of coping with the aversive features of maternal high control and low nurturance may occur raises the question of why, given the same experience, one child adopts one pattern and another child adopts the other? The theory postulates that the adaptive style will be determined largely by the clearness of the mother's communication to the child. If her aversive-control communications are unmistakably clear, the child will protect himself by erecting psychological or physical distance barriers between himself and the aversive stimulus (closed style). If the mother's communication is subtle, blurred, indirect, or inconsistent, the child must maintain an orientation toward her to seek clarification of meaning. This search for meaning blends into an approach orientation toward the mother that involves not only vigilance to cues but concerted attempts to influence their aversive quality (open style).

Related Process-Reactive Schizophrenia Research

Within the voluminous process-reactive schizophrenia literature, the number of studies concerned with maternal communication styles is extremely limited. In fact, only one study (to be discussed at the end of this section) could be found which bore directly upon the proposition that mothers of process schizophrenics are direct in their communication, whereas the mothers of reactives are more subtle and devious in their style of communicating. However, we believe there are other categories of evidence which are reasonably interpreted as consistent with the postulate although hardly direct tests of it.

One case in point is the research which was generated by the hypothesis that a reversal in authority roles occurred in the families of process and reactive schizophrenics (Rodnick and Garmezy, 1957). Process families were thought to include a mother who assumed the dominant parental role with the father being more easy-going and submissive; reactive families tended toward the reverse pattern according to this authority-reversal hypothesis. The evidence in regard to the hypothesis represents a study in equivocation.

When the sons' observations of parental authority patterns have been used, their perceptions have lent full support to the Rodnick-Garmezy proposal in one study (Stockner and Garmezy, 1957). Partial support for fathers only was reported by Johnson and Meadow (1966) who found that reactive schizophrenics saw their fathers as aggressive and overtly rejecting, whereas the fathers of process schizophrenics were described as more passive and covert in their behavior. Jackson (1970) again found partial support in that reactives rated their fathers as more hard and cruel and as more leading, strong, and dominant than their mothers; however, no differences in parent perception were obtained for process schizophrenics. A host of studies failed to find any support for the hypothesized differential parent patterns (Becker and Siefkes, 1969; Bradford, 1966; Cicchetti, 1967; Craig, 1966; Farina and Holzberg, 1967; Fontana, Klein, and Cicchetti, 1967; Klein, Cicchetti, and Spohn, 1967; McKinley, 1964), leaving the hypothesis in serious doubt when tested through filial perception.

Experimental approaches to testing the hypothesized reversal in dominance roles have fared somewhat better in providing positive support. Magaro (1967), adopting the premise that children will be most sensitized to and disrupted by cues associated with the dominant parent, found that process schizophrenics were maximally impaired in their discrimination on a visually presented mother-scolding scene. Reactives were poorer discriminators on a father-scolding scene. The same results were reported by Farina and Dunham (1963). Effects upon subsequent cognitive performance (i.e., digit symbol) of exposure to tape recordings of a simulated mother or father censuring or praising a child were investigated by Goodman (1964). He found that process schizophrenics were maximally impaired following exposure to maternal censure cues and reactive schizophrenics evidenced this effect after hearing the paternal censure cues. Process schizophrenics had differentially higher thresholds for words spoken by a female (mother-surrogate) voice than for words spoken in a male (father-surrogate) voice (Donovan and Webb, 1965). Reactives did not demonstrate differential thresholds. Finally, three studies by Lefcourt and his associates identified sex-linked examiner effects upon the behavior of schizophrenics. Lefcourt and Steffy (1966) found that process schizophrenics rejected more Holtzman Inkblot cards when they were administered by a female examiner than when a male examiner was used. In a similar vein, eye contact with the examiner was more frequently avoided by process schizophrenics when the examiner was female rather than male (Lefcourt, Rotenberg, Buckspan, and Steffy, 1967). Reactive schizophrenics demonstrated more rapid finger tapping when a male examiner was used in a study reported by Lefcourt, Steffy, Buckspan, and Rotenberg (1968). The results of these three studies in which sex of the examiner was varied are relevant here only insofar as sensitivity to sex-gender cues is interpreted in the context of the additional differences in social orientation between process (withdrawing) and reactive (more outgoing) schizophrenics. Given exposure to an adult female, process schizophrenics tended to withdraw more both socially and perceptually. Reactives, in turn, responded positively in their performance to the presence of a male examiner.

Experimental evidence failing to confirm the authority-reversal hypothesis is not without representation. Two studies employing taped presentations of the parent dominance-submission patterns failed to find differences in the influence of these cues upon perceptual-motor performance (Geisinger, 1966) or recall (Cicchetti, 1967) of process and reactive schizophrenics. Several investigations that proceeded methodologically by using pictorial cues depicting maternal or paternal figures have failed to produce differential response. Nathanson (1967) found no process-reactive differences in ratings of mother and father pictures involving rejection, scolding, or feeding of the child. Discrimination performance of these schizophrenic groups on mother and father scenes depicting scolding did not differ in a study reported by Cicchetti, Klein, Fontana, and Spohn (1967). Similarly, exposure to a "severe censure" scene of a mother standing over a boy did not elicit any subsequent process-reactive differences on cognitive tasks for Digiondomenico (1966). I. Z. Goodman (1968) used photographs of maternal and paternal figures in an attempt to influence preferences for various items. Again, process and reactive schizophrenics performed similarly.

Involvement of live parent surrogates in the experimental procedures used to test the authority-reversal hypothesis have also been associated with negative results. Klein, Cicchetti, and Spohn (1967) found no sex-linked experimenter differences in the response of process and reactive schizophrenics. A "mother-figure" experimenter, employed by Sterne (1967), presented praise and censure reinforcement on a paired-associate learning task without obtaining distinct performances from the process and reactive subjects. The same absence of differences resulted from having male and female "authority figures" administer censure during conceptual tasks (DiMauro, 1965). The influence of parent surrogates on autokinesis did not distinguish process and reactive schizophrenics according to a report by Fontana, Klein, and Cicchetti (1967).

Introduction of the actual parents of the schizophrenic into the experimental situation has brought about the clearest support of the Rodnick-Garmezy hypothesis. Stoller (1966), using only mothers, required schizophrenic subjects to perform on a visual discrimination task in the presence of this parent. The mother was required to predict the correctness of each response within the son's range of hearing. Process schizophrenics were more likely than reactives to respond erroneously following the mother's prediction of an error. Direct observation of family interaction led both Farina (1960) and Lerner (1967) to conclude that the families of process schizophrenics were characterized by maternal dominance with the father being the dominant parent in the families of reactives. The "disciplinary fantasies" of the parents of schizophrenics studied by Baxter, Williams, and Zerof (1965) indicated that the fathers of reactives were more likely to respond to crisis situations with verbal censure than were the mothers, whereas the opposite was true of the parents of process schizophrenics.

Tape recordings of family interaction failed to yield any differences in dominance patterns among parents of process and reactive schizophrenics in an investigation by Farina and Holzberg (1968). "Quite limited support" for the pattern opposite to the hypothesis was reported by Becker and Siefkes (1969); there was a suggestion of paternal dominance in process families and maternal dominance in reactive families.

The question remains as to what the equivocal nature of the evidence regarding parent dominance-pattern differences in the families of poor and good premorbid schizophrenics has to do with the theoretical proposal regarding communication under consideration. Let us assume, for the sake of argument, that rather than the Rodnick-Garmezy hypothesized reversal in dominance roles, the true state of affairs was our proposal that the mothers of process *and* reactive schizophrenics are controlling but differ in the directness and subtlety of their influence. This being so, what would we expect to find if dominance-submission patterns among parents were studied by the techniques already described? On the one hand, the devious subtle control mechanisms of the reactive mother are not likely to be recognized and labelled by the son, the husband, or the experimenter as manifestations of dominance. Therefore, she would probably be identified, often inappropriately, as assuming a submissive role in her relationship to her husband. Misrepresentation is also likely to stem from an assumption that the mother's dominance-submission pattern with the father is necessarily the same as she would show in relating to her son. Submission to the father does not preclude subtle control mechanisms directed toward her child.

The process mother, on the other hand, will be easily and appropriately identified as a controlling parent. These conditions surrounding observation of control mechanisms in reactive and process mothers would lead us to expect positive results in some studies bearing upon the authority-reversal hypothesis. However, if the dominance attributes of fathers are not systematically related to process-reactive status in the son, this fact would tend to wash out positive results supporting the Rodnick-Garmezy hypothesis by introducing a random source of sampling error. We would then expect exactly what we found—a sizeable number of studies confirming the hypothesis and a large number disconfirming it.

Fortunately, it is not necessary to depend entirely on the logical assertion that our hypothesis regarding direct and subtle maternal control, if a true state of affairs, would make the equivocal status of the dominance-reversal hypothesis more understandable. There are two corollaries to our interpretation for which clearer evidence does exist. If process mothers are openly dominant but the fathers vary unsystematically over a range of dominance, the coupling of manifestly dominant parents would be a common occurrence for process schizophrenics. The reactive mothers, whose subtler tactics of influence are less likely to be construed as dominance, would less frequently present a dominance match for their husbands. The lack of authority differential between openly dominant parents would lead us to expect that interactions would be more characterized by parental conflict in the family of the process schizophrenic than would be true of the reactive schizophrenic's family. It also would follow that the decision-making role regarding the child would be more equally shared by the two parents in the process family than in the reactive family.

Four investigations of parent interaction patterns have examined the degree of conflict represented in the families of process and reactive schizophrenics. Each has used direct observational techniques as the medium for data acquisition. Without exception, these four studies (Farina, 1960; Farina and Dunham, 1963; Farina and Holzberg, 1968; Lerner, 1967) reported higher conflict between the parents of process schizophrenics than between the parents of reactives.

Decision-making responsibility was investigated by Rodnick and Garmezy (1957) by asking schizophrenics to recall which parents tended to make the day-to-day decisions and the major decisions affecting the child. On a day-to-day basis, the most-responsible parent percentage figures look very much as one would expect if dominance-submission reversal obtained in the families of process and reactive schizophrenics. The mother made these decisions in 28% of the reactive families and the father in 71%; in the process families the figures were reversed, showing the mother responsible in 90% and the father in 10% of the families. However, when asked about the responsibility for major decisions, the results were more in keeping with our point of view. In reactive families, mothers were never (0%) nominated as responsible for major decisions and the father was designated as such by 100% of the schizophrenics. Responsibility for major decisions within the process families was attributed equally often (50%) to mothers and to fathers. Fontana, Klein, and Cicchetti (1967) asked schizophrenics a somewhat different question; which parent made the decisions which affected them the most? Their findings look very much like the day-to-day decision-making results reported by Rodnick and Garmezy. They report that about 83% of the process schizophrenics designated their mothers (as opposed to their fathers or to both) as the critical parent. Some 42% of the reactive schizophrenics indicated that their mothers were primarily or jointly responsible for decisions having the greatest effect on them. All in all, the conflict and decision-making data are consonant with a shared dominance interpretation for parents of process schizophrenics and paternal dominance within the families of reactive schizophrenics, consistent with our expectations.

There are yet other soft signs within the process-reactive research literature that a difference exists in clarity of communicated control between mothers. For example, among the earlier data reported by Rodnick and Garmezy (1957) was a list of maternal attributes applied to their mothers by process and reactive sons. Among the attributes epitomizing the process mother (relative to the father) were "didn't let do things on own," "less likely to be satisfied," and "tried to avoid more." These suggest the process of clear control, rejection, and withdrawal which we have proposed as the dynamics of closed-style adaptation. Among the more characteristic attributes of the mothers of reactives were "turned to talk about problems" and "made you feel guilty for misbehavior" which suggest an intrusiveness and penchant for guilt induction which we will come to identify as major mechanisms of subtle control over the child in open-style adapters.

Farina and Holzberg (1967) identified an interesting distinction between the mothers of process and reactive schizophrenics in the relationship between dominance measured by questionnaire and dominance observed on a structured situational test. Process mothers presented a positive relationship (r = .53) between expressed attitude and actual behavior, whereas the attitudes and behaviors of reactive mothers were inversely related (r = –.45). Farina and Holzberg attributed the difference to greater social alertness of the reactive parents which allowed them to discern the reprehensible nature of domineering attitudes on the child-rearing attitude scale. They further reasoned that the behaviors displayed by the reactive mothers in direct interaction with their spouses was less under their control so that they were less able to suppress domineering behaviors. An alternative to this social desirability interpretation would look to the more blatant control behaviors of the process mothers as the source of consistency between the two modes of measurement and the more subtle and devious (and difficult to measure) forms of control of the reactive mothers as a contributor to the inconsistency from questionnaire to behavioral observation.

Jackson (1970) presented taped parent-surrogate interactions with schizophrenics and tested for influence upon size discrimination responses. The procedure involved the presentation of equal-size angles to the subject with the opportunity to hear a male and female discuss their opinions as to which was the larger. Dominant and submissive roles were varied between the parent surrogates. After recording the choice made by the male and (the opposite) choice made by the female, the schizophrenic was asked to make his own choice. Influence was inferred from the tendency to agree with one person or the other on the tape. The results showed that process schizophrenics were most influenced by sexual gender cues; no matter which person on the tape was cast in the dominant role, they patterned their choices more after the mother surrogate. In contrast, reactive schizophrenics responded primarily to dominance cues. Whichever parent surrogate was dominant served as the prime influence on their behavior. These findings tie into the clarity of communicated control proposal if two things are kept in mind. The more the mother's control directives are clearly communicated and consistently imposed upon the child, the more the mother herself is likely to serve as the organizing cue in mediating influence. If the mother is less clear and more indirect in her control directives, so that the child must search the communication for meaning, the message becomes the focus of attention and not the communicator. In the former case, "motherness" should be the sufficient discriminative stimulus to elicit characteristic filial behaviors (including submissiveness) for the closed-style child or process schizophrenic. In the latter case, the dominance communication would be the focal stimulus in mediating influence for open-style or reactive offspring.

For those less inclined to engage in inferential reasoning or who might choose to interpret the evidence differently, the process-reactive studies cited thus far in this section will not have developed a persuasive picture of maternal communication styles. Obviously, we feel that differential communication clarity levels represent a viable possibility in the developmental histories of good and poor premorbid schizophrenics and, believing this, look at the evidence with preconceptual bias. The issue is best judged by evidence gathered directly from the study of maternal communication styles in process and reactive families. Mishler and Waxler (1968) offer us this opportunity.

The Mishler-Waxler investigation concerned itself with the patterns of communication within families of process and reactive schizophrenics. Live family discussions were tape recorded and subsequently judged for a variety of speech attributes. Two of their major findings are pertinent to our current interest. One of these has to do with the expressive quality of the speech within the families of schizophrenics. (The investigators start from the dictionary meaning of an expressive act as "vividly representing the meaning or feeling to be conveyed.") Mishler and Waxler summarize their evidence on family expressiveness in this way:

> Poor premorbid families . . . show high rates of interpersonal expressive behavior. . . . We have suggested that this reflects a mode or style of behavior oriented to the immediate situation since this rate indicates a disproportionately high allocation of feelings directly expressed toward other persons . . . . good premorbids, who were least expressive but most negative in those feelings expressed, show high rates of indirect interpersonal behavior in the context of lower rates of direct interpersonal behavior; feelings are not expressed toward each other but reappear indirectly in abstract personal references (p. 104-105).

Again, the communication findings included differences in the disruption rates within family discussions with good premorbid families allowing less disruption than the poor premorbid families. Mishler and Waxler conclude:

> . . . the good premorbid families of sons have consistently low rates of speech disruption. . . . The unbroken quality of the good family's speech reflects a high degree of predictability in the sequence of events; there is little uncertainty or ambiguity and also little opportunity for a family member to break out of the rigid sequence and to change the order of events. This pattern in good families is, again, largely reflected in the parents' behavior, particularly the mothers'. The extent to which good families follow a rigid interaction pattern . . . suggests that a strong and consistent effort is being made, especially by the parents, to avoid uncertainty. We may speculate that the parents . . . feel the necessity of avoiding any situation in which uncontrollable events might occur, or unacceptable feelings might be expressed, or forbidden topics might be broached, particularly in relation to the patient. Thus we are suggesting that this ritualistic style of speech serves a defensive function for the good premorbid families. . . (p. 189).

These findings and their interpretation by Mishler and Waxler, taken together, convey a distinction in clarity of communicated meaning to which the reactive schizophrenic is exposed within his family relative to the process schizophrenic. The reactive's parents are the most deficient in conveying meaning or feeling to the child, whereas process parents are direct in their expression of feeling. Again, reactive parents, especially mothers, were viewed as defensively avoiding the expression of unacceptable feelings or broaching forbidden topics; this defensive communication style was not found in process families. Our thesis that the communicated meanings of process mothers will be clearly interpretable by the child while those of reactive mothers will be more subtle or devious receives support from the one study geared to test it directly.

Adaptive-Style Theory Validation Study

The adaptive-style theory, which proposes a congruence between premorbid process and reactive schizophrenic experiences and the experiences of children learning closed and open styles of adapting to aversive maternal control, stipulates that closed-style offspring have been confronted with clearer communicated meaning from their mothers and open-style offspring have been exposed to more diffuse communication. Evidence relevant to this postulate was gathered in an investigation by Heilbrun (1972a). His paper actually incorporated three independent bodies of data which were collected or reanalyzed to test the level of communication hypothesis as it specifically pertains to conveyed control and rejection.

The initial set of data which was considered comes from a dissertation study by McKinley (1964), cited earlier as presenting evidence inimical to the parent-authority-reversal hypothesis. McKinley collected his data from three groups of hospitalized males. Two schizophrenic samples, defined as process and reactive by the Phillips Prognostic Rating Scale, and a sample of patients from medical and surgical services were given the PARI under the same instructional set to describe their mothers as we have used with our normal subjects. The three samples were closely matched for age, the means ranging from 32.4 to 33.1 years.

McKinley was interested in determining whether schizophrenic sons considered their mothers more controlling than normal sons and whether differences in this regard between process and reactive categories could be identified. His results, while confirming the more general difference in attributed control expected for schizophrenics, failed to show any distinction between process and reactive sons on the 16 control scales using conventional statistical standards of significance. A reevaluation of the process-reactive control scale scores on the PARI was conducted for purposes of detecting trends in the McKinley findings without concern in this case for statistical safeguards. Two criteria were employed in identifying the three control scales most exemplary of maternal control experienced by process schizophrenics and the three control scales most exemplary for reactive schizophrenics. The first criterion required that there had to be a statistically significant overall difference in scores for a given scale among the three groups—process schizophrenic, reactive schizophrenic, and hospitalized normal. The second criterion specified that the mean difference in scale scores (relative to the appropriate error term) on a given scale for the process schizophrenic group and the normal controls had to be among the three largest and, in turn, had to be larger than the difference between reactives and the normal controls on the same scale. The latter criterion, directionally reversed, was applied to the selection of the three exemplar scales for reactive mother control.

The items comprising the six PARI control scales identified by these criteria are presented in Table 40. Content analysis of these scale items conforms rather strikingly to the expectations generated by the review of process-reactive literature, especially the Mishler and Waxler study. Process mothers were viewed by their schizophrenic sons as directly and openly controlling of their children and also of their husbands (Fostering Dependency and Ascendance of Mother). Reactive mothers were perceived as engaging in control by indirect manipulation–martyrdom and, we would presume, guilt induction (Martyrdom and Inconsiderateness of Husband). As was the case with process mothers, the type of control mechanisms perceived as characteristic of the reactive mother were employed with both the child and the husband. In further contrast, process mothers tended to be perceived as shutting off the child's attempts to communicate feelings, worries, or upset (Avoidance of Communication), whereas reactive mothers were depicted as requiring complete self-disclosure from the son (Intrusiveness).

It is interesting to recall in the context of these findings which suggest different levels of communicated control that Reichard and Tillman (1950) long ago pointed to patterns of maternal control in schizophrenia involving a distinction in clearness of communicated meaning. They speak of the *overtly rejecting* mother who maintains a cold and sadistically critical attitude toward the child and insists that he meets her excessive demands. The second pattern characterizes the *covertly rejecting* mother, equally dominating as the former, but who exerts her influence in a much more subtle fashion. However, their clinical observations placed the major emphasis upon the obvious or subtle character of rejection rather than control cues; to this juncture, our discussion has been directed to control cues only.

The second study reported in the Heilbrun paper followed directly from the reevaluation of McKinley's schizophrenia data. If process schizophrenic sons have experienced their mothers as manifesting more obvious controls and reactive schizophrenic sons view their mothers as more devious in exerting influence, the adaptive-style theory of schizophrenic development would require the demonstration of the same control patterns when closed-style and open-style HC-LN males are compared.

Subjects for the second study were Emory undergraduates who volunteered their research participation. These 148 males averaged 18.9 years of age. Questionnaire responses were obtained under the usual small-group testing procedures. Assignment to adaptive-style subgroupings was based upon a procedure described in detail within the preceding chapter in which the Stroop Color-Naming Task is performed in combination with the input of aversive maternal cues. One alteration in the experimental procedure was incorporated in this study as well as all other adaptive-style experiments to be reported in this chapter. Rather than a single administration of the Stroop in combination with

Table 40. PARI Scales Best Distinguishing Maternal Control as Perceived by Process and Reactive Schizophrenics

Most Characteristic of Process Mothers

Scale 2 (Fostering Dependency)

1. A good mother should shelter her child from life's little difficulties.
2. A mother should do her best to avoid any disappointment for her child.
3. A child should be protected from jobs which might be too tiring or hard for him.
4. Parents should know better than to allow their children to be exposed to difficult situations.
5. Children should be kept away from all hard jobs which might be discouraging.

Scale 16 (Avoidance of Communication)

1. If you let children talk about their troubles, they end up complaining even more.
2. Parents who start a child talking about his worries don't realize that sometimes it's better to just leave well enough alone.
3. Children pester you with all their little upsets if you aren't careful from the first.
4. If a child has upset feelings, it is best to leave him alone and not make it look serious.
5. The trouble with giving attention to children's problems is they usually just make up a lot of stories to keep you interested.

Scale 19 (Ascendance of Mother)

1. If a mother doesn't go ahead and make rules for the home, the children and husband will get into trouble they don't need to.
2. Children and husbands do better when the mother is strong enough to settle most of the problems.
3. A mother has to do the planning because she is the one who knows what is going on in the home.
4. The whole family does fine if the mother puts her shoulders to the wheel and takes charge of things.
5. A married woman knows that she will have to take the lead in family matters.

Most Characteristic of Reactive Mothers

Scale 5 (Martyrdom)

1. Children should realize how much parents parents have to give up for them.
2. A mother must expect to give up her own happiness for that of her child.
3. Few women get the gratitude they deserve for all they have done for their children.
4. Children should be more considerate of their mothers since their mothers suffer so much for them.
5. Mothers sacrifice almost all their own fun for their children.

Scale 17 (Inconsiderateness of Husband)

1. Mothers could do their jobs better with the children if fathers were more kind.
2. Husbands could do their part if they were less selfish.
3. When a mother doesn't do a good job with the children it's probably because the father doesn't do his part around the house.
4. If mothers could get their wishes, they would most often ask that the husband be more understanding.
5. Few men realize that a mother needs some fun in life too.

Scale 20 (Intrusiveness)

1. A mother should make it her business to know everything her children are thinking.
2. A child should never keep a secret from his parents.
3. An alert parent should try to learn all of her child's thoughts.
4. A mother has the right to know everything going on in her child's life because her child is part of her.
5. It is a mother's duty to make sure she knows her child's innermost thoughts.

the tape, two alternate forms of the Stroop were employed. The first Stroop was administered without distracting cues to establish individual baselines of performance. Then the alternate form was given in conjunction with the distractor tape. Differences in accuracy of performance on the two Stroop tasks were obtained, each subject serving as his own control for cognitive effectiveness. The distribution of difference scores, cut at or near the median value, formed the basis for defining disrupted (open-style) or nondisrupted (closed-style) subgroupings within the aversive-maternal-control group. The difference scores for the general reference group, comprised of subjects from the three remaining control-nurturance child-rearing quadrants, was similarly split into disrupted and nondisrupted components for control purposes.

The hypothesis of parallel differences between open-style and closed-style aversive-control adolescent males and reactive and process schizophrenics was put to test by incorporating the six PARI control scales which best differentiated the two schizophrenic groups into an obvious versus subtle control measure. Scores were based upon the difference between the sum of the scores on obvious Scales 2, 16, and 19 and the sum of the scores on subtle Scales 5, 17, and 20. Obvious-subtle control scores for the entire sample were transformed into standard scores so that the average score was set at 50 with a standard deviation of 10. Higher scores indicate more obvious control experienced by the son and greater similarity to process mothers; lower scores point to more subtle experienced control and greater similarity to reactive mothers.

The pattern of means presented in Table 41, when tested by analysis of variance, contained two significant general effects. Subjects who were disrupted on the Stroop attributed more subtle control to their mothers than nondisrupted subjects, independent of child-rearing pattern ($p < .05$). More importantly though, there was a significant interaction ($p < .05$) among these group averages which required that we look further to determine what the results mean. It is clear by inspection of Table 41 that the interaction was produced by the widely varying levels of clarity in communicated control (51.44 versus 43.88)

Table 41. Obvious-Subtle Quality of Maternal Control for Late-Adolescent Males Varying in Maternal Child-Rearing Experience and Style of Adaptation

Perceived Maternal Child-Rearing Pattern			
High Control-Low Nurturance		Reference Group	
Closed Adaptive Style ($N = 27$) Mean	Open Adaptive Style ($N = 24$) Mean	Nondisrupted Controls ($N = 46$) Mean	Disrupted Controls ($N = 53$) Mean
51.44	43.88	50.80	51.03

NOTE: The lower the score, the more subtle the control attributed to the mother.

experienced by the closed and open adaptive-style males in contrast to the absence of such differences between the reference subgroupings which presented essentially identical means (50.80 versus 51.03). The difference between the aversive-maternal-control subgroups was highly reliable ($p < .01$) and directionally in keeping with our theory. Comparison of each style group with its particular reference group revealed that only the open-style males (43.88) differed ($p < .01$) from its own control (51.03).

In summary, this second set of data in the Heilbrun report was consistent with the adaptive-style theory of schizophrenic development. Late-adolescent males, who are proposed to be the developmental counterparts of the process schizophrenic, describe their mother's control pattern as more obvious and direct in keeping with the process schizophrenics in the first study. Those adolescents proposed to be developmentally aligned with reactive schizophrenics viewed their mothers' control patterns as especially subtle and indirect, the perceived pattern of control elicited from reactive schizophrenics.

The third body of data collected by Heilbrun allowed for an independent test of the proposition that males who have learned different styles of adapting to the mother as an aversive stimulus would have experienced their mothers as differing in distinctiveness of control cues. The 82 Emory male volunteers who served as subjects in this study had an average age of 18.7 years; none had participated in the previous investigation. These adolescents were separated into aversive-maternal-control and general reference child-rearing experience groups by the procedures described for the second study. Further separation into open-style and closed-style subgroupings and their reference disrupted and nondisrupted controls also proceeded in the same way as before.

The experienced communication style of the mother was analyzed in this study by constructing a standard set of six situations involving maternal disapproval and a high probability that the mother would attempt to influence her son's behavior. These six mother-son situations, described in the terms actually presented to the subjects, were as follows:

1. You have been given certain jobs to do around the house and yard which are presented as your responsibilities. Your mother has found out that you have not been doing this work despite having had the time to do so.

2. Your grades in school have fallen noticeably and your mother, who values high grades, is unhappy about the change.

3. Specific deadlines have been laid down for you at home by your mother regarding the time you must be in at night. All your friends have greater freedom in this regard than you, and you have told your mother that you are going to stay out later than the deadline as a regular thing.

4. Your mother has learned that some of your close male friends have gotten into trouble with girls, one of whom has become pregnant. She is worried about your involvement.

5. You have remained undecided about your summer plans for several weeks and your mother is becoming uneasy as the summer approaches.

6. You wish to keep your hair cut longer and to dress in keeping with current "mod" styles. Your mother does not approve of your appearance.

Instructions to the subjects requested them to write down the dialogue which would ensue between their mothers and themselves given the particular situation. No assumption was made that the son would reproduce an exact replica of the content of the mother's verbalizations; it was assumed that he would be able to approximate what he perceived to be his mother's *style* of verbal communication in situations involving her attempts to influence his behavior.

Ten Ph.D. clinical psychologists acted as judges, rating the dialogues along two dimensions. They rated the mother's statements in each situation along six-point scales for how clearly she communicated her control of the son and how clearly rejection of the son was communicated. Control rating scores, summed over the six dialogues, were converted into standard scores with the group mean set at 50 and a standard deviation of 10. Higher scores indicate greater rated distinctiveness of control in the mothers' speech. The same procedure was followed for the rejection rating scores.

Before considering the results of this study (Table 42) in terms of the adaptive-style theory, it might be helpful to consider some evidence bearing upon the usefulness of the communication methodology employed. Certainly the procedure is far less elaborate than those encountered in live family communication studies such as the Mishler and Waxler investigation. Can such a simple research procedure elicit meaningful data? One basis for inferring the usefulness of the communication procedure resides in the relationships which

Table 42. Distinctiveness of Control and Rejection Cues in Maternal Speech Produced by Sons Varying in Maternal Child-Rearing Experience and Style of Adaptation

	Perceived Maternal Child-Rearing Patterns			
	High Control-Low Nurturance		Reference Group	
Rated Variable	Closed Adaptive Style ($N = 13$)	Open Adaptive Style ($N = 13$)	Nondisrupted Controls ($N = 23$)	Disrupted Controls ($N = 33$)
Mean distinctiveness of control cues	55.31	53.23	47.96	49.45
Mean distinctiveness of rejection cues	54.00	54.62	49.48	49.12

NOTE: The higher the score, the more distinct the cues.

exist between the obtained rating scores and the child-rearing questionnaire scores from which the maternal experience categories were derived. The latter questionnaires have long since passed the test of scientific pragmatism when used as we have used them. Referring to Table 42, it seems apparent that the HC-LN males, taken as a whole, depicted their mothers as more distinctively controlling and rejecting in their verbal behavior than the reference group as a whole; statistical analysis verified this conclusion by identifying significant ($p < .05$) main effects of child-rearing group in the analyses of variance. Thus, HC-LN adolescents, who ascribed greater control to their mothers on the PARI, also introduced more distinctive control cues on the maternal communication task. The same subjects, who rated their mothers as more rejecting on the Parent-Child Interaction Rating Scales, also blended clearer rejection into the speech patterns of the mothers. Accordingly, there is internal consistency between perceptual measures.

The second internal basis for evaluating whether the communication task "works" evolves from the expectation, generated by the data of study No. 2, that differences will exist in the experience of the open-style and closed-style sons in the reinforcement extended by the mother for self-disclosure. We would expect closed-style sons to have been discouraged from revealing their feelings and concerns to the mother, whereas open-style sons would have experienced just the opposite, an intrusive need to know what they are thinking and feeling. This would lead us to anticipate greater verbal participation of the son on the communication task as the open-style adolescent reconstructs the character of mother-son exchange relative to closed-style reconstruction. Although a high percentage of the subjects introduced true mother-son dialogue into their constructions, some presented only a maternal monologue in all six situations. A check of child-rearing groups disclosed that 38.5% of the closed-style males indicated no verbal participation by the son compared to 0% of the open-style males. This difference was significant ($p = .05$) when tested by the nonparametric Fisher Exact Probability Test and in the expected direction. The nondisrupted (8.7%) and disrupted (15.2%) reference subgroups fell between the extremes of the adaptive-style subgroups in the incidence of verbal noninteraction and did not differ statistically ($p = .25$) from each other. Again, we can see internal consistency between response to the PARI and the performance on the communication task.

Returning to the Table 42 data, one significant effect was revealed by analysis of variance. A significant ($p < .05$) simple effect was detected which indicated that closed-style males depicted their mothers as more distinctly controlling in their speech (55.31) than were the mothers of their nondisrupted controls (47.96). Open-style males did not differ significantly from their controls ($p < .25$). These results, while not robust, are consistent with theory.

The clarity with which the mother's verbal behavior implied rejection of the son did not distinguish the two adaptive-style groups either compared to each other or as each compared with its appropriate control group. As we have already pointed out, there was a clearer communicated rejection for the combined adaptive-style groups relative to the total reference group. Accordingly, that part of the theory which proposes that children are predisposed toward patterns of coping with aversive maternal control as a function of the degree to which the mother engages in clear communication was supported in the Heilbrun investigation for control cues but not rejection cues.

The lack of results for communicated rejection should be interpreted cautiously, however. It should be borne in mind that the judges in the communication study were asked to rate only the *distinctiveness* of rejection cues, leaving open the possibility that another dimension along which rejection cues might vary would have gone unnoticed. If you consider the item content for the PARI control scales (Table 40), it seems very likely that the kind of mothers being depicted by the obvious versus subtle control scales would also vary in the delivery of contingent versus noncontingent rejection (or contingent versus noncontingent reinforcement as it is more popularly called in the learning literature). The closed-style mother, direct and obvious in her control directives, would be more likely to tie her rejection of the child to explicit failures or shortcomings. Accordingly, felt rejection for the closed-style adolescent should be contingent upon identifiable responses to the mother's control directives which have been evaluated as inadequate. Contingent rejection would have the effect of establishing a close linkage between maternal control cues and the aversive qualities of rejection, the former arousing an expectation of the latter. To be told to do something would come to elicit as much discomfort as subsequent rejection for having done it badly. The tendency toward contingent rejection, if our reasoning is correct, offers some additional insight into the adoption of avoidance-withdrawal strategies for the closed-style child. Such strategies are required not only as a means of avoiding the distress of censure-rejection cues but as a more extended means of avoiding the distress of control directives.

On the other hand, the subtle control scales reported in Table 40 suggest that the open-style mother would not tie her rejection of the child to specific actions or events. As an example, the communication value of the martyred role more characteristic of the open-style mother is not only such as to elicit guilt and dutiful appreciation on the part of the child (and thus control him) but also subtly to reject him by denying that he is important enough to warrant the demands of the maternal role. But this brand of rejection is noncontingent in that the child is not rebuffed for what he has done but simply for being, a state of affairs over which he has no control. The use of noncontingent rejection by the open-style mother would leave open in the child's eyes the possibility of coupling the mother's feelings for him to what he actually does. Thus, the maintenance of a stimulus-seeking orientation toward the mother would be facilitated. The mother's subtle and devious mode of communication requires that the child search for meaning in her words through which he can identify her expectations of him. These expectations, once identified, hold the key to reinstating himself with the mother should he be able to meet them. Noncontingent rejection, then, further solidifies the open-style child's approach orientation to the mother.

STYLE OF ADAPTATION TO AVERSIVE MATERNAL CONTROL AND SOCIAL ORIENTATION

The adaptive-style theory proposes that the child exposed to the mother as a sustained aversive stimulus will learn to cope with the discomfort by adopting one of two complex patterns of social-perceptual behavior. Theoretical expectations regarding the social orientations that help define these styles are that the closed style will entail social withdrawal and the open style will involve a more positive social orientation in which the elicitation of positive responses from others is of major concern.

Related Process-Reactive Schizophrenic Research

It is often difficult to disentangle research findings bearing upon process-reactive differences in withdrawal from social stimulation from the more general case of withdrawal from environmental stimulation. We will review the positive studies in this section which seem to qualify most clearly as falling in the former category.

One investigation (Armstrong, Johnson, Ries, and Holmes, 1967) reports psychometric evidence indicating the greater social withdrawal of process schizophrenics. They emerged as more introverted on the Maudsley Personality Inventory Scale (Eysenck, 1959) than did reactive schizophrenics. Lefcourt, Rotenberg, Buckspan, and Steffy (1967) observed greater social withdrawal within an experimental setting in the form of reduced eye contact for process schizophrenics when the experimenter was female rather than male which would be consistent with adaptive-style theory.

Investigation of recall among schizophrenics identified a deficit in the process group with items having interpersonal significance (i.e., persons' first names), although no differential recall was found between process and reactive groups with items denoting animals, vegetables, or professions (Katahn, Harris, and Swanson, 1967). The same study also reported a relative paucity of associations for process subjects when requested to name acquaintances. Scarcity of associations when asked to name acquaintances for process schizophrenics had also been reported in an earlier study (Judson and Katahn, 1964).

Farina and Dunham (1963), using a family interaction methodology, observed more activity and assertiveness within the family for reactive sons than for process sons. Hellman and Kates (1961) reported behavioral withdrawal by process schizophrenics in an object sorting task involving mild verbal censure. The withdrawal contributed to their impaired conceptual performance. A similar deficit was not found in reactives and normals. Alvarez (1957) studied shifts in preference for initially neutral photographs which came to be associated with censure in a "right-wrong" experimental task. Poor premorbid schizophrenics demonstrated a decrease in preference for all of these social stimuli relative to goods and normals. Finally, Dunn (1965) assessed the responses of process and reactive schizophrenics to the display of their mosaic products either to groups or to individuals. While reactives preferred to have their handiwork evaluated by groups, process schizophrenics shunned group evaluation. Dunn stressed the avoidance of interpersonal involvement on the part of process schizophrenics, especially as this might involve evaluation.

The process-reactive evidence reviewed here, which points to the greater use of avoidance-withdrawal tactics in the face of social stimulation by process schizophrenics (especially in evaluative situations), was collected after the fact of schizophrenic status was established. Heretofore, the point has been made that if accurate case history information is available in the patient's hospital file, the mere assignment of the schizophrenic to the process end of a scale like the Phillips Premorbid Adjustment Scale by the rater requires that he has been more socially alienated prior to onset of the manifest psychotic symptoms than has been the schizophrenic rated at the reactive end. Reference to the Phillips' items in Appendix F will affirm this observation. Thus, the studies cited in this section simply confirm that the premorbid interpersonal differences in process and reactive schizophrenics continue beyond the onset of the full-blown clinical condition.

Adaptive-Style Theory Validation Study (Interpersonal Distancing)

Two earlier studies in our program of research, both described in Chapter 5, produced a common result which on the surface appeared contrary to what we should have expected based upon maternal child-rearing experience. Barker (1965), using an elaborate methodology in which the male subjects were exposed to censure by an adult female authority figure, established that those who perceived their mothers as exerting aversive control subsequently increased the intensity of a floodlight focused upon them relative to their controls. That is, they made themselves more obvious as a social stimulus despite the fact that they still believed themselves under observation by the adult female. Heilbrun and Tiemeyer (1968) used stories told by their subjects to Thematic Apperception Test cards to assess the responses made to censure-control cues from a variety of adult social agents. They found that aversive-maternal-control males were the *least* likely to introduce social withdrawal into their stories among the four child-rearing groups as a resolution to the noxious situations which were depicted.

The commonality between these two results resides in the relative absence of social withdrawal in the group which is presumed to be the most sensitive to the impact of censure or failure cues. The aversive-control males failed to utilize physical means to place interpersonal distance between themselves and the source of the noxious stimulation. It was suggested in Chapter 5 that this paradox might be resolved by distinguishing psychological withdrawal of an attentional nature from social withdrawal involving physical distancing. If the child has learned to detach himself attentionally while in the immediate presence of the censuring mother, there would be less instigation to withdraw from her social presence.

The evolvement of the adaptive-style theory would require that the reasoning outlined above be considerably refined. Closed-style children would be the ones whose perceptual habits would place them in a position to withdraw psychologically and obviate having to place greater physical distance between themselves and a censuring agent to reduce discomfort. On the other hand, open-style adapters should be especially ill-prepared to defend themselves by attentional means and would have to reduce aversiveness by physical distancing if a withdrawal tactic was utilized. However, our theory would lead us to expect that the open-style adapter would engage in withdrawal to censure cues less than the average person, since his dispositions lead him to alter evaluation, not to avoid it. If these further refinements of our thinking are correct, then we would have to assume that the effects of the two adaptive styles were implicit in the Barker and the Heilbrun and Tiemeyer studies, and that both contributed to the same outcome but for different reasons. Less social withdrawal for the HC-LN group was generated by the ability of the closed-style male to disengage himself attentionally and by the disinclination of the open-style male to use social withdrawal.

It is obvious that this post hoc explanation of interpersonal distancing results requires empirical verification using child-rearing groups actually broken down into adaptive styles and an experimental procedure which permits us to distinguish between the responses of the adaptive-style groups to censure. This was the purpose of a very recent experiment by Heilbrun (1972b) in which the methodology was modeled somewhat after that employed by Barker but which included a refinement of the late-adolescent male groupings into child-rearing quadrants *and* adaptive styles (or their control counterparts). Sixty-three Emory undergraduate volunteers acted as subjects, their average age being 18.8 years.

Group questionnaire sessions in which maternal child-rearing materials were completed provided the basis for median-cut assignment of subjects to HC-LN or a general reference group comprised of the three remaining quadrants. Each subject came individually to the laboratory where the female experimenter initially administered the Stroop-tape condition to ascertain the effects of the maternal censure cues upon cognition. The Stroop completed, the experimenter informed the subject that the purpose of the experiment was to establish the effect of relative light intensities upon the accuracy of discrimination. She pointed out to him that a constant light source would be fixed upon a row of angles mounted on the front wall and a variable light source would be focused upon him and a series of angles that he would have to match with the "same-size" angle on the front wall. The information regarding experimental interest in the relative intensities of the two light sources was a diversion from our actual interest in the effects of failure upon illumination preferences for the light fixed upon the subject.

The constant light source on the front wall was furnished by a 60-watt bulb. The variable light source focused upon the subject was a shielded 60-watt bulb in circuit with a voltage regulator. By turning the regulator dial, calibrated in units from 0 to 130 volts output, the light could be varied from maximum intensity (130) to the point where its candescence disappeared (30).

The experimental room was darkened except for the light focused upon the subject and the test stimuli, the lamp fixed upon the standard stimuli on the front wall, and a small lamp used by the experimenter to record responses. The subject lamp was initially illuminated to a voltage regulator setting of 80, midway between maximum and minimum intensity. The subject was told that before he began the angle discrimination task it was of interest to record his personal preference for the brightness of the light to be shown upon him. He was allowed to set the voltage regulator dial at whatever point he wished, and this reading was recorded. However, the light intensity was set again at 80 before beginning the first series of angle discriminations.

The angle discrimination task, which has been described in some detail in an earlier chapter, was so devised that each subject was put on a failing schedule of reinforcement without being aware of the contrived nature of the procedure. Seven of the ten trials on the first series were reinforced as wrong, after which the experimenter pointed out to the subject that performance to this point was deficient and suggested that perhaps the light setting under which he worked might account for this. Each subject was permitted to reset the light intensity to his preferred level. After recording the new setting, the experimenter proceeded to present two additional series of discrimination trials using this preferred level of illumination. These final series were conducted under success conditions (seven and eight of ten correct) in order to alleviate any discomfort in the subject created by the prior failure.

Two scores are considered critical to our understanding of interpersonal distancing in this experiment. The first is the pre-failure preferred light intensity.

This score allows us to estimate how obvious (close) or obscure (distant) the subject's choice made him to the female experimenter as he anticipated performing on a skills task in her presence. The second score important to our purpose is the change in illumination when pre- and post-failure settings are compared. The change score gives us the effect of actual failure upon social distancing. Both the initial and change raw scores were converted to standard scores ($T = 50$ and $SD = 10$) to make them more comparable. This conversion was performed so that a score above 50 on either variable identifies a preference for a higher intensity of light and a score less than 50 indicates a preferred illumination of lower intensity.

Table 43 contains the mean scores for initial preferred illumination level and for post-failure change in preferred illumination level from this baseline. Prior to introduction of the failure condition, the closed-style males did prefer a lower intensity of light than did the open-style males in keeping with their more guarded interpersonal stance in evaluative situations. However, this effect is embedded in a more general effect ($p < .05$) for disruption. This simply means that the same preference difference was found between the two reference control groups as was found between the two adaptive-style groups, for reasons that remain unexplained. After failure was imposed, changes unique to the aversive-control group occurred. The closed-style adapters moved in the direction of increased illumination prior to continuing the task, and open-style adapters changed in opposite fashion toward reduced illumination. Their change scores differed reliably ($p < .05$). In contrast, the two reference subgroups responded almost identically to the failure condition; neither showed any systematic change in preferred light intensity whatsoever.

Table 43. Preferred Level of Illumination as a Function of Failure for Late-Adolescent Males Varying in Maternal Child-Rearing Experience and Style of Adaptation

	Perceived Maternal Child-Rearing Pattern			
	High Control-Low Nurturance		Reference Group	
Illumination Score	Closed Adaptive Style ($N = 10$)	Open Adaptive Style ($N = 12$)	Nondisrupted Controls ($N = 21$)	Disrupted Controls ($N = 20$)
Mean initial (pre-failure) illumination preference	46.30	52.83	47.38	52.75
Mean (post-failure) change from initial illumination preference	54.30	46.33	49.95	49.90

The failure to observe systematic effects of failure upon interpersonal distancing within the reference group is important for two reasons. One is the usual inferential importance of demonstrating that something is happening within the high control-low nurturance group that does not happen within the control group who do not share the same child-rearing history. The second reason, especially germane to the present set of data, is that the aversive-control results taken alone could be interpreted as a "regression to the mean" type effect. Reasoning along these lines would take the form of assuming that the initial difference in light intensity preference was artifactual and that the preferred increase for closed-style males and decrease for open-style males was simply a convergence to a common mean somewhere between the initial extremes rather than having any dynamic meaning. The fact that the two reference subgroups initially demonstrated the same divergence in initial preference but did *not* differentially alter their preferences after failure renders a "regression to the mean" interpretation untenable.

In effect, what Heilbrun has found in this experiment is that the hypothesis previously proposed to account for less rather than more social withdrawal in HC-LN adolescents under conditions involving exposure to censure can be more selectively applied to closed-style adapters. The availability of attentional habits which reduce the immediate impact of aversive social stimulation lessen the instigation to social withdrawal of a physical nature. It must be presumed that the conditions under which withdrawal is to be measured will determine the dominance of one mode of avoidance behavior over the other. Before failure was experienced, closed-style males preferred to make themselves less visible to the female experimenter. If subjects, having been informed of what was ahead, had been given an option of participation or nonparticipation at this point, it is entirely possible that closed-style males would have differentially elected to remove themselves from the experiment. Since no option was forthcoming, attentional defenses of the closed-style adolescent were apparently called into play, sensory thresholds elevated, and increased illumination preference was the result.

STYLE OF ADAPTATION TO AVERSIVE MATERNAL CONTROL AND PERCEPTUAL ORIENTATION

The complex social-perceptual styles which the theory proposes as primary modes of coping with sustained aversive maternal control embrace complementary behavioral systems which must work together before either style can attain its adaptive (if not adjustive) goal of reduction of aversive stimulus input. The closed-style accomplishes only part of its defensive mission insofar as it reduces the discomfort associated with social interaction by predisposing the child to avoidance-withdrawal social tactics. When distressing social interaction cannot be evaded, perceptual defenses are mobilized and the mission is carried on by the mechanisms of selective attention. Closed-style children will demonstrate, according to theory, a tendency to divert their focus of attention away from external cues which they interpret as threatening. By and large, this could mean almost any social cue thought to connote evaluation or control. Selective nonattention to focal extrinsic cues will be mediated either by diverting attention to other (irrelevant) external stimulation or by turning the focus of attention to stimulation having its sources within the organism.

Similarly, the open-style of contending with aversive maternal stimulation requires not only that the child maintain interpersonal contact with the mother as the source of corrective evaluative experience but also that he be sensitive enough to social cues to identify what expectations are being imposed and what the evaluative climate is. Thus, the social orientation could not be conducive to the temporary alleviation of discomfort brought about by low self-esteem without an accompanying vigilance to external social cues denoting expectancy or evaluation.

The proposal that closed-style adapters will make greater use of internal scanning mechanisms than open-style adapters actually evolves logically from the necessary perceptual attributes of the closed style. If one is going to disengage himself from a focal source of aversive stimulation in his immediate external environment, there appear to be only three perceptual strategies which are open to him. All involve the withdrawal of attention from the focal and relevant aversive stimulus and attentional deployment to another source of situationally irrelevant but less aversive stimulation. He may fixate upon another focal stimulus thereby shifting his focus of attention to some less threatening extrinsic input. He may also scan his external environment in an unfocused manner, spreading his attention over a broad range of stimuli. Or he may turn his attention inward and fix upon some internal source of stimulation, probably of a cognitive nature. While all three of these strategies may be equally available to the closed-style adapter, it would be our contention that his general tendency toward social isolation will have enhanced his turning inward as a source of stimulation. Accordingly, the strategy of perceptual disengagement through inward deployment of attention will be dominant. Whether this is so or not, the point remains that the closed-style adapter will be more habitually oriented toward internal scanning than will be the open-style adapter whose priorities require maintaining vigilance to extrinsic social cues.

The theoretical postulates regarding attentional scanning are clear: (1) open-style adapters will be more inclined to engage in external scanning than closed-style adapters; (2) conversely, closed-style adapters will be more predisposed toward internal scanning than open-style adapters. Both patterns will become more pronounced given a potentially evaluative situation.

Related Process-Reactive Schizophrenia Research (External Scanning)

Others who have argued for differences in the perceptual processing of noxious or threatening stimulation between process and reactive schizophrenics have agreed that the process schizophrenic will avoid or disengage himself from such stimulation as a learned pattern of defense (Barry, 1968; Kantor and Herron, 1966; Rodnick, 1967). No proposal conceptualizing the reactive's mode of processing aversive stimulation as a component of a perceptual style is in evidence.

Many investigators have employed a size constancy methodology to investigate perceptual deficit in schizophrenia. Kantor and Herron (1966), in discussing this area of research, point out that visual constancy can be maintained by inhibiting distortions brought about by lack of perspective, poor illumination, or by differences in distance from conscious perception. Constancy, by their formulation, results from more effective inhibition of visual elements which are incongruent with the stable percept. Greater size constancy and presumably more effective visual processing that serves to *maintain* a focal external stimulus has been repeatedly demonstrated in reactive schizophrenics relative to their process counterparts (Crookes, 1957; Johannsen, Friedman, and Liccione, 1966; Lovinger, 1956; Raush, 1952; Sanders and Pacht, 1952; Weckowicz, 1957; Weckowicz, and Hall, 1960; Weckowicz, Sommer and Hall, 1958).

Along somewhat different perceptual lines, Zahn (1959) used size overestimation in process schizophrenics and underestimation in reactive schizophrenics to infer high anxiety and affective responsivity in the latter group and withdrawal in the former. Dwarshuis (1964) reported that the reactive was more capable of integrating extrinsic stimuli when the stimuli are less emotionally arousing but that their superiority to process schizophrenics disappears as the arousal value of the stimuli is increased. This can be taken to suggest an interference effect of heightened affect; the usually more effective scanning of the reactive schizophrenic is counteracted by his susceptibility to emotional arousal. Husni-Palacios, Palacios, and Gibeau (1967) also report that reactives, presented with an auditory scanning task, were superior in their ability to integrate extrinsic stimuli at low arousal levels.

The tendency to deploy attention to external stimulation, as this may be evidenced in more effective perceptual scanning of the environment, can be deduced from another category of studies which use a figure-ground procedure to establish how well the subject can differentiate focal stimuli from surrounding context. The ability to differentiate perceptually figure from ground (i.e., field independence) has been demonstrated more characteristically by reactive rather than process schizophrenics (Bryant, 1962; Feffer, 1961; Gibeau, 1965; Magaro and Vojtisek, 1971).

Superior perceptual processing of extrinsic cues for reactive schizophrenics receives further documentation from studies which have been concerned with the psychological test performance of schizophrenics. The use of unstructured or semistructured projective instruments has led investigators to such conclusions as reactives are more highly organized in their percepts (Fine and Zimet, 1959) or that process patients give greater evidence of irrational thinking in their perceptual responses (Belmont, Birch, Klein, and Pollack, 1964). Both investigations employed standard Rorschach procedures. Lefcourt and Steffy (1966) found that process schizophrenics displayed less ability or willingness to give meaningful percepts to Holtzman Inkblot cards with female examiners (relative to male examiners). Asked to scan pictorial stimuli like those included on the Thematic Apperception Test, process patients were found lacking in "general cognitive ability" (Cohen, 1967). We can conclude that given less structure, process schizophrenics do not organize their visual percepts as effectively as reactives.

The same superiority of reactive schizophrenics is apparent when intelligence-related performance is measured by more clearly structured techniques. Concept formation tasks, requiring a search for common properties among a variety of items in an external sensory field, place a premium upon effective scanning. Reactive superiority on concept tasks to process schizophrenics has been commonly observed (Berman, 1963; Brodsky, 1968; Donoghue, 1964; Herron, 1961; Strain, 1967; Tytko and Spence, 1962). Farina, Holzberg, and Dies (1969) noted the inferior performance of poor premorbids on an anagrams task relative to goods and controls, a type of performance that again requires concerted processing of external stimuli. The three subtests of the Wechsler Adult Intelligence Scale on which Stier (1968) found reactives superior to process schizophrenics were all performance tasks requiring detailed perceptual scanning of extrinsic cues—Picture Completion, Block Design, and Object Assembly. Process subjects also have been found inferior on a memory task for verbal materials in which the presentation placed a premium upon external scanning (Mallet, 1956).

The evidence cited in the present section to this point, while emphasizing the greater effectiveness of reactive schizophrenics in performance situations requiring the perceptual processing of external cues, is not as germane to our theory as data reflecting what happens to external scanning when habitual strategies of defense are called into play. One such category of investigation includes those studies which involve experimenter censure as a systematic methodological procedure and determine its effect upon external scanning behavior. Four studies have reported a greater impairment in the ability to perform abstract and conceptual operations with extrinsic stimuli for process schizophrenics following censure than for reactives (Barry, 1968; Irwin and Renner, 1969; Meichenbaum, 1969; Young, 1962). Ryan (1960), working within the auditory modality, found that process schizophrenics demonstrated a more profound drop in "listening behavior" under conditions of social censure as measured by visual discrimination of orally presented words.

A second type of investigation which should be especially relevant to the question of differential perception among schizophrenics is that which introduces interpersonal content into the perceptual display to which the subject is exposed. Marx (1962) accomplished this at the most general level by introducing social content into a card-sorting task. While this resulted in a performance drop for all schizophrenics relative to normals, the decrement was most pronounced for the process group. A reluctance for process schizophrenics to confront directly verbal or pictorial stimuli that could be interpreted as having interpersonal implications was reported by Levenson (1967).

A somewhat more refined methodology for our purposes is one that assesses the extent to which the subject effectively scans and organizes interpersonal cues. Farina, Holzberg, and Kimura (1966) asked schizophrenics to give the differences between liked and unliked acquaintances. While their results failed to achieve statistical significance, they relate the impression that "poors perceive others in a less differentiated way than do goods." In a study by Gancherov (1963), process schizophrenics were unable to make the discrimination on an adjective check list between an "understanding" and an "authoritarian" experimenter. This was true even though they had performed differently on nontimed problem-solving tasks under the authoritarian condition. In contrast, reactives were able to describe the two types of experimenters accurately but did not respond to them differently. Buck and Kates (1963) found that the ability of process subjects to categorize stimuli indicative of high love was inferior to that shown by reactives and normals, although this difference was not apparent for high anger stimuli. Process schizophrenics also had the greatest difficulty in making semantic distinctions between types of parent figures (e.g., warm-loving versus censorious-rejecting) shown on color slides (Nathanson, 1967).

Cicchetti (1967) presented taped parental dialogues to his subjects and then asked them questions regarding what they had heard. Process schizophrenics made more errors than normals with reactives assuming an intermediate position. Two studies have identified a discrimination deficit for process schizophrenics relative to reactives on scenes depicting a mother scolding her son in contrast to the opposite pattern on a father-scolding scene (Farina and Dunham, 1963; Magaro, 1967). Higher perceptual thresholds were established for process schizophrenics by Friedman (1966) when he exposed his subjects to mother-father-peer interaction cues of nurturance and rejection. In another threshold experiment, Donovan and Webb (1965) isolated a uniquely high threshold for the voice of a mother-figure among process schizophrenics. Reactives and normals did not present differential thresholds for the voices of mother and father figures.

A rather unique experiment has been reported (Mehl, 1967; Mehl and Cromwell, 1969) in which the effects of brief sensory deprivation and sensory stimulation upon schizophrenics were recorded. Process schizophrenics were found to tolerate and often prefer reduction in stimulus input and showed no change in attentional functioning following sensory deprivation. Increased levels of stimulation (including social stimuli) were disturbing to the process schizophrenic and a trend was noted toward deterioration in his level of attentional function. Reactives, in contrast, showed discomfort with reduction of stimulus input and their attention suffered in effectiveness. However, the reactives were found to tolerate increased stimulation with no marked discomfort or alteration in attention.

It seems reasonable to conclude from this substantial number of studies that reactive schizophrenics maintain a more sensitive and effective attentional set toward external stimulus events than do process schizophrenics. Further, the outward deployment of attention under the special situational circumstances of interpersonal stimulation, aversive social cues, or introduction of maternal connotation appears to vary in keeping with the proposed withdrawal of attention for process schizophrenics and attentional vigilance for reactives.

Adaptive-Style Theory Validation Study (Visual Scanning)

The initial validation experiment relevant to the external scanning aspects of the adaptive-style theory (Heilbrun, 1971a) set out to test the hypothesis that aversive-maternal-control late-adolescents, despite a common sensitivity to the quality of evaluative cues, will differ in their ability to recognize such cues as a function of the adaptive style they have learned. Closed-style males will tend to be ineffective in detecting evaluative stimuli presented visually, whereas open-style males will tend to be highly effective.

The experiment included 49 undergraduate male volunteers at Emory University whose average age was 19.0 years. The standardized part of our procedures, group administration of the child-rearing questionnaires followed by individual recall of each subject for the Stroop-aversive tape procedure, was implemented with only one alteration. An additional questionnaire (an abbreviated version of the Minnesota Multiphasic Personality Inventory) was included in the group session to serve as the basis for subsequent instructional manipulation.

Upon completion of the Stroop-tape procedure, the subject was introduced to the final part of the experiment involving the recognition of briefly-exposed words. The personality test taken earlier was recalled to his attention by the female experimenter, and he was informed that a "faculty psychologist," who was quite familiar with the test, had been requested to give his impressions of him as a person by using the results of the questionnaire. Some of the behavioral adjectives used by the psychologist had been put on slides, the bogus instructions continued, and the subject was told to "correctly recognize as many of these words he used to describe you as you can."

The 66 words which had actually been printed on slides were familiar adjectives selected from the Adjective Check List and included 22 words previously judged by college students to reflect favorably upon a person, 22 words of neutral character, and 22 words judged to be unfavorable. Selection of the specific words to be included in each qualitative category proceeded by matching within favorable-neutral-unfavorable triads for word length and initial letter. The 66 words were presented in a fixed order to the subjects using a repeating alternation of neutral-favorable-unfavorable; the order of presentation was unrelated to the original order of matching, however. These words, as originally selected in matched triads, can be found in Table 44. Four additional neutral words were used as practice stimuli to familiarize the subjects with the task.

The 66 words were presented singly upon the screen by means of a slide projector mounted with a four to six inch zoom lens. The exposure time (100

Table 44. Evaluative Words Used in Threshold Recognition Experiment

Qualitative Category		
Favorable	Neutral	Unfavorable
adaptable	assertive	apathetic
cheerful	cautious	careless
calm	cool	cold
capable	contented	cynical
dependable	determined	disorderly
entertaining	excitable	egotistical
frank	formal	fickle
forgiving	forgetful	frivolous
helpful	hurried	hostile
inventive	informal	impatient
imaginative	idealistic	indifferent
insightful	initiative	intolerant
mature	modest	moody
organized	outspoken	obnoxious
patient	precise	prudish
realistic	reserved	resentful
sociable	stubborn	slipshod
sincere	serious	selfish
stable	stolid	stingy
tolerant	trusting	tactless
understanding	uninhibited	undependable
warm	wary	weak

milliseconds) and slightly distorted focus had been selected by means of a pilot study ($N = 7$) as settings most likely to allow for 50% correct word identification over all subjects in the main experiment. Subsequent inspection of the data from the main experiment revealed our approximations to be reasonably precise; accuracy of detection for all subjects turned out to be 29.3 out of 66 or about 44%.

The assignment of subjects to the appropriate child rearing–adaptive style groupings proceeded by the usual median-cut procedures; a general reference group including all quadrants except the HC-LN was employed. The effectiveness of these late adolescents in recognizing evaluative words thought to be self-relevant was assessed in terms of average number of correct recognitions. The top row of Table 45 clearly portrays the open-style male as the most effective and the closed-style male as least effective of all subgroups in recognizing the words, with the two control groups falling in between. Analysis of variance amply documents the support given by these levels of performance to our theory. Starting with a near-significant ($p < .10$) interaction effect, we move to the critical analyses of simple effects. The two adaptive-style groups were clearly distinguishable ($p < .01$) in their recognition of visual cues; the two reference control groups were virtually the same. It is all the more impressive that perceptual scanning of open and closed males diverged sufficiently not only to convey statistical support for the theory but also to suggest differences of practical significance. Open-style adolescents were able to "see" 58% of the words which they presumed the psychologist had used to describe them. Closed-style adolescents, given identical opportunity, recognized but 32% of the authority's descriptive terms.

Turning our attention back to Table 45 again and to the breakdown of correct recognitions by qualitative categories (rows 2-4), it is readily apparent that the differential perception of the adaptive-style groups was almost equally

Table 45. Mean Number of Correct Recognitions of Evaluative Words for Late-Adolescent Males Varying in Maternal Child-Rearing Experience and Style of Adaptation

	Perceived Maternal Child-Rearing Pattern			
	High Control-Low Nurturance		Reference Group	
Qualitative Category of Evaluative Cue	Closed Adaptive Style ($N = 7$)	Open Adaptive Style ($N = 9$)	Nondisrupted Controls ($N = 23$)	Disrupted Controls ($N = 22$)
All words combined	21.29	38.56	26.64	29.50
Favorable	6.43	12.00	8.55	8.82
Neutral	6.71	12.89	8.91	10.27
Unfavorable	8.14	13.67	9.18	10.41

represented in all three categories. The fact that the perceptual effect was a general one rather than specific in character is of importance for two reasons. It is important, on the one hand, from the point of view of scientific inference, because it allows us to distinguish between alternative explanations of the obtained results. One explanation is that which has been assumed correct to this point; different perceptual orientations to extrinsic evaluative cues literally lend themselves to some "seeing" more than others. However, it could be contended (with considerable encouragement from the perceptual defense controversy of the 1950's in which taboo words served as the stimulus) that all groups recognized the words in the Heilbrun experiment to about the same degree, but they differed in their willingness to tell the experimenter what they had seen. The results, according to the latter argument, would be better explained by response suppression than perceptual defense. No credence can be given to the response suppression interpretation of the findings, however, since its basis in avoiding threat or embarrassment would require that unfavorable terms be suppressed more than neutral terms and certainly more than those favorable to the subject. This is clearly not what happened.

The second fact of importance which can be attributed to the general perceptual effect is that it provides some tentative indication of whether the scanning styles work by a general filtering of stimulation or whether there is selective filtering of stimuli that represent some degree of threat to the person. The finding of the same open-style and closed-style differences, whatever the positive or negative character of the cue, argues, of course, against selective attention and for an "all-or-none" registration of stimulus meaning.

That a role was played by central ideational processes in deriving cue meaning was brought to light within this experiment when an analysis was made of those guesses proposed by the subjects which proved to be incorrect. Low self-esteem and sensitivity to esteem-relevant judgments rendered by others for all aversive-maternal-control offspring are basic assumptions of the theory, and the manner in which this child-rearing experience group tended to distort the somewhat ambiguous, briefly exposed words offered an empirical check on these assumptions.

To analyze for possible qualitative differences in cue distortion, all incorrect responses made by the 49 subjects which could be considered descriptive of a person or his behavior were collected. These 251 words were submitted to a new group of 42 Emory undergraduates (31 males, 11 females) with instructions to rate each as favorable, neutral, or unfavorable as applied to a male Emory student. Using the criterion of 80% interjudge agreement, 113 of these words were defined as clearly favorable or clearly unfavorable. The mean number of incorrect guesses representing favorable or unfavorable descriptive words were then determined. Data relevant to cue distortion are presented in Table 46. The summary index of distortion (bottom row of the table), when subjected to

Table 46. Qualitative Distortion of Evaluative Cues for Late-Adolescent Males Varying in Maternal Child-Rearing Experience and Style of Adaptation

	Perceived Maternal Child-Rearing Pattern			
	High-Control-Low Nurturance		Reference Group	
Distortion Data	Closed Adaptive Style	Open Adaptive Style	Nondisrupted Controls	Disrupted Controls
Mean number of distortions	9.29	11.67	9.45	11.18
Mean number of favorable distortions	2.86	2.44	1.36	2.05
Mean number of unfavorable distortions	.71	1.11	1.36	1.64
Mean index (favorable minus unfavorable distortions)	2.14	1.33	.00	.41

analysis of variance, offered one significant effect ($p < .01$). Aversive-control adolescents, whatever their adaptive style, were more prone to favorable distortion of ambiguous cues than the reference group. The defensive character of this systematic distortion of evaluative cues can be logically inferred from the fact that despite the lower self-esteem of the aversive-control male, he introduced more self-enhancing meanings to ambiguous cues in this experiment.

Adaptive-Style Theory Validation Study (Auditory Scanning)

It is necessary at this point to depart somewhat from the format established for this chapter in order to consider in greater detail one of the scanning experiments involving process and reactive schizophrenics which was cited previously. Donovan and Webb's (1965) work represented the target experiment for our adaptive-style investigation of auditory scanning and, therefore, warrants a fuller exposition. These investigators compared the ability of process and reactive schizophrenics to recognize words spoken by the male and female voice. Stimulus ambiguity was introduced by presenting each stimulus word in combination with masking noise. A word was repeated under conditions of increasing clarity (i.e., decreasing masking noise) until recognized by the schizophrenic. A picture of a middle-aged mother figure or father figure was placed directly in front of the subject to correspond with the female and male voice presentations. This was intended to increase the association between the experimental situation and prior exposure of the schizophrenic subject to his own parents.

Table 47, which summarizes the mean recognition threshold scores found by Donovan and Webb, lends itself to several observations. Normals generally performed more effectively than schizophrenics, not in itself an extraordinary finding. Considering only the schizophrenic groups, there was only one exceptional performance; process schizophrenics were uniquely deficient in their ability to recognize words spoken in the voice of a female "mother figure." Stated in a more complete form, process schizophrenics demonstrated a deficit in their ability to recognize "mother"-spoken words (threshold = 6.018) relative to "father"-spoken words (threshold = 5.143). Reactive schizophrenics did not have differential thresholds for the "mother" voice (4.963) and the "father" voice (5.285), although the nonsignificant directional difference favors a greater sensitivity to the female voice.

The Donovan and Webb findings, as they might be replicated in an experiment directly bearing upon the adaptive-style theory, are doubly significant. Replication would offer, first, an increment of proof that common differences do exist between process and reactive schizophrenics and between closed-style and open-style children of the aversive-control mother. But replication of the Donovan and Webb findings would be of special importance in that they offer very clear specifications of perceptual behavior in response to each parent. We have dealt theoretically only with the aversive-control mother, the implicit assumption being that the child's mode of contending with her might be a sufficient basis for explaining schizophreniform development. In the Donovan and Webb experiment we have some confirmation of this assumption.

Table 47. Adjusted Mean Threshold Scores (Corrected for Age and Vocabulary)[a]

Normals to male stimulus complex[b]	4.190	
Normals to female stimulus complex[b]	4.245	
		$p < .01$
Goods to female stimulus complex	4.963	
Poors to male stimulus complex	5.143	
Goods to male stimulus complex	5.285	
		$p < .01$
Poors to female stimulus complex	6.018	

[a]Reproduced from M. J. Donovan and W. W. Webb, Meaning dimensions and male-female voice perception in schizophrenics with good and poor premorbid adjustment. *Journal of Abnormal Psychology*, 1965, 70, 426-431.

[b]Male stimulus complex = "father" voice, female stimulus complex = "mother" voice.

Process schizophrenics, who are hypothesized to be closed-style adapters, did demonstrate perceptual barriers against hearing what the "mother" voice was saying but not against the "father" voice. Conservative interpretation would place reactives as evenly sensitive to the voices of both parent figures. The fact that these data point toward the unique role of the mother in process-reactive differentiation is perhaps best illustrated by yet another way of conceptualizing the Table 47 threshold means. Process and reactive schizophrenics responded almost identically to the "father" voice (5.143 versus 5.285, respectively), but diverged widely in their ability to discern words spoken by the "mother" voice (6.018 versus 4.963, respectively).

The experiment reported by Heilbrun [in press (a)] was devised as a test of whether the differential perception of parent-figure voices found by Donovan and Webb for process schizophrenics would be found in closed-style adolescents and whether the nondifferential perception of reactive schizophrenics would hold for open-style adolescents. Ninety-four male volunteers (mean age = 18.8 years) from the Emory undergraduate body served as subjects, and they were assigned to maternal child-rearing experience groupings and adaptive-style subgroupings by the same procedures as described previously in the present chapter. A combined reference group again was constituted for control purposes.

The voice-recognition task, administered individually to the subjects, involved a tape-recorded series of 66 behavioral adjectives. These were the same words used in the Heilbrun (1971a) investigation of visual scanning and listed in Table 44. Half of the words were recorded in an adult male voice and the remaining half were recorded in the voice of an adult female. The 33 words rendered in each voice included 11 favorable, 11 neutral, and 11 unfavorable terms. The order of presentation throughout the tape was a repeating neutral-favorable-unfavorable sequence. Words were recorded in a clear voice and with neutral intonation. The subject was allowed a 15-second period following the presentation of each word during which time he was to guess the word just presented. A warning signal sounded at the end of the 15-second period to prepare the subject for the next stimulus which was to follow in five seconds.

Stimulus ambiguity was created on this word-recognition task by using an auditory threshold approach. A pilot study established the volume-control dial settings for the male and female voices separately at which 50% of the words would be correctly identified. Looking ahead to the main study, it turned out that these volume levels served their purpose remarkably well. The average figures for correct recognition of the spoken words for the male voice (56%) and the female voice (51%) were both close to the half-correct projection.

Instructions given to the late-adolescent males in the laboratory session introduced the subject of investigation as the effectiveness of communication between their generation and that of their parents. They were given bogus information at this point to the effect that a poll had recently been taken of the parents of college-age children. Furthermore (the instructions continued), the female experimenter had identified the words chosen most often by mothers and most often by fathers to describe their sons. The subjects were told that these words would be presented to them near hearing threshold and that they would be spoken in a woman's voice to represent the mothers' judgments and a man's voice to represent the judgments of the fathers. Finally, the instructions urged the subjects to see how many of these words they could identify correctly as a way of determining how well they could "really hear what their parents thought of them." It was the purpose of these instructions to create two sets in the subjects. First, an evaluative set was desired and, second, a linkage between a state of evaluation and the subjects' own parents was deemed important. Based upon the results of the experiment, the instructions were apparently believable and effective.

Half of the subjects in each subgrouping were presented the male-spoken words first followed by the female-spoken words while half received the words in the opposite order so that warm-up or fatigue effects could not bias the results. Each subject received four neutral practice words spoken in the voice to which he would receive initial exposure.

A single ratio score was used to represent the total performance of the subject on the word-recognition task:

$$\frac{\text{number correctly identified female-spoken words} \;\text{minus}\; \text{number correctly identified male-spoken words}}{\text{total number of correctly identified words}} \times 100$$

This ratio answers the following question for any subject: of those words which the subject was able to identify correctly, what is the percentage difference between those spoken by a female "mother figure" and by a male "father figure"? It can be noted that the ratio score removes the effect of external scanning differences between adaptive-style groups already demonstrated within the visual threshold recognition study (Heilbrun, 1971a), since each person's score is based upon only the total number which *he* was able to recognize.

The top row of Table 48 contains the mean ratio scores on the voice recognition task. Analysis of variance revealed a significant effect ($p < .05$) of child-rearing group but also a significant ($p < .05$) child-rearing by disruption interaction. This led to the critical tests of the predictions for the experiment. One expectation was that the closed-style male would show a unique deficit in recognizing female-spoken words relative to male-spoken words; this was confirmed in that the closed-style mean ratio score (−14.6%) reflected the greatest differential inability to detect the words spoken in the voice of the

Table 48. Accuracy of Detection of Words Spoken in a Female and Male Voice by Late-Adolescent Males Varying in Maternal Child-Rearing Experience and Style of Adaptation

	Perceived Maternal Child-Rearing Pattern			
	High Control-Low Nurturance		Reference Group	
Qualitative Category of Evaluative Cue	Closed Adaptive Style ($N = 18$)	Open Adaptive Style ($N = 15$)	Nondisrupted Controls ($N = 26$)	Disrupted Controls ($N = 35$)
Mean accuracy				
All words combined	–14.6%	–7.6%	+2.8%	–7.2%
Favorable	–11.6%	–2.9%	–2.4%	–.6%
Neutral	–12.3%	+8.1%	+11.4%	+4.0%
Unfavorable	–23.5%	–21.9%	–7.4%	–25.1%

"mother figure" among all groups, and it differed reliably ($p < .01$) from the score (2.8%) contributed by nondisrupted reference controls. In contrast, the mean ratio score for open-style adapters (–7.6%) was almost identical to that provided by the disrupted control group (–7.2%), again consistent with expectation.

Reference to the bottom portion of Table 48 reveals the mean ratio scores as calculated for each qualitative category of word. Inspection as well as statistical analysis by qualitative levels made it clear that the patterns of group differences and similarities found when the total array of words was considered remained the same when the qualitative categories were compared separately. Thus, the faulty perception of the "mother" voice for the closed-style male was a general filtering effect and not contingent upon selective attention to words differing in evaluative connotation. It may be recalled that the same finding was obtained in the visual scanning study; given an evaluative set, the ability to perceive visually presented words for the aversive-maternal-control males appeared as a general effect and was unrelated to the aversiveness of the cue.

There was one clear effect related to qualitative category which assumes importance for us both from a methodological and a theoretical point of view. When by means of the ratio score the recognition rate for the 11 unfavorable terms spoken in the female voice is compared to that obtained for the 11 unfavorable terms verbalized in the male voice, a clear recognition deficit for the "mother" voice becomes apparent for all of our subjects. The recognition differential between the female-spoken negative words and the male-spoken negative words for all subjects was –19.4%. This figure for favorable words was –3.6%. Neutral words elicited a +3.6% differential. This generalized effect speaks tellingly for the unique aversive qualities of censure delivered by the mother for all sons just as our major finding confirms the threatening quality of maternal evaluative cues of any type for the closed-style adapter.

Adaptive-Style Theory Validation Study (Visual Scanning of Simultaneous Cues)

The previously discussed experiments examining visual detection (Heilbrun, 1971a) and auditory detection [Heilbrun, in press (a)] of evaluative cues included a common methodology employing individual presentation of stimuli near recognition threshold to test the perceptual postulates of the adaptive-style theory. It may be recalled that while the evidence for perceptual differences between open-style and closed-style males was forthcoming from these studies, there was no indication in the data that selective filtering of stimulus meaning occurred as a function of the positive or negative nature of the evaluative cue. It remained a possibility that the failure to demonstrate a peripheral screening effect was due to the ambiguity of the words produced by their individual presentation near the threshold of recognition. It might be argued that in such a situation the perceptual styles could only operate on an "all or nothing" basis. The person, in response to his habitual set as an object of evaluation, will either tend to identify word meaning or not, but he is not in a position to select among positive and negative evaluative meanings as these might be clearly and simultaneously made available to him as alternatives. Heilbrun (1972c) implemented a study that sought to clarify the qualitative issue.

Seventy-eight late-adolescent males (mean age = 18.8 years) from the Emory campus participated as subjects; the standard procedures were followed to establish maternal child-rearing experience and style of adaptation (or appropriate control). A combined reference group was employed for comparison purposes.

The perception task, administered individually to subjects, involved the presentation of a visual display board bearing 33 behavioral adjectives. These words were among those used in the earlier perceptual threshold studies and included 11 triads of favorable-neutral-unfavorable evaluative terms matched for initial letter and length. The words, clearly printed in red lettering, were positioned on the board in such a way as to maximally disperse them according to qualitative category.

The female experimenter told the subject that she was studying the "communication gap" between parents and their sons and that she was interested in seeing how well he could perceive and remember words used by mothers to describe their college-age sons. A (fictional) poll was mentioned as the source of the maternal evaluations. Following specific task instructions, the subject was allowed 75 seconds (a time determined by pilot study to give approximately 50% correct recall) to scan freely the visual display. When the exposure period was over, the subject was requested to select exactly 33 adjectives from among those on the Adjective Check List which he recalled as maternal evaluations.

Results of this study are summarized in Table 49. Considering first the

Table 49. Perception of Simultaneously Presented Evaluative Cues by Late-Adolescent Males Varying in Maternal Child-Rearing Experience and Style of Adaptation

	Perceived Maternal Child-Rearing Pattern			
	High Control-Low Nurturance		Reference Group	
Perceptual Performance Score[a]	Closed Adaptive Style ($N = 10$)	Open Adaptive Style ($N = 10$)	Nondisrupted Controls ($N = 27$)	Disrupted Controls ($N = 31$)
Quantitative score	14.50	14.20	16.00	16.29
Qualitative score	.60	–2.50	–1.63	–.84

[a] Quantitative score = number adjectives correctly identified (out of 33); qualitative score = sum of weighted values assigned to correctly identified adjectives (favorable = +1, neutral = 0, unfavorable - –1).

number of correct recognitions (quantitative score), we can see that no difference was found between the two adaptive-style groups when evaluative cues were presented simultaneously and the adolescent was free to selectively attend among alternatives. There was a hint ($p < .10$) of a more general inferiority of the aversive-maternal-control males to all controls with regard to number of correct recognitions.

The qualitative score, explained in the footnote of Table 49, revealed the kind of effects that would be predicted from adaptive-style theory. There was a significant interaction ($p < .005$) between child rearing and disruption which reflected the presence of a significant difference ($p < .01$) between the adaptive-style groups and the absence of any difference between the control groups. If we examine the scores themselves on Table 49, we see that the score of the closed-style males (.60) reflects the tendency to remember more positive and fewer negative words in keeping with their guarded mode of perception. On the other hand, open males (–2.50) demonstrated a strong tendency to selectively retain the negative component of the presumed maternal evaluation as would be expected from generalization of their vigilance to aversive cues from their own mothers. Thus, given the opportunity to selectively attend to evaluative stimuli which are simultaneously presented, the late adolescent males performed qualitatively as would be predicted from adaptive-style theory in contrast to the quantitative confirmation of theory obtained in the prior scanning experiments.

The difference in the qualitative aspects of perception between open-style and closed-style sons identified in this study was interpreted as having its origin in the manner by which the child learned to process maternal evaluative cues. Furthermore, the instructions of the study were intended to elicit a maternal evaluative set so that the results would have theoretical relevance. To make these interpretive and procedural assumptions more compelling, Heilbrun determined whether the predicted qualitative difference between the adaptive-style groups would be found only with those evaluative cues presented as having a maternal source (correct recognitions) or also would be found in the remaining choices made by the subject (incorrect recognitions). The qualitative scoring procedures used for the correct recognition category was applied to the remainder of the words selected by each subject—those words which had not appeared on the display board.

A difference score, which subtracted the qualitative score derived from the nonmaternal evaluative terms from the same score derived from the maternal evaluative words, was ascertained for each subject. The mean intraindividual perceptual pattern score for the closed-style males (+.60) indicated that they were slightly more defended against the negative aspects of evaluative cues when they had a maternal source. In contrast, the mean difference score (−6.30) for the open-style males demonstrated them to be markedly more vigilant to the negative aspect of evaluative cues when mothers were identified as their source. These pattern scores were not only reliably different ($p < .005$) but portrayed the adaptive-style groups as behaving in keeping with theoretical expectation only when the evaluative terms were from a maternal source. Mean pattern scores for the nondisrupted (−3.67) and disrupted (−4.81) reference groups were of intermediate value to those of the adaptive-style groups and did not differ statistically.

By way of concluding this section covering external scanning studies, the evidence concerning adaptive-style differences which has surfaced to date is entirely consistent with the pattern of differences represented in process-reactive schizophrenia research and corroborative of the assumptions contained within the adaptive-style theory.

Related Process-Reactive Schizophrenic Research (Internal Scanning)

Process-reactive research bearing upon internal scanning differences in schizophrenia is far more limited than was the case for external scanning. Probably one reason for this is the greater methodological difficulty of investigating behavior which lends itself so poorly to experimental control. The experimenter maintains little, if any, stimulus control over inwardly directed attentional processes and lacks the means to observe directly or record the scanning response. Broen's (1968) statement on internal scanning behavior helps to resolve some of the inferential problem. He suggests that "much appropriate behavior requires reviewing or scanning of the several possible meanings of symbols or the scanning or searching for different events stored in memory (p. 141)." The nature of the available evidence requires us to consider internal scanning exclusively in terms of the availability of alternate meaning responses to symbolic cues.

Most of the evidence at our disposal comes from investigation of the word associations of process and reactive schizophrenics. Five investigations (Dobecki, Cromwell, and Polidoro, 1968; Dobecki, Polidoro, and Cromwell, 1965; Foley, 1968; Ries, 1968; Ries and Johnson, 1967), while raising some interpretive problems associated with chronicity of illness and instructional set, generally agree that process schizophrenics show less commonality of word associations than do reactives. More remote association of responses for the process group is consistent with a broader range of internal scanning.

While a large number of investigations have followed Loren Chapman's (Chapman, Chapman, and Miller, 1964) lead in studying the use of dominant and secondary meaning responses in schizophrenia, the bulk of this research has been concerned with differences in such usage as a function of chronicity of illness. The Chapman technique involves the presentation of multiple-choice items which include two common meanings of a homograph. One correct meaning of the word in context is the stronger one or the one most commonly used in everyday parlance; in another item the weaker meaning of the word is correct according to context. As an example:

> When the farmer bought a herd of cattle, he needed a new pen. This means that:
> (a) he needed a new writing implement;
> (b) he needed a new fenced enclosure;
> (c) he needed a new pick-up truck.

This item would be correctly answered by foil (b), although foil (a) includes the stronger meaning response. Performance on a series of similar items allows for the assessment of the person's tendency to utilize dominant meanings of words or to engage in the use of more remote (weaker) meanings.

Only one study (Rice, 1970) could be located in which stronger and weaker meaning responses were related to process and reactive status. Rice reports that reactive schizophrenics were the most prone to interpret words in terms of their dominant meanings, although this effect held only for those reactives who were the most emotionally responsive. Process schizophrenics, whether autonomically responsive or not, tended less toward the use of dominant meaning responses. Again, as in the case of word associations, we have an indication of more remote responding to symbols and, thus, broader internal scanning for the process schizophrenic.

One further source of indirect evidence bearing upon process-reactive internal scanning differences can be inferred from studies of intellectual performance in schizophrenia. Despite the inferiority of process schizophrenics to reactives on intelligence measures requiring an attentional focus upon extrinsic task cues (e.g., block design, picture completion), there are several studies which indicate no comparable deficit in process subjects on verbal tasks such as vocabulary which place greater emphasis upon internal processing of information, especially when alternate meanings are involved (Cancro, 1968; Rice, 1970; Schwartz, Hunt, and Walker, 1963). However, when vocabulary is measured by techniques emphasizing external scanning, such as a picture vocabulary test, inferiority of the process schizophrenic is again demonstrated (Digiondomenico, 1966).

Adaptive-Style Theory Validation Study (Internal Scanning)

Heilbrun's [1972d] investigation of internal scanning in late-adolescents involved 56 Emory male undergraduates who served as volunteers. Their average age was 18.7 years. This study, proceeding on the premise that the range of meanings associated with words should reflect the degree to which internal information is scanned, included the two indices of internal scanning which figured most prominently in the process-reactive literature just surveyed.

The first internal-scanning measure was the Willner Unusual Meanings Vocabulary Test (Willner, 1965) which assesses the ability of the person to identify the nondominant meanings of words. The subject was instructed that the correct response to each of the 42 items was an unusual meaning and asked to select his choice from among five alternatives (e.g., shoot–rifle, *sprout,* cap, duck, door). Higher scores on the Willner would indicate broader scanning.

A second index of internal-scanning behavior was developed from a word-association technique. Word-association norms for 200 words, published by Palermo and Jenkins (1964), served as the basic source; from this pool were selected all words that did not have an associated word with a frequency beyond 100 within the normative male college student sample of 500 (i.e., occurred no more than 20% of the time). Seventy-three words met this criterion and were included in the word-association measure. The subject was instructed to write down the first word occurring to him upon reading the stimulus word. (The Palermo-Jenkins norms were based upon written associations of their subjects.) Scores on the word-association task represented the average frequency of association for the 73 responses as determined from the normative table. Lower scores on the word-association measure suggest broader scanning.

The vocabulary test from the Shipley-Institute of Living Scale (Shipley, 1953) was included in the study as a control for vocabulary skills as standardly assessed by calling for the dominant meaning of words. This particular vocabulary test was chosen because of its formal similarities to the Unusual

Meanings Test except for its emphasis upon dominant word meanings. The Shipley is also a self-administered, multiple-choice test of about the same item length as the Willner. The theoretical prediction generated for this study stipulated that closed-style adapters would prove to be broader internal scanners than open-style adapters as evidenced by higher scores on the Willner Unusual Meanings Vocabulary Test and lower commonality scores on the word-association task.

Following the collection of the child-rearing questionnaire data by small-group testing procedures and the individual administration of the Stroop-tape combination, each subject participated in the final phase of the study (again individually). Instructions to the subject introduced this phase as concerned with the relationship between "accuracy and quickness" of thinking and accuracy of spatial perception. The two vocabulary and the word-association tests were administered in combination with a size discrimination task. Performance on the latter was actually irrelevant to our interests. The 30-minute laboratory procedure involved a set order of presentation of the tasks to the subject—Shipley Vocabulary Test, Willner Unusual Meanings Vocabulary Test, the size-discrimination task, and the word-association measure.

The performances of the two HC-LN adaptive-style subgroups and their respective reference control subgroups (made up of the three remaining quadrants) are reflected in the mean scores contained in Table 50. Analysis of variance applied to the Shipley Vocabulary Test scores clearly indicated that no group differences existed. Verbal skills, as assessed by the standard dominant-meaning vocabulary approach, did not prove discriminatory among the child-bearing groups. However, knowledge of word meanings as measured by the Willner did vary; closed-style adapters had a significantly ($p < .05$) higher score than the open-style group. The two reference group Willner means assumed intermediate value and were almost identical to each other. This set of vocabulary findings, which shows the closed-style group to have a superior grasp of nondominant word meanings and the open-style group to be inferior in this regard, gives clear support to the theoretical prediction of broader internal scanning for the closed-style late-adolescent.

The breadth of associated word meanings approached from the vantage point of free word associations conveyed the same set of conclusions. Closed-style subjects responded with the most remote associations and open-style subjects presented the most common set of associations; the mean difference in breadth of association was significant ($p < .05$). Reference control groups again performed at intermediate levels of commonality and did not differ from each other. Free word-association results, like the Willner vocabulary findings, clearly support the theoretical prediction of broader deployment of attention to internal cues for the closed-style youngster.

Table 50. Range of Associated Word Meanings for Late-Adolescent Males Varying in Maternal Child-Rearing Experience and Style of Adaptation

	Perceived Maternal Child-Rearing Pattern			
	High Control-Low Nurturance		Reference Group	
Measure[a]	Closed Adaptive Style ($N = 9$)	Open Adaptive Style ($N = 9$)	Nondisrupted Controls ($N = 20$)	Disrupted Controls ($N = 18$)
Mean score Shipley vocabulary test	32.44	31.89	33.10	32.88
Mean score Willner unusual meanings test	31.22	25.00	28.70	29.00
Mean score word-association test	21.58	26.17	23.99	25.48

[a] Scores on the two vocabulary tests represent the number correct out of 40 and 42 items for the Shipley and Willner, respectively. The score on the word-association task was derived from the mean frequency with which the 73 associations occurred within a normative sample of 500 male college students.

STYLE OF ADAPTATION TO AVERSIVE MATERNAL CONTROL AND EMOTIONAL RESPONSIVENESS

It has been postulated that the defended nature of the closed style of adapting to aversive maternal control would bring with it a reduction in the emotional arousal experienced by the child, since the social and perceptual concomitants of the style decrease the child's exposure to cues having a high potential for evoking negative emotional responses (e.g., cues eliciting feelings of shame, fear, anger, jealousy). Open-style adapters will be emotionally responsive to their external environment, since their behavioral posture will be such as to maintain their sensitivity to the self-relevant meanings in their environment. However, the distinction in emotional responsivity for the adaptive styles would be most salient under conditions which evoke the stylized behaviors, especially evaluative stress.

Related Process-Reactive Schizophrenia Research

Other investigators who have been closely associated with research into schizophrenia have reached conclusions about process-reactive differences in emotional responsiveness consonant with our expectations that process schizophrenics will demonstrate less responsivity. Mednick (1963), for example, has proposed that early-stage (reactive) schizophrenia is characterized by heightened arousal while advanced-stage (process) schizophrenia is associated with reduced arousal mediated by highly learned avoidance of anxiety. More recently, Higgins (1969) cautiously summarized his review of research into process and reactive differences in emotional arousal by saying:

> . . . it is noteworthy that no study of responsiveness has produced contradictory evidence, i.e., greater responsiveness on the part of process schizophrenics. Thus, while the data concerning arousal level remain highly equivocal, there does seem to be slightly less ambiguity with regard to the proposition that reactive schizophrenics are more autonomically responsive than process schizophrenics, a conclusion that is generally consonant with previous research (p. 454).

An actual look at the evidence regarding the deficit in arousal level found for process schizophrenics suggests that Higgins' summary impression might be on the conservative side.

Some of the earliest work bearing upon differential emotional responsiveness in schizophrenia relevant to our interests was reported by Meadow and Funkenstein (and associates). Some 20 years ago, Meadow and Funkenstein (1952) found that schizophrenics who demonstrated a marked physiological reaction to mecholyl injection (e.g., a sizeable fall in systolic blood pressure) showed a good prognosis for recovery (reactive status); minimal autonomic responsiveness to injection, in turn, was correlated with a poor prognosis (process status). A year later Meadow, Greenblatt, Funkenstein, and Solomon (1953), in a subsequent report of a series of experiments, extended their preliminary results to propose two polar types of schizophrenia At one extreme, the patient would show poor abstraction, disorganization of personality, a slight autonomic response to mecholyl, and the poor prognosis of the process schizophrenic. At the other extreme, the patient would be expected to demonstrate good abstraction, good personality organization, a marked response to mecholyl, and the more favorable prognosis of the reactive schizophrenic. Since these early investigations, two subsequent studies confirmed the differential autonomic reaction to mecholyl. Hirschstein (1956), again using response to treatment as the basis for distinguishing among schizophrenics, found the same differences in blood pressure reaction to mecholyl as did the Meadow and Funkenstein group. Diminished physiological responsiveness to mecholyl injection occurred within a process schizophrenic group but not among reactive patients. This result was replicated by King (1958).

A major share of the confirmatory evidence regarding process-reactive differences in arousal level that has appeared in the literature since the earlier mecholyl studies has involved a methodology which exposes the schizophrenic to controlled stimulus input (often aversive) and records his responsiveness, usually in terms of a direct autonomic index. Stephens, Brown, Forster, and Klein (1967), for example, found reactive schizophrenics displayed greater autonomic responsiveness to neutral sound and light stimuli than did process schizophrenics. Similarly, DeVault (1957) described faster resting heart rates for reactives than process. Even more strikingly, he found that while reactives presented accelerated heart rates to experimental stimuli, process schizophrenics demonstrated heart rate deceleration to the same input. Findings by Becker (1959) and Pearl (1962) are also consistent with the picture of greater emotional responsiveness in reactive than process schizophrenics.

Crider, Grinspoon, and Maher (1965) noted the "higher skin potential and faster simple reaction time" for the reactives. As the intensity and rate of the auditory input (noise) increased, it was found that the reaction time of the process group decreased and came to approach that of the reactive group. This was taken to mean that the resting level of arousal for the process schizophrenic, being lower, leaves room for enhancement of his performance by augmented sensory input. Similar results were obtained by Donoghue (1964) who employed a concept-formation task and an unpleasant tone as an accompanying auditory stimulus. Again the more restricted arousal level of the process schizophrenic was indicated. Gromell (1962) investigated arousal from a different perspective, using brain cell activity as his source of information rather than the autonomic nervous system. Here alpha rhythm blocking was measured in response to stressful and nonstressful stimulation, both visual and auditory. While process schizophrenics had a nonsignificantly higher level of activation than reactives, the process group also demonstrated a higher rate of habituation to electrocortical arousal.

The effects of variable stimulus input rates on a discrimination task were investigated by Ward and Carlson (1966) who found that process schizophrenics were the lowest in autonomic responsiveness, normals were intermediate, and reactives were the most responsive. Fenz and Velner (1970) measured emotional response during a rest period and compared this to the responsiveness obtained when the schizophrenic was exposed to auditory or auditory plus visual stimulus stressors. Their findings generally suggested that process and reactives did not distinguish themselves when compared within the discrete resting or stress conditions; a common pattern of variable hyperarousal and hypoarousal was noted for all schizophrenics relative to normals. However, when level of arousal was examined in relative terms, the investigators concluded that the process schizophrenics demonstrated the least change in responsiveness to environmental stress taken from resting level, reactives were intermediate in this regard, and normals showed the greatest autonomic change.

Two investigators have reported differential autonomic response to aversive social cues for the two types of schizophrenics. Reynolds (1963) found that reactives responded more strongly to the stress of failure and criticism than process schizophrenics as evidenced by elevation in systolic blood pressure.

Greater reactive response to verbal censure was also identified by Barry (1968) who used subjective reports of anxiety as his basis for inference. A nonexperimental finding which might be most meaningful inserted at this point is the higher elevation on the Taylor Manifest Anxiety Scale for reactives (Altshuler, 1966).

The final category of studies bearing upon process-reactive differences in arousal require the added weight of conceptualization in learning terms, but despite this requirement the results seem clearly to support the previously noted deficit in emotional responsiveness in process schizophrenics. Struve (1966), using a classical conditioning paradigm, was able to condition increased heart rate to a tone as conditioned stimulus and electric shock as unconditioned stimulus for reactive schizophrenics. Normals were intermediate in demonstrating heart rate conditioning and process schizophrenics were the worst conditioners. Since classical conditioning requires the occurrence of the unconditioned response (in this experiment, heart rate increase), the poor conditionability of the process schizophrenic can be reasonably attributed to his lack of unconditioned responding to the electric shock—his low level of autonomic responsiveness.

DeWolfe (1962) found that reactives displayed increased reaction times ("blocking") to affectively toned verbs relative to neutral verbs but that process schizophrenics did not change their latencies. The data further suggested that the heightened responsiveness of the reactives persisted and augmented subsequent emotional responses to neutral stimuli. Reisman (1960) showed that if reactives were reinforced for faster performance on a card-sorting task, their sorting on criterion trials was slowed. Process schizophrenics and normals failed to demonstrate this effect. The inhibition of performance for reactives, according to Reisman, was attributable to the added stress of reinforcement and their greater vulnerability to stress and anxiety arousal. Process schizophrenics were considered more withdrawn and less vulnerable to stress. Higgins and Mednick (1963) established that reactives provide greater reminiscence effects on a repetitive inverse alphabet printing task; they interpreted this finding as evidence of greater arousal in reactives on the assumption that emotional responses had an initial suppressive effect on performance but subsequently dissipated. A final investigation (Dwarshuis, 1964) reported that reactive schizophrenics were superior in their ability to integrate extrinsic stimuli at low levels of affectivity but that the integrative functions of the process schizophrenic reached the level of the reactive as stimuli became more emotionally arousing. Interpretation of the final equality of the groups under conditions of high arousal either in terms of increased drive for the low-arousal process schizophrenic or the disruptive effects of hyperarousal for the reactive schizophrenic would be consistent with the process-reactive distinction drawn in this section.

Adaptive-Style Theory Validation Study

Since the bulk of the research demonstrating process-reactive differences in emotional responsiveness included external stimulation (often stressful) as part of the procedure, the parallel investigation using late adolescents might be expected to follow a similar procedure. It also should be recalled that the theoretical basis for anticipating differences in emotionality resides in the distinct patterns of processing external stimulation proposed for the two adaptive styles. This further underscores the importance of a methodology which includes systematic application of an extrinsic stimulus stressor.

Iversen (1971) conducted the investigation relevant to the theoretical issue of whether differing arousal levels pertain to late adolescents who have learned open or closed styles of coping with aversive maternal control. His experiment included 33 male Emory undergraduates who averaged 18.9 years of age. This number served as volunteers from the initial pool of 100 subjects who took the two child-rearing questionnaires and included 15 in an aversive-maternal-control group and 18 in a combined reference group. The assignment to adaptive-style subgroupings varied in this one experiment somewhat from our usual procedures in that disruption-nondisruption decisions were based upon the difference in Stroop performance given input of a neutral stimulus (i.e., a male voice counting backwards) and input of the standard aversive mother-child scene.

In brief, Iversen's procedures were as follows. Each subject was tested individually in the laboratory. The first five minutes were used to physiographically record the heart rate under resting conditions in order to establish individual base rates. Following this, the subject was asked to perform on one form of the Stroop while experiencing input of neutral cues. Upon completion of the Stroop-neutral tape condition, a second five-minute resting base-rate period was provided. Finally, the subject performed on the second form of the Stroop while exposed to the taped stimulation of the aversive mother-son scene; electrical recording of heart rate continued throughout.

Each person's base level of heart rate was determined by the beats-per-minute count for the last 60 seconds of the resting period prior to the tape condition in question. Emotional responsiveness to the stimulus condition was specified in terms of the change in heart rate from base level to the stimulus period. Analysis of heart rate obtained during both resting periods indicated no differences in arousal among the four experimental groups. Tables 51 and 52 include the heart rate change data for the neutral-tape and the aversive-tape conditions, respectively. Statistical analysis of changes in emotional arousal for each of the contiguous periods within the neutral-tape condition identified one significant effect related to our interests. The tests of simple effects revealed that the heart-rate change for the closed-style males (14.57) was significantly ($p < .025$) less than for their nondisrupted controls in the reference group (29.56) during the middle phase of the experimental condition. The same effect was noted

Table 51. Emotional Responsiveness[a] to Interfering Neutral Stimulation During Cognitive Performance for Late-Adolescent Males Varying in Maternal Child-Rearing Experience and Style of Adaptation

	Perceived Maternal Child-Rearing Pattern			
	High Control-Low Nurturance		Reference Group	
Period Within Condition	Closed Adaptive Style ($N = 7$)	Open Adaptive Style ($N = 8$)	Nondisrupted Controls ($N = 9$)	Disrupted Controls ($N = 9$)
Pre (15 secs. tape only)	4.00	3.25	6.67	6.78
Initial (15 secs. tape-Stroop)	15.43	18.25	26.44	15.22
Middle (30 secs. tape-Stroop)	14.57	23.25	29.56	20.78
Final (30 secs. tape-Stroop)	12.57	21.00	18.89	16.67

[a]Scores in this table represent mean changes in heart beats per minute during the stimulus condition relative to the last 60 seconds of the resting period. Plus scores show increased heart rate and greater emotional responsiveness.

within the middle period of the aversive-tape condition. Closed-style males were again less aroused (14.71) by the input of task-irrelevant aversive stimulation than their controls (27.11); the difference was reliable ($p < .025$) here as before. No other comparisons in the data of Tables 51 and 52 were significant.

These results are in keeping with the theoretical proposal that closed-style males will be emotionally hyporesponsive under conditions of external stimulation. When the stimulation that served as a distraction was of neutral character, the closed-style adapter was the least autonomically affected over the last 80% of the recorded period among all groups. This pattern held only for the middle 40% of the recorded period for the subsequent aversive input condition. The rather remarkable stability of the closed-style males in heart rate over the last three periods of each condition after an initial acceleration is also apparent.

Iversen, in considering his results, made note of several factors which, taken collectively, lend a more impressive character to this theoretical confirmation. The relatively small number of subjects and the typical wide variability of the physiological measure make statistical significance, when obtained, that much more impressive. One further consideration regarding Iversen's methodology should be noted, since it would be our opinion that it did influence the results and detracted from the predicted effect which was observed in the closed-style

Table 52. Emotional Responsiveness[a] to Interfering Aversive Stimulation During Cognitive Performance for Late-Adolescent Males Varying in Maternal Child-Rearing Experience and Experience and Style of Adaptation

	Perceived Maternal Child-Rearing Pattern			
	High Control-Low Nurturance		Reference Group	
Period Within Condition	Closed Adaptive Style	Open Adaptive Style	Nondisrupted Controls	Disrupted Controls
Pre (15 secs. tape only)	4.71	1.25	8.00	–.67
Initial (15 secs. tape-Stroop)	15.57	14.75	24.44	12.78
Middle (30 secs. tape-Stroop)	14.71	17.50	27.11	17.89
Final (30 secs. tape-Stroop)	12.14	12.75	16.00	9.56

[a] See footnote at bottom of Table 51.

group. Inspection of the arousal levels represented in the neutral-tape and the aversive-tape data suggests that autonomic adaptation to the task-interference procedures occurred not only within each condition but also from one condition to the next. The trend toward extinction of the autonomic response is nowhere more apparent than in the final 30 seconds of the second exposure to the cognitive interference procedures in which all remaining subgroups demonstrated sizeable deceleration of heart rate relative to the closed-style males to the point where none was distinguishable from this low-arousal group.

STYLE OF ADAPTATION TO AVERSIVE MATERNAL CONTROL AND HETEROSEXUAL ORIENTATION

The adaptive-style theory postulates an increasing separation in heterosexual adjustment between closed-style and open-style children during adolescence, particularly in males. The social introversion of the closed-style adapter exerts its general influence by limiting his peer experience to such an extent that heterosexual maturation is curtailed. Specific generalized responses to women, having the mother as their origin, will introduce even more serious obstacles to establishing heterosexual relationships, since the dominant transferred response is avoidance or withdrawal. In contrast, the open-style male will be driven to seek out heterosexual relationships. This follows not only from the approach behaviors which would be predicted from his general social style and from the specific responses transferred from his mother-directed behaviors but also from the potential esteem-building qualities accorded to heterosexual behavior in adolescence. Aside from the obvious implications for palpable heterosexual behavior such as dating, courtship, and marriage, less tangible differences would accompany the two modes of adaptation. We would expect, for example, that the closed-style male would lack the heterosexual experience in adolescence necessary to clearly articulate the object of his sexual drive; the potential for heterosexual and homosexual arousal would be more likely to coexist (although autoerotic behavior would be the most likely sexual outlet). Then, too, the masculine sex-role development of the closed-style child would be retarded by the restricted opportunity to exercise role-relevant behaviors within the context of cross-sex relationships.

Related Process-Reactive Schizophrenic Research

Reference once again to the Phillips Prognostic Rating Scale in Appendix F will attest to the fact that a less adequate premorbid heterosexual adjustment in process schizophrenics than in reactive schizophrenics is a matter of definition, not proof. It is in part by being less heterosexually competent that the schizophrenic comes to be classified as process. However, there are two general classes of studies that add empirical backing if any is needed.

Numerous investigations of prognosis in schizophrenia have reported that the achievement of marital status is a positive prognostic sign (Chapman, Day, and Burstein, 1961; Counts and Devlin, 1954; Farina, Garmezy, and Barry, 1963; Farina, Garmezy, Zalusky, and Becker, 1966; Garfield and Sundland, 1966; Gittelman-Klein, and Klein, 1968; Jenkins and Gurel, 1959; Lindemann, Fairweather, Stone, Smith, and London, 1959; Marks, 1963; Mason, Tarpy, Sherman, and Haefner, 1960; Rassidakis, Lykas, Papadakis, and Kafatou, 1963; Simon and Wirt, 1961). In other words, reactive schizophrenics, who have a more favorable prognosis, will demonstrate a higher incidence of marriage in their history than poorer prognosis process schizophrenics. Reducing this statement to quantitative terms, Meichenbaum (1969) reports a correlation of .78 between reactive-process classification and achievement-nonachievement of marital status. The higher incidence of marriage for reactive schizophrenics conveys a more mature level of heterosexual development than is found for process schizophrenics.

Several psychometric studies using projective techniques have also produced evidence of differential adequacy of process-reactive heterosexual orientation or sex-role adoption. Ussery (1957) collected the fantasy productions of schizophrenics on the Thematic Apperception Test and found his reactive group to be more productive on cards reflecting heterosexual interest. Working with the Semantic Differential ratings of sexually connotative concepts, Query (1962) noted sharper discrimination between the sexual roles for reactive schizophrenics and greater sex-role confusion for process schizophrenics. In a similar vein, Figetakis (1964) detected superior sexual differentiation on the Draw-A-Person Test for his reactive group. Reactives were described as displaying greater heterosexual interest, whereas process schizophrenics appeared narcissistic on the Blacky Picture Test in the same study. Normington (1965), basing his conclusions upon process-reactive performance on a perceptual task, concluded that these groups could be distinguished in terms of "differential love object cathexis"—process toward the self versus reactive toward the opposite sex. The Blacky pictures indicated greater identification with the mother on the part of process schizophrenics.

Adaptive-Style Theory Validation Study (Sexual Arousal)

Gilgun's (1972) master's research was concerned with identifying possible relationships between the aversive-maternal-control experience and subsequent development of heterosexual interest. He reasoned that the aversive qualities of the mother would be generalized to other females, thus serving to diminish the interpersonal attractiveness of any potential heterosexual object. His results, completely negative, were derived from comparing high control-low nurturance males with a reference group perceiving the opposite child-rearing qualities (low control-high nurturance) in their mothers.

What had not been considered at the time Gilgun developed his hypothesis and methodology was the growing body of research indicating that the search for certain hypothesized relationships could be misleadingly barren unless the aversive-maternal-control group was considered in terms of its adaptive-style subgroupings. Since considerable evidence was available pointing toward heterosexual deficit in process schizophrenics, application of adaptive-style theory to hypothesis development might have led Gilgun to a more refined prediction. Fortunately for our present purposes, there was a way to rework the Gilgun data (with his courteous permission) so that the results of an adaptive-style methodology could be approximated.

The 37 male subjects in the Gilgun study were volunteers from among Emory undergraduates. Group-testing procedures for administering the child-rearing questionnaires followed the usual guidelines with each subject returning later for an individual laboratory session with the male experimenter.

The method used to gauge sexual interest was developed originally by Hess, Seltzer, and Shlien (1965). They found that they were able to distinguish between confirmed heterosexual and homosexual men solely on the basis of pupil response to slides of nudes flashed on a screen. The heterosexual males' response to pictures of nude females was pupillary dilation, whereas pictures of male nudes elicited constriction. For homosexuals, pictures of both nude males and nude females led to dilation of the pupils, although the dilation was greater in response to nude males. Actually, the difference between heterosexually oriented and homosexually oriented males was about twice as great when gauged by their responses to the slides of nude males than was found when slides of nude females were shown.

Gilgun's pupillometric technique, in more specific detail, involved the presentation of a series of slides to the subject who sat with his head held by a headrest looking through an aperture to a projection screen. The slides included both male and female nudes (genitalia were not shown) plus some buffer art slides. Each picture slide was preceded by a gray control slide. Pupil size (recorded by a hidden camera) during the exposure of the control slide was used as a baseline to which pupil size during the following nude slide could be compared and a change score calculated.

As previously noted, Gilgun's comparison of pupillary response to the slides for the child-rearing quadrant groups failed to reveal any differences. A method for estimating closed or open style presented itself when the subtle versus obvious control key was developed within the control factor scales of the PARI (see Table 40). These keyed scales were found to differentiate between adaptive-style groups and made possible a post hoc delineation of Gilgun's subjects into open-style and closed-style adapters. Table 53 presents the pupillary change scores for the two child-rearing groups further subdivided into estimated style of adaptation by cutting their respective subtle versus obvious control scale score distributions at the median; more subtle control defined open style and more obvious control defined closed style. No differences emerged when pupillary change to the slides of nude females were considered. The mean scores were, in fact, surprisingly restrained, two groups showing slight pupil dilation in response to nude female cues and two groups demonstrating modest changes in a constricted direction relative to neutral stimulation. However, more robust effects were obtained when nude males were shown, as was the case with the earlier Hess et al. investigation. Analysis of variance identified a significant interaction effect among these mean pupil changes to slides of males ($p < .05$). While all subgroups demonstrated pupillary constriction to pictures of nude males, closed-style males were less "turned off" by homoerotic cues than were open-style males. For some reason, the opposite pattern of pupil response was evidenced by the two low control-high nurturance reference groups.

The reanalyzed Gilgun findings can be interpreted as consistent with the theory inasmuch as the closed-style and open-style late-adolescents were equally aroused by slides of nude females but the open-style adapters were more

Table 53. Pupil Response to Slides of Nude Females and Males for Late-Adolescent Males Varying in Maternal Child-Rearing Experience and Estimated Style of Adaptation

	Perceived Maternal Child-Rearing Pattern			
	High Control-Low Nurturance		Low Control-High Nurturance	
Score[a]	Closed Adaptive Style ($N = 10$)	Open Adaptive Style ($N = 9$)	Nondisrupted Controls ($N = 10$)	Disrupted Controls ($N = 8$)
Mean pupil change to slides of nude females	+2.76	–.77	–5.10	+4.46
Mean pupil change to slides of nude males	–33.95	–46.99	–47.07	–33.59

[a]Plus scores indicate pupil dilation and minus scores pupil constriction.

restrained in their response to slides of nude males relative to their closed-style counterparts. Thus, open-style males demonstrated more differentiation in their sexual interests than did the closed-style males. These results are tempered, of course, by the unexplained reversal of pupillary response to the male nudes found with the two reference groups.

Adaptive-Style Theory Validation Study (Sex-Role Identity and Parent Identification)

There are many aspects of the Gilgun data reanalysis which make it rather surprising that any effect would surface: to name but three, restricted numbers of subjects, a highly variable index of sexual interest, and the necessity to use an estimate (obvious versus subtle control) of an estimate (Stroop-tape performance) to infer prior developmental experience. Even so, the predicted difference in sexual orientation did not emerge as clearly as we would have liked. For that reason, additional evidence regarding the nature of the sex-role behavior of the late adolescent was needed to supplement the sexual arousal observations which the Gilgun data afforded.

Heilbrun (1971b) examined the sex-role identity variable in a sample of 40 Emory undergraduate male volunteers from two perspectives using unanalyzed data from an earlier study (Heilbrun, 1968a). Sex-role identity was considered in terms of conformance to the culturally prescribed behaviors for each sex, the masculinity-femininity dimension. A second approach was to measure the type of parental identification shown by the late adolescent. The latter allows not only a second look at the nature of sexual identity but potentially offers some further clues regarding the family dynamics which obtain when the child is exposed to a sustained aversive-maternal-control experience.

The psychometric indices of masculinity-femininity and parental identification were originally constructed for use with the late-adolescent subject population from which all of our adaptive-style investigations have sampled. The Masculinity-Femininity Scale of the Adjective Check List, derived empirically by Heilbrun (Cosentino and Heilbrun, 1964), has demonstrated its research utility in several studies (Heilbrun, 1964a; Heilbrun, 1965c; 1968b; 1969; 1970a). Similarly, the Identification Scale, also scored from the Adjective Check List, has accumulated a backlog of studies in which significant and psychologically meaningful results have been obtained. A detailed description of scale derivation and review of nine studies cited as evidence of its construct validity has been published (Heilbrun, 1965a). More recent publications [Heilbrun, 1965b; 1968b; 1969; in press (b)] also support the research utility of the Identification Scale. While we feel a healthy skepticism is warranted by any attempt to reduce something as complex as sex-role identity or the parental identification process into simple scores, the Masculinity-Femininity and Identification Scales of the Adjective Check List have probably fared as well as any and better than most psychometric devices in accomplishing these reductions.

The Masculinity-Femininity Scale has been normed for college students and offers a standard scoring system with the mean set at T = 50 and the standard deviation set at 10. Higher scores suggest stronger adherence to culturally prescribed masculine behavioral qualities, whereas lower scores indicate femininity of sex-role identity.

Identification Scale scoring and interpretation is more involved. The procedure involves two components which enter into the final score. First, the personality profile of the child, across 15 important dimensions of normal interpersonal behavior, is compared with that child's ratings of his mother and father on the same dimensions. The summary score reflects the extent to which the child's pattern of personality functioning corresponds more closely to the father's or the mother's characteristic mode of behavior. While a modeling assumption underlies this measure of parent identification (that is, children learn to behave like parents by observation and behavior matching), it is not a necessary assumption of the Identification Scale. Scores are interpreted as meaning stronger identification with parent A relative to parent B as the behavioral similarity between parent A and the child increases, whatever the origins of the corresponding behaviors happen to be (e.g., modeling, genetic influence, common response to cultural prescription).

Identification Scale scores have also been normed for college students with the average behavioral similarity between the son and his father set at T = 50 with a standard deviation of 10. Higher scores in this case correspond to increasing similarity to the father and have been interpreted in prior research as indicating a father-identification for the son. Lower scores, in turn, reflecting increasing similarity between the son and his mother, have been considered indications of a mother-identification.

One conceptual advantage of the Identification Scale to other psychometric approaches to inferring parental identification is the inclusion of a parent-model score which provides an estimate of the masculinity-femininity of the father and mother as models. Consideration of the sex-role attributes of the parents allows the researcher to avoid the naive assumption, often made by default, that all fathers are masculine and all mothers are feminine in their psychological makeup. The parent-model score also is based on the parent descriptions provided by the son. Nine of the 15 personality variables contributing to the similarity score were found to be sex-typed based on the ratings of 400 college students (Heilbrun, 1964b); achievement, dominance, endurance, and autonomy were rated as masculine and affiliation, nurturance, deference, succorance, and abasement as feminine. Thus, the sex-role score for a parent represents the number of ratings out of nine for which the father was judged as better described by the four masculine traits and the mother was judged as better fitting the descriptions of the five feminine traits. Scores can range from 0-9 with high scores reflecting culturally prescribed sex-role patterns in the parents and low scores designated sex-role reversal in the mother and father.

Although the evidence bearing upon the mediating effects of parental identification for subsequent sex-role identity and adjustment in females is difficult to interpret (Heilbrun, 1968c), the contingencies for males are unequivocal (Heilbrun, 1970b). Only one type of parent identification, that with a masculine father model, systematically contributes to a more effective adjustment in the son.

The prediction for the Heilbrun sex-role study, thrice-determined by the adaptive-style theory, the relevant process-reactive schizophrenia research, and the suggestive trends in the Gilgun experiment, was that male closed-style adapters would have established an inadequate (less masculine) sex-role identity. The procedures of this study involved the collection of the Adjective Check List performances and the parent-model descriptions at the same group-testing session as the child-rearing questionnaires, whereas the Stroop-aversive tape condition was administered individually as always.

The sex-role and identification data incorporated in Table 54 are quite revealing. Analysis of variance of scores taken from the Masculinity-Femininity Scale revealed no general between-group effects, but a *t*-test of the mean difference between the closed-style subgrouping and the nondisrupted control subgroup was significant ($p < .05$ one tail). Closed-style males were less masculine in their sex-role identity relative to control males as predicted. They also were the only one of the four subgroups which emerged as feminine in an

Table 54. Sex-Role Identity and Parental Identification of Late-Adolescent Males Varying in Maternal Child-Rearing Experience and Style of Adaptation

	Perceived Maternal Child-Rearing Pattern			
	High Control-Low Nurturance		Low Control-High Nurturance	
Score	Closed Adaptive Style ($N = 10$)	Open Adaptive Style ($N = 10$)	Nondisrupted Controls ($N = 10$)	Disrupted Controls ($N = 10$)
Mean masculinity-femininity score[a]	45.00	52.30	52.90	53.80
Mean identification score[b]	47.90	46.90	52.30	52.90
Mean parent model score[c]	6.20	5.60	7.00	6.70

[a] Greater masculinity is indicated as scores increase above 50; greater femininity is indicated as scores decreased below 50.

[b] Greater father identification suggested as scores increase above 50; greater mother identification as scores decrease below 50.

[c] The higher the score, the more appropriate the sex roles of the parents.

absolute sense, their mean falling a half standard deviation below the male college norm. Open-style males were indistinguishable from their control group with regard to their level of masculinity.

The two component scores of the parent identification measure were also tested by analysis of variance. The parent-child similarity scores evidenced a main effect for child-rearing group ($p < .05$). Aversive-maternal-control males demonstrated an overall tendency to identify more with their mothers and the low control-high nurturance males a general tendency to identify more with their fathers. While the parent model attributes of the HC-LN adolescents appeared to show a trend toward sex-role reversal (5.90) relative to the reference group (6.85), the reliability of this difference could not be established statistically.

The most comprehensive basis for describing parent identification in our data is the combination of both the similarity and parent-model scores to ascertain the *type* of identification characterizing the child-rearing groups. Of special interest is whether the late-adolescent male evidences an identification found to facilitate an effective masculine sex-role identity (primary identification with a masculine father) or one of the other three possible types of parent identification (with a feminine father, a masculine mother, or a feminine mother). Examination of the data for differences in these categorical outcomes (which we shall refer to as facilitative and nonfacilitative types of parent identification) proceeded by determining the mean parent-similarity and parent-model scores for all subjects (50.00 and 6.38, respectively) and using the score nearest the mean as cutting points. Accordingly, scores of at least 50 and 6 were taken to indicate a facilitative identification for the subject; if either or both scores fell below these points, a nonfacilitative identification was inferred. Of the 20 aversive-maternal-control males, only four (20%) presented scores suggesting a facilitative parental identification, whereas 16 (80%) had nonfacilitative combinations of scores. In contrast, 12 (60%) of the low control-high nurturance males showed facilitative identification and only 8 (40%) gave nonfacilitative patterns. Nonparametric chi-square analysis revealed these proportional differences to be statistically significant ($p < .05$).

A frequency table summarizing the specific types of parent identification for the child-rearing groups is provided despite the fact that the breakdown reduces the numbers of subjects per cell beyond possible statistical analysis. Table 55 does at least provide several clues to guide our thinking. It can be observed first that the pattern of specific identification types is almost identical for the two adaptive styles. Although sex-role identity differences were found between

Table 55. Incidence of Parent Identification Patterns for Late-Adolescent Males Varying in Maternal Child-Rearing Experience and Style of Adaptation

Parent Identification Pattern	Perceived Maternal Child-Rearing Pattern			
	High Control-Low Nurturance		Low Control-High Nurturance	
	Closed Adaptive Style	Open Adaptive Style	Nondisrupted Controls	Disrupted Controls
Identified with masculine father	2	2	7	5
Identified with feminine father	3	3	0	1
Identified with masculine mother	1	2	1	1
Identified with feminine mother	4	3	2	3

adaptive-style groups (see Table 54), the common absence of masculine-father identification in both groups raises questions about the source of the apparent masculinity of the open-style adapters. The proposed compensatory nature of the open-style male's heterosexual motivation could provide a possible answer—adoption of culturally sanctioned masculine sex-role behaviors in the absence of a foundation laid down in the parental identification process.

It might be noted next on Table 55 that the incidence of sex-role reversals between parents was considerably higher (45%) for the aversive-control males than for their reference counterparts (15%). (The nonparametric statistic testing this difference approached significance, falling within the 10% confidence interval; this was somewhat more suggestive than the previously reported parametric analysis of the parent-model score means.) Problems created by the absence of an effective model for the son should be more prevalent within the families of the aversive-control mother.

Finally, the Table 55 incidence data fail to indicate that identification with the mother is in any way unique to the aversive-control groups. While 50% of the aversive-control adolescents were considered as mother-identified by our scoring procedures, 35% of the reference group also were so considered. The only trend which is in evidence regarding differential incidence among the deviant identification patterns is the 30% of the aversive-control males with a feminine-father identification as compared with only a 5% figure for the reference males.

STYLE OF ADAPTATION TO AVERSIVE MATERNAL CONTROL AND PARANOID BEHAVIOR

The proposal that the open style of coping with aversive maternal control is dynamically linked to the development of a paranoid character structure is not to be tested by any single experiment. Discussion of paranoid development in the previous chapter outlined seven response dispositions which are thought to coalesce in paranoid behavior and to be contingencies of the open style. These were proposed to be low self-esteem, sensitivity to evaluative cues, broad external scanning, low interpersonal trust, defensive projection, intolerance of ambiguity, and inflexible social ideation. Some of these properties (low self-esteem, low interpersonal trust, sensitivity to evaluative cues) are commonly shared with closed-style adapters, and evidence has been accumulated pointing to these more general effects in aversive-maternal-control adolescents (see Chapters 5 and 6). One of the four proposed differential properties (breadth of external scanning) already has received empirical documentation in the present chapter. Experimental evidence regarding defensive projection and intolerance of ambiguity are treated in a subsequent section of this chapter dealing with personality postulates.

Related Process-Reactive Schizophrenia Research

Much of the evidence needed to establish whether paranoid behaviors are more likely to be observed in reactive than in process schizophrenics is of an indirect nature. For example, there are those studies which demonstrate that the broad external scanning of the reactive (relative to the process) schizophrenic is also found in the paranoid (relative to the nonparanoid) schizophrenic. Price and Ericksen (1966) compared paranoids with nonparanoids on a size-distance discrimination procedure and found that while paranoids were comparable to normals in perceptual sensitivity, the nonparanoids were much less sensitive on this scanning task. Auditory scanning was assessed by Rappaport and Hopkins (1969) who report fewer signal detection errors for the paranoid schizophrenics. Phenothiazine medication failed to affect the auditory acuity of the paranoid group, although it did improve the performance of nonparanoids. Spohn, Thetford, and Woodham (1970) found paranoids inferior to nonparanoids in an information processing task involving the identification of stimuli, apparently in contradiction to the two experiments just cited. Yet these investigators made special note that the nature of their task, involving as it did the brief presentation of stimuli, penalized the broad scanning tendencies of the paranoid schizophrenics. Accordingly, their interpretation places these results in line with other research reporting hyperscanning of external stimulation in paranoids.

Both Goodman (1968) and Wolowitz (1965) provide evidence which suggests differential patterns of influence for parents of paranoid and nonparanoid schizophrenics. These patterns corresponded to the authority reversal found by some investigators to hold for the parents of good (father-dominance) and poor (mother-dominance) schizophrenics. (The reader may recall the highly equivocal nature of the process-reactive research bearing upon this hypothesis.) Both Goodman and Wolowitz suggest that earlier identified process-reactive differences may have been produced by the unidentified presence of many paranoids among reactive groups and the nonparanoid character of the process groups. Wolowitz actually tested this supposition by a reanalysis of earlier authority-reversal data reported by Farina (1960). He was able to demonstrate the same authority reversal previously reported for the schizophrenics' parents when compared by premorbid status when he grouped the patients by the presence or absence of paranoid symptoms.

Size estimation studies have also suggested the commonality of the process-reactive and nonparanoid-paranoid distinctions. Both Harris (1957) and Zahn (1959) reported that process schizophrenics tend to overestimate size and reactives tend to underestimate size on their laboratory tasks. Silverman (1964) established the identical pattern of behavior in his nonparanoid and paranoid schizophrenic groups. Four groups representing the various combinations of process-reactive and nonparanoid-paranoid status were compared on a size-estimation task by Davis, Cromwell, and Held (1967). They report that reactives and paranoids were underestimaters and process and nonparanoid schizophrenics were overestimaters. Although no interaction between the two dichotomous variables was found, their data make it clear that these effects were mediated by two groups. As it turned out, the schizophrenics who were reactive *and* paranoid comprised the only underestimating group. Among the three remaining groups, those schizophrenics who were process *and* nonparanoid overestimated size to about three times the extent as the other two groups. The tendency toward size underestimation in reactive paranoid schizophrenics and overestimation in process nonparanoid schizophrenics was replicated in a subsequent study (Neale and Cromwell, 1968).

In a different realm of perception, paranoid reactives responded to stimulus displays in a less redundant, richer fashion than process nonparanoids (Cromwell, 1968). Preference for complexity in visual designs was the object of study in yet another investigation comparing reactive paranoid schizophrenics with process nonparanoid schizophrenics (Neale and Cromwell, 1969). Subjects were presented with pairs of designs differing with regard to the number of independent turns (3, 6, 10, 20, 40) represented in their randomly generated asymmetrical shapes. After converting these preferences to comparative judgment scores, statistical analysis disclosed a main effect of complexity; there was general preference for less complex designs. However, a significant interaction was also identified which we would interpret, upon inspection of the figure provided in the Neale and Cromwell paper, as a stronger preference in reactive paranoids for the least complex figures and a stronger aversion in the same group for the most complex figures. In fact, the process nonparanoids showed signs of indifference to increased stimulus complexity. Changes in complexity from 6 to 40 was accompanied by only a slight drop in preference, whereas the reactive paranoid group showed a decrement in preference of five to six times this magnitude over the same range of complexity. Thus, reactive paranoids were much more sensitively attuned to changes in extrinsic stimulation than were process nonparanoids.

All of the studies but one reviewed in this section bear upon the processing of external information and point, albeit indirectly, to the conclusion that a commonality exists between the behaviors associated with reactive and paranoid and between process and nonparanoid status. In addition, the evidence emanating from these investigations is entirely in keeping with the process-reactive scanning research previously reviewed; process schizophrenics emerged as more narrow or less effective in their processing of external information and reactive schizophrenics were broader or more effective in this regard. The one study bearing upon preference for stimulus complexity suggested the same conclusions. Process nonparanoids, less responsive to external stimulation, were minimally affected in their preferences by increased complexity. Reactive paranoids, highly responsive to extrinsic stimulation, demonstrated a steep aversive gradient as complexity was increased. It is worth noting that the aversive character of stimulus complexity should be especially compelling during the acute stage of the schizophrenic disorder when stimulus "flooding" is a problem; Neale and Cromwell report the use of acute schizophrenic subjects in this investigation.

One study has been reported which allows us to look directly at the concordance between process and reactive premorbid status and paranoid symptomatology. From two hospitals, Goldstein, Held, and Cromwell (1968) collected data that represent the commonality between good-poor premorbid adjustment and the presence of paranoid delusions as the predominant symptom. The California sample of hospital admissions included acute schizophrenic males, and the Tennessee samples were schizophrenic males of varying chronicity. The contingency data of Table 56, reproduced from the original report, are clearcut. Paranoid delusions are rarely found (8%) in process schizophrenics but are commonly observed (44%) among reactive schizophrenics. The five-fold difference in base rates offers clear testimony to what we have concluded from the indirect evidence. Paranoid behavior is linked with reactive status and its absence with process.

Table 56. The Paranoid-Nonparanoid Status of Good and Poor Premorbid Patients

	UCLA		$Vanderbilt_1$		$Vanderbilt_2$		Subtotal		Total
Diagnosis	Good	Poor	Good	Poor	Good	Poor	Good	Poor	
Paranoid	10	3	5	1	7	0	22	4	26
Nonparanoid	12	13	8	16	8	15	28	44	72
Totals							50	48	98

Note: UCLA ($X^2 = 1.87$, $df = 1$, $p > .05$); $Vanderbilt_1$ ($X^2 = 4.86$, $df = 1$, $p < .05$; Fisher's exact probability test, $p < .04$); $Vanderbilt_2$ ($X^2 = 30.00$, $df = 1$, $p < .001$; Fisher's exact probability test, $p < .003$); Total ($X^2 = 14.20$, $df = 1$, $p < .001$).

Reproduction from Goldstein, M. J., Held, J. M., and Cromwell, R. L. Premorbid adjustment and paranoid-nonparanoid status in schizophrenia. *Psychological Bulletin*, 1968, **70**, 382-386.

Adaptive-Style Theory Validation Study (Late Adolescents)

Two complementary studies have been completed, one using late adolescents and the other schizophrenic patients, which are germane to the hypothesized paranoid character structure of the open-style adapter. The first of these (Heilbrun and Norbert, 1972) used 55 Emory male volunteers whose mean age was 19.2 years.

The major problem which we faced in developing a research methodology which could properly test the hypothesis was one of definition. What behavior could be identified that would find representation among subjects in a nonclinical population and that would be a critical property of the clinical paranoid condition? Standard textbook description in abnormal psychology (Cameron, 1963) affirms that delusional thinking is symptomatically central to the diagnosis of paranoid behavior and that delusional thought can be inferred ". . . when the inferences and the conclusions become fixed, adamant, inflexible, and untouched by contrary evidence. . ." (p. 471). Flexibility of thinking when confronted by evidence contrary to prior judgment seemed to offer the dual advantage of being a criterion in diagnosing a paranoid condition and of providing a dimension of behavior readily observed in clinical and nonclinical populations. What little evidence was available from the developmental literature regarding flexibility of thought suggested only its inverse relationship with maternal child-rearing control (Barclay and Cusumano, 1967; Busse, 1969; Witkin, Dyk, Faterson, Goodenough, and Karp, 1962).

The Heilbrun and Norbert late-adolescent experiment proceeded by the routine questionnaire and Stroop-tape methods, including assignments to HC-LN and combined reference groupings and adaptive-style and disruption control subgroupings by median-cut procedures. At that point in which the laboratory conditions were to facilitate and measure individual differences in thought flexibility, the subject, who was being seen individually by the female experimenter, was asked to record his impression of how he was viewed by other people. After being given a more detailed explanation of this type of social perception, the subject went through the 300 behavioral adjectives of the Adjective Check List and marked those which described how he believed others judged him.

Upon completion of the adjective task, the subject was reminded that he had been administered a personality questionnaire (i.e., an abbreviated version of the Minnesota Multiphasic Personality Inventory) during the group-testing session. He was then given the bogus information that a "faculty psychologist," an expert with this particular personality test, had examined his test responses in the interim and had recorded his impressions of the subject by selecting from among the adjectives on the same check list. The experimenter at this point told the subject that she was going to compare how he thought others viewed him with the view of him provided by the "expert psychologist."

The experimenter then followed a standard sequence of behaviors with all subjects. She removed a manila folder from the top of the pile of such folders and opened it to display a marked check list of adjectives (presumably the subject's description provided by the psychologist but actually a standard form used for all subjects). She proceeded to remove the actual child-rearing questionnaires completed by the subject in the earlier sessions to authenticate the folder as his own. The two completed Adjective Check List forms were then laid side by side, and the experimenter simulated a careful adjective by adjective comparison of the two sets of judgments. Although the experimenter's back was partially turned toward the subject throughout this portrayal, the chair placements were such as to allow the subject to verify what she was doing and that his materials were really included in the folder. After having recorded the actual number of words checked by the subject on his Adjective Check List (which she had counted prior to the simulated comparison), the experimenter determined a figure representing 30% of this total number immediately following her comparison.

All materials were then returned to the folder except the subject's own Adjective Check List, and the experimenter proceeded to inform him that of the ____________ (actual figure) adjectives he had selected as descriptive of how people saw him, the psychologist agreed with only __________ (30% figure). The adolescent was requested to go through the check list again in describing how others saw him and was told in a noncoercive manner that he could change as many or as few as he wished, from none to all. The subject was then given his original check list form back so that his prior choices were available to him as he repeated the task; memory, then, could play no role in response change.

Before proceeding with the results of the experiment, some preliminary consideration of the experimental operations is in order. The degree to which the subject's ideas about his own social stimulus value remain fixed in the face of contradictory evidence from an authority does not automatically qualify as singularly indicative of trends toward paranoid thinking. We will review the arguments and evidence favoring the paranoid interpretation offered by the investigators and add further positive evidence not included in the original source.

Heilbrun and Norbert had two reasons for selecting the particular mode of thinking represented in their experimental procedure. One reason was the expectation of a greater latitude for response change if the initial set of judgments were less firmly fixed; it was assumed that the late adolescent would be less certain of how others saw him than he would be of how he viewed himself, his self-concept. More importantly the perception of how one is construed by others has direct dynamic relevance to the major forms of paranoid delusions (e.g., persecution, grandeur, sex, etc.). Each form is defined by the fixed but incorrect assumption of a particular stimulus value to other people—as an object eliciting inordinate hostility, admiration, sexual arousal, and so forth.

The basic concern with the thought flexibility variable in the Heilbrun and Norbert study, however, is more likely to be voiced in terms of whether a more parsimonious explanation than fixed ideation might not be rendered to account for any results obtained. The only obvious alternative to thinking flexibility, as far as we can see, would be that degrees of change in response from first to second performance represent differences in the tendency to defer to authority. We shall consider some evidence, after the results of the experiment have been reported, which argues strongly against deference as an alternative interpretation.

There was one piece of evidence which was cited in the original study as supporting the paranoid implications of the criterion. When the Paranoid Scale scores taken from the abbreviated Minnesota Multiphasic Personality Inventory were introduced into an analysis of variance, a significant ($p < .05$) effect for perceptual shift was demonstrated. Those males who shifted their choices the least were higher on the Paranoid Scale than those who shifted the most; inflexibility in thinking related to a psychometric index of paranoid status.

To return to the experiment proper, instructions that an expert psychologist had agreed with only 30% of the original choices that went into the subject's perceived social stimulus value elicited a wide range of response. Defining a change on the second time through as either checking an adjective that he had not checked before or not checking an adjective previously checked, subjects varied from 0 to 160 changes. The mean adjective change scores for the adaptive-style groups and their controls, after a square-root transformation to reduce skewness, are presented in Table 57. Comparison of these means by analysis of variance produced one significant effect; open-style males, expected to show paranoid trends, were less flexible in their thinking in the face of contradictory evidence than were their disrupted controls ($p < .05$). Closed-style adapters, for whom no paranoid trends were anticipated, were indistinguishable in their change scores from controls. Gauging these shifts in thinking from the vantage point of practical significance, the results are rather impressive. The open-style group, theoretically linked to paranoid development, on an average changed only about 10 choices compared to the average of 26 changes for their disrupted controls. Both the closed-style group and their controls changed 17 terms on the average.

As indicated previously, group differences in the tendency to defer to authority could satisfactorily account for the change scores reported in Table 57. The Adjective Check List includes a Deference Scale which provides us with the opportunity to examine this personality variable as it may characterize the four experimental subgroups. Table 58 includes these data, collected for but unreported in the sex-role identity study (Heilbrun, 1971b) discussed earlier in

Table 57. Change in Perceived Social Stimulus Value Following Contradictory Evidence for Late-Adolescent Males Varying in Maternal Child-Rearing Experience and Style of Adaptation

	Perceived Maternal Child-Rearing Pattern			
	High Control-Low Nurturance		Reference Group	
	Closed Adaptive Style ($N = 8$)	Open Adaptive Style ($N = 8$)	Nondisrupted Controls ($N = 22$)	Disrupted Controls ($N = 17$)
Mean changes[a]	4.12	3.19	4.14	5.09

[a]These means are based on square-root transformations of the number of changes from first to second performance.

Table 58. Deference Scale Scores for Late-Adolescent Males Varying in Maternal Child-Rearing Experience and Style of Adaptation

	Perceived Maternal Child-Rearing Pattern			
	High Control-Low Nurturance		Reference Group	
Study	Closed Adaptive Style	Open Adaptive Style	Nondisrupted Controls	Disrupted Controls
Heilbrun, 1971b	50.3	45.1	40.2	45.9
Heilbrun and Norbert, 1972	42.5	49.5	41.4	48.2
	High Control-Low Nurturance		Reference Group	
	High Shift	Low Shift	High Shift	Low Shift
Heilbrun and Norbert, 1972	42.5	49.5	47.5	39.4

Note: Deference Scale is normed with the college mean set at 50 and an SD of 10; higher scores indicate greater deference.

this chapter. Also included are the Deference Scale scores based upon the initial perceived social stimulus value ratings from the Heilbrun and Norbert study as well as the Deference Scale means for high-shift and low-shift subjects within the high control-low nurturance and combined reference child-rearing groups in the same study.

Taking the data on Table 58 one set at a time, one finds absolutely no basis for the position that the adjective change scores reported by Heilbrun and Norbert can be interpreted in terms of the deference variable. The reader will recall that the clear difference in fixed ideation was between the open adaptive-style group and the disrupted control group, whereas closed-style males and their controls were almost identical in their performance. Yet it is the open-style (45.1) and disrupted control (45.9) groups who are virtually identical on the deference variable (top row) and the closed-style adolescents (50.3) and their controls (40.2) whose mean Deference Scale scores are at variance ($p <$ .06). Considering deference in terms of how the subject feels others view him (second row), neither adaptive-style group is distinguishable from its control. Finally, relating degree of shift to Deference scores (bottom row) brought a significant ($p < .05$) interaction between child-rearing group and degree of shift. In the reference group, it does appear that low perceived deference (39.4) is associated with less responsiveness to authority. But low deference cannot be used to account for the greater fixation of response for aversive-maternal-control males, since HC-LN low shifters turn out to be more deferent (49.5) than high shifters (42.5). These data, taken collectively, point to two conclusions. Deference to authority is not a viable alternative explanation for the overall pattern of subgroup means obtained by Heilbrun and Norbert. The deference variable may be operating within their experimental procedure to influence change among reference group males in a predictable way, but this variable has no explanatory value within the aversive-maternal-control sample.

Adaptive-Style Theory Validation Study (Schizophrenics)

The treatment of the research evidence on paranoid behavior, as it pertains to the parallel differences between reactive and process schizophrenics and open-style and closed-style adolescents, has proceeded in keeping with our general plan. Evidence has been cited, especially from the Goldstein, Held, and Cromwell study, which places paranoid thinking into the dynamics of the schizophrenic with a good premorbid adjustment. Open-style adaptation to the aversive-material-control experience, the developmental pattern proposed as the premorbid antecedent to reactive schizophrenia, has been uniquely associated with a quality of thinking (inflexibility) which serves to define paranoid thought in its extreme form. The opportunity presented itself to extend the research program beyond our usual boundaries in the case of one hospital investigation.

This one study included a further test of the theory using paranoid schizophrenic subjects.

The logic underlying the prediction in the hospital experiment followed these lines. Cognitive disruption in response to maternal censure cues is the defining operation for open-style adaptation given the life-history experience of sustained aversive control by the mother. Open-style adolescents, thus defined, demonstrate paranoid trends in their thinking. If, then, the open adaptive style is to be considered an etiologic feature of paranoid behavior in schizophrenia, it should be possible to show that paranoid schizophrenics are more cognitively disrupted by maternal censure cues than nonparanoid schizophrenics.

The heightened disruptive effects of verbal censure by a mother figure among paranoid schizophrenics, if demonstrated, would stand in contrast to the results of other studies in which the impact of noxious verbal cues has been examined. Gladis and Wischner (1962) found no difference between paranoid schizophrenics and medical controls in paired-associate learning when aversive words were included. Paranoids were actually less responsive to noxious words than nonparanoid schizophrenics when instructed lever movement was the measure of aversiveness (Silverman, 1964). The perceptual effectiveness of paranoid schizophrenics in detecting homosexual words was reported by Daston (1956) to be superior to that of an unclassified schizophrenic and a normal group.

Heilbrun and Norbert (1971) obtained 31 relatively young male subjects from two state mental hospitals in Georgia. All had an uncontested diagnosis of schizophrenia. Of this number, 12 were further diagnosed as paranoid (mean age of 29.5 years) while the remaining 19 were considered nonparanoid forms of schizophrenia (mean age of 32.1 years). The participating patients were predominantly from lower-middle-class backgrounds and were constituted racially by 28 white and 3 black subjects. All of the schizophrenics had been screened initially by the hospital staff according to their ability to understand and cooperate with experimental instructions. Only two subjects, both nonparanoid, had to be subsequently eliminated because of the failure to respond appropriately to task directives.

Patients were seen individually in a relatively quiet room outside the residence areas of the hospital. The procedure followed that standardly employed to identify the disruptive effect of maternal censure within the adaptive-style investigations. The Stroop Color-Naming Test was first administered alone followed by the alternate form given in combination with the maternal-censure tape. As usual, the task procedures included precautionary checks for the subject's understanding of instructions and for color blindness.

The far greater number of errors evidenced by schizophrenics relative to college late-adolescents made a time-error cognitive efficiency scoring possible for Stroop performance. The subject's effectiveness on each Stroop was determined by dividing his number of correct responses (out of 144) by the number of seconds required to complete the task—the number of correct responses per second. Influence of maternal censure stimulation was represented by a percent change score:

$$\frac{\text{Stroop No. 2 score minus Stroop No. 1 score}}{\text{Stroop No. 1 score}}$$

This ratio score not only compares the schizophrenic's cognitive efficiency rate on the Stroop-tape combination with his rate on the distraction-free Stroop but also removes the effect of initial differences in cognitive level by considering change (numerator) in terms of initial performance (denominator). Plus percent scores represent improvement in performance on the second Stroop (despite the distractor) and minus scores reflect a deterioration in performance. Change scores ranged from a loss of 58% efficiency to a 42% gain. Table 59 includes the initial rate and change score data for the paranoid and nonparanoid schizophrenic samples. A statistical test of the change scores (by one-tail *t*-test) affirmed the experimental prediction; paranoids' performance deteriorated while nonparanoids' performance improved, with their change scores being reliably different ($p < .025$). Accordingly, paranoid schizophrenics were more sensitive to the disruptive effects of maternal censure-control cues than were schizophrenics who did not evidence paranoid symptoms.

Reference back to the initial rate scores in Table 59 points to the possibility of the same interpretive difficulty as we have alluded to before when initial baselines differ. Heilbrun and Norbert acknowledged that the decreased scores for paranoids and increased scores for nonparanoids might be considered a type of "regression to the mean." The assumption of this alternative explanation would be that the superior initial performance of the paranoid schizophrenics inevitably leads to the negative change score because of a type of settling effect, whereas the inferior initial performance of the nonparanoid schizophrenics just as inevitably leads to a positive change score because of a reverse effect. An even more basic assumption of the regression hypothesis is that no true difference in effect of censure cue distractors upon cognitive performance exists between the two schizophrenic groups. This was put to independent test by reference to data

Table 59. Effect of Exposure to Maternal Censure Cues on the Cognitive Efficiency of Paranoid and Nonparanoid Schizophrenics

Schizophrenic Group	Initial Number of Correct Responses Per Second	Percent Change Score
Paranoid	.588	–11.8%
Nonparanoid	.404	+ 5.4%

collected from 50 male college subjects under the standard Stroop-tape conditions. The initial mean Stroop score of .946, considerably higher than that presented by the paranoid schizophrenics (.588), was accompanied within the late-adolescent group by an average change score of +9.0%. Despite their initially high cognitive rate, normals improved when the censure tape was added; the practice effect outweighed the effect of distraction. Thus, the loss of 11.8% efficiency for paranoid schizophrenics (and the disruptive effects of maternal censure cues which it reflects) is even more remarkable in light of the improvement shown by both nonparanoid schizophrenics and normals under the same conditions.

STYLE OF ADAPTATION TO AVERSIVE MATERNAL CONTROL–ADDITIONAL PERSONALITY CORRELATES

The adaptive styles, involving distinct patterns of social and perceptual behavior as they do, theoretically extend a pervasive influence upon personality development in the child. Beyond the more general effects already discussed, three more specific differences in personality growth were proposed as accompaniments to the emergence of coping styles and to the family dynamics which instigated them. The closed-style adapter by contending with evaluative threat by interpersonal avoidance or withdrawal and by attentional disengagement from evaluative stimulus input predisposes himself to:

1. a mechanism of defense based upon avoidance of and disengagement from disturbing symbolic cues (repression);
2. a tolerance for ambiguity in the meaning of extrinsic cues;
3. shame responding given the failure to achieve a standard.

Open-style adaptation with its contrasting interpersonal approach and attentional vigilance for self-esteem-relevant cues promotes:

1. a mechanism of defense consistent with outward orientation toward people; denial of the unacceptable and attribution to others (projection);
2. intolerance for ambiguity of meaning of extrinsic cues;
3. guilt responding given the failure to achieve a standard.

Related Process-Reactive Schizophrenia Research (Mechanisms of Defense)

Kantor and Herron (1966), whose book serves as a review of much of the earlier research into process and reactive schizophrenic differences, address themselves to defensive processing of ego-alien stimulation in these terms:

> Clearly, schizophrenics will avoid threatening inputs if possible. Process schizophrenics will do so by disengagement and reactive schizophrenics by

disavowal. But in those experimental conditions where such avoidance is impossible, and where specific feedback is immediately available, test performances of both groups will tend to improve. Schizophrenics maintain an adaptive alertness to distressing stimuli, but they show it only when their usual schizophrenic defenses are not permitted to function (p. 34).

The "usual schizophrenic defenses" of process disengagement from and reactive disavowal of noxious symbolic meanings seem readily translated into repression and projection as primary defenses. Unfortunately, investigation of the defense mechanisms utilized by process and reactive schizophrenics has been so limited and of such a nature as to deny us any direct evidence in this regard. As we have done before, we will cite whatever indirect evidence we can to bolster the Kantor and Herron position.

For example, we can appeal to the perceptual scanning literature which has provided us with convincing evidence that reactive schizophrenics are broad scanners and process schizophrenics deploy their attention to external events in a more limited way. With this in mind, the conclusion reached by Gardner and Long (1962) that broad scanners, those individuals sensitive to their environment, employ projection to relieve discomfort points to the utilization of this mechanism by reactives. In a similar vein, the accessibility of repressive defenses in process schizophrenia is implied by a study reported by Luborsky, Blinder, and Schimek (1965) which suggested a relationship between repression and narrow scanning.

Differences in field dependency-field independency also have been established as a function of premorbid status (Bryant, 1962; Feffer, 1961; Gibeau, 1965; Margaro and Vojtisek, 1971). Reactive schizophrenics, generally more capable of processing extrinsic stimulation, have been found to be field independent, better able to isolate perceptually focal stimuli from the background in which they are embedded. Process schizophrenics have emerged as field dependent. This distinction is bolstered by the size constancy studies cited earlier which concurred in finding that reactives were given to greater size constancy, also thought to require effective inhibition of visual elements, in this case to maintain the sameness of an external focal stimulus (Crookes, 1957; Johannsen, Friedman, and Liccione, 1966; Lovinger, 1956; Sanders and Pacht, 1952; Weckowicz, Sommer, and Hall, 1958).

Keeping in mind the contingencies between reactive schizophrenia and field-independency and between process schizophrenia and field-dependency, we can note Schonbar's (1965) finding that field-dependent subjects reported dreams less frequently than field-independent subjects. This was interpreted as evidence that field-dependent persons are more prone to repression of emotionally charged events. Minard and Mooney (1969) conducted a tachistoscopic study of words matched in structure but having either neutral or emotionally toned stimulus value for the individual subject. Field-dependent subjects were able to identify fewer emotional words than neutral words, but the field-independent subjects recognized both kinds to the same extent. The repressive character of field-dependent performance is again suggested, but the investigators' interpretation of the field-independent pattern is also interesting within the context of the present discussion.

The equal recognition of neutral and affect-arousing words was made possible, according to Minard and Mooney, by the field-independent group's tendency to "isolate" affect, to separate affect from the cognition of experience. The same tendency toward isolation of affect in field-independent persons was also observed by Bertini (1961) using Rorschach evidence. A representative definition of defensive projection, like that provided by Maddi (1968, p. 160), alerts us to the fact that this defense does operate to separate the cognition of experience from distressing affect: ". . . the defense of projection involves attributing to others characteristics that are really your own (maintaining the cognition), in order that you can remain unconscious of their presence in you, and therefore free of anxiety (separated from distressing affect)." (Parenthetic comments our own.)

In summary of the field dependency studies, we can observe that field-dependent persons, such as process schizophrenics, are disposed to the use of repressive mechanisms of defense. Field-independent persons, such as reactive schizophrenics, are more inclined to projective tactics of defense.

One final piece of indirect evidence supports the conclusion that projection is the major mechanism of defense in reactive schizophrenia. The paranoid and reactive status concordance data of Goldstein, Held, and Cromwell, it may be recalled, indicated that if paranoid symptoms are going to occur in schizophrenia, they are most likely to do so in a reactive schizophrenic. Paranoid conditions are defined by the presence of projective defenses in a manner secondary in importance only to the occurrence of delusional thinking (see the *Diagnostic and statistical manual: mental disorders,* 1952). Projection, then, must be a more common defense among reactive schizophrenics to the extent that major paranoid symptoms are more prevalent in this psychotic group.

Adaptive-Style Theory Validation Study (Mechanisms of Defense)

The rather formidable job of devising experimental paradigms for both repression and projection within the scope of a single investigation was undertaken by Heilbrun (1972a). (Only the defensive projection data is reported in the journal reference because of the substantive orientation of the article.) The study of projection, at least, has a research history characterized by considerable conceptual problems, a fact ably documented by Holmes (1968). Issues of more critical concern have revolved around whether or not defensive projection should be thought of as occurring beyond the person's awareness and whether this mechanism should be considered operative whether the traits attributed to others are characteristic of the person or not. The Heilbrun experiment circumvented these conceptual and paradigmatic pitfalls by patterning its procedures in a general way after those which have proven useful in recent experimental approaches to the study of projection (Bramel, 1963; Edlow and Kiesler, 1966; Secord, Backman, and Eachus, 1964). Their common method involved the delivery of (false) information to the subject regarding an undesirable characteristic and identifying the effect this had upon the attribution of that trait to members of an immediate reference group.

The 72 Emory undergraduate male volunteers were 18.9 years of age on the average. Small-group questionnaire sessions and the individually administered Stroop-tape condition proceeded in standard fashion, as did the subgrouping into adaptive styles and general reference controls by median-cut procedures imposed on the distribution of cognitive disruption scores.

The individual experimental procedures from which defense mechanism scores were derived involved the taped presentation of 66 behavioral adjectives (see Table 44) recorded in an adult female voice. These words were presented at five-second intervals and at a volume level conducive to clear understanding. The list included, as may be recalled, 22 favorable adjectives, 22 neutral adjectives, and 22 unfavorable adjectives ordered in repeating triads of neutral-favorable-unfavorable. Instructions by the female experimenter structured the procedures as an investigation of memory for maternal communications. The subject was told that the words on a check list of adjectives most frequently selected by mothers to describe their college-age sons in a recent poll would be presented to him on a tape. (The poll was fictional.) The subject's task was to listen to the tape, following which he was to identify the words which he remembered having heard. His memory for the taped words was to be assessed by his ability to recognize them among the entire list of 300 words purportedly made available to the mothers. He was to check exactly 66 words from the total array.

After listening to the taped series of words, the subject was given the Adjective Check List and told to check the 66 words he recalled as representative of mothers' opinions of their college-age sons. The final procedural step was a request that the subject review the 66 evaluative words which he had selected and to make a binary judgment about each word; was this trait more characteristic of him than of his college male peers or more characteristic of his college peers than of him?

These procedures were designed to accomplish three objectives. (1) They were intended to elicit an evaluative response set similar to that characteristic of the subject with his own mother by reference to the generalized "mother of the college-age male" as the source of the evaluative words. (2) They established 2 categories of evaluative terms from the 66 identified by the person. One category ("hits") would include those correctly recognized from the taped list and would represent the relevant set for inferring the operation of repression or projection. The remaining category ("misses") would be those words misidentified as being on the taped list or simply selected to comply with the requirement of checking 66 words. This set of words, not being maternal evaluative terms to which subjects were exposed in this experiment, would be available as a check on the importance of evaluative source. (3) By allowing the subject free recognition of words and a choice between self-attribution or peer-attribution of traits varying in level of desirability, a special proclivity toward selective recognition or toward peer-attribution of negative traits could be detected.

Before proceeding with the discussion of the defense mechanism results, several preliminary analyses will be reported. None of these was included in the original paper because of space limitations.

Pilot Data on Endorsement of List-Relevant Adjectives

Veridicality of both the repression and projection measures, which have yet to be described, involves a necessary assumption regarding the self-attribution of the 66 evaluative terms presented to the subject as evolving from a maternal source. It is necessary to assume that selective recognition of unfavorable terms (repression) or differential self- versus peer-attribution of such terms (projection) do not actually represent self-conceptual differences rather than defensive operations. For example, the person's preexisting acceptance or disavowal of a term as self-descriptive could make that term more salient and more easily recognized if it appeared on the list presumably representing maternal opinions. Further, self-endorsement of a descriptive adjective could certainly affect the use of the word as characteristic of the self as opposed to the use of the adjective as a characteristic of one's peers. For these reasons, it is important to determine whether there were self-attribution differences among the 4 subgroups for the 66 tape-listed words by comparing self-descriptions on the Adjective Check List administered under standard conditions.

Problems of contamination with the experimental procedure made it impossible to administer the Adjective Check List to subjects in the main experiment under standard conditions of self-description. File data were accessible, however, which allowed for an analysis of the frequency with which the unfavorable, favorable, and neutral words on the taped list had been endorsed by subgroups of late-adolescent males entirely comparable to those in the main study. The mean self-attribution figures (Table 60) produced no significant differences when statistically analyzed within each qualitative category. One general effect approached significance; reference group males endorsed more favorable adjectives than aversive-control males ($p < .10$) consistent with previously established self-esteem differences in the two groups. Accordingly, there is nothing in these figures to suggest that any emergent relationships between subgroup status and mode of defense could be attributed to preexisting self-conceptual differences.

Table 60. Mean Endorsement Frequency of List-Relevant Words by Qualitative Category for Late-Adolescent Males Varying in Maternal Child-Rearing Experience and Style of Adaptation

	Perceived Maternal Child-Rearing Pattern			
	High Control-Low Nurturance		Reference Group	
Qualitative Category	Closed Adaptive Style ($N = 10$)	Open Adaptive Style ($N = 10$)	Nondisrupted Controls ($N = 10$)	Disrupted Controls ($N = 10$)
Favorable	12.60	13.40	14.20	17.60
Unfavorable	4.40	4.10	2.20	3.90
Neutral	9.00	9.30	9.10	10.80

Note: Twenty-two words are included in each qualitative category.

Preliminary Analyses of Recognition Data

Two further preliminary analyses bear upon the reliability of the recognition data which served as the raw material from which defensive operations were to be inferred. The first of these is addressed to the question of whether the requirements of the memory task had been reasonably well met by the subjects, the alternative being that it was of such extraordinary difficulty as to unduly limit the number of remembered words. The second analysis bears upon the possibility of a special sensitivity to the noxious evaluative words which might lead the aversive-maternal-control subjects to selectively fail to retrieve the unfavorable words, seriously limiting the number of negative terms. Table 61 presents data relating to these preliminary concerns. The range of mean total recognitions of about 36 to 40 was quite narrow and suggested equivalent performances on the memory task among the groups; this was confirmed by statistically nonsignificant differences. All subgroups performed well above the level expected given random performance, since merely guessing on the 300-item check list should have led to average group scores of less than 15. The immediate recognition task was clearly within the competence range of the subjects. The second statistical analysis, having to do with mnemonic retrieval of negative words also substantiated the absence of relative differences among the four subgroups in recognition scores. The absolute values of the recognition score means for negative traits across groups, each representing at least a third of the total words recognized, further allays any concern about selective failure to retrieve noxious terms and about problems with stability of the defense mechanism scores.

Table 61. Frequency of Correct Recognitions of List-Relevant Words for Late-Adolescent Males Varying in Maternal Child-Rearing Experience and Style of Adaptation

	Perceived Maternal Child-Rearing Pattern			
	High Control-Low Nurturance		Reference Group	
	Closed Adaptive Style ($N = 9$)	Open Adaptive Style ($N = 12$)	Nondisrupted Controls ($N = 26$)	Disrupted Controls ($N = 25$)
Mean total number of correct recognitions	40.00	39.25	38.58	36.24
Mean number of unfavorable terms correctly recognized	14.23	14.08	12.92	13.04

Repression

That aspect of the data which bears upon repressive tendencies is the extent to which the subject failed to recognize unfavorable terms which had just been generally applied to him by a maternal source. The index of repression reflected the relationship between the number of unfavorable words and the number of neutral words correctly remembered. The latter term constitutes an individual base line control for memory ability given low evaluative impact of the stimulus.

The repression score was given by the ratio of unfavorable "hits" divided by the number of unfavorable plus neutral "hits." A score under 50% would suggest a selective failure to recognize negative words (relative to neutral words) and repression, whereas a score above 50% would point to a special recognition pull of the negative terms. The same type of score was determined for favorable words relative to neutral as a control for high evaluative impact. In other words, if an effect were identified suggesting a selective loss of negative words, the effect could not be defined as evidence for repression unless it were shown that the same effect did not emerge for the free recognition of any high-impact evaluative words, in this case those words having a positive connotation.

The repression index data (Table 62) indicate that the closed-style males, for whom repression as the primary defense would be predicted, had the lowest index score among the four subgroups, lower scores being indicative of repression. Analysis of variance established that the difference between closed-style and open-style males was significant ($p < .05$); the same comparison between the two reference subgroups failed to identify a reliable difference.

Another way to portray the group differences on the repression index is to define repressor or nonrepressor in terms of a .50 score and to ascertain the

Table 62. Selective Recognition of Words Having High and Neutral Evaluative Impact for Late-Adolescent Males Varying in Maternal Child-Rearing Experience and Style of Adaptation

	Perceived Maternal Child-Rearing Pattern			
	High Control-Low Nurturance		Reference Group	
	Closed Adaptive Style	Open Adaptive Style	Nondisrupted Controls	Disrupted Controls
Mean repression index[a] score	.49	.54	.52	.55
Percent in group defined as repressor	50%	9%	38%	8%
Mean "repression index"[b] score using favorable words	.50	.51	.54	.53
Percent in group defined as "repressor"	40%	55%	15%	28%

[a]Repression index = number unfavorable "hits" / number unfavorable plus neutral "hits"

[b]"Repression index" = number of favorable "hits" / number favorable plus neutral "hits"

composition of each subgroup relevant to these types. Defining repressors as those whose index scores fall at or below the score of .50, the percentage of subjects meeting this criterion is given in the second row of Table 62. These figures portray the relatively high incidence of repressors among closed-style males, especially when compared with open-style males.

The parallel statistical analysis of scores based upon the same scoring procedures as the repression index but substituting positive words (the "repression index") failed to uncover any effects whatsoever. As the scores in row 3 of Table 62 attest, all 4 subgroups evidenced means indicating retrieval of favorable terms at or beyond their level of recognition for neutral words on the mother list.

The percentage of closed-style males displaying a deficit in recognition of favorable words, reported in row 4, is somewhat higher (40%) than their control group (15%), an effect shared with the open-style males (55%) relative to their controls (28%). There is a suggestion, not confirmed statistically, of a more general disinclination on the part of closed-style adapters to retrieve any high-impact evaluative term, negative or positive.

The most striking feature of the comparison of repressor percentages, however, is the suggestion of a counterrepressive tendency in open-style males. Whereas 91% of the open-style adapters recognized more negative than neutral terms spoken by the woman's voice on the tape, only 45% of the same group identified more positive than neutral terms from the same list.

In brief summary, the repression analysis was consistent with the theoretical expectation that closed-style males would more commonly employ repression as a mechanism of defense. There also were indications in these results that closed-style males may have a more general set against retention of high-impact evaluative terms, positive or negative. Finally, open-style males are unlikely to utilize repression to protect against distressing information relevant to themselves.

Projection

Just as a tendency toward repression can be inferred from whether the person selectively fails to remember the more noxious evaluative terms from the taped list, projection is suggested by selective peer attribution of those noxious terms from the tape which are remembered. However, there is a special problem encountered in deriving a projection score. The defensive projection of negative traits for low self-esteem subjects must be distinguished from the disproportionate attribution of negative traits to peers which is to be reasonably expected from high self-esteem subjects who are forced to decide whether negative terms are more aptly applied to themselves or to their general peer group. The scoring procedure, including a correction term to get around this problem, was as follows:

$$\left[\begin{array}{l}\text{Unfavorable traits}\\ \quad\text{attributed to peers}\end{array} \text{ minus } \begin{array}{l}\text{Unfavorable traits}\\ \quad\text{attributed to self}\end{array}\right] \text{ minus }$$

$$\left[\begin{array}{l}\text{Favorable traits}\\ \quad\text{attributed to self}\end{array} \text{ minus } \begin{array}{l}\text{Favorable traits}\\ \quad\text{attributed to peers}\end{array}\right]$$

The initial set of brackets includes the projection term which indicates the differential peer-self attribution of negative traits. The second set of brackets contains a correction term involving the self-peer attribution of positive traits. If a person cognitively processes positive and negative terms in the same way, then the tendency to attribute unfavorable traits to peers should be accompanied by an equal tendency to attribute favorable traits to oneself. Similarly, the tendency to attribute unfavorable traits to oneself should correspond to the tendency to attribute favorable traits to peers. Under these conditions the corrected projection score should approach zero. A plus projection score would result from peer-attribution of negative traits in excess of self-attribution of positive traits and would indicate the use of a projective defense mechanism. A minus score, in turn, would mean that the person engages in self-attribution of negative traits in excess of his peer-attribution of positive traits and would contraindicate defensive projection.

The projection index data, presented in the top row of Table 63, clearly confirm our theoretical position. Open-style males showed a tendency to attribute the negative qualities presented on the list as maternal evaluations of their peers rather than of themselves–in short, to project. Closed-style males, in contrast, reacted in just the opposite fashion: negative traits were deemed more characteristic of the self than of others. Analysis of variance revealed a child rearing by disruption interaction ($p < .05$), but, of greater importance, a significant ($p < .025$) difference on the projection index between the two adaptive-style subgroups. The two reference subgroups did not differ statistically.

The same scoring procedures were imposed upon the peer-self attributions for the evaluative words identified by the subjects but which had not in fact appeared on the taped list. This scoring procedure served as a control for source of the evaluative terms. No differences among the group means (Table 63, row 2) could be statistically identified. Accordingly, the indication and contra-indication of defensive projection found in the open-style and closed-style adolescents were apparent only when the adolescents had to process traits that had been presented to them as judgments of mothers.

Joint consideration of the results for both mechanisms of defense allows one

Table 63. Mean Projection Index Scores for Traits Evolving and Not Evolving from a Maternal Source Given by Late-Adolescent Males Varying in Maternal Child-Rearing Experience and Style of Adaptation

	Perceived Maternal Child-Rearing Pattern			
	High Control-Low Nurturance		Reference Group	
Source of Evaluation[a]	Closed Adaptive Style	Open Adaptive Style	Nondisrupted Controls	Disrupted Controls
Maternal	–2.30	+1.91	–.15	–.52
Nonmaternal	–1.50	–2.27	–3.12	–3.12

[a]Maternal source refers to the words that were actually on the taped list, whereas the nonmaternal source includes the words incorrectly recognized as appearing on the list.

observation which is worth emphasizing. Not only did these sets of data identify one adaptive-style group as more strongly disposed to the use of repression and the other as more strongly inclined toward projection, but in each case there was a contra-indication of the defensive form in the remaining adaptive-style group. Clearer support for our theory is generated by the findings that open-style males are not only projectors but also counterrepressors and that closed-style males are not only repressors but also counterprojectors.

Finally, the results of this investigation taken in combination with those of the visual scanning study (Heilbrun, 1972c) discussed earlier in this chapter offer further solidity to the model for paranoid development which has been proposed within the more general adaptive-style theory. The open-style adapters in the present investigation demonstrated counterrepressive tendencies as far as retrieving unfavorably connotative words from memory store just as open-style adapters selectively attended to unfavorable evaluative terms within the scanning experiment. Selective attention to environmental cues signalling hostility, threat, or disparagement describes a major characteristic of paranoid behavior which has reached clinical proportions. It seems no wonder that an individual prone to engage consciously so much potentially distressing information must protect himself by assignment of its relevance to others through the mechanism of projection.

Related Process-Reactive Schizophrenia Research (Tolerance of Ambiguity)

The process by which meaning is assigned to perceptual input, considered as a series of events which occurs sequentially over time, has received modest attention in research on schizophrenia, and, unfortunately, some of what has been done is not even indirectly applicable to our current interest in process-reactive distinctions. Only three relevant studies could be located which addressed themselves to preference for ambiguous stimuli or to premature assignment of meaning to ambiguous stimulation.

Wilton (1966) used a tachistoscopic recognition task to compare preferences for ambiguity among schizophrenics. He concluded that reactives preferred less ambiguity and process schizophrenics preferred more ambiguity. Psychiatric patients, rated as paranoid or nonparanoid, were given a sorting task in which predetermined reinforcement schedules were used in an investigation conducted by Hilf, Wittner, and Kopell (1969). Subjective feelings of certainty were obtained following trials in which 30%, 50%, and 80% correct reinforcement was delivered. Paranoids were found to be more certain at the lower reinforcement levels, whereas the certainty levels of nonparanoids were more in keeping with the level of reinforcement. The investigators concluded from their findings that paranoids are underresponsive to their environment and more prone to cognitive "closure" when presented with ambiguous perceptual stimulation. McReynolds,

Collins, and Acker (1964) presented delusional and nondelusional schizophrenics with 44 incomplete pictures of common objects and found that delusional patients attempted more identifications and identified more correctly. They concluded that delusional schizophrenics had a stronger tendency to organize ambiguous stimuli in a meaningful way than did nondelusional schizophrenics.

While restricted in number, all of the studies cited point toward a greater tolerance for ambiguity in process schizophrenics and a lesser ability to tolerate ambiguity in reactive schizophrenics. There is a greater need to impose meaning upon ambiguous stimuli in schizophrenics with paranoid symptoms, a contingency of reactive status.

Adaptive-Style Theory Validation Study (Tolerance of Ambiguity)

The manner in which the individual processes ambiguous perceptual input assumes critical importance within the parallel differences approach we have chosen to demonstrate the viability of the adaptive-style theory. Perhaps more than any other variable which has been subjected to experimental analysis, the difference in tolerance of ambiguity between open-style and closed-style adapters is theoretically overdetermined as far as directional prediction is concerned. To begin with what scanty evidence we were able to uncover, reactive or paranoid schizophrenics emerged as less prone to delay the assignment of meaning to ambiguous stimuli than process or nonparanoid schizophrenics. The method of parallel differences would require that we demonstrate a lesser tolerance for ambiguity among open-style adolescents than among closed-style adolescents.

Further, the evidence and theory regarding subtle versus obvious control in the mothers of open-style and closed-style children involves the assumption that open-style adapters have oriented toward the mother, motivated by the need to clarify the meaning of her communication; such motivation literally leads them to impose meaning on ambiguous messages. On the other hand, closed-style children, confronted by the clear and aversive communication of their mothers, are not presented with the same problem of ambiguity. Rather their defended perceptual and social style, which functions as a buffer against the mother's clear but aversive messages, would serve to reduce the clarity of her communication. In short, the closed-style male would seek ambiguity.

Finally, the model for paranoid development subsumed under the adaptive-style theory proposes that the open-style male maintains a vigilance for directive and evaluative cues from his social environment. His hyperattentiveness in combination with an inability to delay the assignment of meaning to ambiguous cues bear the weight of explanation within the model for the predicted overload of information which he cannot effectively process. The delusion, a fixed ideational framework in which he can integrate disorganized information, further increases his tendency to assign premature meanings to events. The delusional framework allows a ready if incorrect basis for rapid interpretation of a broad range of significant and insignificant events.

Tolerance for ambiguity, then, is viewed within the theory as a bipolar dimension with open-style adapters falling near the low extreme and closed-style adapters near the high extreme with controls, taken as a group, assuming an intermediate position. This was tested experimentally (Heilbrun, in press c) using a technique modeled after that reported by Frederiksen (1966). A tape recording was devised upon which a series of words, spoken in an adult female voice, were blended with masking noise. The words (commerce, beauty, revenge, suspicion, remorse, finance, grateful, artist, analysis, numbness, feeble, kindly, spying, useful) represented 14 of the 16 originally selected by Frederiksen as especially conducive to alternate word identification when presented under threshold conditions. Masking noise was constituted by an adult male voice and an adult female voice reading random passages at the same time. The adult female voices used to record the individually spoken words and the masking noise were contributed by different women.

Each of the 14 words was repeated 9 times at 15-second intervals. On the first presentation, the stimulus word and the masking noise were recorded at the same decibel level of intensity. Each subsequent presentation of the word was associated with a one decibel reduction in the masking noise. Accordingly, maximum ambiguity of the stimulus word was achieved on its initial appearance with each subsequent presentation providing a somewhat clearer basis for identifying the word.

The usual group and individual procedures were followed for establishing the aversive-control and general reference child-rearing experience groupings and adaptive-style and disruption control subgroupings for the 63 Emory male undergraduates (average age = 18.8 years) who participated in the investigation. The tolerance of ambiguity part of the experiment was introduced to the subject by the female experimenter as an effort to understand the degree to which sons are perceptive of maternal communication. In explaining what he was going to hear on the tape, stress was placed upon the fact that the stimulus words would be spoken in the voice of a woman "about your mother's age." Instructions, which were intended to leave some room for individual interpretation, urged the subject to do as well on the task as he could and that just as soon as he was reasonably sure of the word spoken in the "mother's" voice, he should guess what the word is. He was told that he could change his mind whenever he wished but that the experimenter would not tell him whether he was right or wrong. However, in the actual conduct of the task, the proper identification of a word on three consecutive presentations served as the criterion for correctness, and the tape was moved ahead to the next word. The subject was warned each time that the stimulus word was to change.

Two tolerance of ambiguity scores were used; both were determined by whether the late-adolescent, upon hearing the ambiguous stimulus, refrained from rendering a judgment to the experimenter. The initial delay score represented the cumulative number of stimulus presentations across the 14 words which occurred prior to the subject's first guess as to their meaning. The total tolerance of ambiguity score represented the cumulative number of occasions for all word presentations in which the subject refrained from guessing. Reference to the upper two rows of Table 64 allows us to compare the child-rearing subgroupings on these two measures.

Analysis of variance applied to the initial delay scores revealed both the main effects of child rearing and disruption and the interaction effect to be significant ($p < .05$). The basis for these effects obviously resided in the departure of the closed-style group mean from all the others. Testing of simple effects disclosed the predicted difference ($p < .01$) between the adaptive-style groups; closed stylers were clearly more tolerant of ambiguity than were open stylers. The two combined reference subgroups performed in an essentially identical manner in terms of initial delay in imposing meaning.

Overall tolerance of ambiguity performance responded to analysis quite similarly. The importance of a main effect for disruption ($p < .05$) was obviated by a significant interaction effect ($p < .05$). Of considerably more importance, the difference between the adaptive-style groupings was highly significant ($p < .01$) in the absence of any difference between the reference control groups. The

Table 64. Tolerance of Ambiguity in Late-Adolescent Males Varying in Maternal Child-Rearing Experience and Style of Adaptation

	Perceived Maternal Child-Rearing Pattern			
	High Control-Low Nurturance		Reference Group	
Score	Closed Adaptive Style ($N = 10$)	Open Adaptive Style ($N = 12$)	Nondisrupted Controls ($N = 21$)	Disrupted Controls ($N = 20$)
Mean initial delay[a]	50.70	29.33	31.19	30.50
Mean total tolerance of ambiguity[a]	58.80	38.25	44.57	44.05
Mean number correct recognitions	11.40	16.58	15.24	15.35

[a]Means refer to the number of word presentations on which the subject did not make a guess as to meaning.

total tolerance of ambiguity scores also conveyed the anticipated extreme values for the means of the two adaptive-style groups and the intermediate mean values of the two control groups far more clearly than had the initial delay scores.

Table 64 (row 3) presents the average number of correct recognitions for each group. The only significant ($p < .05$) effect was the difference between the open- and closed-style males; open-style subjects were able to detect more of the masked words than were the closed-style subjects. This finding of superior auditory detection of cues is in keeping with the earlier experiment (Heilbrun, 1971a) which demonstrated the greater visual accuracy of open-style males with briefly-exposed words. Yet it marks the tolerance of ambiguity results as especially revealing in that despite superior perceptual acuity the open-style group made many more perceptual errors of commission (mean number = 54.50) than their closed-style counterparts (mean number = 44.90) because of their apparent inability to refrain from imposing meaning on highly ambiguous stimuli. This finding is reminiscent of the McReynolds, Collins, and Acker (1964) study which found that delusional schizophrenics attempted more identifications *and* correctly identified more incomplete pictures than did nondelusional schizophrenics.

There is a danger in both the McReynolds et al. and the present tolerance-of-ambiguity studies of a confounding between number of attempts to guess the meaning of ambiguous stimuli and number of correct recognitions. Making more guesses could be thought of as mechanically generating more correct identifications without invoking the interpretation of superior perceptual acuity. A positive correlation of .78 between number of guesses and number correct reported by McReynolds et al. would appear to support the mechanical interpretation, although these investigators believed otherwise. The lack of correlation between total attempts and total correct in the Heilbrun study ($r = -.11$) removed all doubt regarding interpretation. Intolerance of ambiguity, which introduces substantial perceptual inaccuracy because it produces premature judgments, and perceptual acuity coexist in the open-style late-adolescent just as McReynolds and his colleagues felt this to be true for the delusional schizophrenic.

OVERVIEW OF THEORY VALIDATION EVIDENCE

Table 65 summarizes the programmatic research conducted to date that has a bearing on the adaptive-style theory of schizophrenic development. Even a cautious posture, noting that the theory has received support at each point it has been subjected to test, would allow us to conclude that the theory remains a viable interpretation of how it is possible to learn to be schizophrenic.

Table 65. Presence or Absence of Predicted Effects in Investigations Relevant to the Adaptive-Style Theory

Investigation	Performance Variable	Predicted Effect	Findings
Heilbrun (1972a)	Maternal communication	Subtle (open style) versus obvious (closed style) communicated control	As predicted
Heilbrun [1972b]	Interpersonal distancing	Less physical distancing for closed style	As predicted
Heilbrun (1971a)	External scanning	Broad (open style) versus narrow (closed style) scanning	As predicted
Heilbrun [in press (a)]	Differential perception of maternal voice	Only in closed style	As predicted
Heilbrun [1972d]	Internal scanning	Broad (closed style) versus narrow (open style) scanning	As predicted
Iversen (1971)	Emotional responsivity	Low responsivity in closed style	As predicted
Gilgun (1972)	Heterosexual orientation	Less sexual differentiation for closed style	As predicted
Heilbrun (1972c)	External scanning of simultaneous cues	Selective attention to negative cues (open style) versus positive cues (closed style)	As predicted
Heilbrun (1971b)	Sex-role identity and parental identification	Greater deviance for closed style	As predicted
Heilbrun and Norbert (1972)	Fixed ideation	Only in open style	As predicted
Heilbrun and Norbert (1971)	Cognitive disruption by maternal censure cues	Greater disruption in paranoid schizophrenics	As predicted
Heilbrun [1972e]	Defensive projection and repression	Projection in open style, repression in closed style	As predicted
Heilbrun [in press (c)]	Tolerance of ambiguity	Open style low and closed style high	As predicted

The compilation of adaptive-style research in table form illustrates a point about research and theory building in contemporary psychology. One can notice that no study is cited between the original adaptive-style paper in 1968 and 1971, despite the fact that research has been continuous since the earlier date. While this may in small part be related to publication lag, it has much more to do with resistance to the ideas and the research methodologies used to test them on the part of psychologist colleagues. Poincaré pointed out that while natural scientists argue about their results, social scientists argue about their methods. This still seems to hold true.

The invaluable opportunity offered by collating all our research and theory in a single source is that the theoretical framework, as far as it goes, will emerge as logical and reasonably comprehensive, and the scientific evidence, despite the limitations of any given study, will generate a consistency and cohesion that is impressive. Further elaboration or alteration of the theory would be greatly facilitated by enlisting the interest of additional researchers or clinicians.

REFERENCES

Altshuler, H. Competitional and non-competitional paired associates learning in process and reactive schizophrenics. (Doctoral dissertation, Illinois Institute of Technology) Ann Arbor, Mich.: University Microfilms, 1966. No. 65-8878.

Alvarez, R. R. A comparison of the preferences of schizophrenic and normal subjects for rewarded and punished stimuli. Unpublished doctoral dissertation, Duke University, 1957.

Armstrong, H. E., Jr., Johnson, M. H., Ries, H. A., and Holmes, D. S. Extraversion-introversion and process-reactive schizophrenia. *British Journal of Social and Clinical Psychology,* 1967, **6**, 69.

Barclay, A., and Cusumano, D. R. Father-absence, cross-sex identity, and field dependent behavior in male adolescents. *Child Development,* 1967, **38**, 243-250.

Barker, C.L. Maternal child-rearing history and subsequent sensitivity to shame in college males. Unpublished doctoral dissertation, University of Iowa, 1965.

Barry, R. R. The effects of a stress condition on process and reactive schizophrenics. (Doctoral dissertation, Fordham University) Ann Arbor, Mich.: University Microfilms, 1968. No. 68-3677.

Baxter, J. C., Williams, J., and Zerof, S. Child-rearing attitudes and disciplinary fantasies of parents of schizophrenics and controls. *Journal of Nervous and Mental Disease,* 1965, **141**, 567-579.

Becker, J., and Siefkes, H. Parental dominance, conflict, and disciplinary coerciveness in families of female schizophrenics. *Journal of Abnormal Psychology,* 1969, **74**, 193-198.

Becker, W. C. The process-reactive distinction: A key to the problem of schizophrenia? *Journal of Nervous and Mental Disease,* 1959, **129,** 442-449.

Belmont, J., Birch, H. G., Klein, D. F., and Pollack, M. Perceptual evidence of CNS dysfunction in schizophrenia. *Archives of General Psychiatry,* 1964, **10,** 395-408.

Berman, G. Conceptual functioning of schizophrenics classified along the process-reactive continuum. (Doctoral dissertation, Stanford University) Ann Arbor, Mich.: University Microfilms, 1963, No. 63-4583.

Bertini, M. Il tratto defensivo dell' isolamenta nella determinizione dinamica e strutturale. *Contributi dell' Institute di Psicologia,* 1961, 25.

Bradford, N. H. Comparative perceptions of mothers and maternal roles by schizophrenic patients and their normal siblings. (Doctoral dissertation, University of Minnesota) Ann Arbor, Mich.: University Microfilms, 1966. No. 65-15,244.

Bramel, D. Selection of a target for defensive projection. *Journal of Abnormal and Social Psychology,* 1963, **66,** 318-324.

Brodsky, M. Sorting decrement in schizophrenia as a function of social climate. *Journal of Clinical Psychology,* 1968, **24,** 162-165.

Broen, W. E., Jr. *Schizophrenia: research and theory.* New York: Academic Press, 1968.

Bryant, A. R. P. An investigation of process-reactive schizophrenia with relation to perception of visual space. *Dissertation Abstracts,* 1962, **22,** 2460.

Buck, L., and Kates, S. L. Perceptual categorizations of love and anger cues in schizophrenics. *Journal of Abnormal and Social Psychology,* 1963, **67,** 480-490.

Busse, T. V. Child-rearing antecedents of flexible thinking. *Developmental Psychology,* 1969, **1,** 585-591.

Cameron, N. *Personality development and psychopathology—a dynamic approach.* Boston: Houghton-Mifflin Company, 1963.

Cancro, R. The relationship between premorbid adjustment, presenting picture, and outcome in schizophrenia. *Proceedings of the 75th Annual Convention of the American Psychological Association,* 1968, **3,** 495-496.

Chapman, L. J., Chapman, J. P., and Miller, G. A. A theory of verbal behavior in schizophrenia. In B. A. Maher (Ed.), *Progress in experimental personality research.* Vol. 1. New York: Academic Press, 1964.

Chapman, L. J., Day, D., and Burstein, A. The process-reactive distinction and prognosis in schizophrenia. *Journal of Nervous and Mental Disease,* 1961, **133,** 383-391.

Cicchetti, D. V. Reported family dynamics and psychopathology: I. The reactions of schizophrenics and normals to parental dialogues. *Journal of Abnormal Psychology,* 1967, **72,** 282-289.

Cicchetti, D. V., Klein, E. B., Fontana, A. F., and Spohn, H. E. A test of the censure-deficit model in schizophrenia, employing the Rodnick-Garmezy visual discrimination task. *Journal of Abnormal Psychology,* 1967, **72**, 326-334.

Cohen, R. M. The emotional effect of conflictual material upon process and reactive schizophrenic patients. Paper read at the 38th Annual Convention of the Eastern Psychological Association, Boston, April, 1967.

Cosentino, F., and Heilbrun, A. B. Anxiety correlates of sex-role identity in college students. *Psychological Reports,* 1964, **14**, 729-730.

Counts, R. M., and Devlin, J. P. Sexual experience as a prognostic factor in psychosis. *Journal of Nervous and Mental Disease,* 1954, **120**, 364-368.

Craig, J. E. Perceived parental attitudes and the effects of maternal versus paternal censure and approval in good and poor premorbid hospitalized female schizophrenics. (Doctoral dissertation, University of Wisconsin) Ann Arbor, Mich.: University Microfilms, 1966. No. 66-7641.

Crider, A. B., Grinspoon, L., and Maher, B. A. Autonomic and psychomotor correlates of premorbid adjustment in schizophrenia. *Psychosomatic Medicine,* 1965, **27**, 201-206.

Cromwell, R. L. Stimulus redundancy and schizophrenia. *Journal of Nervous and Mental Disease,* 1968, **146**, 360-375.

Crookes, T. G. Size constancy and literalness in the Rorschach test. *British Journal of Medical Psychology,* 1957, **31**, 99-106.

Daston, P. G. Perception of homosexual words in paranoid schizophrenia. *Perceptual and Motor Skills,* 1956, **6**, 45-55.

Davis, D., Cromwell, R. L., and Held, J. M. Size estimation in schizophrenics and emotionally disturbed children. *Journal of Abnormal Psychology,* 1967, **72**, 395-401.

DeVault, S. Physiological responsiveness in reactive and process schizophrenia. *Dissertation Abstracts*, 1957, **17**, 1387.

DeWolfe, A. S. The effect of affective tone on the verbal behavior of process and reactive schizophrenics. *Journal of Abnormal and Social Psychology,* 1962, **64**, 450-455.

Diagnostic and statistical manual: mental disorders. Washington, D. C., American Psychiatric Association, 1952. (Special printing, 1965)

Digiondomenico, P. A. Variables associated with maternal-censure induced performance interference in schizophrenia. (Doctoral dissertation, Pennsylvania State University) Ann Arbor, Mich.: University Microfilms, 1966. No. 66-8711.

DiMauro, J. T. The effects of verbal censure on the conceptual ability of process and reactive schizophrenics. (Doctoral dissertation, Temple University) Ann Arbor, Mich.: University Microfilms, 1965. No. 65-1404.

Dobecki, P. R., Cromwell, R. L., and Polidoro, L. G. The chronicity and premorbid adjustment dimensions as they relate to commonality and stability of word association responses in schizophrenics. *Journal of Nervous and Mental Disease,* 1968, **146**, 310-311.

Dobecki, P. R., Polidoro, L. G., and Cromwell, R. L. Commonality and stability of word association responses in good and poor premorbid schizophrenics. *Journal of Abnormal Psychology,* 1965, **70,** 312-316.

Donoghue, J. R. Motivation and conceptualization in process and reactive schizophrenia. (Doctoral dissertation, University of Nebraska) Ann Arbor, Mich.: University Microfilms, 1964. No. 64-8875.

Donovan, M. J., and Webb, W. W. Meaning dimensions and male-female voice perception in schizophrenics with good and poor premorbid adjustment. *Journal of Abnormal Psychology,* 1965, **70,** 426-431.

Dunn, R. E. Schizophrenia, socio-sexual adjustment, evaluation, and involvement with people. (Doctoral dissertation, University of Washington) Ann Arbor, Mich.: University Microfilms, 1965. No. 65-5417.

Dwarshuis, L. The affect-arousing value of the stimuli as a determiner of affective complexity in schizophrenics and normal subjects. Paper read at the 72nd Annual Convention of the American Psychological Association, Los Angeles, September, 1964.

Edlow, D., and Kiesler, C. Ease of denial and defensive projection. *Journal of Experimental Social Psychology,* 1966, **2,** 56-69.

Eysenck, H. J. *Manual for the Maudsley Personality Inventory.* London: University of London Press, 1959.

Farina, A. Patterns of role dominance and conflict in parents of schizophrenic patients. *Journal of Abnormal and Social Psychology,* 1960, **61,** 31-38.

Farina, A., and Dunham, R. M. Measurement of family relationships and their effects. *Archives of General Psychiatry,* 1963, **9,** 64-73.

Farina, A., Garmezy, N., and Barry, H. Relationship of marital status to incidence and prognosis of schizophrenia. *Journal of Abnormal and Social Psychology,* 1963, **67,** 624-630.

Farina, A., Garmezy, N., Zalusky, M., and Becker, J. Premorbid behavior and prognosis in female schizophrenic patients. *Journal of Consulting Psychology,* 1966, **30,** 18-24.

Farina, A., and Holzberg, J. D. Attitudes and behaviors of fathers and mothers of male schizophrenic patients. *Journal of Abnormal Psychology,* 1967, **72,** 381-387.

Farina, A., and Holzberg, J. D. Interaction patterns of parents and hospitalized sons diagnosed as schizophrenic and nonschizophrenic. *Journal of Abnormal Psychology,* 1968, **73,** 114-118.

Farina, A., Holzberg, J. D., and Dies, R. R. Influence of the parents and verbal reinforcement of schizophrenic patients. *Journal of Abnormal Psychology,* 1969, **74,** 9-15.

Farina, A., Holzberg, J. D., and Kimura, D. S. A study of the interpersonal relationships of female schizophrenic patients. *Journal of Nervous and Mental Disease,* 1966, **142,** 441-444.

Feffer, M. H. The influence of affective factors on conceptualization in schizophrenia. *Journal of Abnormal and Social Psychology,* 1961, **63**, 588-596.

Fenz, W. D., and Velner, J. Physiological concomitants of behavioral indices in schizophrenia. *Journal of Abnormal Psychology,* 1970, **76**, 27-35.

Figetakis, N. Process-reactive schizophrenia: Ego-strength and selected psychosexual dimensions. (Doctoral dissertation, Michigan State University) Ann Arbor, Mich.: University Microfilms, 1964. No. 64-7504.

Fine, H. Q., and Zimet, C. N. Process-reactive schizophrenia and genetic levels of perception. *Journal of Abnormal and Social Psychology,* 1959, **59**, 83-86.

Foley, L. J. Study of the word associations of schizophrenic dimensions with varied instructions. (Doctoral dissertation, Rutgers–The State University) Ann Arbor, Mich.: University Microfilms, 1968. No. 67-9248.

Fontana, A. F., Klein, E. B., and Cicchetti, D. V. Censure sensitivity in schizophrenia. *Journal of Abnormal Psychology,* 1967, **72**, 294-302.

Frederiksen, J. R. A study of perceptual recognition in two sense modalities. Princeton, N.J.: Educational Testing Service, 1966. (Monograph RB-66-32).

Friedman, M. Perceptual and psychogalvanic responses of schizophrenic and normal subjects to cues of nurturance and rejection in interaction with mother, father, and peer figures. (Doctoral dissertation, University of Massachusetts) Ann Arbor, Mich.: University Microfilms, 1966. No. 66-7628.

Gancherov, B. S. "Authoritarian" and "understanding" test administration in relation to problem-solving ability and interpersonal discrimination in process and reactive schizophrenics and non-schizophrenics. (Doctoral dissertation, University of Southern California) Ann Arbor, Mich.: University Microfilms, 1963. No. 62-6055.

Gardner, R. W., and Long, R. I. Control, defense and centration effect: a study of scanning behavior. *British Journal of Psychology,* 1962, **53**, 129-140.

Garfield, S. L., and Sundland, D. M. Prognostic scales in schizophrenia. *Journal of Consulting Psychology,* 1966, **30**, 18-24.

Geisinger, D. L. The effect of maternal versus paternal dominance on the performance of good and poor premorbid schizophrenics. (Doctoral dissertation, Syracuse University) Ann Arbor, Mich.: University Microfilms, 1966. No. 66-9847.

Gibeau, P. J. Field dependency and the process-reactive dimension in schizophrenia. (Doctoral dissertation, Purdue University) Ann Arbor, Mich.: University Microfilms, 1965. No. 65-8603.

Gilgun, L. J. An investigation of the influence exerted by aversive maternal characteristics on heterosexual interest in the male offspring. Unpublished master's thesis, Emory University, 1972.

Gittelman-Klein, R., and Klein, D. F. Marital status as a prognostic indicator in schizophrenia. *Journal of Nervous and Mental Disease,* 1968, **147**, 289-296.

Gladis, M., and Wischner, G. J. Schizophrenic and normal response patterns to "aversive" and "neutral" associations in two paired-associate paradigms. *Journal of Abnormal and Social Psychology,* 1962, **64**, 249-256.

Goldstein, M. J., Held, J. M., and Cromwell, R. L. Premorbid adjustment and paranoid-nonparanoid status in schizophrenia. *Psychological Bulletin,* 1968, **70**, 382-386.

Goodman, D. Performance of good and poor premorbid male schizophrenics as a function of paternal versus maternal censure. *Journal of Abnormal and Social Psychology,* 1964, **69**, 550-555.

Goodman, I. Z. Influence of parental figures on schizophrenic patients. *Journal of Abnormal Psychology*, 1968, **73**, 503-512.

Gromell, H. F. The process-reactive dimension of schizophrenia in relation to cortical activation and arousal. *Dissertation Abstracts*, 1962, **22**, 3741.

Harris, J. G. Size estimation of pictures as a function of thematic content for schizophrenic and normal subjects. *Journal of Personality,* 1957, **25**, 651-671.

Heilbrun, A. B. Conformity to masculinity-femininity stereotypes and ego identity in adolescents. *Psychological Reports,* 1964, **14**, 351-357. (a)

Heilbrun, A. B. Perceived maternal attitudes, masculinity-femininity of the maternal model, and identification as related to incipient psychopathology in adolescence. *Journal of General Psychology,* 1964, **70**, 33-40. (b)

Heilbrun, A. B. The measurement of identification. *Child Development,* 1965, **36**, 111-127. (a)

Heilbrun, A. B. An empirical test of the modeling theory of sex-role learning. *Child Development,* 1965, **36**, 789-799. (b)

Heilbrun, A. B. Personality factors in college dropout. *Journal of Applied Psychology,* 1965, **49**, 1-7. (c)

Heilbrun, A. B. Cognitive sensitivity to aversive maternal stimulation in late-adolescent males. *Journal of Consulting and Clinical Psychology,* 1968, **32**, 326-332. (a)

Heilbrun, A. B. Sex-role, instrumental-expressive behavior, and psychopathology in females. *Journal of Abnormal Psychology*, 1968, **73**, 131-136. (b)

Heilbrun, A. B. Sex-role identity in adolescent females: a theoretical paradox. *Adolescence,* 1968, **3**, 79-88. (c)

Heilbrun, A. B. Parental identification and the patterning of vocational interests in college males and females. *Journal of Counseling Psychology,* 1969, **16**, 342-347.

Heilbrun, A. B. Adjective Check List correlates of social conflict problems in college students. *Measurement and Evaluation in Guidance,* 1970, **3**, 158-163. (a)

Heilbrun, A. B. Identification and behavioral effectiveness of college students. In E. D. Evans (Ed.), *Adolescence: Readings in behavior and development.* Hinsdale, Ill.: Dryden, 1970. Pp. 70-79. (b)

Heilbrun, A. B. Style of adaptation to perceived aversive maternal stimulation and selective attention to evaluative cues. *Journal of Abnormal Psychology,* 1971, **77**, 340-344. (a)

Heilbrun, A. B. Style of adaptation to aversive maternal control, parental identification, and sex-role identity in late-adolescent males. Currently unpublished manuscript, 1971. (b)

Heilbrun, A. B. Style of adaptation to aversive maternal control and interpersonal distancing following failure. *Journal of Nervous and Mental Disease*, 1972, **155**, 177-184. (b)

Heilbrun, A. B. Style of adaptation to perceived aversive maternal control and female-male voice perception. *Journal of Genetic Psychology,* in press. (a)

Heilbrun, A. B. Style of adaptation to perceived aversive maternal control and internal scanning behavior. *Journal of Consulting and Clinical Psychology,* 1972, **39**, 15-21. (d)

Heilbrun, A. B. Parental identification and educational dissatisfaction in troubled college students. *Journal of Genetic Psychology,* in press. (b)

Heilbrun, A.B. Defensive projection in late adolescents: Implications for a developmental model of paranoid behavior. *Child Development*, 1972, **43**, 880-891.(e)

Heilbrun, A. B. Tolerance for ambiguity in late-adolescent males: implications for a developmental model of paranoid behavior. *Developmental Psychology*, in press. (c)

Heilbrun, A. B. Distinctiveness of maternal control: a further link in a theory of schizophrenic development. *Journal of Nervous and Mental Disease,* 1972, **154**, 49-60. (a)

Heilbrun, A. B. Effects of adaptation to aversive maternal control upon perception of simultaneously presented evaluative cues: a replication and extension. Currently unpublished manuscript, 1972. (c)

Heilbrun, A. B., and Norbert, N. Sensitivity to maternal censure in paranoid and nonparanoid schizophrenics. *Journal of Nervous and Mental Diseases,* 1971, **1**, 45-49.

Heilbrun, A. B., and Norbert, N. Style of adaptation to aversive maternal control and paranoid behavior. *Journal of Genetic Psychology,* 1972, **120**, 145-153.

Heilbrun, A. B., and Tiemeyer, E. B. Relationships between perceived maternal child-rearing experiences and projective responses to censure-control cues in normal males. *Journal of Genetic Psychology,* 1968, **112**, 3-14.

Hellman, B. M., and Kates, S. L. Conceptual performance of schizophrenics as a function of premorbid adjustment level and mild verbal censure. *American Psychologist,* 1961, **16**, 354.

Herron, W. G. Bibliography pertaining to process-reactive schizophrenia. *Journal of Psychological Studies,* 1961, **12**, 61-64.

Hess, E. H., Seltzer, A. L., and Shlien, J. M. Pupil response of heterosexual and homosexual males to pictures of men and women: a pilot study. *Journal of Abnormal Psychology,* 1965, **70**, 165-168.

Higgins, J. Process-reactive schizophrenia. *Journal of Nervous and Mental Disease,* 1969, **149**, 450-472.

Higgins, J., and Mednick, S. A. Reminiscence and stage of illness in schizophrenia. *Journal of Abnormal and Social Psychology,* 1963, **66**, 314-317.

Hilf, F. D., Wittner, W. K., and Kopell, B. S. Feedback utilization styles of paranoid patients. *Journal of Nervous and Mental Disease,* 1969, **149**, 491-495.

Hirschstein, R. The significances of characteristic autonomic nervous system responses in the adjustment, change and outcome in schizophrenia. *Journal of Nervous and Mental Disease,* 1956, **122**, 254.

Holmes, D. Dimensions of projection. *Psychological Bulletin,* 1968, **69**, 248-258.

Husni-Palacios, M., Palacios, J. R., and Gibeau, P. J. Auditory perceptual patterns of process and reactive schizophrenics. *Journal of Projective Techniques,* 1967, **31**, 86-91.

Irwin, L., and Renner, K. E. Effect of praise and censure on the performance of schizophrenics. *Journal of Abnormal Psychology,* 1969, **74**, 221-226.

Iversen, C. A. Style of adaptation to aversive maternal stimulation and affective arousal in late adolescents. Unpublished master's thesis, Emory University, 1971.

Jackson, N. L. P., Jr. Sex and dominance cues in good-poor premorbid schizophrenia. *Journal of Abnormal Psychology,* 1970, **75**, 78-82.

Jenkins, R. L., and Gurel, L. Predictive factors in early release. *Mental Hospital,* 1959, **10**, 11-14.

Johannsen, W. J., Friedman, S. H., and Liccione, J. V. Visual perception as a function of chronicity in schizophrenia. Cited in R. E. Kantor and W. G. Herron, *Reactive and process schizophrenia.* Palo Alto, Calif.: Science and Behavior Books, 1966.

Johnson, M. H., and Meadow, A. Parental identification among male schizophrenics. *Journal of Personality,* 1966, **34**, 300-309.

Judson, A. J., and Katahn, M. Levels of personality organization and production of associative sequences in process-reactive schizophrenia. *Journal of Consulting Psychology,* 1964, **28**, 208-213.

Kantor, R. E., and Herron, W. G. *Reactive and process schizophrenia.* Palo Alto, Calif.: Science and Behavior Books, 1966.

Katahn, M., Harris, J. H., and Swanson, R. T. Production of associative sequences in process-reactive schizophrenic and nonschizophrenic groups. *Journal of Consulting Psychology,* 1967, **31**, 104.

King, G. Differential autonomic responsiveness in the process-reactive classification of schizophrenia. *Journal of Abnormal and Social Psychology,* 1958, **56**, 160-164.

Klein, E. B., Cicchetti, D., and Spohn, H. A test of the censure-deficit model and its relation to premorbidity in the performance of schizophrenics. *Journal of Abnormal Psychology,* 1967, **72**, 174-181.

Lefcourt, H. M., Rotenberg, F., Buckspan, B., and Steffy, R. A. Visual interaction and performance of process and reactive schizophrenics as a function of examiner's sex. *Journal of Personality,* 1967, **35**, 535-546.

Lefcourt, H. M., and Steffy, R. A. Sex-linked censure expectancies in process and reactive schizophrenics. *Journal of Personality*, 1966, **34**, 366-380.

Lefcourt, H. M., Steffy, R. A., Buckspan, B., and Rotenberg, F. Avoidance of censure by process and reactive schizophrenics as a function of examiner's sex and type of task. *Journal of General Psychology,* 1968, **79**, 87-96.

Lerner, P. M. Resolution of intrafamilial role conflict in families of schizophrenic patients. II. Social maturity. *Journal of Nervous and Mental Disease,* 1967, **145**, 336-341.

Levenson, R. L. Some variables influencing selective attention in schizophrenia. (Doctoral dissertation, Yeshiva University) Ann Arbor, Mich.: University Microfilms, 1967. No. 67-9666.

Lindemann, J. E., Fairweather, G. W., Stone, G. B., Smith, R. S., and London, I. T. The use of demographic characteristics in predicting length of neuro-psychiatric hospital stay. *Journal of Consulting Psychology,* 1959, **23**, 85-89.

Lovinger, E. Perceptual contact with reality in schizophrenia. *Journal of Abnormal and Social Psychology,* 1956, **52**, 87-91.

Luborsky, L., Blinder, B., and Schimek, J. Looking, recalling, and GSR as a function of defense. *Journal of Abnormal Psychology,* 1965, **70**, 270-280.

Maddi, S. R. *Personality theories: a comparative analysis.* Homewood, Ill.: Dorsey Press, 1968.

Magaro, P. A. Perceptual discrimination performance of schizophrenics as a function of censure, social class, and premorbid adjustment. *Journal of Abnormal Psychology,* 1967, **72**, 415-420.

Magaro, P. A., and Vojtisek, J. E. Embedded figures performance of schizophrenics as a function of chronicity, premorbid adjustment, diagnosis, and medication. *Journal of Abnormal Psychology,* 1971, **77**, 184-191.

Mallet, J. J. Verbal recall of hostile and neutral thematic contents by schizophrenic and normal subjects. Unpublished doctoral dissertation, Duke University, 1956.

Marks, J. Predicting outcome in schizophrenia. *Journal of Abnormal and Social Psychology,* 1963, **66**, 117-127.

Marx, A. The effect of interpersonal content on conceptual task performance of schizophrenics. Unpublished doctoral dissertation, University of Oklahoma, Norman, 1962.

Mason, A. S., Tarpy, E. K., Sherman, L. J., and Haefner, D. P. Discharges from a mental hospital in relation to social class and other variables. *Archives of General Psychiatry,* 1960, **2**, 1-6.

McKinley, R. A. Perceived parental attributes of schizophrenics as a function of premorbid social adjustment. *Dissertation Abstracts,* 1964, **24**, 4800.

McReynolds, R., Collins, B., and Acker, M. Delusional thinking and cognitive organization in schizophrenia. *Journal of Abnormal and Social Psychology,* 1964, **69**, 210-212.

Meadow, A., and Funkenstein, D. H. The relationship of abstract thinking to the autonomic nervous system in schizophrenia. In P. H. Hoch and J. Zubin (Eds.), *Relation of psychological tests to psychiatry.* New York: Grune and Stratton, 1952. Pp. 131-149.

Meadow, A., Greenblatt, M., Funkenstein, D. H., and Solomon, H. C. Relationship between capacity for abstraction in schizophrenia and physiologic response to autonomic drugs. *Journal of Nervous and Mental Disease,* 1953, **118**, 332-338.

Mednick, S. A. A learning theory approach to research in schizophrenia. *Journal of Abnormal and Social Psychology,* 1963, **66**, 314-317.

Mehl, M. M. The effect of brief sensory deprivation and sensory stimulation on the cognitive functioning of chronic schizophrenics. (Doctoral dissertation, George Peabody College for Teachers) Ann Arbor, Mich.: University Microfilms, 1967. No. 67-3617.

Mehl, M. M., and Cromwell, R. L. The effect of brief sensory deprivation and sensory stimulation on the cognitive functioning of chronic schizophrenics. *Journal of Nervous and Mental Disease,* 1969, **148**, 586-596.

Meichenbaum, D. H. Validational study of marital status and the self-report scale for process-reactive schizophrenia. *Journal of Consulting and Clinical Psychology,* 1969, **33**, 351-356.

Minard, J., and Mooney, W. Psychological differentiation and perceptual defense: Studies of the separation of perception from emotion. *Journal of Abnormal Psychology,* 1969, **74**, 131-140.

Mishler, E. G., and Waxler, N. E. *Interaction in families: An experimental study of family processes and schizophrenia.* New York: John Wiley, 1968.

Nathanson, I. A. A semantic differential analysis of parent-son relationships in schizophrenia. *Journal of Abnormal Psychology,* 1967, **72**, 277-281.

Neale, J. M., and Cromwell, R. L. Size estimation in schizophrenia. *Journal of Abnormal Psychology,* 1968, **73**, 44-48.

Neale, J. M., and Cromwell, R. L. Preference for complexity in acute schizophrenics. *Journal of Consulting and Clinical Psychology,* 1969, **33**, 245-246.

Normington, C. J. Some aspects of psychosexual development in process-reactive schizophrenia. (Doctoral dissertation, Michigan State University) Ann Arbor, Mich.: University Microfilms, 1965. No. 65-711.

Palermo, D. S., and Jenkins, J. J. *Word association norms: grade school through college.* Minneapolis: University of Minnesota Press, 1964.

Pearl, D. Stimulus input and overload in relation to classifications of schizophrenia. *Newsletter for Research in Psychology,* 1962, **4**, 44-56. (Kecoughtan, Va.: VA Center)

Price, R. H., and Ericksen, C. W. Size constancy in schizophrenia: A reanalysis. *Journal of Abnormal Psychology,* 1966, **71**, 155-160.

Query, J. M. N. Role perception: A comparative study of good and poor pre-morbid schizophrenic men. Paper read at the 70th Annual Meeting of the American Psychological Association, St. Louis, August, 1962.

Rappaport, M., and Hopkins, M. S. Drug effects on auditory attention in paranoid and nonparanoid schizophrenics. *Journal of Nervous and Mental Disease,* 1969, **148**, 597-605.

Rassidakis, N. C., Lykas, C., Papadakis, E., and Kafatou, A. A. A follow-up study of schizophrenic patients: Relapse and readmission. *Bulletin of the Menninger Clinic,* 1963, **17**, 33-40.

Raush, H. L. Perceptual constancy in schizophrenia. *Journal of Personality,* 1952, **21**, 176-187.

Reichard, S., and Tillman, C. Patterns of parent-child relationships in schizophrenia. *Psychiatry,* 1950, **13**, 247-258.

Reisman, J. M. Motivational differences between process and reactive schizophrenics. *Journal of Personality,* 1960, **28**, 12-25.

Reynolds, D. J. An investigation of the somatic response system in chronic schizophrenia. *Dissertation Abstracts,* 1963, **23**, 4746.

Rice, J. K. Disordered language as related to autonomic responsivity and the process-reactive distinction. *Journal of Abnormal Psychology,* 1970, **76**, 50-54.

Ries, H. A. Commonality of word associations and length of hospitalization in neurotics and schizophrenics. *Journal of Consulting and Clinical Psychology,* 1968, **32**, 722-724.

Ries, H. A. and Johnson, M. H. Commonality of word associations and good and poor premorbid schizophrenia. *Journal of Abnormal Psychology,* 1967, **72**, 487-488.

Rodnick, E. H. Cognitive and perceptual response set in schizophrenics. In R. Jessor and S. Feshback (Eds.), *Cognition, personality, and clinical psychology.* San Francisco: Jossey-Bass, 1967. Pp. 173-209.

Rodnick, E. H., and Garmezy, N. An experimental approach to the study of motivation in schizophrenia. In M. R. Jones (Eds.), *Nebraska symposium on motivation,* Lincoln: University of Nebraska Press, 1959. Pp. 109-184.

Ryan, L. R. An exploratory study of some aspects of listening of schizophrenics. Unpublished doctoral dissertation, University of Colorado, Boulder, 1960.

Sanders, R., and Pacht, A. R. Perceptual size constancy of known clinical groups. *Journal of Consulting Psychology,* 1952, **16**, 440-444.

Schonbar, R. Differential dream recall frequency as a component of "life style." *Journal of Consulting Psychology,* 1965, **29**, 468-474.

Schwartz, M. L., Hunt, W. A., and Walker, R. E. Clinical judgment of vocabulary responses in process and reactive schizophrenia. *Journal of Clinical Psychology,* 1963, **19**, 488-494.

Secord, P., Backman, C., and Eachus, H. Effects of imbalance in the self-concept on the perception of persons. *Journal of Abnormal and Social Psychology,* 1964, **68**, 442-446.

Shipley, W. C. Shipley-Institute of Living Scale for Measuring Intellectual Impairment. In A. Weider (Ed.), *Contributions toward medical psychology: theory and psychodiagnostic methods.* Vol. II. New York: Ronald Press, 1953, Pp. 459-485.

Silverman, J. The scanning control mechanism and "cognitive filtering" in paranoid and nonparanoid schizophrenia. *Journal of Consulting Psychology,* 1964, **28**, 385-393.

Simon, W., and Wirt, R. D. Prognostic factors in schizophrenia. *American Journal of Psychiatry,* 1961, **17**, 887-890.

Spohn, H. E., Thetford, P. E., and Woodham, F. L. Span of apprehension and arousal in schizophrenia. *Journal of Abnormal Psychology,* 1970, **75**, 113-123.

Stephens, J. H., Brown, C., Forster, J. W., and Klein, H. G. Orienting responses in "process" and "nonprocess" schizophrenics. *Conditioned Reflex,* 1967, **2**, 166 (abstract).

Sterne, A. L. Paired-associate learning by hospitalized schizophrenics under conditions of response-specific verbal censure and approval. (Doctoral dissertation, Vanderbilt University) Ann Arbor, Mich.: University Microfilms, 1967. No. 67-7463.

Stier, S. A. Developmental attainment, outcome and symbolic performance in schizophrenia. (Doctoral dissertation, University of California, Los Angeles) Ann Arbor, Mich.: University Microfilms, 1968. No. 68-7486.

Stockner, C., and Garmezy, N. Unpublished data cited in E. H. Rodnick and N. Garmezy, An experimental approach to the study of motivation in schizophrenia. In M. R. Jones (Ed.), *Nebraska symposium on motivation,* Lincoln: University of Nebraska Press, 1957. Pp. 109-184.

Stoller, F. H. Relationship between mothers' predictions and the performance of schizophrenics and their siblings. *Proceedings of the 74th Annual Convention of the American Psychological Association,* 1966, **1**, 169-170.

Strain, G. S. Performance of process and reactive schizophrenic subjects in an extended learning situation. Paper read at the 13th Annual Convention of the Southeastern Psychological Association, Atlanta, April, 1967.

Struve, F. A. Classical cardiac conditioning with process and reactive schizophrenics and normals. *Dissertation Abstracts,* 1966, **26**, 4082.

Tytko, T. A., and Spence, J. T. The performance of process and reactive schizophrenics and brain injured subjects on a conceptual task. *Journal of Abnormal Psychology,* 1962, **65**, 387-394.

Ussery, L. Data cited in Rodnick, E. H., and Garmezy, N. An experimental approach to the study of motivation in schizophrenia. In M. R. Jones (Ed.), *Nebraska symposium on motivation,* Lincoln: University of Nebraska Press, 1957. Pp. 109-184.

Ward, W. D., and Carlson, W. A. Autonomic responsivity to variable input rates among schizophrenics classified on the process-reactive dimension. *Journal of Abnormal Psychology,* 1966, **71**, 10-16.

Weckowicz, T. E. Size constancy in schizophrenic patients. *Journal of Mental Science,* 1957, **103**, 475-486.

Weckowicz, T. E. and Hall, R. Distance constancy in schizophrenic and nonschizophrenic mental patients. *Journal of Clinical Psychology,* 1960, **16**, 272-276.

Weckowicz, T. E., Sommer, R., and Hall, R. Distance constancy in schizophrenic patients. *Journal of Mental Science,* 1958, **104**, 1174-1182.

Willner, A. Impairment of knowledge of usual meanings of familiar words in brain damage and schizophrenia. *Journal of Abnormal Psychology,* 1965, **70**, 405-411.

Wilton, M. M. Differential preference for ambiguity in process and reactive schizophrenics. (Doctoral dissertation, Boston University Graduate School) Ann Arbor, Mich.: University Microfilms, 1966. No. 66-11,327.

Witkin, H. A., Dyk, R. B., Faterson, H. F., Goodenough, D. R., and Karp, S. A. *Psychological differentiation.* New York: John Wiley, 1962.

Wolowitz, H. Attraction and aversion to power: A psychoanalytic conflict theory of homosexuality in male paranoid schizophrenics. *Journal of Abnormal Psychology,* 1965, **70**, 360-370.

Young, H. D. The effects of oral censure on the conceptual performance of chronic schizophrenics as a function of premorbid adjustment and current mental health. (Doctoral dissertation, Columbia University) Ann Arbor, Mich.: University Microfilms, 1962. No. 62-3708.

Zahn, T. P. Acquired and symbolic affective value as determinants of size estimation in schizophrenics and normal subjects. *Journal of Abnormal and Social Psychology,* 1959, **58**, 39-47.

CHAPTER 9

Current Status and Future Implications of the Theory

It seems ironic to me that a theory built with such concern for the empirical verdicts of research should leave as many questions unanswered as does the adaptive-style theory. Perhaps this is so because the penchant for laboratory demonstration at each conceptual step of the way diverts thinking more into the detail-oriented analytic mode of the researcher than into the broadstroke synthesis mode of the theoretician. In any case, residual questions may have beneficial effects in the long run. Curiosity, I hope, will involve others in the formidable task of filling out the skeletal network of the present theory.

There is one question that has been raised more often in our thinking than any other. This has had to do with the role of the father in our theory of schizophreniform development. We will concern ourselves with this question now, and then will bring this book to a close with consideration of a variety of implications of our research.

THE ROLE OF THE FATHER IN THE CHILD'S ADAPTATION TO AVERSIVE MATERNAL CONTROL

The adaptive-style theory, which proposes a learning basis for the development of schizophreniform behaviors and, ultimately, schizophrenic disorders of psychotic proportions, has not been extended to include the role of the father within the family dynamics. The omission can be traced to two factors. First, the theory as it stands is a skeletal one, tied as closely as possible to research evidence. The scientific capacity of the program has not been sufficient to generate the research necessary to bear the added weight of relating the child's development to either the paternal child-rearing experience or the pattern of experiences presented by the parents taken in combination. Second, we have maintained that the mother's influence is primary in our culture so that while the father may play an auxiliary and occasionally a critical role in the child's pathological development, his generalized effect should be more difficult to identify and to reduce to lawful terms. All of these protestations to the contrary, a sprinkling of evidence bearing on the relationship between the paternal child-rearing experience and subsequent child behaviors has been gathered over the years, possibly enough to allow for some conservative guesswork about the father's contribution to schizoid development.

Aversive Paternal Control and Cognitive Deficit

Heilbrun, Orr, and Harrell (1966), in a paper discussed in Chapter 5, reported that late-adolescent males who had experienced aversive maternal control were disrupted more in their conceptual performance on a right-wrong reinforced task than the other child-rearing groups. A second independently conducted experiment was described in that paper in which similar questionnaire and concept-identification procedures were employed except the late-adolescent groups were separated into control-nurturance groupings based on perceptions of their fathers. Seventy-four male volunteers from the University of Iowa campus (mean age = 19.8 years) served as subjects.

Paternal child-rearing patterns were generated by inferring child-rearing control from the father form of the Parent Attitude Research Instrument and nurturance from the Parent-Child Interaction Rating Scales. The father form of the Research Instrument devised by Schaefer and Bell (Cline, Richards, and Needham, 1963) did not show the promise of their mother form for our purposes in that no major control factor emerged from factor analysis. Instead of the 16-scale, 80-item maternal control cluster extracted from the 23 scales on the mother form, Cline, Richards, and Needham were able to identify only 4 scales (20 items) from among the 23 scales represented on the father form which converged into a paternal control factor. The 115 items of the father form are included in Appendix G.

While the reduction in scales introduces some concern about stability of the paternal control score, another implication should not go unnoticed. The difference in the results of factor analysis suggests that perceived child-rearing control does not have the ubiquitous quality for fathers as was apparent in the case of mothers. Stated another way, much more of what mothers do in rearing their children seems to be experienced as a means of control than is true for fathers.

Not only does maternal control appear to be a more pervasive aspect of the child-rearing experience than does paternal control, we can point to some evidence which suggests that maternal control is a more salient experience for sons than for daughters. Heilbrun and Hall (1964), using median-split definitions of high and low maternal control on the PARI, compared the ratings of these groups for two maternal variables—degree of verbal punitiveness and degree of nurturance (using the Parent-Child Interaction Rating Scales). They found that

67% of the sons who experienced their mothers as high in control rated them as high in verbal punitiveness, whereas only 38% of the sons in the low-control group did so; the proportional difference was significant ($p < .05$). For daughters, 50% of the high-control group and 53% of the low-control group rated their mothers as high punitive. Thus, high maternal control for males was associated with high verbal punitiveness which was not the case for females.

Heilbrun and Hall also report that the sons of high-control mothers perceived them as significantly ($p < .001$) less nurturant (28.8) than low-control mothers (32.4). However, the rated nurturance of the mothers of high control (32.2) and low control (33.8) daughters did not vary reliably from each other.

The combination of findings reported by Heilbrun and Hall suggests that the control experience is mediated by systematic application of verbal punitive behavior and withholding of nurturant behaviors when the mother is contending with her adolescent son. Neither punishment nor nurturance is systematically linked to differences in experienced maternal control for the daughter. Whatever the basis for maternal control of the daughter, it lacks the power-assertive qualities apparent in the control experience of the son. Our contention that maternal control of the son would be a more salient experience than maternal control of the daughter stems from this observation. The more manifest qualities of maternal control directed toward the son could be explained by the greater resistance to parental authority for adolescent males relative to females. The son is under increasing social pressure to behave independently in keeping with the requirements of the adult masculine sex role; this would be especially compelling as far as female domination was concerned. Greater resistance to the mother's authority would be expected to elicit more blatant controls.

The lingering question is whether paternal control would also demonstrate a more salient quality vis-a-vis the son. Data available from a study (Heilbrun, Harrell, and Gillard, 1967) to be discussed at greater length later in this chapter allow us to examine the paternal nurturance by level of control relationship. By doing so we note that for sons the perceived nurturance of 45 high-control fathers (26.0) is less than that attributed to the 57 low-control fathers (27.8), but the difference fails to achieve statistical significance ($p > .05$). For daughters, however, the nurturance of 63 high-control fathers (27.8) was significantly less ($p < .01$) than the nurturance of 61 low-control fathers (30.5). Accordingly, we are led to conclude that while a modest inverse relationship between parental control and nurturance is generally to be expected, this is most clearly represented in the mother's relationship with her son and the father's relationship with his daughter.

The narrow band of four paternal control scales (fostering dependency, deification, exclusion of outside influences, and deception) represent rather clear and direct mechanisms of influence, as might be expected from fathers. However, the manipulative character of deception as a form of control can be noted. Three of these four scales were among the eight (out of 23) which discriminated between the perceived paternal attitude ratings of schizophrenics and normals (McKinley, 1963); schizophrenics perceived their fathers as more controlling on each.

Table 66 allows us to compare the average effectiveness of the four paternal child-rearing groups on the reinforced concept task in the Heilbrun, Orr, and Harrell investigation. Statistical analysis proceeded by comparing each of the three remaining groups with the low control-high nurturance reference group. By doing so it was established that only the aversive-paternal-control group had demonstrated significantly ($p < .05$ one tail) inferior performance as gauged by both performance indices. Comparison of the results of this experiment with those reported for males in the companion experiment (see Table 13) suggests a similar sensitivity to evaluative cues and consequent thinking deficits for sons experiencing aversive control in the context of either parental relationship.

A parallel study of the relationships between the father's perceived child-rearing approaches and the daughter's cognitive control under evaluative stress appeared a year later (Heilbrun, Harrell, and Gillard, 1967). This investigation allowed a somewhat more comprehensive look at child rearing and cognitive control in that the questionnaire battery included both the paternal and maternal forms. The pattern of child-rearing experiences with the mother and the father could be determined for each subject.

The 123 female undergraduates from the University of Iowa were exposed to the evaluative stress of performing on the Stroop task before a group of peers. Motivational conditions were such as to reasonably insure that quality of performance assumed more importance to these girls than would be expected in a typical psychological experiment. Each time a girl made an error on the Stroop, the male experimenter would say "wrong," and the girl had to correct her error. Paternal child-rearing group differences in susceptibility to cognitive

Table 66. Concept Identification Performance of Late-Adolescent Males Varying in Paternal Control-Nurturance Child-Rearing Experience

	Perceived Paternal Child-Rearing Pattern			
Score[a]	High Control-Low Nurturance ($N = 19$)	High Control-High Nurturance ($N = 16$)	Low Control-Low Nurturance ($N = 20$)	Low Control-High Nurturance ($N = 19$)
Mean total error	2.92	2.46	2.62	2.16
Mean total correct	2.51	1.68	1.49	1.77

[a] A square-root transformation ($\sqrt{\text{score} + .5}$) was applied to all individual scores to reduce the skewness of the frequency data.

error under the stress of public social reinforcement are summarized in the top row of Table 67. The aversive-control group was the most susceptible to error, but statistics verified that it differed only from the high control-high nurturance ($p < .01$) and low control-low nurturance ($p < .01$) groups in this regard. The low control-high nurturance pattern group, commonly found at the opposite pole of performance from aversive-control subjects when maternal child-rearing was under investigation, demonstrated a level of cognitive disruption comparable to aversive-paternal-control females. However, the most reasonable conclusion to draw from the cognitive error scores, in light of all the previously presented evidence relating to aversive control, is that the aversive-paternal-control experience is associated with a special sensitivity to evaluative situations and to thought interference in daughters just as it was with sons.

The combined effects of each child-rearing pattern when it occurs in both parents is reported in the bottom row of Table 67. Statistical analysis of these means reported in the original paper did not include a direct comparison of the joint-pattern groups. However, that the female adolescents who attributed aversive control to both parents made more errors than any other group is clear; calculation of the t statistic for the smallest intergroup mean difference (2.82 versus 2.15) substantiated its significance ($p < .02$).

The remainder of our discussion of the relationships between parental patterns and cognition under evaluative stress will be based on a reanalysis of the original Heilbrun, Harrell, and Gillard female data, and the reporting of previously unanalyzed male data collected under the same conditions as that imposed upon the females. The wisdom of hindsight has led us to modify our mode of analysis in two ways: (1) to use independent median cutting scores for control and for nurturance rather than nurturance high-low dividing points within the high-control group and, independently, within the low-control group; and (2) to recombine our data in a more complete fashion so as to include the

Table 67. Stroop Color-Naming Test Mean Error Scores for Late-Adolescent Females Varying in Paternal Child-Rearing Experience

	Perceived Paternal Child-Rearing Pattern							
	High Control-Low Nurturance		High Control-High Nurturance		Low Control-Low Nurturance		Low Control-High Nurturance	
	N	Mean	*N*	Mean	*N*	Mean	*N*	Mean
Pattern in father	31	2.87	31	2.27	28	2.14	33	2.55
Pattern in father and mother	16	2.82	13	2.04	11	1.88	14	2.15

NOTE: Means based on square-root transformations ($\sqrt{\text{score} + .5}$) of raw error scores.

Stroop error scores for an additional group of subjects for whom neither parent was experienced as high control-low nurturant. Table 68 presents the mean error scores for the four possible parent patterns relevant to the presence or absence of experienced aversive parental control in the dynamics of the family of the subject—present with both parents, present with the mother but not with the father, present with the father but not with the mother, or present with neither parent. There is little in which to take comfort as far as lawful ordering within the male data is concerned, since there are clearly no additive effects of experienced aversive control with both parents relative to the mother (or the father) alone. In fact, these data do not even reflect any differences when both parents were perceived as high control-low nurturant and when neither parent was perceived in this way. The female results, however, do suggest some incremental effects of aversive paternal control when taken in combination with the maternal counterpart. Cognitive disruption in the daughter was an increasing function of the number of aversive-control parents.

Paternal Child-Rearing Experience in Reactive and Process Schizophrenia

McKinley's (1963) investigation of child-rearing experience, which was discussed previously in terms of its bearing upon the mother-son relationship, also included the father's perceived child-rearing within its empirical scope. Those scales on the father form of the PARI for which significant differences ($p < .05$) among process, reactive, and control group means were found are listed in Table 69. Three of the eight scales (fostering dependency, breaking the will, excluding outside influences) for which schizophrenic-normal differences were established comprise 75% of a control factor, and inspection of the mean scores points up the contingency again between experienced parental control and schizophrenic status.

Table 68. Stroop Color-Naming Test Mean Error Scores for Late Adolescents Varying in Parental Child-Rearing Experience Patterns

	Combinational Parental Pattern Relevant to Presence or Absence of Aversive Control							
	Aversive Control Experienced with Both Parents		Aversive Control Experienced with Mother, not Father		Aversive Control Experienced with Father, not Mother		Aversive Control Experienced with Neither Parent	
	N	Mean	*N*	Mean	*N*	Mean	*N*	Mean
Male	14	2.52	13	2.55	13	2.77	48	2.42
Female	22	2.65	16	2.36	17	2.46	68	2.16

NOTE: Means are based on a square-root transformation of the raw error scores.

Table 69. Mean Perceived Paternal Child-Rearing Attitude Scores for Process Schizophrenic, Reactive Schizophrenic, and Hospitalized Normal Sons

PARI Father-Form Scale Number[a] and Description	Patient Group		
	Process Schizophrenics ($N = 18$)	Reactive Schizophrenics ($N = 17$)	Hospitalized Normals ($N = 18$)
2. Fostering dependency	21.17	22.00	15.72
4. Breaking the will	19.44	19.88	16.39
11. Excluding outside influences	21.33	20.06	17.22
14. Equalitarianism	14.55	17.82	13.39
16. Possessiveness of the wife	19.55	20.23	16.67
17. Avoidance of affection	21.50	21.00	18.22
18. Suppressing of affect	21.22	20.35	17.78
23. Deception	16.83	18.94	12.17

[a]The five items comprising each scale may be identified in Appendix G by starting with the scale number and proceeding by numerical increments of 23.

Much like McKinley's findings with perceptions of the mother, process-reactive differences in reported paternal attributes on the PARI were rare. Only one of the eight scale comparisons for which overall significance was obtained included a reliable difference between the schizophrenic groups. With regard to Equalitarianism, reactives' fathers were attributed higher scores. Despite the paucity of statistically significant differences between process and reactive perceptions, some interesting characteristics of the paternal patterns suggest themselves. Portrayal of the reactive father as both high on control and on equalitarianism suggests a felt inconsistency in expectation and a problem in communication with the father to accompany the reactive's problem with the subtle and devious communications of his mother which we have proposed. The reactive's attribution of high deception to his father as a control mechanism also adds to the impression that the reactive father complements the reactive mother as a manipulative and "double-binding" parental agent. This complementarity could further explain the high incidence of trust problems for reactive schizophrenics who are especially prone to paranoid disturbances. The process father emerges as controlling but without the same inconsistency introduced by equalitarianism and deception found in the reactive father. In short, both fathers look much like the prototypic mothers we have proposed for the reactive and process schizophrenic.

Another implication of the paternal data is the void of affectional interchange experienced by reactive and process sons alike. Not only were the fathers considered more restricted in their own affectional display toward the son but also more suppressive of affectionate behavior on the part of the son. This assumes importance in that it allows us to infer that the schizophrenic's experience with his father had high control *and* low nurturance properties in the absence of a measure of nurturance.

Paternal and Maternal Child-Rearing Experiences and Style of Adaptation

While the evidence reviewed so far relevant to the father's child-rearing role points to the formal similarities in the effects of aversive-control experiences with either parent, the more important theoretical question to be answered is whether aversive paternal control is functionally related to the adaptive styles. The only empirical inroad that we can make into answering this question is to extend and refine the mode of data analysis used in the basic adaptive-style experiment (Heilbrun, 1968) to consider parental aversive-control patterns.

The first tactic to be employed is to take the significant Minnesota Multiphasic Personality Inventory scale differences, critical to the original theoretical description of adaptive styles to aversive maternal control, and to discern whether these differences are influenced by refinement of the comparison groups to include also aversive paternal control. The reasoning involved would follow the line of this example. The combination of cognitive nondisruption in the Stroop-tape condition and high Depression Scale scores in aversive-maternal-control late-adolescents defines the closed adaptive style. The contribution of aversive paternal control to style adoption can be gauged by what happens to Depression Scale scores within the closed-style group for those individuals who have experienced both parents as high control-low nurturant. Table 70 presents the critical Multiphasic scale data for open-style and closed-style males experiencing only the mother or both the mother and the father as aversive-control parents.

Recalling that peak scores on Hypomania paired with censure-induced disruption defined open-style adaptation and a similar pairing of elevated Depression scores and insensitivity to censure cues defined closed-style adaptation, Table 70 includes remarkably clear indications that the combined experience of aversive control in both parents promotes an even stronger style adoption than when the mother alone has this particular child-rearing impact. Columns 1 and 3 not only reflect a clearer differentiation of Depression and Hypomania scores than Columns 2 and 4, but the more prominent elevations on Schizophrenia within the joint parental aversive-control groups are also evident.

Two further effects of this refined grouping are also clear. Social introversion was a common property of the entire maternal aversive-control group in the

Table 70. Mean Scores of Selected Minnesota Multiphasic Personality Inventory Scales for Late-Adolescent Males Varying in Parental Child-Rearing Expereience and Degree of Disruption by Maternal Censure Cues

	Style of Adaptation to Aversive Maternal Control			
	Closed Style		Open Style	
MMPI Scale	Aversive Maternal Control Combined with Aversive Paternal Control (*N* = 4)	Aversive Maternal Control Not Combined with Aversive Paternal Control (*N* = 6)	Aversive Maternal Control Combined with Aversive Paternal Control (*N* = 6)	Aversive Maternal Control Not Combined with Aversive Paternal Control (*N* = 4)
Depression	76.25	61.33	54.17	56.25
Hypomania	52.75	56.83	73.50	62.25
Schizophrenia	66.00	62.50	65.17	57.25
Social introversion	58.00	50.83	49.33	57.50
Paranoia	53.75	57.33	65.17	52.25

original analysis; in the present analysis high Social Introversion scores become empirically aligned only with the socially alienated closed-style male who has experienced aversive control in both parents. Finally, high Paranoid scores for open-style males were only of suggestive significance ($p < .10$) in the original analysis relative to closed-style males. However, considerable evidence, discussed in Chapter 8, lends confidence to a functional tie between open-style adaptation and paranoid behavior. We can see that the expected elevation on the Paranoid Scale occurs only when both parents assume aversive-control properties.

The availability of only very small samples to represent the aversive-control patterns within adaptive styles and the consequent futility of applying statistical tests require conservative conclusions from these Multiphasic shifts. Yet we have identified one clear implication: adaptive styles are most readily discernible when both parents are construed by the child as imposing high control in a low nurturant context. There is a possibility of a confounding in the evidence on this point which must be acknowledged. The generalization of perceived attitudes from one parent to the other would lead to the same results in our analysis as would independent contributions of aversive-control experiences with both parents. In the former case, those who have felt the greatest impact of an aversive-control experience with the mother might be expected to generalize their perceptions to the father or, for that matter, to authority figures in general. This high-impact group would be expected to show the more deviant scores in our MMPI analysis.

In the latter case, the joint contribution of aversive control which had actually been experienced with both parents also would have the effect of producing more deviant MMPI performance; greater pathology in the family dynamics breeds greater pathology in the child. Accordingly, we cannot be certain whether the subjects whose scores are presented in columns 1 and 3 of Table 70 are those who had a high-impact aversive-control experience with their mothers and generalized their perceptions to their fathers or are those for whom the actual properties of the parental relationships led them to experience both as controlling and rejecting.

More recently analyzed data collected at the time of the original 1968 adaptive-style experiment (Heilbrun, 1971) will now be considered in the hope of shedding further light on parental patterning contingencies. In addition to the father form of the PARI and the nurturance ratings of the father on the Parent-Child Interaction Rating Scales, two other types of psychometric evidence can be reported. The Need Scales for the Adjective Check List (Gough and Heilbrun, 1965) represent a broad spectrum of 15 personality variables relevant to normal interpersonal behavior. Rotter's Internal-External Locus of Reinforcement Scale (Rotter, 1966) data are also available; the scale score gives us an estimate of the extent to which the person views the rewards and punishments which befall him as contingent on his own actions (an internal attitude) or whether he feels a lack of such control over how events turn out (an external attitude). Table 71 summarizes these scale means for parental aversive-control combination groups.

Although exceptions are to be found, the general drift of the data in Table 71 is in keeping with our prior observations—the combination of maternal and paternal aversive control mediates a stronger differential patterning of behaviors between open and closed styles than when the mother alone is perceived in this way. The substance of this patterning (using a half standard deviation difference as our guide) points to the open-style adapter's greater concern with egocentric reinforcement-oriented activities (higher need achievement and exhibition), his greater disdain for shared or institutionalized values (higher autonomy), and, surprisingly, his lower level of kinship with people (lower nurturance and heterosexuality). Turning the pattern around, we observe the lack of peer contact (lower affiliation) or leadership qualities (lower dominance) of the closed-style male as well as the presence of "soft" qualities which reflect emotional dependency and felt limitations relating to other persons (higher succorance, abasement, and deference).

A reversal in the comparison of aversive-control pattern groups can be noted for the locus-of-control measure. Those sons who experienced the mother alone as an aversive-control parent emerged as more external in their attitudes than when both parents were perceived in this way. Externality is usually considered the more ineffectual pole of this bipolar dimension.

Table 71. Further Personality Scale Mean Scores for Late-Adolescent Males Varying in Parental Child-Rearing Experience and Degree of Disruption by Maternal Censure Cues

	Style of Adaptation to Aversive Maternal Control			
	Closed Style		Open Style	
Personality Scale[a]	Combined with Aversive Paternal Control ($N = 4$)	Not Combined with Aversive Paternal Control ($N = 6$)	Combined with Aversive Paternal Control ($N = 6$)	Not Combined with Aversive Paternal Control ($N = 4$)
Achievement	48.50	41.83	53.67	47.00
Dominance	44.50	44.50	53.00	48.50
Endurance	48.00	43.67	51.00	47.50
Order	50.25	44.83	51.17	49.50
Intraception	48.25	49.67	47.67	54.25
Nurturance	47.25	51.67	41.83	44.50
Affiliation	39.75	41.50	46.00	39.50
Heterosexuality	50.25	53.00	44.00	46.50
Exhibition	47.50	49.50	57.00	47.25
Autonomy	49.50	50.33	57.50	53.25
Aggression	51.00	52.83	55.50	54.75
Change	48.75	50.50	51.17	44.25
Succorance	57.25	54.33	45.83	49.50
Abasement	54.75	53.50	46.00	47.00
Deference	56.50	51.33	41.67	47.25
Internal-External	10.00	12.00	7.67	12.75

[a]College Norm for 15 Need Scales set at T = 50. Higher scores indicate greater externalization of control on Internal-External Scale.

The masculine-appearing personality functioning of the open-style male with two aversive-control parents is confirmed by a Masculinity-Femininity Scale mean score of 53.00, substantially higher than their closed-style counterparts with two aversive-control parents (44.50). Strangely enough though, all four of the late-adolescents in the more feminine closed-style category had identified with their fathers, but three of the father models presented more feminine sex-role models. The masculine open-style group identified in four out of six cases with their mothers and only in one instance with a masculine father. The absence of the normal mechanisms for mediating masculinity and femininity through the parent modeling process are nowhere more apparent than in these results.

One final observation may be made following our analysis of the previously collected psychometric data. We have not taken the opportunity until this point to reflect upon the possible effects of aversive paternal control in the absence of experienced aversive-control in the mother, and we have only the barest of information to provide the basis for doing so. There were five subjects in the maternal low control-high nurturance group within Heilbrun's 1968 experiment that portrayed their fathers as having demonstrated aversive control. Three of these were defined as nondisrupted by the Stroop-tape procedure and two as disrupted. Scanning of the psychometric data given by the 24 Minnesota Multiphasic Personality Inventory, Adjective Check List, and Internal-External Control scales with which we have been concerned in this chapter offers no hint of the adaptive-style patternings which have been detected when the mother's aversive control impact is evident. This simply adds to our conviction that the father's child-rearing impact, if of an aversive-control nature, primarily serves to increment the deleterious effects of a similar child-rearing impact of the mother. Obviously though, the issue is still an open one.

IMPLICATIONS OF THE RESEARCH

In trying to summarize my own thoughts upon completion of this theoretical presentation, several considerations have occurred to me which relate to the probability that the theory will prove to be accurate and to the implications, if this is so. These reflections may be ordered into three categories—scientific, professional, and humanistic.

Scientific Implications of the Research

Considerable attention has been given throughout the earlier chapters to the general issues surrounding research into psychopathological development and to the specific research strategies which we actually employed over the years. However, there remain a number of considerations generated by the research program which were better withheld until after the evidence was in and the theory articulated. Foremost among these are some striking characteristics of the evidence which has been presented to the reader. Every investigation which I or my student associates have conducted has been reported in this book. This means that to my knowledge there is no backlog of negative or contradictory evidence that has been excluded from consideration. There are differences to be sure among the reported studies in weight to be placed on the evidence, but I am struck at least by the consistency of the findings in a scientific field where the ephemeral quality of empirical relationships is an occupational hazard.

Another most important characteristic of the evidence which bears on the credibility of the theory has to do with the effects of increased refinement of the theory on the precision of the data generated by our research. Inspection of summary Tables 18 and 38 convey an interesting fact which has received our attention earlier in the book. Although all the studies cited present evidence that is consistent with hypothesized effects of the aversive-maternal-control experience, these effects were not confined exclusively to the high control-low nurturance child-rearing group. This situation was rectified to some extent within the investigations summarized within the second of these two tables, presumably because of some methodological and statistical changes which were introduced in order to tighten up our procedures and sharpen our inferences.

The real test of whether further refinement of theory influenced the precision of our data resides within the investigations listed in Table 65. The table, as it stands, tells us only that all studies found some support for the adaptive-style theory. This fact fails to distinguish the evidence cited from the previous summary tables. We will concern ourselves at this point with a closer look at the precision of the evidence stemming from the adaptive-style validational studies.

Statistical analysis of the results of adaptive-style research has proceeded in a reasonably standard way from one study to the next. Adaptive-style high control-low nurturance subgroupings have been constituted and a reference group has been similarly broken down into subgroups to control for level of cognitive disruption. Statistical treatment of the theoretical proposition has then resolved down to tests of the "simple effects" of an analysis of variance, the direct comparison of two subgroupings. Such subgrouping comparisons could proceed in either of two ways to test a theoretical proposition. The two adaptive-style subgroups could be compared directly with each other, a directional prediction tested, and the presence or absence of the same directional difference in the two reference control subgroups established. As an alternative, each adaptive-style subgroup could be compared directly with its control group, and the presence of a directional difference in one comparison and its absence in the other would be the object of statistical test. Both approaches to statistical analysis have been employed, and we have been willing to accept the statistical verdict of either procedure as supporting evidence for the theory if the direction of difference and probability level indicated.

A more demanding requirement for ascertaining the precision with which the empirical data of the adaptive-style research met expectations generated by the theory is available to us, at least in retrospect. Two categories of theoretical expectations and, thus, predictions were possible within these studies. If the behavioral dimension under investigation was one in which open-style adolescents were expected to fall at one extreme and closed-style adolescents were expected to fall at the other, the most reasonable set of predictions would be that these adaptive-style subgroups would demonstrate a difference and that their respective control groups, whose performances should assume intermediate status, would not differ. If the behavioral dimension were one in which only one of the adaptive-style subgroups should deviate, then the prediction that this subgroup would differ from its control group and the remaining adaptive-style subgroup would not differ from its control would be appropriate.

Table 72 summarizes the adaptive-style research findings organized in such a way as to elucidate the patterns of results by the two categories of theoretical expectation. Organized in this way, we would consider the table to be quite revealing. Among the 11 behavioral dimensions for which there was a theoretical basis for expecting bipolar positioning of the adaptive-style groups, 10 of the demonstrated effects involved significant differences between the two coping

Table 72. Patterns of Effects in Investigations Relevant to the Adaptive-Style Theory

Behavioral Dimension	Mean Obtained Values: Closed Style	Open Style	Nondisrupted Controls	Disrupted Controls	Specific Effect Reported as Consistent with Theory
Theoretical Expectation of Bipolar Positioning of Adaptive-Style Subgroups on Behavioral Dimension Under Investigation					
Clarity of communication					
Subtle-obvious scale	51.44	43.88	50.80	51.03	closed > open
Rated clarity of control	55.31	53.23	47.96	49.45	closed > controls
Interpersonal distancing	54.30	46.33	49.95	49.90	closed > open
External scanning					
Threshold cues	21.29	38.56	26.64	29.50	open > closed
Simultaneous cues	.60	–2.50	–1.63	–.84	closed > open
Internal scanning					
Nondominant meanings	31.22	25.00	28.70	29.00	closed > open
Word association frequency	21.58	26.17	23.99	25.48	open > closed
Defense mechanisms					
Repression	.49	.54	.55	.52	open > closed
Projection	–2.30	1.91	–.52	.15	open > closed
Tolerance of ambiguity					
Initial delay	50.70	29.33	30.50	31.19	closed > open
Total score	58.80	38.25	44.05	44.57	closed > open
Theoretical Expectation of Deviation for Only One of the Adaptive-Style Subgroups on Behavioral Dimension Under Investigation					
Differential perception of mother-father voice	–14.6%	–7.6%	2.8%	–7.2%	closed < controls
Emotional responsivity					
Neutral interference	14.57	23.25	29.56	20.78	closed < controls
Aversive interference	14.71	17.50	27.11	17.89	closed < controls
Heterosexual orientation (response to nude males)	–33.95	–46.99	–47.07	–33.59	closed > open (interaction unpredicted)
Sex-role identity	45.00	52.30	52.90	53.80	closed < controls
Fixed ideation	4.12	3.19	4.14	5.09	open < controls

styles. For nine of these 10 demonstrated effects, the open-style and closed-style groups actually established themselves at the extremes of the dimensions, with the two control groups assuming intermediate status. Further, the control groups presented virtually identical mean scores in every set of data.

When there was a theoretical basis for predicting that only one of the adaptive-style groups would deviate, as was the case for six sets of data, the demonstrated effect involved a comparison of an adaptive-style group with its control group in five of these. Again we find nearly identical mean scores for the remaining adaptive-style group and its control group.

The conclusion we derive from this examination of patterned effects within the adaptive-style research is that the theory has not only received consistent support from the data but support of a remarkably precise nature considering the unsophisticated character of our scientific tools. We again would point to the robustness of the behavioral laws necessary for precision under these conditions.

Recognition also should be given to the fact that despite the acknowledged limited power of psychometric procedures, almost all research employing the standard control and nurturance scales has proceeded without introducing extreme measures to generate the power to demonstrate the relationship under test. For example, psychological research, in which a psychological measure is used as an independent variable as we have done, often requires the establishment of extreme cutting scores in order to include sufficiently contrasting groups. It has never been necessary to eliminate a subject from one of our studies in order to gain power, except in those two investigations when a priori decisions meant only high control-low nurturance and low control-high nurturance groupings participated (Heilbrun, 1968; Gilgun, 1971). There are two meanings which can be imposed upon this attribute of the research. One of these would be that we have used powerful psychological measures which got us closer to the natural behaviors we are trying to assess than most psychometric devices. I seriously doubt that this is so. The alternative, previously entertained, would be that the underlying behavioral relationships are powerful and emerged in our studies despite the limitations of the psychological scales and without resorting to special measures to increase power.

The other side of the same coin is the fact that our research with late-adolescents has proceeded with high-low definitions of experienced control and nurturance which qualify in a relative but not an absolute sense. Thus, our median-cut procedure for assigning subjects to child-rearing quadrants has resulted in absolute levels of experienced maternal control and hostility-rejection which generally fall short of intensity levels expected for induction of serious psychopathology. Thus, the lawful relationships that have been established between the aversive-control experience and deviant aspects of development would lead us to expect more extreme effects of the same kind if we concerned ourselves with more extreme experiences. The emergence of systematic relationships in the absence of extreme psychological provocation in the histories of the adolescents studied adds to their significance for psychopathogenic explanation.

Having a theory based upon a reasonably sound foundation of research evidence opens the way to reversing the direction of the inferential process. Heretofore our concern has been in the implications of the evidence for theory building and validation. It should be possible now to look to the theory to generate new ideas about adolescent development or about process and reactive schizophrenia that can be tested by research or clinical observation. This is not to suggest that efforts to extend the theoretical network or to further validate its postulates should abate. In fact, longitudinal investigation of the adaptive-style theory of schizophrenic development, described earlier in the book as unfeasible for theory development, could be implemented now on a long-range basis for evaluating the predictive power of the theory. The difference resides in the fact that sufficient properties of the aversive-control experience and the adaptive styles can now be stipulated so that selection of adolescents from a nonclinical population who demonstrate all or most of these properties should lead to a marked increase in base rate for schizophrenia from the 1% incidence level. The heavy investment of time and personnel required to establish the presence of these attributes should be repaid in a scientific sense by the emergence of schizophrenic behavior in such proportions as to allow reliable conclusions to be drawn.

Earlier in the book we considered the problems inherent in scientific attempts to separate the contribution of genetic and experiential factors to the development of schizophrenia. While the evidence supporting the relationship between genetic endowment and schizophrenia was acknowledged, the point was made that the understanding of the formal characteristics of the disorder seemed to require explanation couched in learning terms. Further, we ventured the assumption that the schizophrenic condition could occur in the absence of genetic flaw.

The program of research which has been described in this book has at no point presumed itself to test the genetics versus learning question. Yet in retrospect one relevant fact emerges regarding this issue. To the extent that we have been able to identify subgroups of normal late-adolescents who demonstrate predictable schizophreniform behaviors, we have done so by sampling from a most unlikely population for genetic flaw. Although the information has never been requested, the chances seem remote that we would find high incidence for schizophrenia in the families of roughly those 25% of the subjects who are selected as having experienced high control and low nurturance of the mother. In fact, it is not our impression that the families of matriculating college students offer that much grist for the geneticist's mill to begin with, at least as far as familial transmission of psychopathology is concerned.

Professional Implications of the Research

In a way, the concerted attention devoted to explaining why psychopathology occurs is out of step with the times. Professional psychologists are turning in significant numbers to the application of learning principles to the modification of ineffective behavior. Systematic application of learning strategies directs attention away from how the person developed ineffectual behavior and toward a precise analysis of what his current behavior is and how he can learn to behave otherwise. Whether behavior modification techniques are or are not successful is not at issue here. That they are re-active rather than active most certainly is. The relative absence of concern with historical explanation of psychopathology and the emphasis upon post facto alleviation deters us from the ultimate goal of all helping sciences, the prevention of the distress state. Any theory that engages the question of why distress states come to be has the potential for bringing prevention a step closer to realization. Theories which contend with the nature of current distress states or their modification will make little if any contribution to this end.

The prevention of schizophrenia, to the extent this is possible through the control of learning conditions, is a distant hope and is unlikely to command the attention accorded to immediate treatment possibilities by those who are placed in a position to contend with psychotic patients. I would point out with this in mind that adaptive-style theory could generate new approaches to the treatment of schizophrenia which have not to my knowledge been attempted. For example, perceptual-attentional accomodation to evaluative stress has assumed central importance in explaining the selective loss or unselective overload of information postulated as the basis for the autistic or paranoid anomalies of thought observed in schizophrenia. Perceptual-attentional retraining involving procedures that will allow schizophrenic patients to learn to more effectively attend to the stimulus properties of their environment or to more effectively blend the external and internal scanning of information would seem to be called for. Accomplishing this kind of retraining might require a new kind of specialist—a psychological systems engineer competent in the technocracy of information field simulation and corrective programming.

Humanistic Implications of the Research

The singular concern of our research with the mother as the child-rearing agent and the abundant evidence of her involvement with the psychopathology of the child could be construed as an indictment of the female parent. This is quite untrue, of course. It must be reemphasized that the decision to work within the perceptual experience of the adolescent magnifies the child's contribution to the deviant developmental outcomes with which we have been concerned. The manner in which the mother's actions, communication, attitudes, and feelings register with the child are certainly open to his misrepresentation. Trying to assess the degree of contribution of the mother and the child is impossible. Yet the critical importance of the mother in our family system of child-rearing is such that her aberrant behavior *or* the child's interpretation of it as aberrant may have disastrous results.

Belief in the critical contribution made by the mother to the healthy and unhealthy development of the child leads me to be quite concerned about the signs of increasing rejection of the maternal role, embraced particularly within the protestations of the women's liberation movement. There would be no argument with a woman's decision not to marry. Nor could exception be taken to her decision to marry and not to bear children, if this were a matter of mutual agreement reached by both the man and woman prior to marriage. But the abdication of child-rearing responsibilities after the fact for the individual woman is not a decision to be made lightly or unilaterally. More than this, the advocation of changes to be more generally applied to the woman's culturally defined child-rearing role should always be accompanied by constructive alternatives which promise to facilitate child development.

REFERENCES

Cline, V. B., Richards, J. M., Jr., and Needham, W. E. A factor analytic study of the father form of the Parental Attitude Research Instrument. *Psychological Record,* 1963, **13**, 65-72.

Gough, H. G., and Heilbrun, A. B. *Manual for the Adjective Check List and the need scales for the ACL.* Palo Alto, Calif.: Consulting Psychologists Press, 1965.

Heilbrun, A. B. Cognitive sensitivity to aversive maternal stimulation in late-adolescent males. *Journal of Consulting and Clinical Psychology,* 1968, **32**, 326-332.

Heilbrun, A. B. Style of adaptation to aversive maternal control, parental identification, and sex-role identity in late-adolescent males. Currently unpublished study, 1971.

Heilbrun, A. B., and Hall, C. L. Resource mediation in childhood and identification. *Journal of Child Psychology and Psychiatry,* 1964, **5**, 139-149.

Heilbrun, A. B., Harrell, S. N., and Gillard, B. J. Perceived child-rearing attitudes of fathers and cognitive control in daughters. *Journal of Genetic Psychology,* 1967, **111**, 29-40.

Heilbrun, A. B., Orr, H. K., and Harrell, S. N. Patterns of parental child-rearing and subsequent vulnerability to cognitive disturbance. *Journal of Consulting Psychology,* 1966, **30**, 51-59.

McKinley, R. Perceived parental attributes of schizophrenics as a function of premorbid social adjustment. Unpublished doctoral dissertation, University of Iowa, 1963.

Rotter, J. B. Generalized expectancies for internal versus external control of reinforcement. *Psychological Monographs,* 1966, 80 (1, Whole No. 609).

APPENDIX A

Parent Attitude Research Instrument (Mother's Form)

INVENTORY OF ATTITUDES ON FAMILY LIFE AND CHILDREN

Mother's Form

Read each of the statements below and then rate them as you think your mother would as follows:

A	a	d	D
Strongly Agree	Mildly Agree	Mildly Disagree	Strongly Disagree

Indicate your opinion by drawing a circle around the "A" if she would strongly agree, around the "a" if she would mildly agree, around the "d" if she would mildly disagree, and around the "D" if she would strongly disagree.

There are no right or wrong answers, so answer according to what you think her opinion would be. It is very important to the study that all questions be answered. Many of the statements will seem alike but all are necessary to show slight differences of opinion.

	Agree	*Disagree*
1. Children should be allowed to disagree with their parents if they feel their ideas are better.	A a	d D

2. A good mother should shelter her child from life's little difficulties.
3. The home is the only thing that matters to a good mother.
4. Some children are just so bad they must be taught to fear adults for their own good.
5. Children should realize how much parents have to give up for them.
6. You must always keep tight hold of a baby during his bath for in a careless moment he might slip.
7. People who think they can get along in marriage without arguments just don't know the facts.
8. A child will be grateful later on for strict training.

9. Children will get on any woman's nerves if she has to be with them all day.
10. It's best for the child if he never gets started wondering whether his mother's views are right.
11. More parents should teach their children to have unquestioning loyalty to them.
12. A child should be taught to avoid fighting no matter what happens.
13. One of the worst things about taking care of a home is a woman feels that she can't get out.
14. Parents should adjust to the children some rather than always expecting the children to adjust to the parents.
15. There are so many things a child has to learn in life there is no excuse for him sitting around with time on his hands.
16. If you let children talk about their troubles they end up complaining even more.
17. Mothers would do their job better with the children if fathers were more kind.
18. A young child should be protected from hearing about sex.
19. If a mother doesn't go ahead and make rules for the home the children and husband will get into troubles they don't need to.
20. A mother should make it her business to know everything her children are thinking.
21 Children would be happier and better behaved if parents would show an interest in their affairs.
22. Most children are toilet trained by 15 months of age.
23. There is nothing worse for a young mother than being alone while going through her first experience with a baby.
24. Children should be encouraged to tell their parents about it whenever they feel family rules are unreasonable.
25. A mother should do her best to avoid any disappointment for her child.
26. The woman who wants lots of parties seldom makes a good mother.
27. It is frequently necessary to drive the mischief out of a child before he will behave.
28. A mother must expect to give up her own happiness for that of her child.
29. All young mothers are afraid of their awkwardness in handling and holding the baby.
30. Sometimes it's necessary for a wife to tell off her husband in order to get her rights.
31. Strict discipline develops a fine strong character.
32. Mothers very often feel that they can't stand their children a moment longer.
33. A parent should never be made to look wrong in a child's eyes.
34. The child should be taught to revere his parents above all other grown-ups.
35. A child should be taught to always come to his parents or teachers rather than fight when he is in trouble.
36. Having to be with children all the time gives a woman the feeling her wings have been clipped.

37. Parents must earn the respect of their children by the way they act.
38. Children who don't try hard for success will feel they have missed out on things later on.
39. Parents who start a child talking about his worries don't realize that sometimes it's better to just leave well enough alone.
40. Husbands could do their part if they were less selfish.
41. It is very important that young boys and girls not be allowed to see each other completely undressed.
42. Children and husbands do better when the mother is strong enough to settle most of the problems.
43. A child should never keep a secret from his parents.
44. Laughing at children's jokes and telling children jokes makes things go more smoothly.
45. The sooner a child learns to walk the better he's trained.
46. It isn't fair that a woman has to bear just about all the burden of raising children by herself.
47. A child has a right to his own point of view and ought to be allowed to express it.
48. A child should be protected from jobs which might be too tiring or hard for him.
49. A woman has to choose between having a well run home and hobnobbing around with neighbors and friends.
50. A wise parent will teach a child early just who is boss.
51. Few women get the gratitude they deserve for all they have done for their children.
52. Mothers never stop blaming themselves if their babies are injured in accidents.
53. No matter how well a married couple love one another, there are always differences which cause irritation and lead to arguments.
54. Children who are held to firm rules grow up to be the best adults.
55. It's a rare mother who can be sweet and even tempered with her children all day.
56. Children should never learn things outside the home which make them doubt their parents' ideas.
57. A child soon learns that there is no greater wisdom than that of his parents.
58. There is no good excuse for a child hitting another child.
59. Most young mothers are bothered more by the feeling of being shut up in the home than by anything else.
60. Children are too often asked to do all the compromising and adjustment and that is not fair.
61. Parents should teach their children that the way to get ahead is to keep busy and not waste time.
62. Children pester you with all their little upsets if you aren't careful from the first.

63. When a mother doesn't do a good job with children it's probably because the father doesn't do his part around the home.
64. Children who take part in sex play become sex criminals when they grow up.
65. A mother has to do the planning because she is the one who knows what's going on in the home.
66. An alert parent should try to learn all her child's thoughts.
67. Parents who are interested in hearing about their children's parties, dates, and fun help them grow up right.
68. The earlier a child is weaned from its emotional ties to its parents the better it will handle its own problems.
69. A wise woman will do anything to avoid being by herself before and after a new baby.
70. A child's ideas should be seriously considered in making family decisions.
71. Parents should know better than to allow their children to be exposed to difficult situations.
72. Too many women forget that a mother's place is in the home.
73. Children need some of the natural meanness taken out of them.
74. Children should be more considerate of their mothers since their mothers suffer so much for them.
75. Most mothers are fearful that they may hurt their babies in handling them.
76. There are some things which just can't be settled by a mild discussion.
77. Most children should have more discipline than they get.
78. Raising children is a nerve-racking job.
79. The child should not question the thinking of his parents.
80. Parents deserve the highest esteem and regard of their children.
81. Children should not be encouraged to box or wrestle because it often leads to trouble or injury.
82. One of the bad things about raising children is that you aren't free enough of the time to do just as you like.
83. As much as is reasonable a parent should try to treat a child as an equal.
84. A child who is "on the go" all the time will most likely be happy.
85. If a child has upset feelings it is best to leave him alone and not make it look serious.
86. If mothers could get their wishes they would most often ask that the husbands be more understanding.
87. Sex is one of the greatest problems to be contended with in children.
88. The whole family does fine if the mother puts her shoulders to the wheel and takes charge of things.
89. A mother has a right to know everything going on in her child's life because her child is part of her.
90. If parents would have fun with their children, the children would be more apt to take their advice.
91. A mother should make an effort to get her child toilet trained at the earliest possible time.

92. Most women need more time than they are given to rest up in the home after going through childbirth.
93. When a child is in trouble he ought to know he won't be punished for talking about it with his parents.
94. Children should be kept away from all hard jobs which might be discouraging.
95. A good mother will find enough social life within the family.
96. It is sometimes necessary for the parents to break the child's will.
97. Mothers sacrifice almost all their own fun for their children.
98. A mother's greatest fear is that in a forgetful moment she might let something bad happen to the baby.
99. It's natural to have quarrels when two people who both have minds of their own get married.
100. Children are actually happier under strict training.
101. It's natural for a mother to "blow her top" when children are selfish and demanding.
102. There is nothing worse than letting a child hear criticisms of his mother.
103. Loyalty to parents comes before anything else.
104. Most parents prefer a quiet child to a "scrappy" one.
105. A young mother feels "held down" because there are lots of things she wants to do while she is young.
106. There is no reason parents should have their own way all the time, any more than that children should have their own way all the time.
107. The sooner a child learns that a wasted minute is lost forever the better off he will be.
108. The trouble with giving attention to children's problems is they usually just make up a lot of stories to keep you interested.
109. Few men realize that a mother needs some fun in life too.
110. There is usually something wrong with a child who asks a lot of questions about sex.
111. A married woman knows that she will have to take the lead in family matters.
112. It is a mother's duty to make sure she knows her child's innermost thoughts.
113. When you do things together, children feel close to you and talk easier.
114. A child should be weaned away from the bottle or breast as soon as possible.
115. Taking care of a small baby is something that no woman should be expected to do all by herself.

APPENDIX B

T-Score Norms for the Parent Attitude Research Instrument (Mother's Form)

College Males (N = 300)

Raw	T	Raw	T	Raw	T	Raw	T	Raw	T	Raw	T
320	101	293	90	266	79	239	68	212	58	185	47
319	100	292	90	265	79	238	68	211	57	184	46
318	100	291	89	264	78	237	68	210	57	183	46
317	100	290	89	263	78	236	67	209	56	182	46
316	99	289	88	262	78	235	67	208	56	181	45
315	99	288	88	261	77	234	66	207	56	180	45
314	98	287	88	260	77	233	66	206	55	179	44
313	98	286	87	259	76	232	66	205	55	178	44
312	98	285	87	258	76	231	65	204	54	177	44
311	97	284	86	257	76	230	65	203	54	176	43
310	97	283	86	256	75	229	64	202	54	175	43
309	96	282	86	255	75	228	64	201	53	174	42
308	96	281	85	254	74	227	64	200	53	173	42
307	96	280	85	253	74	226	63	199	52	172	42
306	95	279	84	252	74	225	63	198	52	171	41
305	95	278	84	251	73	224	62	197	52	170	41
304	94	277	84	250	73	223	62	196	51	169	40
303	94	276	83	249	72	222	62	195	51	168	40
302	94	275	83	248	72	221	61	194	50	167	40
301	93	274	82	247	72	220	61	193	50	166	39
300	93	273	82	246	71	219	60	192	50	165	39
299	92	272	82	245	71	218	60	191	49	164	38
298	92	271	81	244	70	217	60	190	49	163	38
297	92	270	81	243	70	216	59	189	48	162	38
296	91	269	80	242	70	215	59	188	48	161	37
295	91	268	80	241	69	214	58	187	48	160	37
294	90	267	80	240	69	213	58	186	47	159	36

College Males (N = 300) (continued)

Raw	T	Raw	T	Raw	T	Raw	T	Raw	T	Raw	T
158	36	144	30	131	25	118	20	105	15	92	10
157	36	143	30	130	25	117	20	104	14	91	9
156	35	142	30	129	24	116	19	103	14	90	9
155	35	141	29	128	24	115	19	102	14	89	8
154	34	140	29	127	24	114	18	101	13	88	8
153	34	139	28	126	23	113	18	100	13	87	8
152	34	138	28	125	23	112	18	99	12	86	7
151	33	137	28	124	22	111	17	98	12	85	7
150	33	136	27	123	22	110	17	97	12	84	6
149	32	135	27	122	22	109	16	96	11	83	6
148	32	134	26	121	21	108	16	95	11	82	6
147	32	133	26	120	21	107	16	94	10	81	5
146	31	132	26	119	20	106	15	93	10	80	5
145	31										

College Females (N = 100)

Raw	T	Raw	T	Raw	T	Raw	T	Raw	T	Raw	T
260	95	237	86	214	76	191	67	168	57	145	47
259	95	236	85	213	76	190	66	167	56	144	47
258	95	235	85	212	75	189	66	166	56	143	46
257	94	234	85	211	75	188	65	165	56	142	46
256	94	233	84	210	74	187	65	164	55	141	46
255	93	232	84	209	74	186	65	163	55	140	45
254	93	231	83	208	74	185	64	162	54	139	45
523	93	230	83	207	73	184	64	161	54	138	44
252	92	229	82	206	73	183	63	160	53	137	44
251	92	228	82	205	72	182	63	159	53	136	43
250	91	227	82	204	72	181	62	158	53	135	43
249	91	226	81	203	72	180	62	157	52	134	43
248	90	225	81	202	71	179	61	156	52	133	42
247	90	224	80	201	71	178	61	155	51	132	42
246	90	223	80	200	70	177	61	154	51	131	41
245	89	222	80	199	70	176	60	153	51	130	41
244	89	221	79	198	69	175	60	152	50	129	40
243	88	220	79	197	69	174	59	151	50	128	40
242	88	219	78	196	69	173	59	150	49	127	40
241	88	218	78	195	68	172	59	149	49	126	39
240	87	217	77	194	68	171	58	148	48	125	39
239	87	216	77	193	67	170	58	147	48	124	38
238	86	215	77	192	67	169	57	146	48	123	38

College Females (N = 100) (continued)

Raw	T	Raw	T	Raw	T	Raw	T	Raw	T	Raw	T
122	38	112	33	102	29	92	25	82	21	73	17
121	37	111	33	101	29	91	25	81	20	72	17
120	37	110	32	100	28	90	24	80	20	71	16
119	36	109	32	99	28	89	24	79	19	70	16
118	36	108	32	98	27	88	23	78	19	69	15
117	35	107	31	97	27	87	23	77	19	68	15
116	35	106	31	96	27	86	22	76	18	67	14
115	34	105	30	95	26	85	22	75	18	66	14
114	34	104	30	94	26	84	22	74	17	65	14
113	34	103	30	93	25	83	21				

APPENDIX C

Parent-Child Interaction Rating Scales

Directions:

It is known that there are differences in affectional give and take between members of various families within American cultures. We are interested here in your impressions regarding the way your parents (or parent substitutes) related to you during your formative years from the age of earliest recall until you graduated from high school. You will be asked to rate the way your parents related to you along several dimensions and even though a parent may have changed during your formative years it still should be possible to find some rating point which best typifies this parent over most of these years. If you cannot recall a parent or parent substitute of a given sex, no ratings for a parent of that sex are expected. Remember, these ratings should reflect only the way you feel your parents related to *you*.

Turn to the next page and begin.

1. Affection I. Please place an X in the space which best represents the degree of affection which your father and mother felt for you.

Father		Mother
______ 1	This parent felt little affection for me. Raising me was a social requirement only.	______ 1
______ 2	This parent probably felt some affection for me, but I often was uncertain of it.	______ 2
______ 3	This parent definitely felt some affection for me, but it was not strong nor often expressed.	______ 3

Father		Mother
______ 4	This parent felt a fairly strong affection for me which I was certain of most of the time. There were times, though, when I wished to be reassured.	______ 4
______ 5	This parent felt a strong affection for me, and I rarely felt uncertain of it.	______ 5

2. *Affection II.* Please place an X in the space which best represents the degree of affection which was physically expressed toward you by your father and your mother. Physically-expressed affection would include kissing, hugging, holding hands, holding on his (her) lap, stroking, etc.

Father		Mother
______ 1	This parent was highly affectionate physically.	______ 1
______ 2	This parent quite often expressed affection physically.	______ 2
______ 3	This parent fairly often expressed physical affection.	______ 3
______ 4	This parent occasionally expressed affection physically but, generally speaking, was reticent to do so.	______ 4
______ 5	This parent rarely showed any physical signs of affection.	______ 5

3. *Approval.* Please place an X in the space which best represents the degree of approval of you which your father and your mother felt.

Father		Mother
______ 1	This parent rarely seemed to approve of me or the things I did.	______ 1

Father		Mother
______ 2	This parent occasionally seemed to approve of me or the things I did, but, in general, there was clear disapproval.	______ 2
______ 3	This parent sometimes approved of me or the things I did, but at times there was clear disapproval.	______ 3
______ 4	This parent usually showed approval of me or the things I did, and only rarely was there clear disapproval.	______ 4
______ 5	This parent almost always seemed to approve of me or the things I did; it is difficult to recall any clear disapproval.	______ 5

4. *Sharing of experiences.* Please place an X in the space which best represents the degree to which you and your father and you and your mother discussed personal feelings and experiences with each other.

Father		Mother
______ 1	There was an almost complete freedom of discussion of personal feelings and experiences between this parent and me; I rarely felt that a matter could not be discussed.	______ 1
______ 2	Personal feelings and experiences were usually discussed between this parent and me and only occasionally did it seem necessary to keep matters to ourselves.	______ 2
______ 3	Personal feelings and experiences were often discussed between this parent and me but just about as often we kept these matters to ourselves.	______ 3
______ 4	Occasionally there was discussion of personal feelings and experiences between this parent and me, but mostly we kept these matters to ourselves.	______ 4

Father		Mother
______ 5	There was little discussion of personal feelings and experiences between this parent and me.	______ 5

5. *Concrete giving.* Please place an X in the space which best represents the amount of concrete giving (e.g., gifts, money, clothing) done by your father and your mother.

Father		Mother
______ 1	This parent rarely gave me things beyond the minimum necessary to meet everyday requirements of living.	______ 1
______ 2	This parent occasionally gave me things beyond the necessary requirements of living but only on special occasions like birthdays.	______ 2
______ 3	This parent was fairly generous in giving me things beyond the necessary requirements of living, but many times I was denied extra things I felt I should have.	______ 3
______ 4	This parent was quite generous in giving me things beyond the necessary requirements of living and only occasionally was I denied extra things I felt I should have.	______ 4
______ 5	This parent was extremely generous in giving me things beyond the necessary requirements of living and only rarely was I denied things I felt I should have.	______ 5

6. *Encouragement.* Please place an X in the space which best represents the amount of positive encouragement which your father and your mother expressed in your attempts to meet responsibilities in school, around the home, in social relationships, etc., or in pursuing personal interests such as sports, hobbies, clubs, etc.

Father		Mother
______ 1	This parent was almost always positively encouraging in my attempts to meet responsibilities or in my pursuit of personal interests, and I have difficulty remembering when I ever was left too much on my own.	______ 1
______ 2	This parent quite often expressed positive encouragement in my attempts to meet responsibilities or in my pursuit of personal interests, and I seldom was left too much on my own.	______ 2
______ 3	This parent fairly often expressed positive encouragement in my attempts to meet responsibilities or in my pursuit of personal interests, but occasionally I was left too much on my own.	______ 3
______ 4	This parent occasionally expressed positive encouragement in my attempts to meet responsibilities or in my pursuit of personal interests, but I was usually left too much on my own.	______ 4
______ 5	This parent rarely expressed any positive encouragement in my attempts to meet responsibilities or in my pursuit of personal interests.	______ 5

7. Trust. Please place an X in the space which best represents the degree of trust which your father and your mother placed in you. Examples suggesting a lack of trust would be an undue number of reminders to do (or not do) something, doing things for you which children of a given age should do for themselves, or obvious concern and worry over your success in most ventures.

Father		Mother
______ 1	This parent rarely seemed to trust me to do what was expected.	______ 1

Father		Mother
______ 2	This parent occasionally seemed to trust me to do what was expected, but most of the time there was a lack of trust.	______ 2
______ 3	This parent often seemed to trust me to do what was expected, but many times there was a lack of trust.	______ 3
______ 4	This parent usually trusted me to do what was expected, and there seldom was a lack of trust.	______ 4
______ 5	This parent almost always seemed to trust me to do what was expected.	______ 5

8. Security. Please place an X in the space which best represents the degree of security you experienced with your father and with your mother. Security refers to a feeling of being loved, wanted, and protected by the parent in question.

Father		Mother
______ 1	It is difficult for me to remember any time when I was not secure in my relationship with this parent.	______ 1
______ 2	I almost always experienced a feeling of security in my relationship with this parent, and only occasionally was I somewhat insecure.	______ 2
______ 3	I usually experienced a feeling of security in my relationship with this parent, but at times I was somewhat insecure.	______ 3
______ 4	I occasionally experienced a feeling of security in my relationship with this parent, but I usually was somewhat insecure.	______ 4

Father		Mother
______ 5	I rarely experienced a feeling of security in my relationship with this parent, and I usually was quite insecure.	______ 5

APPENDIX D

T-Scale Norms for Maternal Nurturance Ratings on the Parent-Child Interaction Rating Scales

College Males (N = 300)				College Females (N = 140)			
Raw	T	Raw	T	Raw	T	Raw	T
40	73	24	27	40	67	24	32
39	70	23	24	39	65	23	30
38	67	22	21	38	63	22	28
37	64	21	19	37	61	21	26
36	62	20	16	36	59	20	24
35	59	19	13	35	56	19	22
34	56	18	10	34	54	18	19
33	53	17	7	33	52	17	17
32	50	16	4	32	50	16	15
31	47	15	1	31	48	15	13
30	44	14	0	30	46	14	11
29	41	13	0	29	43	13	8
28	39	12	0	28	41	12	6
27	36	11	0	27	39	11	4
26	33	10	0	26	37	10	2
25	30	9	0	25	35	9	0
		8	0			8	0

APPENDIX E

Scripts of Aversive and Neutral Maternal Dialogue

AVERSIVE SCRIPT

Mother: You received your report card today, didn't you? Hurry up! Go on, bring it to me. I bet you don't want me to see how you have been doing in school. Bring it to me! (slight pause) My Gawd! You're doing awful–even worse than I expected. These grades are unbelievably bad–beyond imagination. I might expect you to foul up one subject but you messed up all of them. This card is an utter disgrace. You just look here. Look here! A "C" in English! How can anyone raised in my home fail to even understand how to speak? *Explain that* to me. You don't even know enough English to do that, do you? And here–a "B" in gym. You don't even do well in courses which don't take any brains. What is the matter?

Son: Well . . . . (pause)

Mother: Don't answer. Your answer probably wouldn't be worth anything anyway. I don't think you have the brain power to know what is going on. Now I've got to do something about your schoolwork. You are either not trying or you are just plain stupid–maybe both for all I know. But I just can't believe that I could have an idiot for a son. It couldn't happen to me–what would my friends say if they knew. You don't realize that receiving good grades is important in order to get places in this world–a well paying job as well as achieving status and friends. I don't want a complete failure for a son. Now I'm going to wait until you give me a decent explanation for this dreadful situation. (slight pause) I'm waiting, damn you!

Son: But mom . . . . (pause)

Mother: I don't have to wait. I know! You act bored in class and daydream and don't pay attention to what the teacher is saying. Lord knows I should know. You sit around the house moping, not doing one worthwhile thing unless I'm there to tell you every last thing you have to do. What are you ever going to do when I'm not there to lead you by the hand?

Son: Well, I . . . .

Mother: Just sit there on your rear end and dream your life away. What you could be thinking about I don't know. Probably about those dirty pictures I found hidden in your desk drawer this morning. If your mind is in the gutter, how are you ever going to make me proud of you as a son! School! That's the only way you can prove to me that you're worthy of being my flesh and blood. Listen and mark my words! I can't be standing over you every minute telling you what's right and wrong, but you should know that teachers consider class participation as well as tests when they give grades. Do you contribute to class discussions?

Son: Yes . . . .

Mother: Well, you must not be participating enough in class. Be more assertive and not such a weak sissy. Raise your hand and answer the teacher's questions more often, providing you can give the correct answer and I am beginning to doubt that on the basis of this report card. But for gawd's sake don't be a trouble maker like you are around home. Only do what the teacher tells you to do but do it well. I just wish you could live up to your younger sister. Everything she does makes you look sick. I tell her something once and she does it and does it well. You should see the report card *she* brought home. Kids come over and want to play with her—she's a leader—but who comes to see you? Those worthless tramps down the street that you follow around like a sheep. Try to remember that you're from a respectable family if you possibly can. I guess I will have to do again what I *always* have to do with you—tell you exactly what to do. First, you have to study a lot more at home. I'll make a study schedule for you to follow starting tonight. After this you will come home immediately after school and you can study for a good hour before supper. Then after supper you can study until *I* tell you to stop. No more T.V., no more daydreaming, no more trashy magazines, no more of those trampy friends of yours. If your test grades don't improve, you know what you'll be doing on weekends, don't you? Studying! I've also been thinking that being on the baseball team probably doesn't help matters. You aren't even on the first team anyway. You might as well give that up and spend the time doing something useful which *I* could be proud of rather than just sitting on the bench and watch the good athletes play.

Son: But gee, Mom . . . .

Mother: Stop talking back!

Son: (Cries)

Mother: Stop your whimpering. Don't add being a baby to your list of failures. I'm getting tired of being humiliated by having a failure for a son. Come to think about it, I'd better go to school and talk with your teacher. She would be a better informant about what is actually going on with you than you are. I will take you to school tomorrow morning, and tell her exactly what I've told you to do. Maybe if she keeps an eye on you, she can make you do the things that I've told you.

Son: Mom, please don't do that. What will the other boys say?

Mother: Shut up! I've got to do something. It is for certain you can't do anything on your own that is worthwhile.

NEUTRAL SCRIPT

Mother: Let's see, it's been two months since school started. The semester is well underway, and I wonder whether the subjects are interesting? As I recall you told me you were taking American History as one of your classes.

Son: Uh-Huh. (affirmative)

Mother: When I was a girl we had history as one of our classes too. *I* thought it was interesting to learn about our country and how it developed into the country it is today. I had to memorize the Preamble to the Constitution of the United States. The test to see if we had perfected it was to write it without a single error. You couldn't leave out a single period, comma or semicolon. That was really something!

Son: You did?

Mother: Well, we had other things to study too. Such as the Indians who occupied the land that became America. I can remember to my surprise that the Indians were really quite resourceful which was just the opposite from the cowboy and Indian type stories that I had read about them. They taught the American pioneers a lot of things–like planting corn and tomatoes. By the way how's math coming?

Son: OK.

Mother: As I remember, the math teacher is new this year. He seems very nice. I met him in the grocery store the other day and he said "hello." It turned out that his wife and I had met before.

Son: He seems OK.

Mother: It's a shame in a way that you didn't have Mrs. Evans for your math teacher, but she retired last year. She was my math teacher when I was in school at Jefferson. Of course, the building is gone now. It used to be at the corner of Jefferson and 2nd Street, where the shopping center is now. Mrs. Evans used to drill us and drill us and drill us. She would print various math problems on pieces of cardboard with the answer to the problems printed on the back of the cardboard. I can remember how boring it seemed to me but the technique worked—you learned your math. Your sister seems to be enjoying her math class. This is her first math class. She's got Mrs. Johnson, the teacher you liked so much when you had her two years ago. It's too bad she only teaches one grade level. When I was young and first learning my multiplication tables I got sick with whooping cough and the measles. As a result, I missed two months of school. And to this day I still have trouble with multiplication. Next semester you should be getting Mr. Brown for math. Is he also going to coach the baseball team again this year or is the new gym teacher going to take over as coach?

Son: The new gym teacher is.

Mother: I wonder what kind of team you'll have this year. I guess it would depend upon whether many of last year's team members graduated. I hear the sporting goods store is thinking of donating new uniforms this year for the team. They're supposed to have a little emblem of an Indian on the arms and on the cap so they ought to be pretty sharp looking. Baseball is a game that's hard for me to understand—all these things about balls and strikes and fouls and all that. It's just like anything else. I guess—you have to grow up playing a game to really understand it. Is that a new English book I saw on the coffee table?

Son: Yeh, we just started a new unit on poetry.

Mother: I've always enjoyed sitting down and reading poetry. It is a relaxing pasttime. I think one has to learn how to appreciate poetry. I suppose this will be what you will be doing in class—learning the finer points of poetry such as rhythm, rhyme and alliteration. It's funny how the poems you enjoy and like very much become committed to memory. Maybe it's because you read them so many times. Anyway, they're available so that you can enjoy them anytime, regardless of what you are doing. I wonder if you will find some poems which have more meaning to you and which will become your favorites. I can still remember snatches of "Abu Ben Adam" and "The Daffodils" after all these years. I used to spend a lot of time alone with my poetry books—poems helped fill up my time pretty well. You were telling me

7. No desire to be with boys and girls; never went out with girls 6

C. Social Aspects of Recent Sexual Life: 30 Years of Age and Above

1. Married and has children, living as a family unit 0
2. Married and has children but unable to establish or maintain a family home 1
3. Has been married and had children but permanently separated 2
4. a. Married but considerable marital discord 3
   b. Single, but has had engagement or deep heterosexual relationship but emotionally unable to carry it through to marriage 3
5. Single, with short engagements or relationships with women which do not appear to have had much emotional depth for both partners, i.e., "affairs" 4
6. a. Single, consistent deep interest in male attachments, no interest in women 5
   b. Single, has gone out with a few girls but without other indications of a continuous interest in women 5
7. a. Single, occasional male contacts, no interest in women 6
   b. Single, neither interested in men or women 6

D. Social Aspects of Recent Sexual Life: Below 30 Years of Age

1. Married, living as family unit, with or without children 0
2. a. Married, with or without children, but unable to establish or maintain a family home 1
   b. Single but engaged or in a deep heterosexual relationship (presumably leading toward marriage) 1
3. Single, has had engagement or deep heterosexual relationship but has emotionally been unable to carry it through to marriage 2
4. Single, consistent deep interest in male attachments, with restricted or lack of interest in women 3
5. Single, casual male relationships with restricted or lack of interest in women 4
6. Single, has gone out with a few girls casually but without other indications of a continuous interest in women 5
7. a. Single, never interested in or never associated with either men or women 6
   b. Antisocial

E. Personal Relations: History

1. Always has had a number of close friends but did not habitually play a leading role 1
2. From adolescence on had a few close friends 3
3. From adolescence on had a few casual friends 3
4. From adolescence on stopped having friends 4
5. a. No intimate friends after childhood 5
   b. Casual but never any deep intimate mutual friendships 5
6. Never worried about boys or girls; no desire to be with boys or girls 6

F. Recent Premorbid Adjustment in Personal Relations

1. Habitually mixed with others, but not a leader	1
2. Mixed only with a close friend or group of friends	3
3. No close friends; very few friends; had friends but never quite accepted by them	4
4. Quiet; aloof; seclusive; preferred to be by self	5
5. Antisocial	6

APPENDIX G

*Parent Attitude Research Instrument (Father's Form)**

INVENTORY OF ATTITUDES ON FAMILY LIFE AND CHILDREN

Father's Form

Read each of the statements below and then rate them as you think your father would and as follows:

A	a	d	D
Strongly Agree	Mildly Agree	Mildly Disagree	Strongly Disagree

Indicate your opinion by drawing a circle around the "A" if you believe your father would strongly agree, around the "a" if you think your father would mildly agree, around the "d" if you think your father would mildly disagree, and around the "D" if you believe your father would strongly disagree.

There are no right or wrong answers, so answer according to your own opinion. It is very important that all questions be answered. Many of the statements will seem alike but all are necessary to show slight differences of opinion.

	Agree	*Disagree*
1. Children should feel absolutely free to gripe about rules which their parents make.	A a	d D
2. A father should do his best to avoid any disappointment for his child.		
3. The home is the only thing that matters to a good father.		
4. Children need some of the natural meanness taken out of them.		
5. If small children refuse to obey, parents should whip them for it.		

*The four paternal control scales are: Fostering Dependency (items 2, 25, 48, 71, 94), Deification (items 10, 33, 56, 79, 102), Exclusion of Outside Influences (items 11, 34, 57, 80, 103), and Deception (items 23, 46, 69, 92, 115).

6. Parents who allow their children to grow up with the idea that other people will always help them just encourage them to become failures.
7. Sometimes it's necessary for a husband to tell off his wife in order to get his rights.
8. Few young men realize how much of a burden the responsibility of a family can be.
9. It's a father's job to see to it a boy has the courage to fight.
10. More parents should teach their children to have unquestioning loyalty to them.
11. There is no excusing someone who upsets the confidence a child has in his parents' ways of doing things.
12. The things wives and children ask of a man after a hard day's work are enough to make anyone lose his temper at times.
13. It isn't going to hurt children to see each other or their parents undressed.
14. A parent should always treat a child as an equal because the child is helpless.
15. A father's duty is to see to it that the whole family does what he knows is best.
16. Few wives realize that husbands are part of the family too and need some looking after.
17. Kissing and tender treatment of children should be kept within limits if children are to develop properly.
18. Parents should keep out of children's activities as much as possible so that children can learn to do things on their own.
19. The main thing wrong with today's homes is the wife tries too much to run everything.
20. A child who can keep calm on the surface no matter what happens, will do well in life.
21. The best attitude for a child to learn is to take things as they are.
22. A man should be careful that his marriage doesn't result in his losing interest and close contact with his own mother and father.
23. It's best to trick a child into doing something he doesn't want to do instead of having to argue with him.
24. Parents should ask for and take into account the opinions of children on all questions of how the family should be run.
25. A child should be protected from jobs which might be too tiring or hard on him.
26. Too many men forget that a father's place is with his family when he is not working.
27. Many children, like horses, must be broken in order to be trained.
28. Spanking a child immediately when he is cross and nagging is better than letting him get into the habit of acting like that.
29. The child who grows up with the idea he will have to do almost everything for himself gets much further in life.
30. It's natural to have quarrels when two people who both have minds of their own get married.

31. Most young fathers are bothered more by the feeling of being tied to the home than by anything else.
32. A boy has to be taught to use his fists when someone else is asking for it.
33. A child soon learns that there is no greater wisdom than that of his parents.
34. It's best for a child if he never gets started wondering whether his father's views are right.
35. There are times when any husband or father gets to the point where he feels he can't stand his marriage or family a moment longer.
36. You have to give children sexual freedom or they will not develop properly.
37. In a well-run home children should have things their own way as often as the parents do.
38. There always has to be a boss and, in the family, that person should be the father.
39. Spending a lot of time with her parents' family is a good way for a wife to lose out with her husband.
40. It's quite possible for a parent to overdo love and affection for children.
41. If children plan their own work and do it without the direction of parents they are more willing to help and they do more.
42. The trouble with wives nowadays is they don't have any respect for a man's right to have his say so.
43. Parents who teach their children to think at least twice before expressing how they feel help them to get along better in life.
44. One important thing for a child to learn is that about all you can expect to do is make the best of what you have.
45. The responsibilities of taking care of his wife and children should not keep a husband from spending plenty of time with his own parents.
46. Often you have to fool children to get them to do what they should without a big fuss.
47. A child has a right to his own point of view and should never be kept from expressing it.
48. Parents should know better than to allow their children to be exposed to difficult situations.
49. A man can't do a father's job and have an active social life too.
50. A child is better off if he has a healthy fear of adults.
51. The wise parent will not hesitate to whip a child to teach him to change his ways.
52. A child should be taught never to depend on others for anything he can do for himself.
53. Even in marriage a person must fight for his rights at times.
54. Men don't have any idea when they get married about the obligations and problems they are taking on.
55. A father should never tolerate his son's running away from a fight.
56. Loyalty to parents comes before anything else.
57. A child should not question the thinking of his parents.

58. A man may need to "blow his top" once in awhile around the home just to clear the air a bit.
59. A child who isn't curious about sex is the one you should worry about.
60. Grown-ups should treat their children the same way they treat other grown-ups.
61. The old fashioned family in which the father is in charge is best for everyone.
62. Wives too often use the children as an excuse for ignoring the father.
63. Giving children love and affection can be carried too far just like anything else.
64. Managing their own affairs without interference develops responsible children.
65. Most wives would do better if they would quit trying to act smarter than their husbands.
66. A parent can be very helpful to a child by teaching him how to keep from showing it when he is "boiling" inside.
67. Children should know that happiness is a result of being satisfied with life as it is and not in always trying to change it.
68. There is no excusing a wife who tries to come between a man and his parents.
69. You have to fool children into doing many things because they wouldn't understand anyway.
70. A family is at its best when the children say what they think about things no matter what the subject is.
71. A child is most lovable when he is small and helpless.
72. Most fathers shouldn't have much time left for anything else by the time they take care of their jobs and their families.
73. A stubborn child has to have some punishment or he may not learn anything.
74. Children who are always breaking their parents' rules will remember them after a good whipping.
75. A child will take care of himself much better later on if he never gets started in the first place expecting help from others.
76. A woman will just take advantage of a man if he doesn't let her know very firmly what he will and will not stand for around the home.
77. A father has enough to do just supporting a family without being held to blame for everything his children might do.
78. If a child doesn't learn to strike back good and hard when hit he will end up being the one the others pick on.
79. A child should always love his parents above everyone else.
80. A child's trust in his parents should be safeguarded better by not having so many people around with different ideas.
81. Raising children is a nerve-wracking job.
82. There is no need for a parent to spend a lot of time explaining sex to children except to tell them what kinds of sex play are prohibited.
83. When a parent asks a child to do something the child should always be told why.

84. The ideal home is one in which it is clear to all that the father is head of the household.
85. Too many wives are so busy with friends, relatives or the children that they forget all about the man they married.
86. A proper child does not like a lot of kissing and hugging.
87. Most of the time when parents try to supervise what children are doing they just keep the children from developing independence.
88. Women too often get the idea from books and magazines that they don't have to respect what their husbands say.
89. A child who always looks calm and cool no matter how upset he feels inside gets along best.
90. The main thing in growing up is to learn there isn't too much you can do except take things as they are.
91. A man must consider his own parents' view just as much as those of his wife when making family plans.
92. There's no excuse wasting a lot of time explaining when you can get kids doing what you want by being a little clever.
93. If a child has been trained properly, he will speak right up and disagree with his parents when he feels they are wrong on some matter.
94. Parents should try to prevent all difficulties which might make a child unhappy.
95. A man should get his happiness out of his wife and children and not out of stag parties and vacation trips with other men.
96. If you are soft-hearted with children, they will just find out they can push you around.
97. A child deserves to be slapped when he talks back to his parents.
98. Sooner or later a child must learn if he doesn't look out for himself no one else will.
99. A marriage in which there are no arguments is usually one which is pretty dull.
100. A man should not get married until he really knows what it means to take care of a family and is ready for it.
101. If you teach a child to always be friendly he won't be able to handle himself when there is a quarrel on the playground.
102. A child should grow up convinced his parents always know what is the right thing to do.
103. Children should never learn things outside the home which make them doubt their parents' ideas.
104. It's natural for a father to "blow his top" when the wife or children are selfish and demanding.
105. Children are going to find out anyway so you might just as well tell them what grown-up sex life is like.
106. Parents have to respect the wishes of children even more than the child respects their wishes.
107. The happiest homes are those in which the father has the final word on all important decisions.

108. The biggest trouble with most wives is they forget they belong to their husband and not to their parents or other people.
109. A parent has to learn to keep his affection for his children under control or he sets a bad example for the children.
110. A child can only become self-confident if allowed to do things his own way.
111. Modern education has taught many women to think they are not only equal to men but even brighter and more capable.
112. Parents should teach a child to control his feelings as soon as he can understand.
113. Children should be taught to be content with just what they happen to have and not expect to get much more.
114. No matter what his wife may think, a man has to see to it that his own mother's requests and wishes are carried out as much as is possible.
115. When a child is doing something he shouldn't one of the best ways of handling it is to just get him interested in something else.

Author Index

Subject Index

DATE DUE

DEC 12 '74	APR 2 1981	AP 19 '03	
MAR 20 '75	MAR 16 1981	MR 31 '04	
JUL 22 '75	APR 06 1981	AP 15 '04	
MAR 30 '7?	OCT [illegible]	APR 24 '05	
		JAN 31 '07	
APR 6 '78	FEB 27 '85		
FEB 24 '78	MAR 20 '85	APR 23 '07	
APR 2[illegible]	APR 23 '86		
APR 19 '78	OCT 21 '87		
APR 26 '78	APR 4 '90		
	SEP 30 '92		
DEC 1[illegible] 1978	NOV 15 '95		
FEB [illegible] 1979	MAR 5 '97		
MAR [illegible] 1979	MAR 26 '97		
MAR 26 1980	AP 24 '02		
APR [illegible] 1980	OC 28 '02		
APR 2[illegible] 1980	NO 11 '02		
	NO 18 '02		
APR 8 1981	DE 08 '02		

GAYLORD PRINTED IN U.S.A.